JAMES JOYCE

A PORTRAIT OF THE ARTIST

'Love is a cursed nuisance, especially when coupled with lust also.'

J.J.

En Amérique, professeur;
En Angleterre, journaliste;
C'est à grands pas et en sueur
Que vous suivrez à peine ma piste.

T. S. ELIOT, 'Mélange Adultère de Tout'

JAMES JOYCE

A PORTRAIT OF THE ARTIST

Stan Gébler Davies

STEIN AND DAY/*Publishers*/New York

Grateful acknowledgment is made for the use of the following copyrighted material:Lines from "Mélange Adultère de Tout" from *Collected Poems 1909-1962* by T. S. Eliot, copyright, 1936, by Harcourt Brace Jovanovich, Inc., copyright, 1963, 1964, by T. S. Eliot; reprinted by permission of the publisher, and by Faber & Faber Ltd. Excerpt from *Our Friend James Joyce* by Padraic and Mary Colum, copyright © 1958 by Padraic Colum; reprinted by permission of Doubleday & Company, Inc. Lines from "Songs for Informal Gatherings" from *Pound/Joyce: Letters of Ezra Pound to James Joyce*, edited by Forrest Read; copyright © 1967 by Ezra Pound; reprinted by permission of New Directions Publishing Corporation. Lines from "Down by the Sally Gardens" and "Who Will Go Drive with Fergus Now?" from *Collected Poems* by William Butler Yeats, copyright, 1906, by Macmillan Publishing Co., renewed, 1934, by William Butler Yeats; reprinted with permission of Macmillan Publishing Co., Inc., and M. B. Yeats, Miss Ann Yeats and the Macmillan Company of London and Basingstoke. Lines from "Because your voice was at my side" and "All day I hear the noise of waters" from *Collected Poems* by James Joyce, copyright 1918 by B. W. Huebsch, Inc., copyright renewed 1946 by Nora Joyce; all rights reserved; reprinted by permission of The Viking Press, Inc. Lines from "A Flower Given to My Daughter" and "Ecce Puer" from *Collected Poems* by James Joyce, copyright 1927, 1936 by James Joyce; all rights reserved; reprinted by permission of The Viking Press, Inc. Dialogue extracts from *Exiles* by James Joyce, copyright 1918 by B. W. Huebsch, Inc., copyright 1946 by Nora Joyce; all rights reserved; reprinted by permission of The Viking Press, Inc. Excerpts from *Giacomo Joyce* by James Joyce, copyright © 1959, 1967, 1968 by F. Lionel Monro as administrator of the Estate of James Joyce; all rights reserved; reprinted by permission of The Viking Press, Inc. Lines from "The Holy Office" and "Gas from a Burner" and nine lines of prose from *The Critical Writings of James Joyce* edited by Ellsworth Mason and Richard Ellmann, copyright © 1959 by Harriet Weaver and F. Lionel Monro as administrators of the Estate of James Joyce; all rights reserved; reprinted by permission of The Viking Press, Inc. Excerpts from *The Letters of James Joyce*, Volume I, edited By Stuart Gilbert, copyright © 1957, 1966 by The Viking Press, Inc; all rights reserved; reprinted by permission of The Viking Press, Inc. Excerpts from *The Letters of James Joyce*, Volume II and III, edited by Richard Ellmann, copyright © 1966 by F. Lionel Monro as administrator of the Estate of James Joyce; all rights reserved; reprinted by permission of The Viking Press, Inc.

First published in the United States of America, 1975

Copyright © 1975 by Stan Gébler Davies

Printed in the United States of America

Stein and Day/ *Publishers*/ Scarborough House, Briarcliff Manor, N Y. 10510

Library of Congress Cataloging in Publication Data

Davies, Stan Gébler.

James Joyce: a portrait of the artist.

1. ✓ Joyce, James, 1882-1941 – ~~Biography.~~

PR6019.09Z5286   823'.9'12 [B]   75-11940

ISBN 0-8128-1828-8

Contents

Illustrations

Preface

Believe it or not, there have only been two other full biographies of James Joyce. The first, by Herbert Gorman, was written under Joyce's direction and is for that reason more or less worthless, being distinguished chiefly by its omissions and evasions, and its presentation of James Joyce as a plaster saint. The unfortunate Gorman is not entirely to be blamed: when he had done he swore he would never again choose as a subject a living man.

Professor Richard Ellmann's biography, first published in 1959, is altogether a different kettle of fish. It is an admirable, scholarly work but it has, to my taste, too much of the monument about it. Nor is it free from error, though none is glaring. Professor Ellmann, for instance, is mistaken in assuming that there was no carnal communication between Joyce and Marthe Fleischmann in Zurich in 1919. Joyce's friend, Frank Budgen, provides positive evidence to the contrary. One might even say that Professor Ellmann had no business making any such assumption, given the passionate nature of Joyce's addresses to the lady, and her known character: she was the sort of woman who exists almost solely for that use which Joyce found for her. The fact that James Joyce dallied with a lady other than his wife is scarcely likely now to make many think the less of him. 'Every married man has his Marthe Fleischmann,' as Frank Budgen said.

A minor difference, perhaps. This book differs from Professor Ellmann's on certain other points of fact, emphasis and interpretation (of *Finnegans Wake* in particular), and these differences will be principally of interest to Joyce scholars, who are happily legion, and to critics, who are paid to detect such differences. They will seem of lesser importance to persons who simply consider that James Joyce was a great writer (or suspect that he may have been) and know (or suspect) that he had an 'interesting' life. He did, and I hope I have made it seem so. My book is short on critical waffle and I do not recommend it to seekers after a PhD in Eng. Lit., except possibly as an example of how not to write a thesis.

7

There seems to me no particular reason why the biography of a great man should be tedious: after all, that is no compliment to the subject. Joyce himself did not dismiss the concept of 'readability' so vehemently as one would expect from certain Mandarin interpretations of his aesthetic philosophy. He took time off from the composition of *Finnegans Wake* to read *Gentlemen Prefer Blondes* and, particularly at the end of his life, displayed joyously bad taste in his choice of musical and theatrical entertainments, much as Dylan Thomas displayed an extraordinary preference for the works of Micky Spillane above all other literature.

It is possible that some people will discover the works of James Joyce after reading my book who have not discovered them before. I will omit the usual hypocritical footnote to the effect that I hope this will be so. As I explain in the text I do not think that Mr Joyce needs assistance or exegesis, apart from the special case of *Finnegans Wake* and the happy task of explaining that monstrous production I leave gratefully to others, apart from the bare few pages necessary to demonstrate the nature of the monster on which the greatest novelist of the century wasted seventeen years of his genius: it is as if Mozart had not died at thirty-six, but lived on seventeen years to produce, instead of another *Die Zauberflöte* or *Don Giovanni*, the sort of mournful howls, whistles, moans, silences and thunderous bangs of the likes of Karl-Heinz Stockhausen. *Finnegans Wake* is a monument to perversity, the apotheosis of the crossword puzzle. I leave it to its admirers.

I have synopsized here the plot of Joyce's play *Exiles*, believing that it is not so widely known as his other works. I apologize for any tedium this causes to those who know it already.

Readers of this book will find a bibliography at the end of the text, listing numerous volumes of reminiscence by Joyce's friends. The dialogue quoted in this book comes either from those reminiscences or from Joyce's own account in those volumes of letters so admirably edited by Stuart Gilbert and Richard Ellmann. Appended also is a list of critical works, for those who are unwilling to take my word on the simple readability of James Joyce.

STAN GÉBLER DAVIES
Dublin, 1975

Chapter One
'Here's Me'

'For the second half of his life my father belonged to the class of the deserving poor, that is to say the class of people who richly deserve to be poor,' pronounced Stanislaus Joyce, James's younger brother. John Stanislaus Joyce, father of James and Stanislaus, was born the only child of an entrepreneurial family, in Cork, in 1849. He inherited certain traits from his father James, one of those being a tendency to bankruptcy. He would have inherited his Christian name too, but for a blunder of the drunken clerk who registered his birth, or so he said. James Joyce, grandfather of the writer, handsome and hedonistic, went bankrupt twice, the second time on his wife's money.

The lady was an O'Connell from Kerry, supposedly related, at some remove, to Daniel the Liberator (of whom it was said you could not throw a stick over a poor-house wall without hitting one of his bastards). She was older than her husband, pious and not beautiful, but she had a fair pile of money and some wit. Stranded by a rainstorm with her new husband, she took refuge in a peasant cottage.

'Sure that's a fine young man, God bless him,' said the sly peasant woman within, glancing after Mrs Joyce's husband. 'I suppose now, ma'am, you're his mother?'

'No, faith,' growled Mrs Joyce, 'I'm his grandmother.'

James Joyce had a serene disposition, a gift which skipped a generation to his grandson (who was known in his youth as 'Sunny Jim'). He died of typhoid at the age of thirty-nine, urging his son from his deathbed to attend an opera performance instead of waiting for his death.

That son, John Stanislaus, like himself, was musical, handsome and athletic, but as a child he was delicate. His father saw to it that he went out in pilot boats to meet the trans-Atlantic liners which called at Queenstown (now called Cobh). His health improved and so, under the tutelage of the pilots, did his vocabulary. John Joyce attended Queen's College, Cork, supposedly studying medicine. He spent three years at it, taking few exams and passing fewer, but doing rather well at sports and theatricals, breaking the record for the hop, step and jump (the hop was claimed to be eighteen feet, a prodigious leap by anyone's standards), and attracting the favourable notice of the *Cork Examiner* and other newspapers for his histrionic efforts. He had a fine voice and a pronounced comic talent.

In 1870 he ran away with three college friends to fight for the French in the Franco-Prussian war, but got only as far as London before his mother caught up with him and dragged him back by the ears. His ardour undiminished, he offered himself to the Fenians, but there was little prospect of insurrection at the time. There was, however, a good deal of talk, which is almost as pleasant and rather less dangerous.

In a year or so his mother moved to Dublin, taking John Stanislaus with her, his medical career abandoned, in the hope of finding him useful employment. His voice had been much praised: he took it to a teacher. It was much praised again. He could with work be the successor to the great Campanini, then the rage of Covent Garden. Like most Irishmen, the praise and the possibility of future glory were quite enough to satisfy him. He did not persevere in his studies, and his splendid voice, splendid even when it was blurred with booze, graced the saloon bars and front parlours of Dublin instead of the Opera House.

His immediate ambition now was to become secretary to the Lord Mayor, a cousin of his mother's, but he did not achieve it. Instead he invested £500, the remains of a coming-of-age gift from his O'Connell grandfather, in a new distillery at Chapelizod on the Liffey outside Dublin (a location which his son made the centre of the world in *Finnegans Wake*). He became secretary of the company on a salary of £300 a year, until that foray into capitalism came to an unhappy end. The manager, discovered by Joyce to have embezzled most of the funds, departed suddenly, apparently ungrateful for Joyce's having previously saved his life. Joyce's story was that the workmen, who hated their manager, had dropped a beam on him from some height. But Joyce, as luck would have it, was close enough to pull him under a shed in the nick of time. The hero of this saga enjoyed the retailing of it, for all the good it did him. He got nothing from the wreckage of the company beyond a vote of thanks from the directors for saving them from worse loss. In order to improve the story he invented a bank account containing money to which he, as trustee of the company, was entitled, but which was unfortunately hedged around with legal restrictions and therefore not worth worrying about. There was no such sum.

So far as it is possible to trace the Joyce ancestry, there is a bankruptcy or two in every generation. John's father was a bankrupt, and his father before him. James Joyce was to inherit the family ineptitude at business, and the family confidence in its business talents.

Having nothing better to do, John Joyce now became secretary to the National Liberal Club. The Liberals were at that time more or less in tune with Nationalist sentiment and rejoiced, at the election of 1880, unwisely called by Disraeli, in the ousting of two Conservative members from a Dublin constituency, one of them Sir Arthur Guinness, also in the drink trade. Joyce was given credit for his organizational energy and awarded 200 guineas, 100 for each elected candidate, a handy sum. The gratitude of his party did not extend, as he had hoped, to the offer of a safe seat in Parliament, which was just as well: politicians are expected to pay some attention to their business, and Joyce could not long have survived in London. He became a partisan of the obnoxious but effective Nationalist politician, Charles Stewart Parnell.

With time on his hands, Joyce amused himself well, living off his mother and the income from his property, as yet unmortgaged, in Cork. He sailed in a boat in Dublin Bay, and sang at concerts, and drank with his friends. 'He belonged,' said his son Stanislaus, whose disapproval we have already noted, 'to that class of men regarding whom it is impossible to postulate any social system of which they could be active members. They are saboteurs of life though they have the name of *viveur*.'

John Joyce was precisely the sort of character about whom it is said, particularly in Ireland, that there is nothing wrong with him that marriage would not cure. Many unfortunate women have been nailed to that particular cross. John Joyce's choice was no exception. Mary Jane Murray, called May, was the daughter of John Murray, a wine and spirits agent and a customer at the Chapelizod distillery.

11

His daughter was fair and pretty, good at singing and playing the piano. She was nineteen when she met her ruin. Her father (naturally) had better sense and forbade her seeing him, but she was obstinate under the spell of Joyce's charm.

Finding them together in Grafton Street, where the better class of Dubliner, then as now, do their shopping, he called a cab to take her out of Joyce's company. Dublin is a dull town and its citizens are eager to savour any sort of diversion. One of the spectators enquired into the causes of the drama.

'Oh nothing serious,' said Joyce, enjoying himself, 'just the usual story of the beautiful daughter and the irascible parent.'

John Murray, however irascible, had eventually to reconcile himself to the loss of his daughter and put up with Joyce's vitriolic animosity for the rest of his life. 'The old fornicator', his son-in-law called him because he had married a second time after his first wife died. 'Bottle-washer in a paper hat' was another amiable epithet.

John Joyce married the beautiful daughter in May 1880, a month after the election. Joyce, with money in his pockets, took her on honeymoon to London, where she was introduced to the less gallant side of his nature and the scatological fluency of his language. Joyce's mother, disapproving of the marriage on the grounds he had married beneath himself, went back to Cork and stayed there. Her son got a job in Dublin as rate-collector, supposedly for life. The hours were easy and elastic and the duties such that he could plausibly disappear into bars for hours at a time. Since the job involved the collecting of money, there were frequent dippings into the satchel, and the consequent necessity of replacing what was taken out with the assistance of money-lenders and mortgage brokers. One by one the properties in Cork were hocked and Joyce began the long descent from comfort to poverty.

The Joyce children, as is not unusual in Irish Catholic families, appeared with the maximum speed which nature and the constitution of women allow. The first, a boy, was born in 1881, while the Joyces were resident in Kingstown (now Gaelicized to Dun Laoghaire, and known to the natives as Dunleary, a pronunciation which only approximates the Gaelic and infuriates the Gaels), and died before he could be baptized. 'My life was buried with him,' said the father, weeping into his whiskey, and got on with the business of procreation. James Augustine Joyce duly appeared on 2 February, 1882. The Joyces had by then moved back into town, to the suburb of Rathgar, the first of many displacements which were to follow one another at decreasing intervals, accompanied by the raising of mortgages, the birth of children and the complaints of unpaid landlords. (The Irish are not scrupulous about the paying of rent.)

A further eleven children followed, of which nine survived birth. Margaret was born in January 1884, Stanislaus eleven months later (Joyce *père*, whatever else he lacked, did not lack potency), Charles in 1886, George in 1887, Eileen in 1889, Mary in 1890, Eva in 1891, Florence in 1892 and Mabel in 1893. There was a last son born in 1894 who lived long enough to be christened Frederick, but no longer, after which May Joyce, with one lapse, was allowed relief from fecundity, probably by the normal Irish method of abstention from sexual intercourse. (There was one more still-birth, four years later. Possibly John Joyce was drunk enough to be amorous but not drunk enough to be impotent.) She was thirty-five, she had ten children to look after in circumstances of accelerating poverty, with more hindrance than help from a drunken and occasionally brutal husband. She had less than ten years to live.

While the job in the rates office lasted there was a period of relative stability. John Joyce ought to have been solvent on his salary of £500 a year, even without the added income from his properties, but his tastes were too rich. The family moved south again, to the seaside town of Bray, then a fashionable resort in a small way. The sea was across the road, the strands were fine and the countryside began at the end of every lane.

He had chosen Bray, he said, because the price of the train fare would keep his wife's relatives away. Of course it did not. Bray is some sixteen miles from Dublin and well serviced by trains. Joyce spent his time fishing in the company of a bottle of whiskey, rowing in regattas (he won a race at the age of forty), entertaining friends down from Dublin, and singing, as always. Stanislaus preserved a Boat Club concert programme from 1888. Mr and Mrs Joyce both sang, and so did Master James Joyce, then aged six.

The convivial life of Bray did not improve Mr Joyce's temper when he was drunk, though his capacity for drink was large and overt violence consequently rare. Stanislaus nevertheless remembered his foul moods, his habit of grinding his teeth and glaring at his wife with mutterings of 'Let's finish it now'. She was on occasion terrified to be alone in the house with him. No doubt these moments were not pretty, but May Joyce, in the twenty-three years she was married to him, made only one attempt to leave him. Whenever else she was tempted, she was dissuaded by priests full of the sanctity of family life but not having to endure it themselves.

Stanislaus loved his mother and could not stand his father. Nor did his father like him. 'What a loving son!' said John Joyce when his second son made his disappearance to avoid his father's company. His elder brother was less inclined to be upset by domestic trauma, liked his father and was liked in turn. After his mother's death, James discovered his father's love letters, read them all and passed them to his brother with the comment, 'nothing', meaning nothing of literary value. Stanislaus burnt them without reading them.

Mr Joyce was inclined to be jealous of the attention his pretty wife attracted. 'Will you introduce me to that pretty young lady?' asked a guest of his hostess at a dance the Joyces attended. 'Certainly,' said the hostess, 'but let me tell you that pretty young lady is the mother of four children.' Joyce, told the story, professed to be amused, but made a fuss about it when he got home, and continued to do so for months. He kept on the piano the photographs of former girl-friends, all of them pretty, from whom he had broken off in fits of petulant jealousy. Mrs Joyce did not object, as women sometimes do not object to the evidence that their man had been sought after by other women. Nevertheless, the trophies suddenly disappeared.

'Where are the photographs?' demanded Joyce when he noticed their absence.

'Burnt,' said his wife.

'Who burnt them?'

'I did.'

'No you didn't,' said Joyce, who knew his household better. 'It was that old bitch upstairs.'

It was, in fact, the 'old bitch upstairs', Mrs Conway, a distant relation of Joyce's, known to the children as Dante (probably a corruption of 'Auntie'). She, out of Catholic propriety and a concern for the morals of growing children, had insisted on the destruction of images more appealing than her own. She was James's first teacher. She taught him to read and write, gave him some arith-

metic and geography and was blamed by Stanislaus for having in-
culcated a degree of bigoted Catholicism and anti-English patriotism
(there is no other sort in Ireland). Fat and unlovely, she was clever
enough, but certainly bigoted in the Irish Catholic puritan direction.
Considering her history, her prejudice was not surprising. She had
entered a convent with the intention of becoming a nun, but withdrew when her brother died and left her a fortune, a decision she
later had cause to regret. She married a bank clerk who went off to
South America to better himself, taking her money with him to
smooth the way. He neglected ever to send for her. One under-
stands, therefore, her severe opinion of philandering males. But, by
the time she managed to destroy the evidence of John Joyce's past
successes, we may assume it had registered with her precocious
pupil that God put many pretty women into the world and did
not necessarily limit a man to only one of them; not, at least,
his father.

In order to teach patriotism, Dante took to illustrating it herself.
She banged an elderly gentleman over the head with her parasol at
a concert for uncovering for *God Save The Queen*, an offence to her
Irish sensibilities. There was also an incident when a servant-girl
reported a woman driven almost to suicide because her child had
died unbaptized. Dante explained that the child on that account
could not be admitted to Heaven. Stanislaus, who appeared from an
early age to be less taken with religion than his brother, said they
were all suitably impressed. 'It seemed the most natural thing in
creation that God should be some kind of drunken ogre with less
mercy even than the small mercy of men.'

God had made some impression on Jim, as the family called him.
He was petrified by thunderstorms until he was twelve or thirteen.
That, his brother put down to Dante's religion of terrorism. His
reaction was to run upstairs, refusing to be comforted by his mother,
and hide in a cupboard until it was over. Cross yourself, said Dante,
and repeat, 'Jesus of Nazareth, King of the Jews, from sudden and
unprovided-for death, deliver us, O Lord.' Jim did so but it did not
make the thunder or the lightning go away. The anxiety persisted
into later life. Jim would say to Stannie, if he were standing at an
open window, enjoying a storm, 'would you be kind enough to close
that window, like a good bloody fool?' To Alessandro Francini-Bruni,
a friend in Trieste twenty years later, he said 'You know my brother

15

thinks that a thunderbolt knocks at the door before coming in. (Francini-Bruni later improved the story to have Joyce in his maturity still hiding under the bedclothes at the first rumble of thunder. He was not the first or the last to decorate the truth.)

Joyce when young displayed inherited histrionic ability. While still in the nursery he got up a dramatization of Adam and Eve with himself playing the Devil (that being the best part). Visitors to the house in Bray were likely to be treated to his 'playing' the piano and singing when his parents' backs were turned. Even at the age of four or so, coming down the stairs with his nurse-maid (a luxury which did not survive long in the family), he would call out 'here's me!'

He began his formal education at Clongowes Wood College, the most distinguished Catholic boarding school in the country, run, naturally, by the Society of Jesus. It was a Jesuit who made the rash remark that, given a child before the age of seven, the Society would determine the man he was to be. The Jesuits' educational intentions were not precisely realized in the case of James Joyce, no more than they were with Voltaire, another charge of theirs.

James Joyce was delivered to Clongowes at the age of six and a half. Asked how old he was he answered 'Half past six' and was given that as a nickname by his contemporaries. He experienced the usual sense of trauma at first, but soon got over the homesickness. When his parents arrived, with Stanislaus, to see him, he was glad to see them, but his letters home, after brief expressions of hope that everyone was well, were principally lists of items he considered necessary to his continued wellbeing. His mother, in the manner of mothers, complained she would like a more detailed account of his condition. The Reverend T. P. Brown SJ, who was in charge of the pupils' health, attempted to browbeat him into obliging her, reporting meanwhile – in 1890 – that 'he is very well – his face being, as usual, very often well marked with any black thing that comes within reach. He has been taking the cod liver oil regularly.'

The pleasures of female company dawned on him early. He was less inclined than his brother to run around in gangs assaulting other gangs. He accumulated his first girl-friend at Bray, a pale-faced girl called Eileen Vance, with long dark hair. She was aware, as most seven-year-old ladies are, of her attractions, and of Jim's. Her

16

winsomeness did not endear her to Mrs Conway, nor did her Protestant religion. Jim, Dante informed him, would most certainly burn
in hell if he did not give up her company. He was willing to take
the risk.

Miss Vance, still smitten back in Bray while the object of her
affections disported himself at Clongowes, attempted a correspondence with him, but it was intercepted by his mother and read to the
family with some amusement. Eileen (or her father) had adopted a
popular ballad to express her feelings:

> Oh Jimmy Joyce, you are my darlin',
> You are my looking-glass night and mornin'.
> I'd rather have you without a farthin',
> Than Johnny Jones, with his ass and garden.

That at least is one version. It could be that the idea and the
authorship was entirely her father's. At any rate, poor Eileen was
mortally embarrassed by the publicising of her feelings and hence-
forth avoided Jim's company. Fickle young gentleman, he did not
seem to notice.

Back for the summer holidays he demonstrated that, in his
enthusiasm for his studies, which was by now very evident, he had
not lost his taste for fun. Lacking a football to kick around the
green, he appropriated a tall hat belonging to William O'Connell,
John Joyce's maternal uncle, a gentleman of advanced years. When
Jim and his friends had done with it it was in a bad state. Thoughtfully they filled it up with stones before putting it back on the
hallstand. William O'Connell was not delighted at the destruction
but preferred not to have his nephew find out about it, so he sent
it to a hatter who promised to have it back good as new in time
for a picnic due in a few days. When the hat got back it was
covered with some messy stuff which attracted the local flies the
way whiskey did John Joyce.

'My God, man,' said Joyce, squinting at the mass of insects.
'What's the matter with your hat? All the flies on Bray Head are
swarming over it.'

'Musha, let them alone, John,' said the old man. 'Sure the cray-
thurs are taking their tay.'

So long as he was at Clongowes, James remained at the top of
his class and accumulated for his family's sideboard a collection of

17

trophies won at school sporting events. The image of the hero in *A Portrait of the Artist as a Young Man* and *Ulysses* (which are not quite so autobiographical as they seem), of a delicate youth, was artifice. 'Like him was I,' says Stephen Dedalus to himself in *Ulysses*, regarding one of his pupils, 'these sloping shoulders, this gracelessness . . . ugly and futile: lean neck and tangled hair and a stain of ink, a snail's bed. Yet someone had loved him, borne him in her arms and in her heart. But for her the race of the world would have trampled him under foot, a squashed boneless snail. She had loved his weak watery blood drained from her own.'

Not quite the James Joyce his schoolfellows remembered. He grew up tall and slim. He swam well, ran well at long distance and short, played cricket with enthusiasm, had a mania for walking which never left him. He never went mad about sports like his father and grandfather, preferring to exercise his mind. He had no liking for sports which involved punching, kicking, wrestling or otherwise doing violence on one's opponents, nor to playing in teams, except at cricket which was not in his day nearly so violent as it is now. He detested violence always. Cricket was then the least violent of games, and the most elegant.

There was slight drama at Clongowes when another boy broke his glasses. James was beaten with a pandy-bat (more painful than it sounds) by a priest who so far misread his character as to assume he had broken them himself to avoid study. He protested this injustice to the rector, Father Conmee, and was upheld. The incident finds its way into *A Portrait*. Protesting became a life-long habit.

His career at Clongowes ceased in the summer of 1891 when his father, his property dissipated and his employment about to come to an end, could no longer afford the fees. The rates office was wound up, its functions transferred to the Corporation of Dublin, with only a few employees going with it. John Joyce, by no means a success at the job, was retired at the age of forty-two on a pension of £11 a month. He would not have had even that but for the pleading of his wife. With ten children to support, and without other income, he had sunk now beneath even the level of the genteel poor.

The family retreated once more towards Dublin, to the seaside suburb of Blackrock, taking a house in Carysfort Avenue called Leoville, after a stone lion that stood over the porch. Stanislaus was sent to be taught by local nuns. His elder brother was allowed, for the time being, to conduct his own education. He did so by means of the text-books he had brought with him from Clongowes, employing his mother to examine him on the lessons he had taught himself, even on picnic outings. In the hope of some freedom to get on with her own work, she would set him what she calculated to be two hours, study and find him back in an hour.

He continued his own wide reading and began (he was nine years old) his first attempt, apart from school essays, at writing. The project was a novel, written in collaboration with a Protestant boy next door called Raynold. Raynold, a year or so older than himself, does not seem to have kept on at literature, at least not with conspicuous success. The plot (alas, completely lost) was concocted in conversation between the two, Joyce devoting the afternoon to fleshing out the work at his father's desk in the corner of the dining room.

Either at Blackrock or before that at Bray he first got into print, at his father's expense.

The work was *Et Tu, Healy*, a poem: the hero Parnell, the villain his chief lieutenant in the Irish Party, Tim Healy. Parnell was lately dead, the victim of sexual scandal and the hounding which was the fate of Victorian politicians caught in the wrong bed, so long as humbugs like Gladstone had time to spare from the pursuit and conversion to virtue of prostitutes. Parnell, a dull and chaste man whose principal passion was hatred of England (followed closely by contempt for the Irish) had lived monogamously for ten years with Mrs Kitty O'Shea. The liaison was more or less public knowledge, at least to those who took care to know about such things. The fly in the ointment was that Mrs O'Shea's husband was alive, and kicked. Indeed, he was an MP from Galway, a constituency he had been given by Parnell's party as reward for keeping his mouth shut.

Parnell, with many enemies, many followers, but few friends, was too tempting a target. Gladstone did not like him because he was an adulterer; the Irish bishops did not like him because he was a Protestant; his wretched peasant followers, who granted him loyalty because he was the leader of the only party that offered them hope, did not love him because he was a landowner.

O'Shea sued for divorce, and got it. The hounds were let loose.

Parnell hung on for a while, until Healy turned on him at the in-sistence of their sanctimonious English ally, Gladstone, and brought down the uncrowned King of Ireland. "Twas Irish humour, quick and dry', wrote Joyce years later, in one of the sets of doggerel he composed to get bile out of his system, 'flung quicklime into Par-nell's eye'.

> *This lovely land that always sent*
> *Her writers and artists to banishment*
> *And in a spirit of Irish fun*
> *Betrayed her own leaders, one by one.*

The drama was closely observed in the Joyce household, John Joyce remaining a partisan of Parnell and no respecter of the Church. (He was reprimanded by a pious friend for blaspheming when it began to rain. 'Hush John,' said the friend. 'Do you not know that God could drown the world?' 'He could,' said Joyce, 'if he wanted to make a bloody fool of Himself.') It is difficult to speculate to what degree his nine-year-old son understood the ins and outs of adultery, but it is not difficult to imagine the spates of histrionic obscenity, oiled by alcohol, which the destruction of his hero brought forth from John Joyce and his friends. He is said to have approached Healy in a Dublin theatre to shout 'traitor' in his face, but since that is his own story there is no way of knowing if it is true.

The infant writer, enraged as much as his father by Parnell's death (in October 1891), wrote his poem eulogizing him and damn-ing Healy. It was received with enthusiasm by his father's circle, so much so that John Joyce had it printed in broadsheet and arrived home with thirty or forty copies which were freely distributed, but not so freely that some were not left, to be trampled into the floor by the boots of the removal men when the time came to decamp from Blackrock (the Joyces could still afford removal men). No copy survives, but only those lines which Stanislaus and the author could remember, imperfectly. They describe the late Parnell, elevated in death, gazing down in contempt upon the swinish mass of former colleagues, from

> *His quaint-perched aerie on the crags of Time*
> *Where the rude din of this . . . century*
> *Can trouble him no more.*

The lines, no worse than those produced by contemporary laureates

20

seven times Joyce's age, were a souce of much amusement to him when his critical sense was better established.

Mrs Conway's stay with the Joyces did not long survive the death of Parnell and the attendant scenes. She left after a monumental row over his death, at Christmas dinner, 1891, heard by the neighbours across the street, and described in *A Portrait of the Artist*. She had two brushes, one maroon-backed for Davitt of the Land League, one green-backed for Parnell (an inappropriate choice if only she had known it; one of his complaints against the Irish was that they had chosen green, which he considered sinister, as their national colour). When knowledge reached her of his ultimate sin against the Holy Ghost, as carnality, or what is taken to be carnality, is regarded in Ireland, she tore off the green backing, rowed, wept, and left. Stanislaus in particular was not sorry to see her go. So long as she remained, her Catholic enthusiasm had imposed on the family, every evening, the Rosary and the Blessed Litany.

The stay at Blackrock lasted less than a year, before the family moved once again back into Dublin, to Fitzgibbon Street, off Mount-joy Square. Stanislaus, when writing his memoir, compiled a list of nine addresses gone through in about eleven years. The threats of landlords and creditors increased in stridency, but ruin was not yet complete. John Joyce still had a little left from what was raised on the last of the Cork property and he was able to supplement his slight income with occasional odd jobs given to him by old cronies. The family had crossed the Liffey, which was a bad sign in a city where the better class of person preferred to keep south of the river. But there were respectable addresses to the north, and Mount-joy Square was by no means bad. For a few months before moving in, the family lived in lodgings. In the temporary nature of things there seemed little reason to worry about sending the children to school.

Jim's holiday continued. With Stannie in tow, he spent the time exploring the streets of Dublin. Such absences were not taken seriously by the authorities, but eventually, after a few months, John Joyce felt obliged to provide some sort of education. James and Stanislaus had to suffer the indignity of attending the Christian Brothers' school close by in North Richmond Street. It was an episode both preferred to forget. The Brothers are celibate but not priests, which may explain their savage discipline and unsubtle instruction. A traditional method of punishment with them was to force a child to immerse his hands in a bucket of cold water before beating them. The classes were so large, said Stanislaus, he heard little and learnt nothing.

They were rescued by a chance meeting between John Joyce and Father Conmee, no longer rector at Clongowes, now prefect of studies at Belvedere College, two streets away from Mountjoy Square. Father Conmee, distressed to hear his brilliant former pupil was at the mercy of the Christian Brothers, offered to take James and Stanislaus free of charge. James Joyce was now back with the Jesuits, where he felt he belonged. 'I began with the Jesuits,' he said, when the Dominicans, hearing of his brilliance, wanted to poach him away to a school of their own, 'and I want to stay with them'.

Joyce was found, unsurprisingly, to be good at English composition and well enough dedicated to subjects he did not like (like mathematics). He began to win prizes. There was a system in Ireland of having all the pupils in the country compete against one another at national examinations for money prizes. The first he won at the age of twelve in the Intermediate examinations, the very useful sum of twenty pounds. It might have gone into his father's pocket, but John Joyce was inclined to be generous, and allowed his son to spend the money as he pleased. He made the remark, somewhat inappropriate coming from himself, that it was time Jim learnt how to handle money.

Jim financed trips to the theatre, displaying fine taste by choosing whenever possible the better Shakespearian productions. Dublin was still a town visited by actors like Henry Irving and Herbert Beerbohm-Tree, with flourishing theatres and music halls and its own opera company. He bought boots and dresses for the family and, taking his father's advice, played at being a banker, pressing small loans on brothers and sisters and entering the transactions into an account book. The habit of keeping track of money he maintained to the end of his life. (It is always useful to know to whom you owe how much, even if there is no possibility or intention of paying.)

One composition of his survives from this time, on the sort of theme with which teachers of English plague their pupils – 'Trust Not Appearances'. Later Joyce was to be allowed to write on what he liked, but for the time being the prodigy turned the unappetising

22

theme into an overblown discussion of *Fortune,* pretty awful but no worse than his teacher deserved.

'The fickle tide of ever-changing fortune,' he wrote, 'brings with it – good and evil. How beautiful it seems as the harbinger of good and how cruel as the messenger of ill! The man who waits on the temper of a King is but a tiny craft in that great ocean. Thus we see the hollowness of appearances.'

Neat, but little sign so far that young Mr Joyce was going to produce masterpieces. His efforts, nevertheless, were so much better than those of his fellows that his instructor was in the habit of reading them out to the class. Some, naturally, were jealous. A band of them intercepted him on his way home.

Who was the best writer of prose, they enquired, 'Marryat?'

'Newman,' said Joyce, a choice that could not be faulted without insult to the Church, though it was not for his ecclesiastical distinction that Joyce admired him, just his style.

'And who is the best poet, Tennyson?' suggested one.

'No,' said Joyce, 'Byron.'

Now, since Byron was considered to be a wicked person, even by English Protestants, Joyce could at this point safely be beaten up for having committed, at least, heresy. He was punched and thrown into barbed wire (as reported in *A Portrait of the Artist*) and returned home to be comforted and have his clothes mended by his mother.

They were by now living in Millbourne Lane, Drumcondra, having after a year in Fitzgibbon Street slid further down the social scale, this time into a working-class neighbourhood. There was the River Tolka, then as now a thin trickle of sewage, but there were fields and woods about too (now gone). The neighbours' offspring were in the state of pristine savagery normal to Dublin working-class children. The arrival of decayed gentility they saw as a heaven-sent opportunity to inflict carnage at no risk to themselves. 'Their hostility,' said Stanislaus, who got into a scrap without much delay, 'was due solely to that animosity, observable everywhere in the lower classes, to anyone who is not quite so lousy as they are.'

Stannie's delegated opponent in this peripheral skirmish to the class war was a red-haired brat, one Pisser Duffy. He does not record whether he won or lost, but he took the precaution from then on of going around in the company of a gang formed of members of his

23

own class. His brother remembered the incident and gave him the name Duffy, by way of a private joke, when he made him the central figure of the story 'A Painful Case', in *Dubliners*.

That summer of 1894 James was treated by his father to a trip to Glasgow. He enjoyed traipsing after his father from one pub to another, listening to the songs and the talk. There was no particular point to this trip, except that the captain of the liner was a drinking acquaintance of John Joyce, and gave him free passage. Apparently the captain had more than the usual Irish devotion to duty, since he declined to drink when the ship was on the seas and he in charge of it. John Joyce was under no such constraint, got drunk and quarrelled bitterly with his host, who happened to be an anti-Parnellite. 'By God, man,' recounted Joyce, safely back on dry land, 'if he'd been drinking he would have thrown me overboard.'

Stanislaus would not have wept. He could never see his father's antics with the same amused tolerance as his brother. 'I believe most firmly,' he wrote, 'that when the heart feeds on hatred and contempt, the human being is facing the wrong way. But how is one to blink facts and maintain one's honesty?'

Facts. About that time the last child was born and died quickly. The child was scarcely in his grave when John Joyce, in another drunken fit leapt at his wife roaring 'Now, by God, is the time to finish it,' the chosen expedient being strangulation.

Mrs Joyce was saved by James, who jumped on his father's back and brought all of them tumbling to the floor, the other children screaming in terror. May Joyce fled with the younger children and her eldest daughter, taking refuge with neighbours. Some days later a police sergeant arrived to deliver a lecture to John Joyce on the desirability of keeping the peace and refraining from murder. Unthinkable disgrace in middle-class Ireland. To be lectured by the police in one's own parlour! But the Joyces were no longer in middle-class Ireland.

'We were at last,' wrote Stanislaus, 'on the same level as the navvies and farm-labourers around us.'

It is probably for that reason that the neighbours were, from that point onwards, a degree more civil. The Irish like nothing better than to see their putative superiors dragged down to their own level. It is part of the destructive instinct of the race.

Whatever effect the lecture had on John Joyce, it did not cause him

24

to cut down on the booze. Stanislaus, who sounds from time to time more like a Salvationist (an *atheist Salvationist*) than a lapsed Jesuit, speaks in one of his gentler phrases of 'the imbecility of drunkenness, that malodorous mixture of partial paralysis and semi-insanity.' The practice in dealing with drunks, however, would come in useful some years later, when the drunk would not be his father but his brother. Stanislaus was to become for many hard years, as he described himself, 'my brother's keeper'.

The time came, late that year, to leave Millbourne Lane, the landlord's patience having run out. The neighbours were sorry to see them go. Perhaps after all they had added a little tone to the district. One called to express his regrets over a bottle of stout. He was a big man, the father of Pisser Duffy. Off again, this time back to North Richmond Street, where the awful Christian Brothers were, a stone's throw from Mountjoy Square and Fitzgibbon Street, but not by any means a good address. The Joyces, who began their removals career with two vans and a float, ended it needing only a handcart. In the Dublin tradition the removals took the form of what is known as a 'Moonlight Flit', with as much gaiety as possible, the theory being that defaulted landlords are normally in bed after midnight. It is unusual on these occasions to leave a forwarding address.

James Joyce's chosen role, as befits the son and heir, was to precede the handcart carrying the family history in the form of several oil portraits and a framed coat-of-arms. There is a part of Galway called the Joyce Country. John Stanislaus claimed the arms of these Joyces, though no genealogist could buttress the claim. That did not stop his son carting the coat-of-arms around with him for the rest of his life.

Chapter Two
I Will Not Serve

Joyce in later life gave the Jesuits credit for having developed his mind in an orderly direction, while coming eventually wholly to reject their teachings. The Stephen Daedalus[1] of *Stephen Hero* (the earliest version of *A Portrait*. Only a couple of hundred pages survive.) is closer to himself than the Stephen of *A Portrait* and *Ulysses*. 'He spurned from before him the stale maxims of the Jesuits,' says the first Stephen, 'and he swore an oath that they should never establish over him an ascendancy.'

They had, for a while. Before he discovered what they did not wish him to discover, which necessarily he could not discover until he was past puberty, their emphasis on the cultivation of the soul produced ecstasy in him more often than the annoyance it produced in his brother. (Stanislaus, who was so earnest, lost his faith through the exercise of his intellect. James, who was cerebral, lost it through acquaintance of the flesh.) Catholic ceremony, the inheritance of five thousand years of priestcraft, Pagan, Jewish and Christian, appeals to the sensual. Catholic dogma seduces the mind, Catholic myth the heart; all by skilful design, the cunning of millennia. Joyce served as altar boy and wrote a hymn to the Virgin. It dawned on his mentors that they had the makings of a priest. They had indeed, but he was to choose his own religion. It would not be theirs, and there would be no pope, no bishops, few prophets, and no priest but himself.

James Joyce, as a child, had been remarkably well-behaved, considering his family circumstances. Signs of rebellion appeared about the time of puberty. He became more inclined to independence, in several directions, as his own high opinion of himself was reinforced by the approbation of his elders.

After going with his parents to see Mrs Patrick Campbell in a

[1] Spelt 'Dedalus' in *A Portrait* and *Ulysses*. For the explanation of this switch see pp. 91–2.

play, *Magda*, by Sudermann, he announces, when he gets home: 'The subject of the play is genius breaking out in the home and against the home. You needn't have gone to see it. It's going to happen in your own house.'

His mother might have felt some twinges at this declaration. Her son, convinced by now that he was an artist of some sort (though unsure of *what* sort) was attracted to the possibility of finding a morality suitable for an artist, a morality, in other words, which would allow him license to follow his own inclinations. The philosophy of aggressive decadence which was fashionable at the time provided seeds of rebellion. The idea of immersing oneself in *Sin* is attractive from several points of view. Classical Catholic literature is full of it (followed, of course, by repentance) and every second scribbler or painter of the 1890s, finding repentance unnecessary, was able to excuse his bad behaviour on the grounds it was fuel for his Art. For James Joyce the impetus to rebellion was by no means purely philosophical. His father's blood was in his veins.

Young Joyce, from earliest childhood, had had a pronounced interest in females, of the sort which makes generations of parents more recent than his own anxious that their sons may be homosexually inclined because they spend so much time in the company of girls.

He wrote poetry for Eileen Vance. 'She too wants me to catch hold of her,' thinks Stephen in *A Portrait of the Artist as a Young Man*. 'That's why she came with me to the tram. I could easily catch hold of her when she comes up to my step: nobody is looking. I could hold her and kiss her.'

It is certainly a sign of precocious sexuality to want to kiss girls at the age of ten or so, when it is more normal to hope that such distasteful activities can be put off for many years, or avoided altogether. It is a consequence of Joyce's lifelong obsession with females that we got from him the most brilliant, and complete, portraits of women ever drawn. (Even Leopold Bloom is part-female, but more of that later.) Given a weaker interest in the other sex we might have had instead Father James Joyce SJ, author of a new system of Catholic philosophy, something, perhaps, like Teilhard de Chardin. Better Joyce as he was.

Some time past his fourteenth birthday, Joyce's sexuality got him into trouble for the first time. The object of his lust was a servant girl in the Joyce household (surely one of the last) who was in her early twenties. The source of the story is Stanislaus, who innocently precipitated the crisis. Father William Henry, the rector of Belvedere, had got it into his head that his prize pupil's immortal soul might be in danger. Precisely how he got the idea is a mystery, though certainly Joyce had been increasingly insolent. But Father Henry appears to have been uncommonly shrewd, and the sin of Pride was not the only one that occurred to him.

He summoned Stanislaus to his office and questioned him about his brother's morals. Stanislaus, being scarcely twelve years old, had no idea what he was talking about. Sternly the rector reminded him that he was a priest and that the conversation was 'in the nature of the confessional'. There was the terrible sin to consider of telling a lie to the Holy Ghost. (Surely the Holy Ghost, being omniscient, knew without being told. And was Father Henry promising the secrecy of the confessional or not? Stanislaus realised afterwards he had been taken in by the Jesuitical ploy, and was properly incensed.)

Dredging in his mind for some scrap to offer up to the Holy Ghost, Stanislaus recollected a bit of horse-play between his brother and the servant girl some time previous. They had chased one another around and took turns at catching and spanking one another. Given the differences in ages, young Jim must have got the greater thrill out of it, but Stanislaus was inclined to think there was nothing sexual about it at all.

Father Henry knew otherwise, equipped as he was with the moral zeal of a convert from Protestantism. His suspicions confirmed, he sent for Mrs Joyce and informed her without preamble that her eldest son needed watching, being given to evil ways. The poor woman, seriously worried, asked what form this evil took, but the priest would say no more.

At home Stanislaus confessed himself the source of Father Henry's conviction. Mrs Joyce was inclined to blame it on the servant girl, but vengeance could not be visited on her since she had already left.

John Joyce, when he got home, detected the strained atmosphere and inquired what was going on.

'I am under a cloud at school,' remarked his eldest son laconically.

'What about?' asked John Joyce, playing the concerned parent.

'I don't know,' said Jim. 'You had better ask the rector.'

So John Joyce took himself to Belvedere and quizzed Father Henry, who was not forthcoming, limiting himself to: 'The boy will cause you trouble.'

'No he won't,' said Joyce, 'because I won't let him.'

He was in no position to curb his son's rampant appetite, which later that summer managed to find a fuller expression.

There are arguments among admirers of Joyce about the precise degree of autobiography in *A Portrait of the Artist*. Stanislaus emphasizes that his brother's book is more art than autobiography but there are parts – those describing the hero's chasing after whores, and his subsequent religious crisis – which are plainly accounts of what happened to James Joyce (suitably embroidered, for art's sake) and how he felt about it. For chase after whores is just what the adolescent Joyce did when he had money, and he began at the age of fourteen. The finance was supplied by Exhibition money. He won £20 in 1894 and again in 1895, the second award to run for three years at £20 a year. And in 1897 he won an exhibition of £30 for two years and £3 for writing the best English composition in his grade in Ireland.

In the summer of 1896, with money in his pocket, lust sprang upon him with a fully orchestrated accompaniment of guilt. Stephen Dedalus in *A Portrait* roams the alleyways of the prostitutes' quarter of Dublin in a state of high excitement, looking for instances of sin in the shape of whores, listening for the sounds of illicit coupling. 'He wanted to sin with another of his kind, to force another being to sin with him and to exult with her in sin.' The force which drove Joyce there was not taken away from him by the Catholic fear of doom, which would stay with him a good while yet. Such feelings and passions as he describes do not come from the imagination of one who has not felt them. Joyce is describing experience.

Since the objects of his lust were willing, as they are when gentlemen of any age have money, he found the occasions of sin frequent and indulged them, enjoying, even in his gross sinfulness as he felt it to be, a sense of religious indulgence: 'The yellow gas-flames arose before his [Stephen's] vision against the vapoury sky, burning as if before an altar. Before the doors and in the lighted halls groups were gathered arrayed as for some rite. He was in another world: he had awakened from a slumber of centuries.'

Here art does take over from reality. At this point in the book Stephen is approached by one of the ladies whom he desires. She takes him to her room and he watches her as she undoes her gown, 'noting the proud conscious movement of her perfumed head'. She embraces him with soft round arms and his heart rises in him in joy and relief. Ardently she kisses him. With body and mind both, he surrenders to her.

Well, that is a pleasant fiction. Perhaps later on Joyce was able to find the more expensive sort of prostitute who might correspond to that description. His actual initiation was somewhat different, as confessed to his brother. What did happen was that Joyce, walking home from the theatre with a few shillings in his pocket, chanced upon an outdoor whore on the banks of the Royal Canal and with her put the remains of his innocence behind him. The transaction would not have cost him above two shillings and sixpence. (A Dublin joke of the time runs like this. Potential client: 'Don't bother me, woman. I am the Crown Solicitor for Fermanagh.' Whore: 'Are you now? Well I'm the half-crown solicitor for Stephen's Green.') The experience was to his taste, since he repeated it so often. It is to be doubted that the lady was highly perfumed.

Meanwhile, Joyce, far from abandoning religion, or even con-templating it, had been enrolled in the Sodality of the Blessed Virgin Mary at Belvedere and was elected its prefect in September 1896. Now, how is it possible for a fervent young Marianist, conspicuous for his devotion to the BVM, to be spending his pocket money on prostitutes? Quite possible. Our Lady, after all, is a woman. Indeed, she is normally depicted in cheap Catholic art of the pietistic sort as a good-looking blonde with a kind look in her eye. Joyce, as Stephen Dedalus, displays signs of being in love with the lady. 'The glories of Mary,' he writes of Stephen, 'held his soul captive.' The whores behind Mecklenburgh Street were one part of his pursuit of the female, the BVM another. A religion which did not have a sup-reme Goddess (as Protestantism has not) could not have commanded his allegiance so long or marked him so deep. 'If ever his soul, re-entering his dwelling shyly after the frenzy of his body's lust had spent itself, was turned towards her whose emblem is the morning star, *bright and musical, telling of heaven and infusing peace,* it was when her names were murmured softly by lips whereon there still lingered foul and shameful words, the savour itself of a lewd kiss.' It is a defiant and courageous young man who worships Mary, fears an eternity of hell, spends money awarded for scholastic virtue on prostitutes, and gets aesthetic satisfaction from the juxtaposing of his sin again his desire for grace. Soothed by ritual, Joyce was able publicly to fulfil his function as prefect of the Sodality but unable privately to address prayers to God, or His Mother.

After some months of this split behaviour he felt his soul to be festering in sin. Rescue was at hand. The Catholic Church has evolved an institution called the retreat to attract back to virtue those of its adherents who have strayed from the path of righteousness. One such occurred at the right moment to cause Joyce to suffer a religious crisis, and to cause him to return, for a while, to purity. At retreats the chosen instrument of redemption was terror, induced by graphic and passionate accounts of the tortures of the damned, spread out over several days. On 30 November 1896, Joyce and his companions from Belvedere embarked on their spiritual odyssey. There is some doubt about the name of the preacher who gave the sermons, none at all about his talents. Joyce spends twenty-five pages in *A Portrait of the Artist* describing the two-day sermon he endured. In hell eyeballs burn, intestines glow incandescent, demons gnaw, conscience torments, God mocks most spitefully – all for eternity. None of this is to be doubted, for the greatest doctors of the church have devoted many years of their lives to discovering the precise climate of hell. Certain refinements achieved there and granted in visions to saints outdo in vicious obscenity all the fantasies of all the pornographers that ever lived.

'Dear little brothers in Christ,' the Jesuit tenderly addresses his charges, before trying to frighten the wits out of the more imaginative and gullible among them. It didn't work on Stanislaus, whose robust mind was already capable of detecting fictions, and whose imagination did not extend to embracing mysteries. It did work on his brother.

Overcome with revulsion at his sins, Stephen Dedalus vomits in his bedroom and goes the day afterwards to confession in a strange church, as Joyce did himself, in order not to have to face the rector in the confessional. Then occurs the prototype procession of

31

sins, since imitated by countless Catholic writers of autobiographical
fiction who first found it in Joyce.

'I . . . committed sins of impurity, father.'
'With yourself, my child?'
'And . . . with others.'
'With women, my child?'
'Yes, father.'

He did not get the tongue-lashing he might have expected at
Belvedere, but was heard with a certain compassion and sent on his
way, with a warning that sin was bad for him, and an exhortation to
mend his behaviour. Mary was recommended as an appropriate target
at which to aim prayers. A splendid cycle this seems – sin, guilt,
confession, absolution, penance, prayer, sin – and one known
as a matter of routine only to Catholics. The works of James
Joyce are a fine introduction, for those who do not know it, to the
Roman Catholic religion. He is very sound on matters of doctrine,
having taken the trouble to master many of the more esoteric dogma.
His hellfire sermon would do very well as a textbook for novice
priests, containing, as it does, no instance of heresy.

Feeling that he had had a narrow escape from perdition, Joyce
took to mortifying himself and otherwise indulging in pious acts
to be certain of the paradise he had so nearly lost. Stanislaus remembered him engaging in long talks at the college with Father
Jeffcott, the preacher of the Lenten sermon in 1897 (the conversion
had lasted at least that long), and with Father Conmee, the rector.
Joyce took to attending early morning masses with his mother,
remaining in the chapel when the mass was over to continue with
his own prayers, outdoing his mother in piety as she reminded him
his breakfast was ready. During Lent also he gave up theatres and
newspapers. One of his sisters remembered seeing him in the street
telling his beads. There were other austerities which he practised.
Stanislaus describes them as mild. If they correspond to those
indulged by Stephen Dedalus, they are not quite so mild. Stephen
mortifies his sight by staring at the pavement while he walks, and
avoiding the gaze of women. He mortifies his sense of hearing by
listening to the sharpening of knives, his sense of touch by many
devices, including, when he is telling his beads, walking with his
arms held stiffly by his sides. Joyce's friends and family, much to their

amusement, did notice some manifestations of this behaviour, so the catalogue in *A Portrait* may be a true one. It is also true that the author of that catalogue had a pronounced taste for Sacher-Masoch in later life, but that is skipping ahead .

There was one sense which neither Stephen nor his creator found easy to mortify, and that was smell, both being indifferent to strong odours, particularly those given off by their own bodies. 'All Ireland is washed by the gulfstream,' says Stephen in *Ulysses*, an excuse commonly advanced by the Irish for avoiding bathwater. (Swift, whom the Irish sometimes claim as their own, betrayed his Englishness by fastidiousness.)

In *A Portrait*, Stephen, seeking further mortification, carefully explores the stinks offered both by the outside world and his own person, with a view to selecting one for self-torture. Joyce does not describe these experiments – *A Portrait* is less uninhibited in these matters than *Ulysses* – but they may be imagined. He decides that the only truly revolting smells are those associated with stale urine, human and animal. These he pursues and savours wherever possible. (After the episode in *A Portrait*, where Stephen takes part as the leading actor in a school play – as Joyce did – he is so upset after the performance, apparently because the girl he is smitten with is not waiting for him, that he makes an excuse to his family and runs away to seek solace, in an alleyway, in the inhalation of the odours of horse piss and rotted straw. 'It is an odour to breathe. It will calm my heart. My heart is quite calm now. I will go back.')

In any other country (except perhaps along the Catholic littoral of the Mediterranean or in Hindu India) this behaviour might be put down to incipient lunacy or criminality. In Joyce's own it was thought to be due to an excess of religious fervour, quite natural at his age, and possibly fitting him to be put in charge of the souls of others. He was invited to become a Jesuit.

The invitation came from the director of studies at Belvedere when Joyce was still sixteen, but it had come too late. His conversion had run its course after only a few months. His intellect had rejected Catholic dogma and dismissed his fear of damnation as superstitious terror, and that part of his anatomy whose importance as a driving force in young men is not to be underrated, had dictated that he return to embracing women. By embracing women he was to embrace Life, and for the devotion to the Church which was so

33

large a part of his scheme, he would substitute a devotion to Art. The mass was a drama which was satisfying to the soul. There was a drama of a more satisfying kind which did not require that he lie to himself. 'I will not serve that in which I no longer believe,' writes Stephen. '*Non Serviam,*' said Lucifer, and was thrown out of Paradise in an instant for his impudence, thence to set up his own kingdom. Joyce adopted this motto as his own, and the Church was not all he would not serve.

For a little while the idea of following the priestly vocation had its attraction, which was principally power – a power greater than angels, to bring God down upon the altar and hear and grant absolution for the sins of women and young girls. But the observance of priestly life at the college did nothing to reinforce the temptation. Priests appeared to him to be dessicated creatures, leading dreary lives, incapable of intellectual distinction, men who took cold baths and wore bleached linen. Joyce was employed by his fellow pupils to waste time in class by baiting the priests with abstruse points of catechism.

By the time of the offer the Joyce family had moved again, this time to the district of Fairview, not very well named. Nearby the filthy Liffey slimed its way into Dublin Bay and the smell of sewage exposed to sunlight was not sweet. But there is a place not far distant called Bull Island, reached by a causeway, and there Joyce took to walking on the long strand. It appears many times in his works. Stephen in *A Portrait*, after the interview with the priest, when he is decided against the offer, goes walking there, passing on the way a statue of the Virgin, perched 'fowl-wise' on a pole in one of the garish shrines which disfigure the Irish landscape. Against that is counterpointed the image of a brazen young girl about his own age whom he sees paddling in a stream with her skirts hiked up about her waist. Stephen is most impressed with the sight of her young legs. She does not mind his frank gaze, returns it. His soul bounds free. The BVM loses for good.

That is precisely what happened to Joyce. He had experienced one of his 'epiphanies,' the word he borrowed from theology to describe those moments of transfiguration when life becomes art and art grants truth. These, as he wrote them down, were his first serious excursions into prose. The composition of them, along with his poetry, allowed him to justify to himself the title of artist.

In his writing, as is usual with young writers, he was much given to imitating the style of authors he admired. Newman was one, Ruskin another. To the list were added, as he got older and his reading wider, Tolstoy, Turgenieff, the Elizabethan poets, Verlaine, Maeterlinck, Sudermann, D'Annunzio, Blake, George Moore, Yeats. The greatest influence of all was to be Ibsen. For a while he had a high regard for Thomas Hardy, principally because of his moral stance, and the fact he was frowned upon in Dublin, as is usual with highly moral writers, for his supposed immorality.

At the time the family was living in North Richmond Street Joyce plundered the Capel Street Lending Library, a mile distant, for his reading. One book he got from there was *Tess of the D'Urbervilles*. The librarian, an old man called Grogan, felt this to be a dangerous work and warned John Joyce, who, in one of his occasional attempts at playing paterfamilias, took up the question with his son.

'So,' said James, 'so I have to ask old Grogan what I am to read. The ignorant old clod-hopper, he'd be much more at home in his native bog. I've a good mind to write a letter to the Corporation about him.'

'Well, if you say it's all right . . .' said John Joyce, more at home with racing papers. For breathtaking literary interest, said Stanislaus, he would turn to Wilkie Collins.

James was in the habit of sending Stanislaus to the library for him, with lists of books he wanted, in descending order of preference, claiming he could not afford the time from his studies to make the trip himself. When he found a work he admired he sought out all other works by the same author and read them through. Stanislaus reports that he retained little of what he read. Stanislaus read most of them afterwards, curious to know what engrossed his brother's genius (he had decided by then that James was indeed a genius), and determined to keep up well enough to be able to follow the progress of his brother's mind. He discovered, when he mentioned certain points brought up by his reading his brother's books, that brother Jim had frequently forgotten the passages concerned, and was grateful for the reminder. Even about the age of fifteen, James Joyce was glad to acknowledge his younger brother as a whetstone on which he sharpened his own mind (Stannie's mind was of no account, being hopelessly blunt.

35

His brother did not mind telling him so). Stanislaus was enthusiastic for Dickens, and even Walter Scott. Joyce dismissed both as story-tellers. Storytelling was not art.

One of the lists Stanislaus took to Capel Street contained, a little way down, *Jude the Obscure*, in ambiguous handwriting. As it happened, the first book on the list was available, so Stanislaus was spared the necessity of asking Grogan for *Jude the Obscene*, though he had screwed up his courage to do so. Reporting this back to his brother, he was rewarded with loud laughter. He wished he had been there, said Jim, to see the looks on the stupid faces of the two of them, brother and librarian.

Until the age of fifteen Joyce followed diligently the course of studies prescribed at Belvedere. The last examination for which he took pains was the Middle Grade, when he managed to do well even in mathematics, to win his exhibition. After that the literary interest took over and he read what he liked.

He wrote a good deal of poetry, some of it lyrical, some occasional, after the example of Goldsmith. A classmate called George O'Donnell was the butt of a mock epitaph written by Joyce in the Goldsmith style. Joyce wrote it in the front of O'Donnell's copy of *A Concise History of Ireland*, a school textbook. It reads:

> *Poor little Georgie, the son of a lackey,*
> *Famous for 'murphies', spirits and 'baccy,*
> *Renowned all around for a feathery head*
> *Which had a tendency to become red.*
> *His genius was such that all men used to stare,*
> *His appearance was that of a bull at a fair,*
> *The pride of Kilmainham, the joy of the class,*
> *A moony, a loony, an idiot, an ass.*
> *Drumcondra's production, and by the same rule,*
> *The prince of all pot-boys, a regular fool.*
> *All hail to the beauteous, the lovely, all hail*
> *And hail to his residence in Portland gaol.*

A little crude, what with the references to O'Donnell's unfortun-ate appearance, lack of wit and his family's trade, but O'Donnell was impressed enough at the production to preserve it, and showed it with pride to Padraic Colum, when that friend of his friend was writing his memoir, *Our Friend James Joyce*.

Joyce was writing lyrics as well, and collected them into a note-

book labelled *Moods*. There were fifty or sixty poems of his own
(none survive) and half a dozen translations from Latin and
French. A second volume was called *Shine and Dark*. It was mostly
dark, judging by what Stanislaus preserved of it, his diary being
written in parts on sheets of his brother's discarded poetry. These
poems are much later than the schoolboy efforts and echo his lusts
and his guilts.

> *There are no lips to kiss this foul remains of thee,*
> *O, dead Unchastity!*
> *The curse of loneliness broods silent on thee still,*
> *Doing its utmost will,*
> *And men shall cast thee justly to a narrow tomb,*
> *A sad and bitter doom.*

Awful stuff, but he was serving an apprenticeship and he did have
the taste to throw it away. Another goes :

> *Wind thine arms round me, woman of sorcery,*
> *While the lascivious music murmurs afar:*
> *I will close mine eyes, and dream as I dance with thee,*
> *And pass away from the world where my sorrows are.*

The hero of that one dances himself to death in a jangle of bad
rhymes. The adolescent Joyce is scarcely to be laughed at for wanting
a 'woman of sorcery'. Who doesn't? He had not known love yet,
only whores, and dreamed of a girl who would love him.

Another literary production of a lower order is mentioned in
A Portrait, which has to do with certain tremors of guilt induced
in Stephen by the sound of a pure young girl's innocent laughter.
Stephen admits to the practice, common in adolescent males, of
fishing out dirty pictures secreted in the fireplace, and using them
for what they were intended for. He takes to producing pornography
as well as consuming it, writing down accounts of his encounters
with harlots and leaving them after dark where they might be
picked up by young women and read by them, hopefully with shameful excitement. Stephen, unable to get his hands on the young
maidens of Ireland, liked to satisfy himself by ravishing them at a
distance. This tendency persisted in Joyce, who had a fondness for
the literature of self-abuse and in 1909, when temporarily parted
from his wife, exchanged with her letters designed to assist one
another in masturbation.

37

He tried his hand at 'humorous' dialect poems too; the principal technical device being to drop the final 'g' in certain words:

> *Am I foolish to be hopin'*
> *That you left your window open*
> *To be listenin' to me mopin'*
> *Here and singin', lady mine?*

This he called 'Rebuking,' keeping *that* 'g' for some reason. Stannie, asked his opinion of it, said he thought it would be all right if he changed the 'b' of the title to a 'p'. James, who did not normally react well to adverse criticism, laughed, and wrote no more in that vein, though he kept the habit of doggerel.

He wrote some sketches at Fairview, about the age of sixteen, giving them the title *Silhouettes* after the first, which Richard Ellmann has unkindly called, going on the outline remembered by Stanislaus, 'avant-garde literature of the school of General Booth'. True, Joyce appears to share the Salvationist's detestation of the effect of drink (booze was a later enthusiasm of his, coming a good way after women) but there is a hint too of the realism he was to embrace to a tiresome degree before going beyond it, in the style he called a style 'of scrupulous meanness' which makes the reading of parts of *Stephen Hero* a leaden duty, but suits all but the last story in *Dubliners* perfectly and makes that book high literature.

In the story the narrator sees two figures silhouetted against a drawn blind, a drunken man and a sharp-faced woman. The man strikes the woman, the lights go out. The narrator waits a while for further drama. Faint candlelight appears. The woman is seen with two children in tow (presumably the scene is played on the ground floor). She points a warning finger at her now unconscious spouse. 'Don't waken Pa,' she is saying. End of vignette.

Once again, Joyce, though by no means producing masterpieces, is demonstrating his singularity. A violent saga of some sort would be a more normal production at that age and if not that, then a love story. No plot either. What's the moral? 'He declared bitterly,' said Stanislaus of his brother in his youth, 'that he believed in only two things, a woman's love of her child and a man's love of lies; and he was determined that his spiritual experience should not be a make-believe,' this recollection being perhaps coloured by Stanislaus's own dour view of life, love and lies.

Two of his early stories did in fact have plots, and one of them was to have been submitted to an extremely lowbrow magazine called *Titbits* (so lowbrow, a form of it is still with us), being written in the style favoured by that organ. Stanislaus describes it: 'The plot concerns a man who goes to a masked ball disguised as a prominent Russian diplomat, and when returning home on foot, narrowly escapes assassination at the hands of a Nihilist outside the Russian Embassy. The would-be assassin is arrested, and the masquer, too, as a suspicious character, because in his confusion he forgets about his disguise. But he is rescued by "the laughing witch who is soon to be his bride," who, hearing of the attempt, at once guesses what has happened and hastens to the police station to identify him.'

Joyce, not wishing to acknowledge authorship of this piece, had no objection to being paid for it (Bloom in *Ulysses* reads a story in *Titbits* called 'Matcham's Masterstroke' – 'Matcham often thinks of the masterstroke by which he won the laughing witch who . . .' – and notes, 'seated calm above his own rising smell,' as his bowels ease, that payment has been made to the author at the rate of one guinea a column). He gave it to a friend called MacGinty to post under his own name, but MacGinty apparently neglected to do so. It seems a pity on two counts. First, the yellow press, so-called, which was later to make so much mileage out of the author of a certain 'obscene' book, might have provided him with a sorely needed alternative source of income. Second, John Joyce, whose favourite reading *Titbits* was, would have had the pleasure of knowing early that his son had the makings of a true writer in him.

James and Stanislaus were regular guests at the home of David Sheehy, a Member of Parliament whose two sons attended Belvedere. There were four daughters, and for the youngest, Mary, Joyce harboured fond feelings for some years, without ever letting her know. She was, incidentally, the prettiest. The brighter contemporaries of the Sheehy children were encouraged to congregate in the house on Sunday evenings. They amused themselves with singing, parlour games and dancing. Sometimes they got up plays amongst themselves. Another frequent guest there was Francis Skeffington. He became a close friend, if also something of a butt for Joyce's humour, and duly finds his way into *A Portrait* as MacCann, archetypal Nationalist and bone-headed believer in political solutions to all that ails mankind. The chief attraction for Skeffington at the Sheehy's was the eldest daughter Margaret, whom eventually he married. When he did he changed his name to Sheehy-Skeffington in token of his belief in female emancipation. To his feminism he added teetotalism, vegetarianism, pugnacious pacifism and premarital chastity, none of them (Skeffington's pacifism being too militant for Joyce's taste) likely to recommend him to Joyce, who did, however, respect his intelligence. Sheehy-Skeffington was shot during the First World War by a demented British Army captain on suspicion of being a rebel.

Joyce liked to withdraw into himself for spells of moody intro-spection, which he presented as steely detachment. Stephen Dedalus indulges these moods a great deal and is hardly ever extrovert. Not so Joyce. He enjoyed clowning. Stanislaus describes him at the Sheehy's watching a charade performed by Margaret: 'He was sitting on the floor, half reclining, half resting on one hand, looking up at her with an expression of blank imbecility on his face. Then, following the recitation, his face showed indignation, or astonishment or happiness, always at an imbecile level. At any point of irony he would go into a kink of silly giggles, the perfect reproduction of the laugh of a girl friend of ours, and recovering himself to find that the point of irony was long past and that the tone was now pathetic, fell to weeping and blowing his nose loudly.' He entered into all these entertainments enthusiastically. The company particularly admired his beautiful singing. His repertoire ran from grand opera to Irish comic ballads learnt from his father, and one speciality was *The Man who Broke the Bank at Monte Carlo*.

In the summer of 1898 he took his exams and left Belvedere for university, but not before he had appeared in the leading role in the school's production of Anstey's farce, *Vice Versa*. Playing a school-teacher, he took the opportunity to parody Father Henry, who was sitting in the front row and was said to have enjoyed it. Certainly his fellow pupils did.

He did not do so well in his last set of exams as he had before, but he kept the exhibition he had won in 1897 and won a £4 prize for the best English composition. This dropping off was not sur-prising, since he had a very cavalier attitude to turning up on time, or sometimes, turning up at all. Once, his English teacher lost patience with him and sent him to interrupt Father Henry, who was teaching another class, to report his lateness. Joyce did so. Father Henry told him off. Joyce listened in silence until the end, then added, 'Mr Dempsey told me to tell you, sir, that I was half an hour late yesterday too.' Father Henry tore off another strip while Joyce listened in apparent boredom. 'Mr Dempsey told me to tell you, sir,' he said when the rector had finished, 'that I have not been in time for school any day this month.' A less brilliant pupil might have expected to be beaten unmercifully. Joyce could depend on an unusual degree of indulgence.

His final rebellion at Belvedere was to refuse to sit the college exam in Catholic studies. He claimed he was too busy studying for the Board of Education exams which, being interdenominational, omitted religion. Since this was transparently false the rector lost his temper and refused Joyce permission to sit the examinations he had to pass if he were to proceed to university. He appeared unmoved by the prospect, but was saved by the intercession of his French master, who did not want to see his best pupil wasted. Joyce was allowed to enter the examination hall late. He passed.

Chapter Three
The Master Finds His Master

Catholic Ireland had gone four centuries without its own university before it was provided with one, thanks to the energy of an Englishman, Cardinal Newman, in the mid-nineteenth century. By the time Joyce attended it – he enrolled at University College, Dublin, in September 1898 for his preparatory year – it still had little of the distinction of the Anglo-Irish university down on College Green, Trinity College, which Catholics were forbidden to enter without permission from their bishop. UCD was then run by the Jesuits, so Joyce was still in their care, and students did not live in – there were branches of this Catholic university in Cork, Galway and Belfast – so Joyce was still stuck with his family.

The Church was by now more or less abandoned. Some wag put Joyce's name down for the college Sodality but almost certainly he never attended its meetings. Joyce was no more devoted to his studies at university than he had been in the last year at Belvedere, preferring to skip lectures and spend as much time as possible either idling or in the National Library, a few yards away.

Having now abandoned the Church he did not turn on it, dismissing it, or at least the Irish branch of it, as 'the scullery-maid of Christendom'. His attitude was mere indifference, as he demonstrated to Stanislaus in a conversation as they walked between their home and the National Library. Stanislaus announced with vehemence that he was not going to do his Easter duty for the singular reason that he had decided he did not believe in the doctrine of transubstantiation.

'Don't you think,' inquired the elder brother, more interested in his own business, 'that there is a certain resemblance between the mystery of the mass and what I am trying to do? I mean that I am trying in my poems to give people some kind of intellectual pleasure or spiritual enjoyment by converting the bread of everyday life into something that has a permanent artistic life of its own.'

42

Stanislaus, for once choosing to follow his own thoughts instead of his brother's, repeated that he did not think that the tasteless wafer that is called the Host, and the wine, put into the mouth of the communicant, became the body and blood of Christ. And even if they did, he continued with blunt logic, he did not hold with cannibalism. His brother threw back his head and roared with laughter. A mystery is a mystery, a sacrament is a sacrament. One either accepts or does not. 'Do as you please,' said Jim. 'I certainly don't want to influence you.'

In appearance he was dishevelled. He did not comb his hair and his clothes looked slept in. His Dante-like profile was impressive. So were his steel-blue eyes, though he could not see very far out of them and now refused to wear glasses for vanity's sake, this adding to his apparent air of aloofness. You cannot appear to be very interested in what you cannot see. He maintained his distaste for soap.

In *A Portrait*, where Stephen Dedalus is louse-ridden, he wonders if the girl Emma, whom he desires, has settled for some athlete who every day washes himself 'to the waist', as if that were the furthest anyone would venture. 'Yes, it was her body he smelt, a wild and languid smell, the tepid limbs over which his music had flowed desirously and the secret soft linen upon which her flesh distilled odour and a dew.

'A louse crawled over the nape of his neck and, putting his thumb and forefinger deftly beneath his loose collar, he caught it.'

Scarcely surprising that the lady did not fancy him. Joyce, asked his pet aversion during a parlour game, answered 'soap and water'. He did not care what was thought of him. The workings of his mind were private and precious to him, his person and his outward behaviour were not.

At the college he became known as a champion of Ibsen, by then an old man not far from death (he died in 1906 at the age of seventy-eight), famous throughout Europe but so little known in the fish-pond of Dublin that Joyce's fellow students thought his advocacy due to a desire to appear eccentric. But Stanislaus remembered the arrival in the Belvedere days of William Archer's translation of *The Master Builder* and his brother staying up into the night to read it, armchair, table and lamp pulled over to the fire. In Ibsen he found a morality, or at least a defiance of conventional morality, which suited him quite well. At the same time he felt able to claim that morality had nothing to do with art, performing mental gymnastics to reconcile the two points of view.

Ibsen wrote his plays for publication, regarding that as almost more important than performance. The state of the European theatre made long runs improbable except in the largest cities, but widespread publication ensured that Ibsen's plays sold as well as novels and were known to thousands of enthusiasts who had no chance of seeing them performed. He had even been heard of (if not much read) in Ireland, and his name was used as a handy symbol of modern degeneracy by those to whom conventional morality, thought to be adequately represented in Shakespeare and the Greek classics, was perfectly acceptable.

One such was Arthur Chanel Clery, a student at UCD who took a passing swipe at the master during a debate at the college Literary and Historical Society without betraying any knowledge of the subject. A sample of another of Mr Clery's speeches before the Society will give an idea of the quality of his intellect: 'Though we [the Irish] may sometimes, occasionally, overstep the mark in convivial drinking (laughter) we are totally free from a more desolating vice.' (Applause).

It was unnecessary to mention which vice, but there was one in the audience who was by no means free of it, did not care who knew it, and was annoyed by attacks on Ibsen. Clery's assault was in a paper of his delivered in February 1899, on 'The Theatre, It's Educational Value'. Joyce not only counterattacked on that occasion but determined to deliver a paper of his own, on Ibsen. This, called 'The Drama and The Life', he read before the Society nearly eleven months later, in January 1900. Father William Delany, president of the college, at first refused him permission to read the paper on the ground it did not advance the didactic and uplifting theory of art. That was precisely Joyce's point (or one of his points), but he managed to overcome the priest's objection by quoting Aquinas at him, no mean feat. 'Those things are beautiful the apprehension of which pleases'[1]—*Pulchra sunt quae visa placent.*

'He [Aquinas] seems to regard the beautiful as that which satisfies the aesthetic appetite and nothing more,' says Stephen in *Stephen*

[1] Joyce's translation.

Hero (the episode is left out of *A Portrait*), 'that the mere apprehension of which pleases...'

'But he means the sublime,' says the president, 'that which leads man upwards.'

'His remark would apply to a Dutch painter's representation of a plate of onions.'

'To support Ibsenism on Aquinas,' says the priest, 'seems to me somewhat paradoxical. Young men often substitute brilliant paradox for conviction.' But he relented.

Joyce was asked by the secretary of the Society whom he would like to have preside. He answered, ironically, Henrik Ibsen. The secretary wrote down Henry Gibson and asked where he might get in touch with him.

Joyce wisely read the piece flatly, 'quietly and distinctly,' as he puts it in *Stephen Hero*, 'involving every hardihood of thought or expression in an envelope of low innocuous melody . . . and when he had read out the final sentences in a tone of metallic clearness he sat down.'

Joyce had spent much time and effort on the composition. The labour shows. To read the piece with the gesture and inflection it seems to call for would painfully expose its adolescent enthusiasm and dogmatism; the classical drama, said Joyce, was dead and so was Shakespeare. That was mere spoken literature.

He passed on to the one true master, which was Ibsen.[2]

'*Ghosts*,' he said, 'the action of which passes in a common parlour, is of universal import – a deepset branch of the tree Yggdrasil, whose roots are stuck in earth, but through whose higher leafage the stars of heaven are glowing and astir.' Joyce's enthusiasm for *Ghosts* is presumably based upon the life-embracing message therein, apart from the fact that it is a fine drama, but at the same time he is slanging Shakespeare and in particular, *Macbeth*, which had been chosen by Clery as an example of great drama. Three-quarters of a century later, audiences who see *Ghosts* on the rare occasions it is presented are inhibited from full approval of the drama by the realisation that it is a play about hereditary syphilis and therefore somewhat dated by the discovery of pencillin. Few

---

[2] Peculiarly, Bernard Shaw, who was Joyce's elder and in many ways his opposite, had similarly denounced Shakespeare and embraced Ibsen. Joyce had read his book, *The Quintessence of Ibsenism*, and did not like it.

now suffer from that disability (or, for the time being, from Norwegian Calvinist morality) but murderous ambition is still with us and *Macbeth* has the timelessness Joyce claimed for *Ghosts.*

There is no doubting Ibsen's moral effect on Joyce. Speaking still of *Ghosts*, he continues: 'It may be that many have nothing to do with such fables [he had also mentioned *Lohengrin,* Wagner being another enthusiasm], or think their wonted fare is all that is of need to them. But as we stand on the mountains today, looking before and after, pining for what is not, scarcely discerning afar the patches of open sky; when the spurs threaten, and the track is grown with briars, what does it avail that into our hands we have given us a clouded cane for an alpenstock, or that we have dainty silks to shield us against the eager, upland wind? The sooner we understand our true position, the better; and the sooner then will we be up and doing on our way. In the meantime, art, and chiefly drama, may help us make our resting places with a greater insight and a greater foresight, that the stones of them may be bravely built, and the windows goodly and fair ... "What will you do in our society, Miss Hessell?" ask Rorlund – "I will let in fresh air, Pastor," answered Lona.'

Young Mr Joyce, who has begun by saying it is not the artist's business to preach morality, praises Ibsen for preaching what seems to him a new and necessary morality. The last passage ('The sooner we understand our position the better') is usually taken by Joycean scholars, of whom more later, to deal only with abstract artistic principle. It is, on the contrary, a sign of his embracing a morality which he found truer and more convenient, and which he did not mind proselytizing. Joyce was attracted to the Norwegian for another powerful reason. There is violent emotional drama in the later Ibsen (his epic and poetical drama did not much influence Joyce) even to the extent that his characters are driven to jump off bridges, fall off towers, or take an overdose of morphine, but the drama is sparse, pared down, concerned with people of no great consequence in the world. That also is the direction in which Joyce's talents drove him. 'Even the most commonplace, the deadest among the living, may play a part in a great drama.' It was a fortunate direction: it is always best for a writer to write what he can write best. But was such elaborate justification necessary? The burden that James Joyce took on of Catholic scholasticism, Ibsen-

46

ism and aesthetic theory, most of it of his own manufacture, caught up with him in the end, and with the aid of his adulators spoilt the last twenty years of his work, work that suffered from the arrogant certainty of his theory of art and the self-indulgence it allowed him. An artist may put himself beyond criticism by ignoring it, but he cannot put himself at the same time beyond ridicule and self-parody.

Joyce's audience was not much interested in his aesthetics. Few knew what little work he had produced, by which they could measure his theories. They could, on the other hand, readily detect certain heresies among the rhetoric and fell to attacking him for want of religion and national feeling, due reverence for church and country. Aeschylus was imperishable and *Macbeth* would outlive Scandinavian municipal drama. Joyce made an answer which was said to be brilliant, lasting half an hour beyond the allotted time and was congratulated for his brilliance even by those who disagreed with him. *Stephen Hero* suggests that John Joyce was in the audience. If so, he cannot have had the faintest idea of what his son was talking about. The book, also, curiously omits mention of Joyce's answering speech to his critics.

Joyce read his Ibsen paper a month before his eighteenth birthday. It occurred to him that what he had to say about Ibsen might get a better audience than he was liable to find in the college Physics Theatre on debating night, so he wrote, with brazen cheek, to W. L. Courtney, editor of *The Fortnightly Review*, then the principal English literary magazine, suggesting that he contribute a general article on Ibsen. His own letter is lost but Courtney's reply is preserved. It has been misread by biographers of both Joyce and Ibsen as constituting encouragement, but would scarcely seem so to anyone with much experience of journalism. Courtney, incidentally, was known to take a jaundiced view of the Norwegian master, but perhaps Joyce was ignorant of that. Courtney's letter is dated 19 January 1900, the day before Joyce was due to speak in the Physics Theatre.

> My dear Sir, I am sorry to say that my February number is complete, and that I could not possibly find room for any additional article. I am sorry for this, as I should have liked to have got in some reference to Ibsen's new play. I suppose it would be too late for the following Issue, as Mr Heinemann

tells me it will shortly appear in several languages?
With many thanks and regrets, Believe me, Faithfully yours,
W. L. Courtney[3]

Joyce took this as encouragement to write a review of the new play, *When We Dead Awaken*. He read a French translation of it and fired off an 8,000 word article to Courtney. In content it is quite close to his original intention, being more a review of Ibsen's entire work than of only one play. But his impertinence paid off, and Courtney sent a letter of acceptance dated 3 February, making only two slight suggestions for improvement. He did not trust the French translation Joyce had used, and arranged for the proofs of Archer's Heinemann version to be sent, and did not like an apparently slighting reference to Arthur Wing Pinero, an English playwright of the day whose productions are still occasionally revived by the misguided. Joyce had no objection to using Archer's translation and accepted the slight censorship without demur.

The article appeared in *The Fortnightly Review* (which was in fact a monthly publication) in the issue of 1 April 1900. It created a considerable stir in the academic circles of Dublin, provoking many in the profession of letters to try their hands at the same business. None succeeded, but Joyce had been noticed and the article provided for him an *entrée* into the town's more exalted literary society. It is a remarkable piece. Joyce notes a trait of Ibsen's which he was to share in his own work:

'If one may say so of an eminently virile man, there is a curious admixture of the woman in his nature. His marvellous accuracy, his faint traces of femininity, his delicacy of swift touch, are perhaps attributable to this admixture. But that he knows women is an incontrovertible fact. He appears to have sounded them to almost unfathomable depths. Beside his portraits the psychological studies of Hardy and Turgenev, or the exhaustive elaboration of Meredith, seem no more than sciolism.[4] With a deft stroke, in a phrase, in a word, he does what costs them chapters, and does it better.'

Joyce was in no doubt that Ibsen was the greatest playwright of

[3] Heinemann was the publisher of Archer's translation of Ibsen. *When We Dead Awaken*, Ibsen's last play, was about to appear in English.
[4] Joyce was being very rude. Sciolism, according to the Oxford English Dictionary, means 'a superficial pretence to knowledge'.

48

his age, and said so. 'Appreciation, hearkening, is the only true criticism . . . When the art of a dramatist is perfect the critic is superfluous.'

Ibsen's understanding of English was slight, but he took the trouble to 'spell out' (his own words) his young admirer's review, having no more idea of Joyce's age than Courtney (Joyce had kept quiet on that score), and mentioned his appreciation in a letter to Archer. 'I should greatly like to thank the author, if only I had sufficient knowledge of the language . . .' Archer passed on the message to Joyce, and Joyce answered him, 28 April 1900, not omitting to mention his age as evidence of precosity, now that the article was safely printed.

> Dear Sir, I wish to thank you for your kindness in writing to me. I am a young Irishman, eighteen years old, and the words of Ibsen I shall keep in my heart all my life. Faithfully yours,
> Jas. A. Joyce

He now paid Ibsen the compliment of beginning a study of Norwegian (until Ibsen's time a rude dialect of Danish without a literature of its own), and even German, which he disliked, in order to read Gerhart Hauptmann, considering him to be a follower of Ibsen. In the summer of 1900 he made an attempt to translate two of Hauptmann's plays, but was reduced in parts to the use of asterisks, denoting omissions, thanks to Hauptmann's liberal use of Silesian dialect. Some knowledge of these languages he added to his mastery of Italian and French, and took to declaiming Norwegian lyrics to his friends, who were suitably impressed with his Europeanism. 'Ireland,' he announced, choosing to ignore *Anglo-Ireland*, 'has contributed nothing but a whine to the literature of Europe.'

The large sum of twelve guineas arrived as payment for Joyce's article and he decided to spend it on a trip to London, taking his father with him. They set out in May, leaving May Joyce £1 to sustain the household during their absence. They seem to have had a splendid time, visiting music halls as well as the serious theatre (drink was freely available *during* the performance in music halls), and enjoying the comic acts they saw there as well as Eleanora Duse in D'Annunzio's *La Gioconda*. 'The music hall, not poetry, is a criticism of life,' Jim told Stannie when he got back, perhaps forgetting his remark in the Ibsen article. 'Life is not to be criticized, but to be faced and lived.'

La Duse, in spite of her years, made an impact on Joyce. A slender, dark woman, just on the wrong side of forty, she was celebrated for her high expressiveness on the stage and vile temper off it.[5] She was a champion of D'Annunzio, whom she made famous, and incidentally his lover. Joyce saw her in two of D'Annunzio's plays and was moved to write her a poem of praise which she did not acknowledge, being perhaps a little wary of poets. Joyce burnt his copy of the poem but got for himself a photograph of the lady which he kept for a long time on his desk. When it was reported to him that she had a low opinion of Ibsen he declared, 'if I could have had half an hour's conversation with her, I would have converted her.'

He sent Archer a note requesting an audience and was granted one when Joyce reminded the prickly Scot who he was, but not before. Archer treated Joyce to lunch and fed him wild duck, appropriate meal for a pair of Ibsenites. Archer agreed with Joyce's enthusiasm for Duse, telling him of the time, five years previous, when Sarah Bernhardt had appeared in Sudermann's *Magda* in London while Duse appeared in the same part on another stage in the same city at the same time. 'Duse,' he said, 'could act Sarah off the stage.' Joyce paid a visit to Courtney, who was taken aback by his youth, and another, with his father, to T. P. O'Connor, an unrepentant, block-headed Fenian of the school of 1865, editor of *T.P.'s Weekly*. The idea, probably John Joyce's, was to launch him on a career in journalism. 'T.P.' (or 'Tay Pay', as Yeats derisively called him) dismissed him as too young, so he was saved for literature.

Joyce's brief taste of the greater world beyond Dublin must have exhilarated him. Father and son arrived back in Dublin with twopence between them. Joyce had every intention of making use of his acquaintance with Archer. That summer of 1900 he got busy writing his first play. It was called *A Brilliant Career*, and began with the modest dedication:

5 Shaw on Duse: 'When it is remembered that the majority of tragic actors excell only in explosions of those passions which are common to man and brute, there will be no difficulty in understanding the indescribable distinction which Duse's acting acquires from the fact that behind every stroke of it is a distinctly human idea.'

TO

MY OWN SOUL I

DEDICATE THE FIRST

TRUE WORK OF MY

LIFE

'Holy Paul!' as John Joyce remarked when he saw it.

A Brilliant Career was written in a few weeks at Mullingar, a fine place for intending authors. Possibly the most boring town in provincial Ireland, there is little in the way of distraction. John Joyce found brief employment there revising the voting lists and took his son with him. Since James burnt the play, the only record of it is Stanislaus' rather hazy recollection. Little of the plot remained with him, but he thought the play a rehash of *When We Dead Awaken, A Doll's House* and *The League of Youth*, leaving out, for some unaccountable reason, *An Enemy of the People.*

Stanislaus's account of the play :

> A young doctor, Paul, for the sake of his career, throws over a girl, Angela, with whom he is in love, and marries someone else. He renounces the valiant purposes of his youth, and becomes a time-server. His career is a great success, and, still young, he has been elected mayor of the town, unnamed, in which the scene is laid. There is a serious outbreak of plague in the port (there were some sporadic cases of bubonic plague in Glasgow that year) and the town is thrown into a state of panic. The doctor-mayor copes with the situation energetically, and in a short time the threat of an epidemic is eliminated. From the outbreak of the plague until the end a woman has been organizing assistance for those stricken with plague, and after a public manifestation of gratitude to the mayor, the woman comes to see him. She is Angela, the girl the doctor had jilted. She, too, is unhappily married to a jealous husband. The doctor realises that his brilliant career is dust and ashes. My recollection of the play, especially the end of it, is vague. It ended in psychological disaster, though not in tragedy. After bitter recriminations Angela goes out, leaving the doctor to his thoughts. I seem to remember that the curtain for the last act was that, after Angela had gone, the servant comes in to announce dinner.

Second-hand Ibsen of course, but the eighteen-year-old Joyce is scarcely to be blamed since he had so little experience of his own to go on. He bundled the manuscript off to Archer at the end of August. Archer wrote back a splendidly encouraging and useful letter two weeks later, the eminent critic beginning his letter by apologizing for taking so long to read the play. Joyce had talent, he said, possibly more than talent, but the play was not a success and wildly improbable for the commercial stage.

> But taking it simply as a dramatic poem, I cannot help finding the canvas too large for the subject. It narrows down in the last act into a sort of love tragedy – almost a dialogue – but in order to reach that point you construct a huge fable of politics and pestilence, in which the reader – one reader at any rate – entirely loses sight of what I presume you intend for the central interest of the drama. I have been trying to read some elaborate symbolism into the second and third acts to account for their gigantic breadth of treatment, but if you had a symbolic purpose, I own it escapes me. It may be very good symbolism for all that – I own I am no great hand at reading hieroglyphics.

Prophetic comment for an early critic of James Joyce.

Joyce, Archer remarks, has a gift of easy, natural, yet effective dialogue and 'a certain sense of scenic picturesqueness', but crowds his canvas with so many figures that Shakespeare himself could not differentiate between them. Young men rarely take advice, good, bad or indifferent. Joyce cannot be accused of restricting himself always to a small canvas but it may be that he remembered Archer when he was writing the stories in *Dubliners*, and his one surviving play, *Exiles*, is a drama played out between four souls.

Archer's comment – that he had found the centre of the drama in the scene between Paul and Angela, and that he had found the rest of the characters indistinct – puzzled Stanislaus on two counts. He knew that the love scene was a product of his brother's imagination, since his only experience of 'love' was with prostitutes. And he thought that many of the minor characters were real because he recognized in them portraits of mutual acquaintances. He asked his brother where he got the last scene from 'Here,' said Jim, touching his forehead, 'all here.'

'I think,' said Stanislaus, 'the scene would be more telling for me if I knew it had some basis in reality.'

'How can you know whether Ibsen's scenes have any basis in actual experience or not?'

'I don't know,' said the dogged brother, 'but I have that illusion. I fancy the reality of experience has a way of making itself felt.'

'There are realities of the imagination too.'

'Why, then, do you pour such ridicule on the dreamy dreamers with manuscripts hidden away in their desks?'

'Yerrah,' said the scornful artist, 'what reality of experience do you think I could have in this city?' He recited the names of girls known to them. 'It is with so-and-so and so-and-so? No, thank you. I leave flirting to clerks.'

'I don't mean flirting,' said Stanislaus, Jim knowing perfectly well what he meant.

'Well,' said Jim, 'if you mean anything else you are talking like an idiot.'

Another argument of the time concerned what Joyce called his love poetry. Stanislaus preferred to call it prostitute poetry. 'Well, why not?' says the poet. 'Doesn't a great part of all lyrical poetry correspond to that description? You're a tiresome moralist.'

The reports of these conversations are reasonably accurate, thanks to Stanislaus's habit of keeping his diary. The phrase about the 'reality of experience' is interesting. Joyce uses it in the trumpet blast which is the last page of *A Portrait of the Artist*. 'I go to encounter for the millionth time the reality of experience . . . and to forge in the smithy of my soul the uncreated conscience of my race.'

Chapter Four
The Rabblement by the Door

The brothers were a strange pair, as brothers so close together in age frequently are. 'He used to say that I reminded him of a sluggish saurian whose scaly hide occasionally reflected glints of light,' said Stannie, not minding in the least. Another piece of abuse; after a discussion of Stannie's rejection of God, Jim asks him whether he has considered if he is competent to discuss such questions. 'There's a queer, grim, Dutch touch about your phiz,' he concludes. 'I pity the poor woman who wakes up to find it on the pillow beside her.' John Joyce joined in the abuse, taunting Stanislaus with the observation that he shone only like the moon, with reflected light. Better that, said Stannie, than to shine as his father's nose did, which seemed to generate its own luminosity.

Joyce was writing down accounts of his dreams as well as what he called 'epiphanies'. The brother's presence is plain. 'Something is moving in the pool; it is an arctic beast with a rough yellow coat. I thrust in my stick [Joyce took an ashplant with him everywhere he went, as a kind of trademark] and as he rises out of the water, I see that his back slopes towards the croup and that he is very sluggish. I am not afraid but thrusting at him drive him before me. He moves his paws heavily and mutters words of some language I do not understand.'

In another dream Stannie appears again as a big dog recumbent in the rain (not having the sense to get out of it?), from time to time lifting his muzzle to utter a prolonged and mournful howl. This howl, Stannie offered, might be proceeding not from himself but from his brother's soul. In any case, he didn't mind, because he liked dogs.

The family was driven out of Fairview for the usual reason (there had already been a move from one house in Fairview to another, in 1900), this time to an even smaller house in a worse neighbourhood, John Joyce dealing with the old landlord in the usual way: he could not leave until he was provided with a receipt for the (unpaid) rent, since otherwise no landlord would take him in. Would the old landlord oblige, and save himself the trouble and expense of an eviction? Normally the landlord did. The new house was in a street called Glengariff Parade. They were not there long, but while they were, Joyce took to composing music for some of his poems, and some of those of Yeats and James Clarence Mangan. Stanislaus observed there one morning a butcher's boy walking along the road with his basket on his head, kicking up the dust with his feet and singing:

> *Walkin' along the road*
> *Kicking up all the dust*
> *And there's ne'er a wan in Glengariff Parade*
> *Dar give him a lick in the puss*

'A rival poet,' said Stannie, unamused.

'The Poet,' said Jim, 'of the Rugged Glen.' He had been studying Irish at the urging of a Nationalist friend, and because he liked the look of a certain Nationalist young lady who attended the same class. His teacher was Patrick Pearse, a zealot whose enthusiasm for blood sacrifice reminds one of other European Fascists. One of the leaders of the Easter Rising which began Ireland's twentieth-century agonies, he was executed for his part in it. He drove Joyce from his Irish classes by his attacks on the English language. The friend who introduced Joyce to the study of the 'native' language was George Clancy, who was country-bred, intelligent but unsubtle. He appears in *A Portrait* as Davin, who is presented most sympathetically, the only student allowed the liberty of calling Dedalus 'Stevie'.

'His nurse had taught him Irish and shaped his rude imagination by the broken lights of Irish myth . . . Whatsoever of thought or of feeling came to him from England or by way of English culture his mind stood armed against in obedience to a password; and of the world that lay beyond England he knew only the foreign legion of France in which he spoke of serving.'

Joyce would not make obeisance to the passwords of Nationalism any more than to the passwords of the Church. In Mullingar he had offended the citizenry by rebuking them for their antagonism to the English. 'My ancestors threw off their language and took another,' says Stephen to Davin. 'They allowed a handful of for-

55

eigners to subject them. Do you fancy I am going to pay in my own life debts they made. What for? . . . You talk to me of nationality, language, religion. I shall try to fly by those nets.' Joyce did. Clancy did not. While mayor of Limerick during the war of independence he was murdered by Black and Tans.

What Gaelic Joyce did master found its way into *Finnegans Wake* thirty years later, along with scraps of every other language he had knowledge of, to assist in the bafflement of those who attempt to read that peculiar book.

In 1899, during his first year at the university, Joyce had refused to join his fellow students, led by Skeffington, in a denunciation of Yeat's rather silly play, *The Countess Cathleen,* which the poet had written seven years before, ironically, in order to impress the fiery Nationalist revolutionary Maud Gonne, with whom he had fallen in love. The Countess barters her soul to prevent starving peasants from having to barter theirs. The brilliant young men of University College objected to the play, not because it was silly, but on national and religious grounds. How dare Yeats (who, of course, was Anglo-Irish) suggest that Irish peasants were ignorant and superstitious? Skeffington got up a letter to *The Freeman's Journal,* the principal Catholic newspaper of Ireland. 'The subject is not Irish,' it said in part. 'It has been shown that the plot is founded on a German legend. The characters are ludicrous travesties of the Irish Catholic Celt . . . He [Yeats] represents the Irish peasant as a crooning barbarian, crazed with morbid superstition, who, having added the Catholic faith to his store of superstition, sells that faith for gold or bread in the proving of famine.'

If that was the product of the flower of young Ireland's intellect, no wonder Joyce conceived an ambition to head for a more civilized climate. Skeffington's letter was left out in the college for the students to sign. Joyce had made a point of clapping ostentatiously amid the booing at the play's première: now he made a point of ostentatiously refusing to sign.

His interest in the theatre led him to think of abandoning his university studies and going on the stage himself, after deciding his own first play was a failure. He took this ambition as far as buying a few copies of *The Stage,* the newspaper of the acting profession, and adopting for himself a stage name. This was to be Gordon Brown, after his favourite heretic, Giordano Bruno of Nola. He took the lead role in two plays while he was at college, one of them written by Margaret Sheehy.

Miss Sheehy's play, called *Cupid's Confidante*, got two performances, in March 1900 and January 1901. Joyce played an unscrupulous rake after an innocent young thing on account of her money, her true lover having taken himself off in a huff after a quarrel. Margaret Sheehy played the heroine, in the name part. Friend of the heiress, she unmasks the rake's villainy by getting him to make overtures to her.

Perhaps the part was congenial to Joyce. At any rate, he enjoyed hamming it up and was extravagantly praised by the critic of the *Evening Telegraph*, who compared his technique to that of Charles Matthews, the English comedian whose skill was still celebrated twenty-five years after his death. Joyce was modest about his performance. He told Stanislaus 'the virgin cheeks of my arse blushed for it'. But he kept the clipping in his wallet.

In March 1901 he wrote a long letter of greeting to Ibsen on the occasion of his seventy-third birthday, translating it into Norwegian after writing the draft in English. He confesses he is a very young man and tells how moved he was by Ibsen's message of gratitude for his review, regretting only that it was hastily written and ought to have been something more worthy of the master's praise.

> What shall I say more? I have sounded your name defiantly through the college where it was either unknown or known faintly and darkly. I have claimed for you your rightful place in the history of the drama. I have shown what, as it seemed to me, was your highest excellence – your lofty impersonal power. Your minor claims – your satire, your technique and orchestral harmony – these, too, I advanced. Do not think me a hero-worshipper – I am not so. And when I spoke of you in debating societies and so forth, I enforced attention by no futile ranting.
>
> But we always keep the dearest things to ourselves. I did not tell them what bound me closest to you. I did not say how what I could discern dimly of your life was my pride to see, how your battles inspired me – not the obvious material battles but those that were fought and won behind your forehead, how your wilful resolution to wrest the secret from life gave me heart and how in your absolute indifference to public canons

of art, friends and shibboleths you walked in the light of your inward heroism. And this is what I write to you of now. Your work on earth draws to a close and you are near the silence. It is growing dark for you. Many write of such things but they do not know. You have only opened the way – though you have gone as far as you could upon it – to the end of 'John Gabriel Borkman' and its spiritual truth – but your last play stands, I take it, apart. But I am sure that higher and holier enlightenment lies – onward.

As one of the younger generation for whom you have spoken I give you greeting – not humbly, because I am obscure and you in the glare, not sadly, because you are an old man and I am a young man, not presumptuously nor sentimentally – but joyfully, with hope and with love, I give you greeting.

Faithfully yours,
James A. Joyce

Whether Ibsen was well enough to read the letter is not known, and his copy of it does not survive. Since he hoped to recover his health to the point that he could write another play (he had the themes well fixed in his head) he might not have been pleased with Joyce's callow references to his nearness to the grave, or Joyce's hint that, Ibsen having opened up the way and gone along it as far as he could, there was still some way to go. And Joyce, maybe, was the man to make the going. Still, it was well-intended. Joyce had had a dream about the old man, which he wrote down.

Yes – they are the two sisters. She who is churning with stout arms (their butter is famous) looks dark and unhappy; the other is happy because she had her way. Her name is R . . Rina. I know the verb 'to be' in their language.
'Are you Rina?'
I knew she was.
But here he is himself in a coat with tails and an old-fashioned high hat. He ignores them: he walks along with tiny steps, jutting out the tails of his coat . . . My goodness! How small he is! He must be very old and vain – maybe he isn't what I . . . It's funny that two big women fell out over this little man . . . But then he's the greatest man on earth.

The final episode of his theatrical career in Dublin was an assault on the Irish Literary Theatre.

58

This worthy organization, ancestor of the Abbey, which is now the Irish national theatre, had been founded by Yeats, Edward Martyn (another Irish Ireland zealot) and Augusta, Lady Gregory. Their first production in 1899 had been *The Countess Cathleen.* Lady Gregory, an Anglo-Irish-woman in middle age with a lot of money and energy to spare, had spent much time roaming the west of Ireland with Yeats from her splendid home, Coole Park (a literary landmark since demolished by a grateful Irish nation), collecting peasant folk-lore for inclusion in plays. Most of these plays were drivel (even Yeat's), most were put on very badly in Gaelic, all were short – some only four or five pages long. Joyce called them 'dwarf drama'.

Joyce had hoped that the Irish Literary Theatre, in accordance with a promise of Yeats's, would put on European drama as well as Irish – perhaps even his own translations of Hauptmann. He was disappointed. In October 1901 Yeats announced in his magazine *Samhain* that he and the other authors who wrote for the Theatre had put as much energy into it as they were able. They hoped that some similar theatre would continue the tradition they had established, but the Irish Literary Theatre itself would function no longer. Furthermore, the last two productions, which would get their première on 21 October, would be far from European. Precisely the sort of stuff Joyce abhorred, they were to be *Casadh an t-Sugain,* a bovine 'comedy' nine pages long, by Dr Douglas Hyde, and *Diarmuid* and *Grania,* a longer effort by Yeats and Moore, on the theme of an ancient Irish love story. No room for Joyce.

In one morning he composed an article condemning the theatre for pandering to 'the rabble' and presented it to *St. Stephen's,* the college magazine, no doubt knowing full well it would be rejected. It was, and this time an appeal to the college president got Joyce nowhere. He resolved to publish it himself.

By a fortunate coincidence, Skeffington had also had an article rejected, Skeffington's being a slightly premature feminist appeal to admit women to all faculties. By tacking them together, the two were able to afford the printing of eighty-five copies, each author taking care to dissociate himself from the other's contribution. Skeffington's was called *A Forgotten Aspect of the University Question.* Joyce called his *The Day of the Rabblement.*

'No man, said the Nolan,' it begins, 'can be a lover of the true or the good unless he abhors the multitude, and the artist, though he may employ the crowd, is very careful to isolate himself.' It goes on to attack Yeats and Moore for failing in their promise and describes the Irish as the most belated race in Europe. It ends with a broad hint: 'Elsewhere there are men who are worthy to carry on the tradition of the old master who is dying in Christiania. He has already found his successor in the writer of *Michael Kramer*, and the third minister will not be wanting when his hour comes. Even now that hour may be standing by the door.'

Stanislaus was roped in to help deliver Joyce's copies to the literary élite of Dublin: he noticed that George Moore had a very pretty servant girl to answer the door. The pamphlet got the publicity suppressed documents usually get. The Irish on the whole did not much mind being called debased rabble. There was even a certain amount of amusement among the rabblement. Few had any idea who had written *Michael Kramer* and no more than one or two had the faintest idea who 'the Nolan' was – some guessing he might be the hereditary chief of an Irish clan, like 'the O'Rahilly', others that Nolan who was the porter of the medical school, one of whose duties was preparing corpses for dissection.

'The Nolan' was actually Giordano Bruno of Nola, that hero of Joyce's who had escaped burning at the hands of the Calvinists to be burnt instead by the Pope. Joyce had discussed his enthusiasm for Bruno's aesthetics with Father Ghezzi, the young Italian Jesuit who taught him that language. Ghezzi's Catholicism, being Italian, was less primitive than the Irish variety, yet he was cautious on the subject of the champion heretic. 'But you must not forget,' he reminded his student, 'that he was a terrible heretic.'

'Yes,' said Joyce, 'I'll remember, and also that he was terribly burnt.'

Wouldn't it be better, inquired Stanislaus, to let the rabblement in on the secret? No, said Joyce, let them take the trouble to find out who the Nolan was and then they might be interested enough to read him.

The hint about who was to follow Ibsen aroused some derisive comment. 'Never have I seen so much pretension with so little to show for it,' said Yeats. Margaret Sheehy, more blunt, shouted, 'Even now the rabblement may be standing by the door!'

The fuss lasted a week or so, and was forgotten. Joyce continued to get much pleasure from his association with the Sheehys. There is a story of him walking in the street with Eugene Sheehy when they were accosted by a beggar asking for a penny. 'And why would you want a copper?' asked Joyce.

'To tell yiz the honest truth,' said the beggar, 'I was dyin' for a drink.'

Joyce quite rightly gave him his last penny. 'If he'd said he wanted it for a cup of tea,' he said, 'I'd have hit him.' The Sheehy's and others, at a mock election, nominated him Pope to succeed Leo XIII, who appeared to be approaching death. Asked for his blessing, he said he'd left it in his suitcase.

He would go a little out of the way to shock. He had fallen to some slight extent in love with the youngest of the Sheehy girls, who was dark and very pretty, and had no idea of his admiration. On an excursion into the Wicklow Mountains with the Sheehy girls and Skeffington, coming back late, the object of Joyce's unsuspected passion noticed the pale and wispy moon. She said she thought it looked tearful.

'It looks to me like the chubby hooded face of some jolly, fat Capuchin,' said Jim, being daringly anti-clerical.

'I think you are very wicked,' said the girl, not terribly shocked.

'Not very,' said Jim, 'but I do my best.'

When they had parted he stood under the light of a street lamp to write two stanzas on the back of a cigarette pack.

> *What counsel has the hooded moon*
> *Put in my heart, my shyly sweet*
> *Of love in ancient plenilune,*
> *Glory and stars beneath his feet*
> *A sage that is but kith and kin*
> *…With the comedian Capuchin?*
>
> *Believe me rather than am wise*
> *In disregard of the divine,*
> *A glory kindles in those eyes,*
> *Trembles to starlight, Mine, O Mine!*
> *No more be tears in moon or mist*
> *For thee, sweet sentimentalist.*

It isn't much, but Joyce thought highly enough of it to put it in his first (and second-last) book of poems, *Chamber Music*.

61

Stanislaus tells the story of Skeffington, when the three of them were out walking, discussing the forthcoming trip to Wicklow, suddenly springing: 'Have you ever been in love?' He liked asking what he considered to be profound questions, said Stanislaus, and brother Jim liked answering them, provided he had thought out the answers in advance. This time, evidently, he had, since he was able to rattle off his reply.

'How would I write the most perfect love songs of our time,' declaimed Joyce, modest as usual, 'if I were in love? A poet must always write about a past or future emotion, never about a present one. If it is a regular, right-down, honest-to-God, till-death-us-two-part affair, it will get out of hand and spoil his verse. Poetry must have a safety valve properly adjusted. A poet's job is to write tragedies, not to be an actor in one.'

When Skeffington is gone, Stannie inquires, at the door of the university, 'do you really think your poems are so perfect?'

'Evidently I think highly of them, otherwise I shouldn't be trying to find a publisher for them.'

'I think,' says Stannie, 'that nature abhors perfection, and that most readers agree with her.'

'Is that a quotation from that brilliant diary of yours?'

'No, but it will be. It occurred to me when I was reading Pope's *Essay on Man*.'

'Pope's what?' says Jim scornfully. 'Why on earth are you reading that?'

'Culture,' says his brother grimly.

'You take my mistakes hostage,' said Jim, going back to the more interesting question of love, and his opinion of it. 'Do you expect me to return an intelligent answer when Skeffington asks a damn silly question?'

Stanislaus, in spite of the way his brother wrote about women, never did believe that the female sex was the chief interest in his life, because James had said that he did not expect to be the main purpose of any woman's life. Sooner or later children would take his place. True, but the one thing does not exclude the other. Women with children have been known to maintain an interest in men. But Stanislaus spoke of women always in terms of their functions, as if they were necessary for little else but procreation and the healthy release of the sexual appetite. Stanislaus was a terrible puritan, but his brother was not, and women *were* to constitute the principal interest in his life.

'Women are a great invention,' says one of the medical students with whom Jim goes carousing, 'because they save a lot of manual labour.'

'You exaggerate, Elwood,' answers Stannie, who claims to have given up that vice at a suspiciously early age. 'How often do you go down to the kips, after all? I don't think women save you an awful lot of manual labour in the intervals.'

Stanislaus refused to go on these excursions himself, thinking of the cheerful whores of Dublin as unwilling victims of the white slave trade. 'I determined to give continence a fair trial,' he said, and gave it more than that, preserving himself until the age of twenty-four or twenty-five.

Brother James, however, was getting fed up with prostitutes. Whores, he said, were bad conductors of emotion and he longed to copulate with a soul. He meant he wanted to be in love with a woman who would be in love with him. But he would have to wait three more years for that, and he wanted it so much he was never quite sure he had it when he got it.

Chapter Five
Death and Exile

Another Joyce child died in 1902. George, so called because he was born on the Fourth of July (the Irish remember with approval the American Revolution and George Washington), was a handsome boy of fourteen, and of the Joyce children the closest in temperament and ability to his eldest brother. He was tall, fair and athletic. 'When I first took him for a walk on the esplanade at Bray everybody used to turn and look after him,' said his grief-stricken mother, who was broken by his death and blamed herself for it.

George had an infectious laugh with no trace of malice in it. He was bright enough to skip a year at Belvedere. He strummed away at the piano, demonstrating a keen ear for music. 'Though still a boy,' said Stanislaus, 'he was one of those people whose presence banishes boredom.' Just the sort of person, thought Stanislaus, whom God, if He existed, would choose wantonly to destroy.

When George fell ill his mother was at first undecided whether to send him to hospital. He was now her favourite son, after her religious estrangement with James, and she preferred to nurse him herself if she could. Hospitals were not necessarily the best place for the sick.

When his pains were bad he did not complain but put his arms around his mother's neck and held on tight until they went away. There were long weeks of typhoid fever when he could not eat solids because of the fear of perforating his intestines. When the crisis seemed at last to be over, May Joyce asked the doctor (a countrified blockhead) what she might give him to eat. 'Oh anything,' he said, offhand, 'soup, meat, anything you like.' She gave him soup and a morsel of meat. He felt better and asked Jim to sing for him his setting of Yeats's lyric from *The Countess Cathleen*, 'Who will go drive with Fergus now':

1   May Joyce, the writer's mother, drawn from a photograph twenty-three years after her death by Patrick Tuohy. 'As you so often said I am stupid and cannot grasp the great thoughts which are yours . . .'

2   Joyce playing Rimbaud in Paris, 1902. (p. 77).

3　My Brother's Keeper. Prognathous, pugnacious Stanislaus Joyce before the long struggle to keep his brother out of the gutter wore him down. He always regretted that his inheritance was O'Connell rather than Joyce. Here he looks it.

4　(*below left*) Nora Barnacle in Galway before she ran away to Dublin and met Joyce, thence to become alternatively his 'Fuckbird' and his 'proud blue-eyed queen'. '*Everything that is noble and exalted and deep and true and moving in what I write comes, I believe, from you.*' 5　(*below right*) Lucia and Eva Joyce in Trieste, about 1910. Joyce enlisted three members of his family to prop up his household there.

And pierce the deep wood's woven shade,
And dance upon the level shore?
Young man lift up your russet brow,
And lift your tender eyelids, maid,
And brood on hopes and fears no more.

James sang the melancholy chant which was his version of the lyric from the piano in the parlour, leaving the door open for his voice to reach George and Stanislaus up the stairs. While he was singing his brother began to die. The symptoms of a perforated intestine had appeared.

One of Joyce's epiphanies describes the moment:

> Mrs Joyce: (*crimson, trembling, appears at the parlour door*) . . . 'Jim!'
> Joyce: (*at the piano*) . . . 'Yes?'
> Mrs Joyce: 'Do you know anything about the body? . . . What ought I to do? . . . There's some matter coming away from the hole in George's stomach . . . Did you ever hear of that happening?'
> Joyce: (*surprised*) . . . 'I don't know . . .'
> Mrs Joyce: 'Ought I send for the doctor, do you think?'
> Joyce: 'I don't know . . . what hole?'
> Mrs Joyce: (*impatient*) . . . 'The hole we all have . . . here (*points*)

George was not long in dying, of peritonitis, which killed James thirty-nine years later. He died calmly, saying only to his terrified mother, 'I am very young to die'. Two of his Jesuit teachers came from Belvedere to offer condolences. One of them wept. Mrs Joyce blamed herself for following the doctor's instructions, whom she had sometimes suspected of being drunk as well as stupid. Her son's death hastened her own. She thought James callous because he did not display open grief, but he describes in another epiphany how he stole upstairs after the others were asleep to see the body.

'Poor little fellow! We have often laughed together. He bore his body very lightly . . . I am very sorry he died. I cannot pray for him the way the others do. Poor little fellow! Everything else is so uncertain!'

May Joyce was often found quietly weeping over her housework. Her priest took advantage of her grief to attempt to persuade her to get rid of James and Stanislaus as bad influences on the other children: James was amused, Stanislaus incensed.

Another brother, Charlie, was providing comic relief. A little older than George, he had less than the family quota of brains but had recognized George's brightness and was deeply attached to him. Being about the same age, they spent a good deal of time together. In his grief it dawned on Charlie that he might make a priest. Besides, the idea appealed to his vanity. He left school to enter a seminary of the ordinary sort, not being precisely Jesuit material. He had a fine voice and a fine profile and was able to enjoy the pleasure of parading on Sundays, admired by his sisters and other young females, to the pro-cathedral in the centre of Dublin, dressed up in his soutane and biretta, a prayer-book piously clasped, in the company of other young priestlets. He was more looked at than they were, but looked on with less favour by his tutors. He was in danger of being kicked out of the seminary but left of his own accord, deciding he had no vocation after all (or, more likely, had James and John Joyce's eye for women). John Joyce will have looked back with pain on one particular interview with the rector of his son's seminary, before he left. Joyce went in to pay his son's fees, which the rector was happy to accept, and no doubt surprised to get. John Joyce had commuted half his pension for cash and had bought a small, two-storied house in Cabra, then a reasonably pleasant district. He was even able to buy some old furniture and a good deal of booze, but he was not left with much income.

'A par-ti-cu-lar-ly stu-pid boy,' enunciated the rector as he jingled John Joyce's gold coins in his priestly paw. 'A particularly stupid boy,' said Stanislaus, 'who has a particularly foolish father to pay his gold, as you call it, to a particularly cunning priest.'

'Begad, you're right there, anyhow,' said the old man.

Charlie had a chance of a sort to get on in life, but Stanislaus, censorious and fussy as always, ruined it for him. He was offered a job with a travelling acting company, touring Irish towns and villages, but was required to pay his own fares. Stanislaus had visions of him turning up drunk at some theatre and being thrown out into the hedge without a penny. He prevented Charlie's joining the company, but soon regretted it. The manager, he realized, might have recognized Charlie's talents and, in any case, sleeping in a ditch in the country was scarcely worse than living in the Joyce household.

From one of Stanislaus's rare encounters with the opposite sex came the germ of one of the stories in his brother's book, *Dubliners*. Brother Jim was in the habit of reading Stannie's diary, which was principally an account of *his* comings and goings, not the author's. One experience of his own which Stannie did trouble to record was a few words exchanged with a lady, 'a handsome dark-haired woman between thirty and forty years old' who sat beside him at a concert of Clara Butt's, noticed his enthusiasm for the music and spoke to him during the interval. If she was hoping for anything more than a polite musical chat she had picked the wrong man, but Stannie *did* notice 'her fair skin and the large pupils and very pure whites of her brown eyes'. He spoke to her only once again and seems to have been puzzled both that he had taken the trouble to write the episode down and that his brother chose to make a story of it. That was years later, in Trieste.

The story is 'A Painful Case' and two of Stannie's grim aphorisms, filched from his notes, are included: 'Every bond is a bond to sorrow,' and 'Love between man and woman is impossible because there must not be sexual intercourse, and friendship between a man and a woman is impossible because there must be sexual intercourse.' Stannie, as suits his character always, is made middle-aged in the story, though he was only eighteen at the time of the encounter, and is given the name of Duffy, after Pisser Duffy, his childhood tormentor. Joyce adds a little melodrama by making Mr Duffy responsible for having the unfortunate woman, thanks to his coldness, throw herself under the wheels of a train.

Joyce burnt most of his works, including his play and even some of the poems Archer had praised, before he left university in the summer of 1902. The autumn before, hearing that Archer was going to bring out a book on young poets, he had sent him verses by Irish poets he admired and, naturally, some of his own. Archer wrote telling him the book was long since finished, warning him against certain 'metrical eccentricities' and bad rhymes. One such was 'clothes' and 'those', words which rhyme in Dublin but not in London (or Edinburgh, Archer being a Scot). 'I think the probability is that if you published these poems now you would one day regret it.' Joyce took the advice.

Before he left University College he delivered another lecture before the Literary and Historical Society, which stunned its audience by its brilliance even more than the one he had delivered on Ibsen. He called it 'Poetry and Life' and the subject this time was James Clarence Mangan, an early nineteenth-century Irish poet, much taught in Irish schools but little read outside them. The author of atrocious rhymes ('Bosphorus, Life has lost its gloss for us'), his life was shortened by drink. Some of his lyrics had impressed Yeats, and Joyce set two of them to music. He deserved the mantle of greatness, said Joyce, if only for a few matchless lines he had written. He was a peg for Joyce to hand another aesthetic hat on.

The style of the Mangan lecture is almost as high-flown as 'The Drama and The Life', but the content is a good deal more obscure, deliberately so. Joyce mentions the 'most enlightened of western poets' without enlightening his audience as to the poet's identity (Blake, as a matter of fact). 'All those who have written nobly,' he says, 'have not written in vain, though the desperate and weary have never heard the silver laughter of wisdom.' The point at least is made that the calling to which Joyce intends to devote his life is a noble one, deserving of respect and consideration. This refrain many of his friends were to hear repeated when he needed money, or favours. But that is common in artists of genius (Ibsen and Wagner, to name but two) as well as 'artists' devoid of talent. 'I have sacrificed myself to the noblest calling: give me money'.

He made also an unfortunate reference to 'death, the most beautiful form of life', upon which his critics joyfully seized, one of them remarking that absence was the highest form of presence. Joyce, recognizing a good joke, appropriated it for later use.

He spent a little of his spare time attending backroom meetings of would-be social revolutionaries, but never, after his childhood and the death of Parnell, took politics seriously, though he attached the label 'socialist' to himself for a while. After the First World War he scandalized Stanislaus, who had been complaining about the Italian Fascists, by remarking that he was no longer interested in anything but style. In 'A Painful Case' he pokes fun at a socialist party which splits into three parts, each with its own leader and its own garret.

Much conversation was conducted with friends on the steps of the National Library, not all of it of a philosophical nature. On one occasion an old lady emerging from the Bible Society across the road was so alarmed by the sight and sound of Joyce's manic laughter that she crossed the street to intervene. 'What's the matter with that young man? He must be sick. Take him home and take care of him.'

Various of Joyce's university friends appear in his writings. Apart from George Clancy ('Davin'), who had introduced him to Gaelic, there were, among others, John Francis Byrne, Vincent Cosgrave and Oliver St John Gogarty. Byrne (who becomes 'Cranly') was a quiet person, an admirer of his poems who read a paper on 'The Imitation of Christ' and ended it with a quotation of Joyce's. Cosgrave ('Lynch' – a name he resented. There was a mayor of Galway named Lynch who hanged his own son. Joyce intended the connection) was a companion in the whorehouses, a medical student who shared another interest with Joyce – in Gregorian chant.

> *There is a young fellow named Joyce,*
> *Who possesses a sweet tenor voice.*
> *He goes down to the kips*
> *With a psalm on his lips,*
> *And biddeth the harlots reioice.*

A limerick by Gogarty, who was a tireless composer of scatological verse. Gogarty and Joyce were said by friends to be compiling an anthology on the inscriptions in public lavatories, a pastime indulged in by many young men with literary inclinations and nothing to write. Those who do so in every generation think the idea novel.

In *Ulysses* Gogarty becomes Buck Mulligan, the abandoned medical student who satirizes Stephen Dedalus for his high seriousness and low station (Stephen is the 'bullock-befriending bard' because he is required, as a teacher in a private school, to insert a letter his employer has written on the topic of foot-and-mouth disease into a newspaper with which he is supposed to have influence. Stephen is also 'Kinch the knifeblade' because Mulligan is aware of the power of his Jesuit-sharpened tongue). Gogarty was a natural bully, attracted to Joyce and yet jealous of him. His family had money and sent him to Trinity, the Protestant University, thought to be much better than UCD, and later Oxford. He was a brilliant classicist who could reel off long streams of Greek poetry and used his talent for embroidery to invent outrageous stories about Joyce all his life. He was also an accomplished athlete who had saved two men from drowning in the Liffey, a stream in which it takes a high courage merely to dip your toe. (When he was a senator of the Irish Free State he swam across it in winter to escape murder by his IRA captors.) He was to be useful to Joyce as well as an irritant. Their acquaintance began with a chance meeting at the counter of the National Library.

Joyce met another who was to become a fast friend, Padraic Colum, in the company of Gogarty at a tea party of Lady Gregory's. Yeats was also present, but aloof, discussing with Lady Gregory various projects for the National Theatre, she being so little annoyed by Joyce's scathing pamphlet that she asked him on this occasion to write 'something for our little theatre', a request which amused him mightily. Both Joyce and Gogarty had a certain notoriety already in Dublin, Joyce for his fluent arrogance, Gogarty for his scabrous wit, but Colum was unknown and kept quiet out of shyness. No doubt it was very kind of Lady Gregory to invite all these students to have tea with her. Colum quotes a limerick written by Joyce:

> *There was an old lady named Gregory*
> *Who cried: 'Come, all ye poets in beggary.'*
> *She found her imprudence*
> *When hundreds of students*
> *Cried: 'We're in that noble category'.*

Colum too was a poet. A little while after the tea party he introduced himself to Joyce in the National Library, having heard from George Russell the false and careless opinion that Joyce wrote poetry something like his own. In spite of the closeness of their ages and the lack of any huge achievement on the part of either of them, Joyce took the overture as homage to himself – which it was – and treated Colum to one of his discursive promenades, impressing him by his fluency and his maturity. Colum, being a Nationalist, mentioned the Gaelic League. 'I distrust all enthusiasm,' said Joyce. It was not with any youthful bravado, said Colum. 'It was rather like one giving a single veto after a tiring argument.'

Joyce was not above doing his own accosting. He had chosen

George Russell ('A.E.') as his entrée into Dublin's senior literary society and met him by the simple expedient of knocking on his door at midnight. Russell, fifteen years older than Joyce, had made a considerable reputation as a poet and novelist and gained a certain notoriety by dabbling in mysticism of the Theosophical variety. He was inclined to be indulgent and granted Joyce a long audience, notwithstanding the hour. At the end of it, Joyce produced some of his work, taking care first of all to let Russell know he did not care what his opinion of it was.

Russell was suitably impressed, by Joyce's manner as well as his prose. He described him in a letter to a friend as 'my young genius'. He had known him only a few days but seems quickly to have experienced Joyce's prickly side. 'I wouldn't be his Messiah for a thousand million pounds. He would be always criticizing the bad taste of his deity.'

There was some talk of Theosophy between the two, but Joyce was not looking for a deity in Dublin and found that then (and now) fashionable religion was small beer compared to Roman Catholicism.

Russell wrote to Yeats, whom Joyce had not yet met, that August of 1902, recommending Joyce to his attention. '. . . he has all the intellectual equipment, culture and education which all our other clever friends here lack. And I think he writes amazingly well in prose though I believe he also writes verse and is engaged in writing a comedy which he expects will occupy him five years or thereabouts as he writes slowly . . . Anyway I think you would find this youth of 21 with his assurances and self-confidence rather interesting.' (He was actually twenty.)

Yeats turned up in Dublin in October. Russell arranged a meeting with him at the Ancient Concert Rooms, where Yeats was rehearsing *Cathleen ni Houlihan*, his Fenian playlet, a piece of un- varnished rubbish which he later repented. The burden of it is the old business of dying for Ireland.

> *Did that play of mine send out*
> *Certain men the English shot?*

Joyce chose not to meet Yeats at the theatre, coming across him instead at the National Library. Certainly he would have loathed *Cathleen ni Houlihan*. The two repaired to a café in O'Connell

Street (the principal street of Dublin, then called Sackville Street) for a long talk. Joyce produced and read some scraps of prose and meditation on request and when Yeats offered praise, answered: 'I really don't care whether you like what I am doing or not. It won't make the least difference to me. Indeed I don't know why I am reading it to you.' Or so Yeats remembered his words. 'He is from the Royal University,' thought Yeats, 'and he thinks that everything has been settled by Thomas Aquinas, so we need not trouble about it.'

Yeats attempting to defend his folk plays, Joyce told him abruptly he was deteriorating. Yeats asked Joyce to write a play anyway, for his Irish National Dramatic Society: Joyce said he would do so in five years. 'I am twenty,' he said at the conclusion of the interview. 'How old are you?' Yeats was thirty-seven but knocked a year off the total. 'I thought as much,' said Joyce sadly. 'I have met you too late. You are too old."

Poor Yeats. What Joyce meant was that he had met Yeats too late to have a beneficial effect on his (Yeats's) work. Yeats wrote him a letter of praise (and condescension). 'The work which you have actually done is very remarkable for a man of your age who has lived away from the vital intellectual centres. Your technique in verse is very much better than the technique of any young Dublin man I have met during my time. It might have been the work of a young man who had lived in an Oxford literary set.'

If he did not care what others thought of his work, Joyce was certainly free with his opinion of theirs. Padraic Colum had had a play put on at the National Theatre (or Dramatic) Society, of which Yeats was president, and unwisely gave it to Joyce to read. When he had read it he met Colum in O'Connell Street with the play under his arm. Colum imagined the encounter arranged for maximum effect. Joyce was a degree less courteous than he had been with Yeats. Pointing his ashplant at Colum, he said, 'I do not know from which of them you derive the most misunderstanding – Ibsen or Maeterlinck.' He handed the script neatly rolled to its author. 'Rotten,' he said, 'from the foundation up.'

Mary Colum (not yet married to Padraic) had another story of about the same time illustrating Joyce's adolescent haughtiness. A girl student staying in the same university residence as herself got a postcard from a man unknown to her, suggesting a meeting.

It was signed 'James A. Joyce'. With proper Edwardian indignation, she sent back a haughty answer and got from Joyce an even cooler missive: he never remembered having seen her and in any case did not send communications to girl students unless they were friends of his family. The young lady, comparing the handwriting, decided that the original had not been sent by Joyce. Nevertheless, she was put out. She and all her friends decided Joyce was no gentleman to answer in such a tone. It was held by his contemporaries that he had too high an opinion of himself. 'There is James Joyce, the great genius of University College, in his own estimation,' said the person who first pointed him out to Mary Colum.

Taking his final oral examination in English for his degree, Joyce got in a last sting as the examiner questioned him:

EXAMINER: How is poetic justice exemplified in the play of *King Lear?*
JOYCE: (apparently bored) I don't know.
EXAMINER: Oh come, Mr Joyce, you are not fair to yourself.
JOYCE: Oh yes, but I don't understand your question. The phrase 'poetic justice' is unmeaning jargon so far as I am concerned.

Joyce left university in June 1902 with an undistinguished degree in modern languages. His mark in his final year in English was 344 out of a possible 800 and the results in French and Italian not very much more brilliant, but enough to make him Bachelor of Arts. It was unusual for men to specialize in those days in modern languages, and there was nothing much a graduate could do with that sort of BA except teach. Joyce, improbably, decided to follow in his father's footsteps and study medicine. He was to be even less successful at that study than his father had been. It does not seem to have occurred to him that he was unsuited by his talents to be any sort of physician. His marks in mathematics had been atrocious and he had studied no other science at advanced level. Predictably he found the preliminary science course disagreeable and with fine logic decided he would better be able to study medicine in Paris than in Dublin, at the Sorbonne.

He had no money and his father had less than ever, thanks to the purchase of the house in Cabra. Nor had he any income. Through Skeffington, who was registrar at University College, he was offered evening classes teaching French but declined them, telling Father

Darlington, the English convert who was Dean of Studies, that he was set on a career in letters (it was his idea to be both physician and writer, an ambition which his friend Gogarty, with different talents, achieved).

'Isn't there some danger of perishing of inanition in the meantime?' asked the Dean.

'Of course,' said Joyce, 'that is by tradition one of the ever-present perils of the career, but it has its prizes too.'

Father Darlington suggested journalism (as the Dean does in *A Portrait of the Artist*), citing the example of a law student who had simultaneously written editorials for two newspapers of opposite politics.

'I may not have that gentleman's talents,' said Joyce.

'You never know,' said the Dean, missing the irony, 'you never know till you try.'

Joyce left the interview in jubilation at having escaped distasteful employment, whistling *Solveg's Lied*[1] from Greig's music for *Peer Gynt* (a character with whom he, like Ibsen, had something in common – chronic fecklessness).

He had it in mind to do some tutoring but the College was disobliging, informing him that his services were not required. Bravely he wrote off to the Faculty of Medicine at the Sorbonne, applying for admission without taking the trouble to ascertain if he was applying to the right quarter, or indeed any other relevant detail. Joyce, of course, simply wanted to get to Paris. To discover prematurely that his scheme for medical studies was wholly impractical would take away the excuse.

In November he began the dunning process which he hoped would get him there. First on the list was Lady Gregory. She got a letter announcing his imminent departure. He had been forced to give up his medical studies in Dublin thanks to the machinations of the college authorities. '. . . I had made plans to study medicine here. But the college authorities are determined I shall not do so, wishing I dare say to prevent me from securing any position of ease from which I might speak out my heart.' There follows a plea of poverty dressed up in a good deal of imaginative self-pity. Joyce was to suffer (and his friends more so) all his life from a degree

[1]

74

of persecution mania. 'I am going alone and friendless . . . I am not despondent, however, because I know that even if I fail to make my way such failure proves very little. I shall try myself against the powers of the world. All things are inconstant except the faith of the soul, which changes all things and fills their inconstancy with light. And though I seem to have been driven out of my country here as a misbeliever I have found no man yet with a faith like mine.'

Lady Gregory had little idea of what she could do to help him. She suggested a meeting with John Milicent Synge, who had much experience of narrowly avoiding starvation in Paris when he was writing his plays there, and wrote to Yeats to suggest he feed Joyce on his way through London. 'Poor boy, I am afraid he will knock his ribs against the earth.' She wrote also to friends in Paris to inquire if Joyce could be got a little work teaching English. Most important, she got him some reviewing work for the Dublin *Daily Express,* a Conservative pro-British newspaper with copious literary content, much read for that reason by the cultured, even among the Nationalists.

George Russell obligingly called on George Moore to see if *he* knew anyone in Paris who might be helpful. Moore answered irritably that his friends were writers. Why the devil should he send a medical student to them? Maud Gonne too was in Paris. Russell wrote to her about Joyce's imminent arrival. A lot of people were going to some trouble on his behalf.

Archer wrote to him from London to try to talk him out of the plan. The market for teaching English in Paris, he said, was extravagantly overstocked. 'It is hard enough by giving lessons all day to keep body and soul together in Paris; and how you can expect to do that, and at the same time qualify as a doctor, passes my comprehension.' Yeats wrote too, and offered him breakfast and dinner before he caught the Paris train. There were perhaps a great many people in Paris, he suggested gently, who did not want to learn English. He would give Joyce some literary introductions in London if he wished. Perhaps he would get some work that way.

Archer had been over-pessimistic. When Joyce did get to Paris he was offered a job at the Berlitz School but declined it without stating any reason. There was work in Paris: whether Joyce wanted it was another matter.

On 1 December 1902 he set off from Kingston Harbour on his first exile, the artist as victim, sent out to combat trolls. Lady Gregory had not obliged with cash. He had few clothes with him and very little money.

Yeats was glad enough to see him again, and looking forward to their talk. Joyce had breakfast with him at his nearby apartments after getting off the train at Euston Station. Yeats spent the whole day with him, taking him to see the editors of two journals, *The Speaker* and *The Academy*. Neither interview was a success. Joyce asked C. Lewis Hind, editor of *The Academy*, if he might review books. Hind replied that he had only to put his head out the window to get a hundred young men as reviewers. Joyce resisted with difficulty asking him if he meant a hundred young men would review his head. Hind said he would like from Joyce 'moments of his spiritual life', a suggestion which Joyce found distasteful. He left agreeing to submit such moments from Paris, but never did.

In the evening they went to see Arthur Symons, eminent poet and critic. He offered to submit Joyce's poems to editors and to try to find a publisher for them as soon as Joyce had a volume ready. He talked of poets and artists he had known and played on the piano the Good Friday Music from *Parsifal*, remarking 'when I play Wagner I am in another world'.

Joyce found this encounter amusing. 'Symons always had a longing to commit great sin,' remarked Yeats afterwards, 'but he had never been able to get beyond ballet girls.'

Arrived in Paris, Joyce settled into the 'Grand'[2] Hôtel Corneille, which catered for foreigners with little money, and rapidly became adept at avoiding the proprietress, whom he called 'Baa-baa black sheep', and who objected to his wasting money on food instead of giving it to her. He dropped in at the Sorbonne and was told that his Irish degree was worthless in Paris: he would need a special dispensation, available only from the Minister for Public Instruction. Furthermore he was late in applying for it. But he got a provisional card of admission to lectures in physics, chemistry and biology, and actually attended some of them. He reported back to his family that he was being scrupulously economical. 'No information is to be given about me to anybody,' he adds, 'except—"O, Very nicely, thank you".'

---

[2] 'Grand' only in letters to his mother.

He lost no time making the acquaintance of the whores of the city, sending a scatological description of those ladies in dog Latin to his friend Vincent Cosgrave on the back of a postcard. The postcard is decorated with a picture of himself, settled already into his role as *Parisien*, looking studiously artistic in over-long coat and flat broad-rimmed hat. Two others of these postcards he sent to his family and to another friend, J. F. Byrne. The Byrne postcard was adorned with a poem about Joyce's new-found role as wanderer:

> *All day I hear the noise of waters*
> *making moan,*
> *Sad as the sea-bird is when going*
> *forth alone*
> *He hears the winds cry to the waters'*
> *monotone.*
>
> *The grey winds, the cold winds are blowing*
> *Where I go;*
> *I hear the noise of many waters*
> *Far below,*
> *All day, all night I hear them flowing*
> *To and fro.*

Perhaps there was bad plumbing in the Hôtel Corneille. At any rate Joyce did include that poem in *Chamber Music*. But he regretted most of the poetry he published.

Byrne was pleased to get the card and boasted to Cosgrave that he knew Joyce better than any man in Dublin. Cosgrave, grinning, produced his own filthy postcard and Byrne was deeply upset at what he considered a betrayal. He gave his own card to Cosgrave in disgust, who gave it in turn to Stanislaus. It survives: Cosgrave's does not.

Joyce built from the incident of Byrne giving away his postcard a new fable of betrayal (of himself) and put it in *A Portrait of the Artist*, where Byrne's ('Cranly's') imagined jealousy is explained in terms of a homosexual attraction to Joyce which certainly did not exist. When it comes to devoting imaginative genius to the events of one's own life Joyce ranks with Beethoven, Berlioz and Wagner.

This first exile was not protracted. Two weeks was about enough. He was only twelve days in Paris before he was writing to his mother, alarming her with the recital of a peculiar, painless, malady which prevented his getting up before eleven in the morning and made him weary by two in the afternoon. 'Write again if you like and say if I should go home for Christmas.' Since he had no money for the fare it fell to his father to find it. In the same letter he mentions that his single pupil, M. Douce, a champagne salesman, will advance him ten shillings and the *Daily Express* a guinea. Another pound is due from *The Academy*, he thinks—strange considering he had written nothing for them. With the accumulated largesse, when it arrives, he proposes to buy his mother a new set of false teeth.

Letters are exchanged every day. Mrs Joyce is worried that he will catch some contagion from the Paris water, advises him to buy a small spirit stove with which he could boil water and heat his room, but he must be *very careful* with it. She wishes she could be near him to look after and comfort him, and she gets little back from him in the way of comfort. 'My dear Jim, if you are disappointed in my letter and if as usual I fail to understand what you would wish to explain, believe me it is not from any want of a longing desire to do so and speak the words you want but as you so often said I am stupid and cannot grasp the great thoughts which are yours much as I desire to do so. Do not wear out your soul but be as usually brave and look hopefully to the future.' Joyce, at the age of twenty, was still a precocious brat. He told his impoverished parents he was too fragile to make the long Dieppe crossing. They sent him a ticket for the shorter and more expensive Calais to Dover crossing. To his father he explained that his funds were low, among other reasons, because the Parisian shopkeepers had passed old or foreign coins on him, an excuse which must have amused John Joyce, practised spendthrift that he was himself.

Joyce got back in time for Christmas and stayed a month instead of a week, making the rounds of old friends to impress them with his new Parisian style. At the Sheehy's he sang French songs and amused himself by leaving out perfectly innocuous lines in the knowledge that the assembled company would assume they contained French smut.

Back in Paris again in January, he abandoned the pretence of medical studies on learning that he was required to pay certain fees in advance, and took instead to spending his time reading Aristotle, Aquinas and Ben Jonson, Paris being a fine place to read such authors. He did not bother to call again on Maud Gonne, who had been nursing a cousin with diphtheria when first he called, but who had sent profuse apologies. 'I am very sorry for Mr Russell and Mr Yeats have both spoken and written to me so much about you that I have been looking forward to making your acquaintance. However, as I hear you are thinking of staying in Paris for some time, it is only a pleasure deferred.' Not so. He was not going to be in Paris very much longer and preferred in any case to imagine Miss Gonne had slighted him in some fashion.

Joyce remained in Paris three months, the whole time bombarding his unfortunate mother with a stream of letters describing his privations in horrific terms. The only money coming in was from reviews in the *Daily Express*, one review in *The Speaker*, and the proceeds of his teaching—but since he never advanced beyond having two pupils, that was not much.

His twenty-first birthday (2 February 1903) went unheralded except for a letter from his father, some cards, and a cigarette-case from his aunt, Josephine Murray. Even so, he was full of hopes. Shortly he would be making £200 a year from journalism. There was the *Express* and the *Speaker*, and the *Irish Times*, if all went right, would make him Paris correspondent. There was a new magazine coming out in London called *Man and Woman*, and they would pay him the grand sum of two guineas a thousand words. None of this happened, and what pieces of Joyce's did appear appeared with agonising slowness. He suffered the torments of the hungry free-lance journalist who knows he will not be paid until his work appears in print, and cannot understand the savagery of editors in holding it over.

In his *Daily Express* reviews he took occasional swipes at the Nationalists, but in March picked on an unfortunate target, knowing quite well what he was doing. Lady Gregory had brought out a work called *Poets and Dreamers* and Joyce did not like it. It contained long and boring accounts of peasant storytellers from the west of Ireland who had managed to irritate even the author by their nonsensical ramblings. It contained also a translation of Douglas Hyde's play *Casaidh an t-Sugain* (*The Twisting of the Rope*) whose appearance in the theatre eighteen months before had so incensed Joyce. Reading it in English and understanding it did not improve his temper. It was in this review that Joyce christened such

79

productions 'dwarf drama'. Lady Gregory, who had gone to the trouble of getting him the reviewing job in the first place, was not amused. The editor of the paper at least knew on which side his bread was buttered and broke precedent by signing the articles with Joyce's initials, a hint to Lady Gregory that the opinions were Joyce's and not his own.

By the middle of February Joyce was writing vilely whining letters to his mother, who was by now fatally sick as well as destitute: 'Dear Mother, Your order for 3/4d, of Tuesday last was very welcome as I had been without food for 42 hours (forty-two). Today I am twenty hours without food . . . With the utmost stretching your last order will keep me Monday midday . . . then, I suppose, I must do another fast. I regret this as Monday and Tuesday are carnival days and I shall probably be the only one starving in Paris.' Money arrived from his father in time to celebrate the tail end of the carnival, so much so that Joyce suffered a fit of vomiting and 'neuralgia'. This he put down to his periods of fasting.

'As a by-product of that sojorn in Boheme,' said suffering Stanislaus, 'there must be noted an attitude towards money that to me, with my middle-class ideas on the subject, was like a hair-shirt during all our life together.'

Joyce was by now complaining of toothache, which he said kept him in agony. He had no money to pay a dentist but disregarded his mother's advice to seek free treatment. He met Synge, who had by then written four plays. The only great playwright so far produced by the Irish national movement, he was almost as poverty-stricken as Joyce, and desperately unhealthy. He was less inclined to levity and more interested in writing than in aesthetic theory. Synge showed Joyce the manuscript of *Riders to the Sea*, whose plot is certainly improbable – a tragedy of drowning fishermen in the Aran Islands, lugubrious almost to the point of risibility. It is written in splendid language for all its faults, and Synge might have expected some compliment from his young acquaintance. He got none. Joyce rudely pointed out that the play was an imperfect tragedy since it did not conform to Aristotelian convention. 'I am glad to say that ever since I read it I have been riddling it mentally till it has not a sound spot,' Joyce wrote gleefully to Stanislaus. He was being more than usually obnoxious. He had more admiration for the play than he admitted. He memorized speeches from it and translated the whole into Italian. Synge didn't mind anyway: he was too weary.

He passed some time with other young gentlemen who described themselves as writers and engaged in animated debate over cheap wine. One of them, a Triestine Austrian with the splendid name (for a would-be poet) of Daubler was considering challenging Joyce to a duel after one of Joyce's celebrated sallies, but did not get round to it. His immediate reaction, said Joyce very sensibly, would have been to get on the first train for Dublin. In the absence of wine (and whore) money he spent the time walking the streets reciting poetry he liked, including his own, or in the Bibliothèque Nationale, reading and taking notes for an essay on aesthetics which, in the end, he never wrote. He had spent long enough contemplating the theory of how art ought to be produced. It was time he began instead to produce some.

The last work he did in Paris was an interview with Henri Fournier, a French motorist who was to race in Ireland in July. It was printed in the *Irish Times*. It is obvious from the piece that Joyce could have made a little more money from journalism if he had wanted to, since plainly he knows nothing about motor-racing and cares less; and yet he has that knack indispensable in journalists of turning out passable copy anyway.

On Good Friday 1903 Joyce returned late in the evening to the Hôtel Corneille to find a telegram from his father, 'Mother dying come home Father.' He roused Douce, one of his two pupils, from bed and succeeded in borrowing the fare back to Dublin, arriving there on Easter Sunday, 12 April.

Chapter Six

Lost Angel of a Ruined Paradise

May Joyce was indeed dying, of cancer of the liver (or, conceivably, syphilis – see Appendix), at the age of forty-four, medical science unable to save her, her system battered by all those years of drudgery and worry. But she did not die for the time being. Her son meanwhile had no burning desire to return to starvation in Paris. Instead he went back to his old existence of whoring and drinking, principally with medical students, providing literature in that way with the night-town material for *Ulysses*. Gogarty and Colum were glad to see him back. He made friends again with Byrne.

Colum introduced him to James Cousins, who was a poet, had a household unlike his bachelor friends, and indulged in vegetarianism, like Skeffington and Russell ('Damn vegetable verse,' said Joyce, 'and double damn vegetable philosophy!'). Cousins took Colum and Joyce to that sort of lunch and got more conversation than he bargained for over the nut cutlets. Like Colum he was one of the company of Gaelic revivalists contributing to the national theatre movement. One of the staples of that theatre was a wandering vagabond poet (as in *The Twisting of the Rope*) who seems to decorate every third play of that sort and whose curses, in verse, are as much feared as his blessings are sought after.[1] Joyce, by way of comment on this fey excuse for drama, quoted to them a curse he claimed to have composed and laid on the head of a whore who had dissatisfied him. After that, the mock turkey washed down with coffee, he treated them to one of his impressive aesthetic lectures. Afterwards, Cousins regarded with regret the figure of Joyce going away from them down the street.

'Lost angel of a ruined paradise,' he murmured, and one can imagine his sententious head wagging in sadness from side to side.

[1] The best satirist of this sort of stuff is Flann O'Brien, in *At Swim Two Birds* and other works.

Later, he was to be useful to his lost angel, when the angel needed a roof over his head.

Sometimes Joyce went prowling in the hope of picking up non-commercial ladies. Colum went with him on one of these expeditions and reported they got nowhere near success. Standing beside Joyce in the National Library he had left down a copy of *The World as Will and Idea*. Joyce was with a companion. 'You see before you two frightful examples of the will to live,' he said. Colum walked with them a while and then left them to their apparently hopeless chase. But Joyce was to meet his future wife by accosting her in the street.

While May Joyce declined, her husband's behaviour was not impeccable. For a while he behaved himself until he came home one night towards the end after a relapse into vicious drunkenness. He paced his wife's room muttering to himself, until he turned at the end of her bed.

'I'm finished! I can't do any more! If you can't get well, die. Die and be damned to you!'

That was too much for Stanislaus. 'You swine!" he shouted in the best melodramatic manner, rushing for his father, but his mother prevented his delivering the thumping the old ruffian deserved. To his horror he saw her struggling to get out of bed and went to her while James led his father out of the room.

'You mustn't do that,' she said. 'You must promise me never to do that. You know that when he is that way he doesn't know what he is saying.'

She died on 13 August 1903, surrounded by a large gathering of relatives. One of them, John Murray, an elder brother of hers, was a reformed drunkard and atheist, only occasionally given to relapse. His piety was conspicuous. He knelt on the floor to pray in a loud voice and, seeing that James and Stanislaus were not following his example, motioned angrily to them to do so. They ignored him. It cannot have given their mother any offence: she was already unconscious. But much was made of it in so hypocritical a country and Joyce was accused of unpardonable cruelty when the story was embroidered to the point of having him refuse his dying mother's last request to pray for her. Gogarty ('Mulligan') appears in *Ulysses* as the principal author of this fiction, which, strangely, is presented as being more or less true, perhaps because Joyce himself chose disdainfully not to deny it: after the death of Stephen's mother Mulli-

83

gan has spoken of Stephen, who is visiting his house: 'O, it's only Dedalus whose mother is beastly dead.' He justifies himself to Stephen:

> – And what is death, he asked, your mother's or yours or my own? You saw only your mother die. I see them pop off every day in the Mater and Richmond and cut up into tripes in the dissecting room. It's a beastly thing and nothing else. It simply doesn't matter. You wouldn't kneel down to pray for your mother on her deathbed when she asked you. Why? Because you have the cursed Jesuit strain in you, only it's injected the wrong way. To me it's all a mockery and beastly. Her cerebral lobes are not functioning. She calls the doctor Sir Peter Teazle and picks buttercups off the quilt. Humour her till it's over. You crossed her last wish in death and yet you sulk with me because I don't whine like some hired mute from Lalouette's. Absurd! I suppose I did say it. I didn't mean to offend the memory of your mother.

> He had spoken himself into boldness. Stephen, shielding the gaping wounds which the words had left in his heart, said very coldly:
> – I am not thinking of the offence to my mother.
> – Of what, then? Buck Mulligan asked.
> – Of the offence to me, Stephen answered.

John Joyce was at least affected by his wife's death. Stanislaus found him sitting up in the parlour after a drinking expedition, as he said – 'whining'. He lost his temper and berated his father for his crimes. John Joyce listened in silence and said simply, when his son had finished, 'You don't understand, boy'.

The youngest child, Mabel, was most grieved, and only her eldest brother was able to calm her. She would creep up the stairs weeping, to find a place to cry alone. James, seeing that, went after her and said, according to Stanislaus, who was listening, in a very matter-of-fact voice: 'You must not cry like that, because there is no reason to cry. Mother is in Heaven. She is far happier now than she has ever been on earth, but if she sees you crying it will spoil her happiness. You must remember that, when you feel like crying. You can pray for her, if you wish. Mother would like that. But you mustn't cry any more.' Stanislaus, that militant atheist ('We have only one life and all talk of another is just a priestly swindle'), held his peace and the child was comforted as well as

84

she could be. She died herself only a few years later, at the age of fourteen.

The principal burden of looking after the family now fell on Poppie (Margaret) the eldest daughter, who was twenty. Stanislaus felt able to compliment her on her 'unselfish, patient goodness' and commiserated in his diary with what he imagined to be the source of her discontent, her 'forced virginity' (Margaret escaped eventually, no doubt grateful for the peace, into a nunnery), but joined James in idleness by quitting his meagrely paid post with the Apothecaries' Company five months after his mother's death. What he got for those months he did at least contribute to the family upkeep. His elder brother would occasionally hand over a few shillings from the proceeds of his reviews in *The Daily Express,* accompanying the gift with the remark it was no part of his duty to support the family since he had already done enough in that direction. He meant the exhibition prizes of his schooldays.

Colum remarked to him that he had seen one of those articles. 'I received for it thirty thillings,' said Joyce, 'which I immediately consecrated to Venus Pandemos.' Some appetites are more compelling than others: thirty shillings was a steep price to pay for a whore in those days. One of the characters in *Dubliners* buys himself a meal consisting of a plate of peas and a bottle of ginger ale, and is content with it. The bill is two-pence halfpenny. That is to say – less than a quarter of a shilling.

There were days when the children went with less than a plate of peas. Stanislaus complained in his diary of going whole days without food and hearing with hatred his drunken father return late at night – but made little effort to do anything about it. There was one day when he was deprived even of footwear. His father's shoelaces having given out, he appropriated Stanislaus's boots. St Peter's Terrace was dirty, dilapidated and bereft of furniture. John Joyce was reduced to selling the piano.

Josephine Murray made some effort to help the children, in spite of having six of her own. Discreetly, she fed James. Nor was Stanislaus beyond visiting the Murray household to scrounge a crust and had fallen in love in his morose way, most unsuitably, with his fourteen-year-old cousin, Katsy Murray. That added to his misery.

John Joyce addressed his younger children, when he spoke to them, as wastrels and little bastards, complaining of the injustice of his being expected to fill their bellies. He had got it into his head that he could somehow dispose of all responsibility and retire to Cork, where he had been happy, and would be again. 'I'll get rid of you all and go back to Cork. But I will break your hearts before I go. Oh yes, by God, see if I don't! I'll break your hearts but I'll break your stomachs first!'

The elder brothers were required to take it in turns in the evenings to protect their sisters. Stanislaus calculated that his father was drunk four nights out of seven and when drunk was in the habit of flinging anything to hand – pokers, plates, cups or pans – at his children. James, Stanislaus and Charlie were big enough to look after themselves, but were frequently threatened with eviction by their father.

'Pappie has been drunk for three days,' records Stanislaus on 31 July 1904. 'He has been shouting about getting Jim's arse kicked. Always the one word. "Oh yes! Kick him, by God! Break his arse with a kick, break his bloody arse with three kicks!"'

The artist, however, was not always around to have his arse kicked, had his father been capable of it. Stanislaus *was* capable, being physically robust, but held off from that remedy for another couple of years. He was having a bad time of it. John Joyce and James had now been joined at the bottle by Charlie, who spent some time as a clerk in a wine office, testing to the limit his capacity for drink, and, released from his vows of chastity, whores. He spent three nights running, recorded Stanislaus, with a whore in Tyrone Street, and four in jail for drunkenness before the fine was paid. At the same time he was proud of the religious expertise he had picked up in his brief stay at the seminary and took to imitating the speech of one Father Breenan, who had trouble with his breathing. 'Oh you know (puff)' he told his sister May, 'you can make the seven visits without going any further than Phibsboro here (puff), without going to a single other chapel (puff). But of course you're supposed to go to seven chapels if you can (puff). Now today, for instance (puff), I went to . . . etc.' Poppie was aware of the excursions (non-religious) of both wayward brothers. No wonder she chose the cloistered life.

John Joyce was not pleased at his sons' taking after him. 'Another, perhaps,' said Stanislaus, 'might have been able to distill low comedy out of a situation in which a drunken father rails at two drunken sons for being drunk,' but he did not get the joke. It occurred to the ex-seminarist too to cultivate writing. 'In the silvery moonlight that flooded the room,' ended one of his pieces, 'I took off her drawers.'

James's literary career was somewhat limping. The last of his reviews appeared in the *Daily Express* in November 1903, after which the editor, for some insolence, threatened to kick him downstairs if he ever showed up again. His medical career he attempted to resume but that, once again, foundered on the rock of chemistry.

There were always pawn shops, those brokers to the poor with which the Joyces were intimately acquainted. Joyce went once to Colum bearing a pawn ticket donated in lieu of money by a medical student. It represented books which were redeemable for the sum of six shillings, plus interest. Undoubtedly they were medical text books which could be sold at a profit, the drawback being that Joyce had not got six shillings, plus interest. Colum was able to scrape up seven.

They took themselves to Terence Brady's pawnshop, paid the seven, got the package, eagerly opened it. No medical text books. Instead, a set of Scott's Waverley novels, one missing – worth nothing.

These they took away to George Webb's bookshop, Webb being generally considered fair.

'Some of your Italian books, Mr Joyce?' the dealer asked hopefully.

'No, Webb, these are special,' said Joyce loftily, exhibiting his offering.

Webb was kind and had the books rewrapped. 'Take them back to Terence Brady,' he said. 'Maybe you can get him to let you have back the six shillings.' They were lucky and suffered the loss of only one shilling (Colum's).

Dismal times. Joyce went to Colum's workplace at Lent to ask if he could share his supper. Colum said yes but his landlady, being religious, was zealous to see her lodgers kept to the dictates of denial. The meal was tasteless fish. Joyce ate it glumly and in silence.

'Where have you been for two days?' Gogarty inquired in this grim season. 'Were you ill?'

'Yes,' said Joyce.

'What were you suffering from?'

'Inanition.'

Joyce astonished Colum by coming to him with a project to start a new daily newspaper for Dublin, to be published, on the continental model, in the afternoon. He had precisely calculated not only the exact cost of the project (£2,000, a fantastic sum, it seemed to Colum. Indeed it was), but the format and the tone of the articles which would appear (in return for Skeffington's co-operation he had agreed to some Socialist and Feminist content). More, he had registered (or claimed to have registered) the name of the newspaper, not that anyone was likely to appropriate it. He wanted it called *The Goblin.*

Colum's part in the scheme was to put Joyce in touch with moneyed people. Alas, said Colum, he knew no one with money. Well then, said Joyce, who knew better, did he know any Jews? Jews had money ('It is odd,' remarks Colum, 'that the creator of the most outstanding Jew in modern literature did not at that time know any of the Jewish community in Dublin.'). Colum did know two Jews, brothers called Sinclair who had an antique shop in Nassau Street and were considered intellectuals. He took Joyce along to meet them. One was present. What he thought of this remarkable overture is not recorded but evidently he did not have £2,000 to spare, or, if he did, did not care to part with it. He must have been civil because he gets a favourable mention in *Ulysses,* when Bloom contemplates a visit to his co-religionist, 'a well-mannered fellow'.

No newspaper appeared. It is difficult to imagine any editorial policy Joyce and Skeffington were likely to concoct failing to infuriate nine-tenths of Dublin and bankrupt their backers.

Joyce was aware that Colum did have a patron, an American millionaire called Thomas Kelly, resident at Celbridge in County Kildare, who had undertaken to subsidize Colum's existence for three years while Colum, after the example of Synge, studied the aboriginals of the true Ireland and wrote about them. Kelly, in return for this generosity, was to have title to the American copyright of all masterpieces subsequently produced by Colum. Joyce having prised Kelly's address out of Colum made the fourteen-mile trek to Celbridge, unannounced, and was told to go away by Kelly's lodge-keeper. He trudged back through the December night to Cabra, turning up in rather a bad mood. (One of the phobias he listed was 'country roads at night'.)

Joyce had fired off an indignant letter from Celbridge post office before he left, and was answered by telegram and letter from Kelly, who had no previous knowledge of his existence and intended no insult. In Colum's apartment in Paris, the two did meet, Joyce and the wealthy American, years afterwards. Each was astonished and Joyce was amused by the remembrance of his newspaper project.

(The business manager was to have been one Gillies, editor of the *Irish Bee-Keeper*. Joyce offered to translate for him Maeterlinck's *La Vie des Abeilles*. Gillies read it and commented 'I don't think Maeterlinck ever kept a bee in his life'. He offered Joyce by way of consolation the position of sub-editor on his own paper. Joyce accepted and kept the job twenty-four hours.)

The months following Joyce's return from Paris had not been very productive of anything in the way of literature .'It is always a little troublesome getting a first start in literature,' Yeats had loftily advised him, 'but after the first start one can make a pittance if one is industrious.' Industrious he was not. He went as far as asking Stanislaus to suggest some titles for essays in the hope of selling them. One suggestion was 'World-troubling Semen', a pun of the brother's on Yeats's phrase 'World-troubling Seamen', in a ballad of his. This piece of uncharacteristic humour on his brother's part did not inspire Joyce actually to write anything. Neither for the time being did 'A Portrait of the Artist' or *'Contra Gentiles'*. But the last did tempt him and he mentioned it to Gogarty, who promptly stole it for the title of an essay of his own. When this was presented to Joyce for his approval, Joyce, after reading it, neatly tore off the title. Gogarty protested that they all used the same alphabet.

'I did not tear it off because he borrowed it,' Joyce explained to Stanislaus. 'I tore it off because he had wasted it. What he had written was all nonsense.'

Gogarty was at the time his most frequent companion, his money allowing him to be patronisingly generous to Joyce, who did not mind scrounging off him, whether it was for money, drink or cast-off clothes. Gogarty felt free to make slighting remarks about Joyce to Yeats, as when Yeats made a remark about some writer who was making three hundred a year in London writing clever articles.

'It is a pity Joyce couldn't get something like that,' said Frederick Ryan, another Dublin *littérateur* who was present. 'He could write the articles all right, but then he couldn't keep sober for three days together.'

'Why put it at three days?' said Gogarty. 'One day.'

Gogarty made conversation for the sake of having his talk admired: Joyce did not care who admired him and who did not. Besides, Gogarty was coarse. Joyce affected the belief that gentlemen do not use bad language because they like the sound of it, only because it precisely expresses what other language cannot. The sentiments he chose to express were certainly coarse enough. 'She's very warm between the thighs, I fancy', was a remark his brother regarded with distaste. Joyce's attitude to Gogarty, as he realized the degree of his own superiority, became one of condescension. Gogarty, in turn, had decided that one way of putting Joyce in his place was to encourage him to drink as much as he did himself. Joyce did so with enthusiasm: but Gogarty was an athlete, robust, better fed, and far better able to hold his drink. Joyce for a while drank sack, Falstaff's drink, which he found in a wine bar, then found it more economical to stick to porter, the cheap beer once brewed by Guinness for the Irish poor.

Stanislaus, christened 'Thug' by Gogarty (on account of his squat appearance and phlegmatic manner), detested his brother's companion and blamed him for James's dissipation: when brother Jim gets home Stannie lectures him: 'Last night when Byrne brought you home you were scarcely able to stand. Don't you know that you are disgusting?'

Jim: 'You are a tiresome Puritan . . . What's the matter with you is that you are afraid to live, you and the people like you. This city is suffering from hemiplegia of the will. I'm not afraid to live.'

Stannie: 'The fact remains that except for those reviews you haven't written anything for months.'

Jim: 'You would like me to put on a nice clean collar and take the tram at nine o'clock down to some office, like a Second Division clerk, and then come home in the evening and be a "pote" and write "pomes" . . . I don't care if I never write another line. I want to live.'[2]

'But for the life of me,' Stannie explodes at the end of this conversation, 'I can't imagine what you have to say to those drunken yahoos of medical students. That stumps me.'

'At least,' says Jim, 'they don't bore me as you do.'

In January of 1904 Joyce got around to writing something again, his first extended piece of prose since the essays on Ibsen and Mangan, but equally overblown and infected with the same stylistic

[2] Erhart in *John Gabriel Borkman*: 'I *won't* work. Only live, live, live!'

flatulence. He had heard of a new literary paper called *Dana*, to be edited by Frederick Ryan and William Magee, sub-librarian at the National Library, who preferred to be known as John Eglington. In one day he dashed off his contribution, calling it *A Portrait of the Artist* after his brother's suggestion. It was the beginning of the novel which metamorphosed through *Stephen Hero* into *A Portrait of the Artist as a Young Man*.

Ryan and Eglington promptly turned it down on the grounds it contained mention of prostitutes and apostasy. The hero (unnamed), like the hero of the two later works, rejects the Virgin Mary and is inspired by the thought of female beauty to embrace whores. Not the sort of thing to please an Irish audience in 1904, even supposing they could wade through the prose:

> For this fantastic idealist, eluding the grunting booted apparition with a bound, the mimic hunt was no less ludicrous than unequal in a ground chosen to his disadvantage. But behind the rapidly indurating shield the sensitive answered. Let the pack of enmities come tumbling and sniffing to the highlands after their game. There was his ground and he flung them disdain from flashing antlers.

The muse is Paranoia. Flash defiance at the enemy. Otherwise he might not know you existed. 'I can't print what I can't understand,' said Eglington. Eglington and Ryan, however, according to Joyce, were pleased with the style of his effort. The *real* reason for rejecting it was that it was all about himself. By his twenty-second birthday, 2 February 1904, which he spent drinking tea and playing cards while his father slept off a drunk upstairs, he felt able to announce to his brothers that he had begun a novel. It was to be autobiographical and based on *A Portrait of the Artist*. It now seemed to him a happy accident that the editors of *Dana* had rejected it. He and Stanislaus passed the time dreaming up the title of the new book and the names of the characters who were to appear in it. The title, again suggested by Stanislaus, was to be *Stephen Hero* after Stephen Daedalus, the name Joyce had chosen to call himself in the book. The title was meant to be satirical. As for the name Daedalus, Stanislaus objected to it on the perfectly reasonable grounds that no Irishman was ever surnamed Daedalus. But James wished to identify himself with the Greek hero – artificer, magician, inventor who gave Man wings (like Daedalus, Joyce was fascinated by the idea of flight but never tried it himself). By way of compromise he struck out the first 'a' in the name to make it seem less fanciful, but still has Mulligan in *Ulysses* comment on the preposterousness of it.

By 29 March he had got through eleven chapters of *Stephen Hero*. 'It is a lying autobiography and a raking satire,' recorded Stanislaus. 'He is putting nearly all his acquaintances in it, and the Catholic Church comes in for a bad quarter of an hour.'

This new industry weaned him away from drink for a while, as urgent work did for the rest of his life. His accession to virtue was not total, since he had to ask Gogarty in March for the name of a doctor willing to treat ailments of a sexual nature,[3] but Stanislaus noted with approval that he had been drunk only once in two months and showed signs of drink barely three times.

He had been taking a few voice lessons from Benedetto Palmieri, said to be the best voice teacher in Dublin, for a few (borrowed) shillings a lesson, and had made the acquaintance of John McCormack, then at the beginning of his career. McCormack had won the tenor competition at the Feis Ceoil, the nationalist music festival, the year previous and encouraged Joyce to try his luck. He scraped up the entrance money by selling the tickets to some books he had pawned, having failed to borrow ten shillings from Colum for that purpose. Gogarty retailed Joyce's economic woes to a whore called Nellie known to both of them. Nellie liked Joyce and was dismayed to hear he had to enter the Feis and feed himself, as Gogarty said, from what he got by selling his books. She offered to do her bit.

'But you couldn't suggest that to him,' she said, 'he's too - - - in'[4] proud.' Nellie particularly admired his voice. He had 'the - - - - inest best voice' she had ever heard. 'I could sit listening to you all night, Kiddie.' (Nellie had a fine voice herself. In moments of excitement she exclaimed 'God's truth I hate you. Christ, God's truth I do hate

---

[3] Ulick O'Connor, biographer of Gogarty, tells me that he was able to oblige. The ailment was syphilis (see Appendix). This could have contributed to Joyce's later eye trouble. There is also the possibility that he may have inherited the disease. Arthur Power tells me that he remembers speaking to a Dr Sullivan, a Dublin physician, who told him that he had treated John Joyce for syphilis. Dr J.B. Lyons in his *James Joyce in Medicine* (Dublin, 1973) says there is no evidence that Joyce had syphilis.
[4] Stanislaus's deletion. The story is from his diary.

you.' And one time when Joyce was about to give voice offered the accompaniment of herself on the pisspot.)

The Feis Ceoil was not a success for Joyce. He sang better than the other contestants but refused to attempt the sight-reading test, losing many marks for that reason. He won an honourable mention and a bronze medal which, being unpawnable, he threw away, and spent the evening railing at the judges for their presumption in asking an artist to sing a piece he had not prepared. Aunt Josephine rescued the medal and later Joyce asked for it back.

There being no alternative (except starvation) Joyce took his first job that spring of 1904, as a teacher in a private school at Dalkey, a pleasant seaside suburb on the southern tip of Dublin Bay. The headmaster was Francis Irwin, an Ulster Scot who, like many members of that nation, counted his pounds in shillings and pence. Joyce, at least, had some money in his pocket and stayed on until the end of the summer term, now resident in a large room in the Shelbourne Road, rented from a family called McKernan who insisted, from time to time, on being paid rent. The episode at Clifton School duly finds its way into the first part of *Ulysses*, with Dedalus/Joyce extracting his pay from Irwin/Deasy (as he rather oddly renamed him: Deasy is a southern Catholic name) before setting out to spend it in the kips. Mr Deasy asks Stephen if he can say to himself, *I owe nothing*. 'Mulligan, nine pounds, three pairs of socks, one pair brogues, ties,' thinks Stephen. 'Curran, ten guineas; McCann, one guinea; Fred Ryan, two shillings; Temple, two lunches; Russell, one guinea; Cousins, ten shillings; Bob Reynolds, half a guinea; Kohler, three guineas; Mrs McKernan, five week's board. The lump I have is useless.'

The description of Stephen's finances is an accurate reflection of Joyce's at the time. Curran, Ryan, Russell, Cousins and of course McKernan (his landlady) are all the names of Joyce's acquaintances, unchanged. Mulligan is Gogarty, McCann – Skeffington, Temple – John Elwood, medical student companion in the kips, and Kohler probably T. G. Keller, from whom Joyce had tried to extract £5 in return for a future £6, the proceeds of stories as yet unsold. Keller, having no money, was able to refuse this bargain. There is a splendid photograph of Joyce taken then by Constantine Curran, who had been a student with Joyce at University College and was, in spite of many differences, to be a fast friend all his life. Joyce frowns quizzically, feet planted wide apart, hands stuffed in baggy trousers. Asked what he was thinking when the photograph was taken, he answered: 'I was wondering would he lend me five shillings'.

John Eglington left a fine sketch of him: 'A pair of burning dark blue eyes, serious and questioning is fixed on one from under the peak of a nautical cap, the face is long, with a slight flush suggestive of a dissipation and an incipient beard is permitted to straggle over a very pronounced chin, under which the open shirt collar leaves bare a full womanish throat. The figure is fairly tall and very erect and gives an impression of seedy hauteur.'

The beard did not last long. Joyce had come back with it from Paris and refused his mother's request to remove it. But the impression of seedy hauteur it may have been that was responsible for the National Library's declining his services. He had asked for a job and was dismissed as entirely unsuitable. The beard, at any rate, had gone by the time Curran took his photograph. Later Joyce grew the pencilled goatee which we remember from his portraits of the 'twenties and 'thirties.

Joyce stayed with the McKernans until the end of August. Part of the time he had with him a grand piano, rented from Piggott's music shop (he found a grand piano necessary to accompany himself as he practised singing in spite of being capable of only a few chords) until Piggott's, inevitably, took it back for non-payment of rental fees. 'Dear Roberts,' reads a Joyce letter to George Roberts, later a director of the Dublin publishers Maunsel (with whom Joyce was to have an unfortunate association), 'be in the "Ship" tomorrow at 3.30 with £1. My piano is threatened. It is absurd that my superb voice should suffer.' Presumably Roberts was less than distraught at the threat to Joyce's superb voice.

To Gogarty, who was in Oxford, Joyce disclosed yet another scheme for advancing himself. He was going to travel the resort towns of the south of England 'from Falmouth to Margate', singing old English songs and accompanying himself on the lute. The lute was to be made for him by Arnold Dolmetsch, the great antiquarian musician and instrument maker. Joyce did indeed sing the songs of Dowland and Henry VIII very well, but there were slight snags to the plan. To begin with, Joyce did not know how to play the lute. Dolmetsch pointed out in a letter that it was very difficult to play and that furthermore he was not particularly anxious to make one, having made only one other before: and if he did, it would be very expensive. A simple harpsichord or a very early type of piano would be more practicable. This Dolmetsch could supply fairly easily. The sum of £30 to £60 would suffice. Joyce dropped the plan.

In the same letter to Gogarty (3 June) Joyce renews a request for money and if possible, clothes. He is singing at a garden fête and has nothing to wear. He wants to visit Gogarty at Oxford but hasn't the fare. He passes on the gossip of the town: Elwood is nearly recovered from the clap. Jenny, a young widow friend of his and Gogarty's, notable for her sexual athletics, is leaving town soon. He will call and say *adieu*. Jenny was another lady with a chamber pot, and had used it in Gogarty's presence while Joyce read his poems. 'There's a critic for you!' said Gogarty. Joyce had already decided to call his first volume of poems *Chamber Music*. 'You can take it as a favourable omen,' said Stanislaus, told the story.

Chamber Music was in the hands of Arthur Symons, who thought it ought to be published and was thinking about who might publish it. In September he got around to suggesting Grant Richards, not long in business in London, to whom Joyce hopefully sent this, his first complete work which he thought worth publishing. In July George Russell asked him to write a short story for the *Irish Homestead*, a magazine whose principal editorial concern was to avoid giving offence to anyone at all. The fee was to be one pound. The story was to be 'simple, rural, live-making, pathos.' Joyce wrote 'The Sisters' which we now know as the first story in *Dubliners*. It is neither simple, rural nor live-making, but concerns the death of a priest. 'I felt my soul receding into some pleasant and vicious region; and there again I found it waiting for me [the heavy grey face of the dead priest]. It began to confess to me in a murmuring voice and I wondered why it smiled continually and why the lips were so moist with spittle. But when I remembered that it had died of paralysis and I felt too that I was smiling feebly, as if to absolve the simoniac of his sin.' Uplifting or not, the *Irish Homestead* printed it, and the two that followed, 'Eveline' and 'After the Race', stories dealing respectively with a woman who is to run away to Buenos Aires with a man she hardly knows, but loses her nerve at the last moment – and with an all-night drinking and card-playing party on board a yacht. Joyce announced optimistically to Constantine Curran that he was writing a series of ten stories, to be called *Dubliners,* which would 'betray the soul of that hemiplegia or paralysis which many consider a city.' But the readers had had enough after three betrayals of their paralysis and the volume of their complaining letters induced the editor to inform Joyce his contributions were no longer needed. So optimistic had he been that his literary career had finally started that he had attempted to form a joint-stock company of an informal sort and sell shares in himself. There were no takers.

The subject matter of 'Eveline' is interesting. Joyce, when a child in North Richmond Street, had known a girl there called Eveline Thornton, who had fallen in love as Eveline does in the story. But she had neither run away with her lover nor failed to run away : she had married him and settled down in Dublin. So why the change in the story?

Because Joyce had met the love of his life, and by September 1904 he was contemplating running away with her. If she could be persuaded to run away with him. She was Nora Barnacle, from Galway.

7 The author engaged in Joycean research at what remains of No 7 Eccles Street, January, 1975, at some risk to his person. (p. 238).

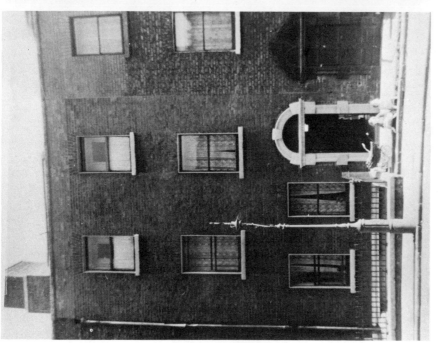

6 No 7 Eccles Street before being demolished by nuns. J. F. Byrne took Joyce back here one evening in 1909 and by doing so set the scene for *Ulysses*. (p. 160).

8　The newly famous author of *Ulysses* en famille, Paris, early 'twenties. George in the uniform of an aspiring bank clerk, Lucia demonstrating the beauty she inherited from her mother.

9　Joyce and Sylvia Beach at Shakespeare and Company, behind them a poster advertising the *Pink 'Un's* opinion of *Ulysses*.

Chapter Seven

The North Wall

Walking into eternity along Sandymount Strand, Stephen Dedalus muses in *Ulysses*: 'God becomes man becomes fish becomes barnacle goose becomes featherbed mountain,' the thought put into his head by the knowledge that out in the bay a drowned man is decomposing, 'bag of corpsegas sopping in foul brine. A quiver of minnows, fat of a spongy titbit, flash thought the slits of his buttoned trouserfly . . . Dead breaths I living breathe, tread dead dust, devour a urinous offal from all dead. Hauled stark over the gunwhale he breathes upwards the stench of his green grave, his leprous nosehole snoring to the sun.'

A strange paragraph into which to introduce the name of his wife but James Joyce, curious as always about words, had gone to the trouble of finding out the curious derivation of the name Barnacle.[1] It is rare even in Galway and honours an animal made dear to the Catholic Irish by a strategy worthy of that sometimes cunning race – the barnacle goose. Until recently it was Catholic law that meat might not be eaten on a Friday. But some inventive Irishman, fed up with fish and preferring fowl, concocted a dubious but at the time then apparently plausible life-cycle for a species of goose found in the west of Ireland. Unlike other animals with wings, this goose was not born from an egg but was the mature form of the sea-creature known as a barnacle. Hence it was not a bird at all – it was a fish and could be eaten without offence to God on Fridays. Such is the story of how the Barnacle family came by its name, and no doubt it is no more far-fetched than most Irish stories.

At any rate, there was Nora Barnacle, fresh from Galway, a tall, striking young woman with a splendid head of dark red hair. She

[1] At least I presume he had done so. I got the explanation from the late Martin O'Cadhain, Gaelic scholar, whose own name derived from the Irish for barnacle goose, as do O'Kane and Kane.

was walking down Nassau Street, by Trinity College on 10 June 1904, when Joyce spotted her and moved in hopefully. The blue eyes impressed her, though she thought at first, because of the second-hand yachting cap, he might be a sailor. Miss Barnacle was a skivvy in Finn's Hotel, not a very exalted institution, and only six months escaped from the clutches of her family, so was not inclined to be distant. The conversation progressed well enough for them to be able to agree to meet four days later on the street outside the former residence of Sir William Wilde in Merrion Square, a Dublin landmark.

But she didn't turn up. Joyce, smitten, wrote her a note:

> 60 Shelbourne Road
> I may be blind. I looked for a long time at a head of reddish brown hair and decided it was not yours. I went home quite dejected. I would like to make an appointment but it might not suit you. I hope you will be kind enough to make one with me – if you have not forgotten me!
> James A. Joyce

She had not, and on the evening of the 16th they went out walking at Ringsend, which is by the sea and close to town but has little else to commend it. One does not know what they discussed but it would have come more as a relief than a disappointment to Joyce to discover that Miss Barnacle had no interest in literature and little in art beyond the normal Irish liking for the sentimental, the facile and the humorous. It was only fools like Skeffington, said Joyce, who expected women to think. Joyce in turn will have charmed Miss Barnacle and perhaps he was allowed a kiss or two or a stray arm around her waist. He had lately been sarcastic about sexual love, quoting to friends the epigram of a Dublin joker, one Dr Perse, typical, in its vicious ignorance, of the Irish male attitude to women; 'Woman is an animal that micturates once a day, defecates once a week, menstruates once a month and parturates once a year.'[2] But he yearned still to find that pure sexual love he had wanted, like all men of high imagination who are not homosexual, since first he knew what female was.

---

[2] Apart from the impossibility of women menstruating in a state of pregnancy, the science is deficient in another respect. Micturition is a morbid, not normal, state of urination. Joyce, who was fond of parading his scant medical knowledge, should have known better.

That second meeting was enough to plant in his mind the idea that he had found sexual love, and for that reason he glorified 16 June 1904, to his own satisfaction, by making it the date of all the action of the greatest novel of the twentieth century, *Ulysses*. That, of course, was many years later, and Nora, being no great connoisseur of the works of James A. Joyce never did quite understand all the fuss about 16 June.

Nora Barnacle's father was a baker who drank his family into poverty in the classic Irish manner. Nora's mother when pregnant farmed her out to her own mother when she was five, and afterwards separated from the drunken father, so that the arrangement with the grandmother continued. Nora attended a convent school until the age of thirteen when, being deemed sufficiently educated for a girl of her station, she was sent to work as a portress for another lot of nuns, in Galway City.

Nora's first experience of sexual passion had been the intrusion of a curate's hand up her skirt: afterwards he asked her to omit in confession the fact it had been a priest. She had had two boyfriends in Galway. The first was Michael Bodkin, a handsome student of University College, Galway, with a head of wavy black hair and a romantic disposition. He stole in the rain from his tubercular deathbed to serenade her from her garden and is immortalized in 'The Dead' – the last story of *Dubliners*. Joyce, in his perverse way, dwelt jealously on her memory of her dead lover, buried at Oughterard and was inspired to fine prose[3] and verse. Nora had been too young for Bodkin (and certainly there was no carnality) but wept sometimes in sad guilt at the thought of having caused his death. Her second boyfriend was Willie Mulvey, from whom she extracted boxes of chocolates to share with her friend Mary O'Holleran, who provided her with alibis while surreptitiously she went walking with Mulvey. With Mary she would also dress up in men's clothes and wander the town. One evening, in this costume, they managed to deceive Nora's uncle, Thomas Healy, since Mary, fortunately, had a rather gruff voice. Healy was in the habit of patrol-

---

[3] 'The Dead': 'Yes, the newspapers were right: snow was general all over Ireland. It was falling on every part of the dark central plain, on the treeless hills, falling softly upon the Bog of Allen and, farther westward, softly falling into the dark mutinous Shannon waves. It was falling too on every part of the lonely churchyard on the hill where Michael Furey lay buried.'

ling the town with a heavy stick and a sharp eye out to see his niece got up to no devilment. He was not long deceived, caught her out with Mulvey and followed her home, stick twitching. Mulvey, God help us, was a Protestant. Miss Barnacle was soundly thrashed and ran away a week later to Dublin, preferring the life of a slavey to her existence in Galway. She took care to keep her address secret from her family.

The courtship of Jim and Nora (though she was not allowed to call him Jim yet) advanced speedily. Two weeks after she met him she was addressing him in a note as 'My Precious Darling', but signing herself N. Barnacle. By 8 July he is calling her 'Little Pouting Nora' and 'dear little brown head' but signing himself J. A. J. A few days later she is 'My dear little Goodie Brown Shoes' – a little too good for Joyce's taste as he has evidently attempted more liberties than he was allowed. He has slept with her glove beside him all night, and it has conducted itself very properly – like Nora. '*Please* leave off that breastplate as I do not like embracing a letterbox.' He plants kisses on her neck, being allowed not much further, and seems quite soon to have gone too far – or to have let his hand go too far – since his 'particularly pouting Nora' withdraws her company for four days without explanation and Joyce is 'trying to console his hand but can't.'

It would be pleasantly romantic to be able to record that love had entirely and immediately transformed Joyce's behaviour, but it had not. On the 15th, the day before the second momentous meeting with Nora, the MacKernans, their patience for the moment exhausted, suggested he leave until he could pay the rent. He sought refuge in the Cousins' vegetarian household. Tiresome as it might be, it was not so tiresome at St. Peter's Terrace. Five days later he created a drunken disturbance at the rehearsal rooms of the National Theatre Society, whence he had gone with Gogarty. 'Joyce gets drunk in the legs, not in the head,' said one of his companions to Padraic Colum. 'The other night I took him home and he was curled up in the cab like a tobacco spit.' It was his legs that betrayed him on his visit to the National Theatre Society. Their rehearsals were conducted in a small room approached by a narrow passageway. However much he mocked the aspirations of the 'National Theatre' Joyce was tolerated there because he sang and talked to please the company in between their exertions. Some of the actresses, no doubt an attraction to him, were recruited from a group of Nationalist young ladies, called, in English, the Daughters of Erin.

Joyce's legs gave out on him in the dark corridor. He was, however, conscious, so that one of the daughters of Erin was surprised to hear grunting noises issuing from the object she stepped over. W. G. Fay, the stage manager, one of the two brothers who ran the theatre, was annoyed at this affront to the high seriousness of the national drama and had Joyce roughly thrown out and the door locked after him. Joyce took his ashplant and banged on the door, roaring for admission until, in kindness, two of the company took him home.

This incident he celebrated with a brace of limericks (as well as mentioning it in *Ulysses*):

> *O, there are two brothers, the Fays,*
> *Who are excellent players of plays,*
> *And, needless to mention, all*
> *Most unconventional,*
> *Filling the world with amaze.*

> *But I angered those brothers, the Fays,*
> *Whose ways are conventional ways,*
> *For I lay in my urine*
> *While ladies so pure in*
> *White petticoats ravished by gaze.*

There was only one lady, a Miss Esposito, and she did not ravish his gaze. When years later he met her again in Paris and was reminded of the incident he shook his head ruefully and said: 'I was too drunk to see your legs. What drink makes us miss!'

The turbulence persisted. The same day in June that Nora was writing to him as her precious darling, he was writing to Constantine Curran complaining of a black eye, sprained wrist, sprained ankle, cut chin and cut hand, the souvenirs of an encounter in Stephen's Green. Joyce was full of resentment at Cosgrave, who had been with him but had stood by with his hands in his pockets while Joyce was dealt with by his assailants. Cosgrave, living up to Joyce's assigned role as traitor, sowed the seeds of a future jealousy drama by attempting Nora himself, but got nowhere. The reaction of Joyce's other friends was less positive. They thought Nora Barnacle beneath the bard.

'Miss Barnacle has a very pretty manner,' allowed Stanislaus in his diary, 'but the expression of her face seems to me a little common. She has magnificent hair.' – 'I never saw Jim manage any affair so badly as he had managed his affair with Miss Barnacle,' he adds in July. Cunning Cosgrave told Joyce that he was not the man for one enduring affair: Nora would be only the first of a hundred. Joyce heard out these counsels in dignified silence.

'Certain people who know that we are much together insult me about you,' he told Nora. 'I listen to them calmly, disdaining to answer them but their least word tumbles my heart about like a bird in a storm.'

Suspecting he had too enthusiastically attempted her breastworks, Joyce sent her two poems to make up for the boldness of his advances, one by Yeats, one by Henry VIII, both gentlemen who had trouble with women. Henry, he remarked, was a brutal and lustful king. 'It is strange from what muddy pools the angels call forth a spirit of beauty.' The Yeats, by way of apology, was *Down by the Sally Gardens*, which has the lines:

> *She bade me take love easy as the leaves grow on the tree*
> *But I, being young and foolish, with her would not agree . . .*
>
> *She bade me take love easy as the grass grows on the weirs,*
> *But I was young and foolish and now am full of tears.*

This lyric he sang at a concert in August, when Nora heard him sing in public for the first time and was pleased. She used to tell him frequently in their years together that he (and she) would have been better off if he had stuck to singing. The concert was something of a shambles, with the accompanist departing in a huff early in the evening, and her replacement turning out to be incompetent. Joyce sat down at the piano to accompany himself and gave a lugubrious account of 'The Croppy Boy', a patriotic ballad. The *Freeman's Journal* reported he was the possessor of a sweet tenor voice. He tended to force it on the high notes to gain maximum effect, like his father. The incident of the departing pianist became the germ of 'A Mother', also from *Dubliners*.

Leaning on Nora, he implored her to write him something heartening, and, being an obliging young lady (up to a point) she sent him a treacly love letter, carefully calligraphed onto flowered notepaper: 'My dearest, My loneliness which I have so deeply felt, since we parted last night seemed to fade away as if by magic, but, alas, it was only for a short time, and I then became worse than ever.' And so on. Apart from the foreignness of the syntax, Nora was not normally much given to the use of commas. Joyce mentioned his suspicions to Byrne who said, of course, the epistle must come from a letter-writing book. So Nora was told off and promised to do nothing of the sort again.

Joyce, on his part, had to face the fact that the attachment was considerable. He had been half planning to go away with some travelling troupe of actors. 'I could put no energy into the plan because you kept pulling me by the elbow.' Nora was treated to a recital of his sexual history, which, naturally, upset her. He confessed to a perverse desire to ruin her opinion of himself, and added a denunciation of the church, to which she still felt loyalty. 'My mind rejects the whole present social order and Christianity – home, the recognized virtues, classes of life and religious doctrines.'

Sexually he had made some progress, since Miss Barnacle had conferred on him some favour which he appeared to have enjoyed more than herself.

He notices a certain shyness in her manner, as if the recollection of a certain night, and what happened on it, troubled her. 'I however consider it a kind of sacrament and the recollection of it fills me with amazed joy. You will perhaps not understand why I honour you so much on account of it as you do not know much of my mind. But at the same time it was a sacrament which left in me a final sense of sorrow and degradation – sorrow because I saw in you an extraordinary, melancholy tenderness which had chosen that sacrifice as a compromise, and degradation because I understood that in your eyes I was inferior to a convention of our present society.'

Advanced petting, 1904? It seems that Joyce wasn't doing too badly, but felt the necessity of pleading higher motive. 'I honour you very much but I want more than your caresses. You have left me again in an anguish of doubt.'

Nora heard similar speeches during their meetings, and reacted with phrases which Joyce thought to be painfully rude.

'I know what's talking now,' she said. She was, in ancient but now, for the time being, outmoded tradition, nailing her man down before she granted the last favour.

Joyce, inspired by Nora, wrote and sold some poems, one of them appearing in the August issue of Eglington's *Dana*. Rather than behave with gratitude, Joyce, with the assistance of Gogarty, insulted Eglington in a manner which quickly went the rounds of Dublin and reinforced the common view of Joyce as a young rake impetuously set on the road to ruin. Eglington was an adherent of a group of would-be mystics calling themselves the Hermetic Society and known less reverently to others as the Emetic Society. The leading light was George Russell, who prided himself on an imaginary skill for filling empty heads with airy rubbish, much as Aldous Huxley and Timothy Leary similarly reverenced themselves in later generations for preaching a different, but related brand of nonsense. Joyce dismissed mysticism as the refuge of apostate protestants. Gogarty, equally rude, said Eglington had to fart before he could think[4] – but did not say it to Eglington's face.

George Moore and Eglington apparently found the topic of Joyce's excesses interesting enough to talk about. It was their opinion, they said, that Joyce drank too much. Gogarty, who was present, mentioned helpfully that his companion was given not only to drink but to women as well.

'We have all kissed women,' announced Moore, who liked to be thought a lady-killer. 'If we have not kissed them on the mouth we have kissed them otherwhere.'

Not Eglington. 'I never did it,' he protested (Moore, for that matter did not do it so frequently either, but had the unenviable reputation of *not* kissing and telling anyway). This unfortunate phrase of Eglington's, passed around the town by Gogarty, created much merriment. Joyce christened Eglington 'the horrible virgin.' On a trip to the rooms (or, to be more accurate, room) of the Hermetic Society in search of Russell (and some innocent amusement), the two, Joyce and Gogarty, found that the members had stepped out for some reason. Present, however, was the travelling bag of George Roberts, the same who had declined a loan of £1 for the salvage of Joyce's piano. Roberts was not yet manager of Maunsel the publishers but was passing the time in the uncongenial occupation of traveller in ladies' underwear. His samples were contained in the bag. Joyce and Gogarty fell upon it and

---

[4] A witticism stolen from Swift, by the way.

extracted one particularly voluminous pair of bloomers. These they stretched between two chairs, with an upended broom inserted.

'I never did it,' read the attached notice, signed 'John Eglington'.

Russell was not amused. 'I found,' he said, 'an obscene effigy set up by Joyce.' Neither were Eglington nor Roberts pleased. None of which prevented Joyce from asking all three for help when shortly he needed it for the great escape.

For the time being he had taken refuge with Gogarty in the Martello Tower at Sandycove which is the setting of the first chapter of *Ulysses*. The room at the McKernan's was no longer available, and neither the Joyce nor the Cousins household was appealing, one for the reason of squalor, the other excessive virtue.

The tower is still there, and likely to remain unless removed by Irish vandalism. It is presently a well-appointed Joyce museum. Martello towers were built by the British in the Napoleonic wars as coastal defences against a possible French invasion. Solid stone walls eight feet thick are surmounted by ramparts containing a gun rest, an oven for heating cannon-balls and a channel for pouring molten lead or boiling oil on incautious attackers. There is a perilous staircase, built into the wall, leading the two stories up to the top, and the only entrance is twenty feet up from the ground. Entry was via a ladder, and a door which could be opened only by a copper key, copper so that it would not give off sparks which could ignite gunpowder. At the end of the nineteenth century the British Government, deciding that the possibility of French invasion was slight and the towers of doubtful military value, removed the artillery and leased the towers. They were taken mostly by young men attracted by the cheap rent and the proximity of the sea.

The tower where Joyce stayed (very briefly) in September 1904 is a twenty minute train ride from Dublin. It was leased for £8 a year by Gogarty, who allowed Joyce to stay there rent free on condition that Joyce did the housework while he got on with his novel, or so Gogarty claimed. Joyce, too, was to be fed. It was costing Gogarty, Stanislaus recorded, no more than a few shillings a week, but Gogarty found it a bad bargain, as is scarcely surprising: James Joyce does not strike one as the ideal room-mate, or ideal housekeeper. Joyce has it in *Ulysses* that he contributed his share to the domestic economy from his salary as schoolmaster, but he had by that time given up that profession. There was certainly ill-feeling, which was not helped by the presence of a second lodger, Samuel Chenevix-Trench.

Diarmuid Trench, as he called himself, was yet another unhinged Anglo-Irish convert to nationalist Celticism, scion of a distinguished family, one of whose members had been Archbishop of Dublin. Trench had taken his enthusiasm to the point of fluent mastery of Gaelic and had recently returned from a canoeing trip of the island which had given him, he was certain, a proper understanding of the 'real' people of Ireland. Just the sort of person Joyce could be calculated to loathe. Apart from his other faults, Trench was demented, suffered from violent nightmares and was dreadfully earnest. He played the part – in Irish, of course – of the wandering vagabond poet, before mentioned, in Douglas Hyde's *Casadh an t-Sugain*. Colum liked him.

Joyce made him Haines, the block-headed Englishman full of apology for England's sins, symbol of Ireland's conqueror in a chapter stuffed as full of symbols as any in *Ulysses*: Dedalus renounces Ireland, Mulligan betrays her. The symbol of Irish art is the cracked looking-glass of a servant and Cathleen ni Houlihan is the old milk-woman with shrunken paps who takes Haine's Gaelic greetings to be French.

'. . . I'm ashamed I don't speak the language myself. I'm told it's a grand language by them that knows.'

'Grand is no name for it,' said Buck Mulligan. 'Wonderful entirely.'

From this acid comedy Joyce omitted the manner of his going. On the night of 15 September Trench woke up screaming about a black panther, took up a revolver and loosed off a few shots at the phantom. Joyce was understandably terrified, with bullets richocheting around the small stone room. Gogarty disarmed Trench and soothed him back to sleep, but when the panther reappeared Gogarty said 'Leave him to me,' and banged away at some pans over Joyce's head. Considering this marksmanship an invitation to leave, Joyce got up and dressed, and walked through the rain back to Dublin.[5]

[5] Ulick O'Connor disputes this story as one of Joyce's inventions. He points out that their friendship appears to have ruptured as early as 16 August, when Gogarty wrote to a friend: 'I have broken with Joyce. His want of generosity became to me inexcusable. He lampooned Yeats, "A. E.", Colum, and others to whom he was indebted. A desert was revealed which I did

All ye who dig for treasure trove
Beneath the tower of Sandycove,
What joy if you could only seize
One Sapphic fragment, or unroll
A tender twilight-litten scroll
Of Starkey's hazel trees!

So much for Gogarty's boast. James Starkey, who called himself Seumas O'Sullivan was an occasional resident at the tower and a poet whom Gogarty regarded highly, though it was not Starkey who would make the place memorable. Joyce had hoped to spend a year under Gogarty's roof, completing *Stephen Hero*. Now he had made up his mind that he could count on no Irish friendship, and determined to leave Ireland immediately. He sent Starkey a note demanding that Starkey put Joyce's possessions in his trunk and rope it up (it had no lock). The trunk would be collected the following morning. The possessions were – a pair of black boots, a pair of brown boots, a blue peaked cap, a black cloth cap, a black felt cap, a raincoat, and the manuscript of *Chamber Music*. 'Also see that your host has not abstracted the twelfth chapter of my novel from my trunk.'

Another souvenir of the tower appears to have been a renewed outbreak of the pox. Mr Mervyn Crofton, who died in Dublin in 1974 at the age of ninety-three, told Ulick O'Connor of a conversation with Gogarty: 'Gogarty told me he had a beautiful girl in the tower – "Hair all up her spine, Crofton, but she has syphilis".' Gogarty had the sense to keep off, but Joyce did not, or so Gogarty said. If Joyce was still suffering from syphilis in the late summer of 1904 he must have been hoping for a quick cure, since his ardour for Nora did not diminish.

Joyce lost no time in extracting from Nora a declaration of love which, for the time being, he declined to return, assuring her instead that he had great respect for a love which he hoped to deserve and return. She had to be content for the time being with the knowledge that her soul seemed to him to be the most beautiful and

---

not think existed amid the seeming luxuriance of his soul.' More likely, I would think, that Joyce had in some way offended Gogarty rather than Yeats, 'A. E.' or Colum. He may also have left the tower more than once and returned again. It is his own account that puts the stay at only a few days. As to whether the story is true or not, he retailed it himself, frequently, and with relish.

simple soul in the world. However puzzled by her lover's equivoca-
tion, Nora knew her own heart well enough. She told him she would
go abroad with him, and spent part of the evening of the 16th
(a Saturday) evading her employers in Finn's Hotel while she stole
the time to read his latest missive. (In those days of primitive
technology letters were delivered on the same day they were
posted.)

Joyce wrote off to a scholastic agency in Lincolnshire which
advertised teaching posts on the continent. A Miss Gilford, who ran
the agency, answered immediately. She had reserved, with astonish-
ing speed, a post for him with Berlitz and would tell him where it
was on the payment of a two-guinea fee. Properly suspicious, he
telegraphed the Lincolnshire police, asking Gilford's credentials and
repeated the enquiry to Berlitz headquarters in London, along with a
request for a job in Paris. The police telegraphed that the person
was well known and respectable. Berlitz said they didn't know the
agency and sent Joyce a registration form. Joyce sent Gilford her
two pounds, two shillings. Nora was offered some sort of job in
London. Joyce wrote off accepting it for her, but did not want to go
there if they could avoid it. Perhaps London too was suffering from
hemiplegia of the will. He saw his place in Europe.

Nora was excited at the thought of her impending romantic
adventure: 'Dear Jim I feel so lonely to night I dont know what to
say it is useless for me to sit down to write when I would prefer to be
with you I hope you will have good news when I see you to morrow
night I will try and get out 8.15 Giving you all my thoughts till
then Nora.' Joyce, suffering from a cold as a result of his wanderings
in the rain, was more sober; 'I often wonder do you realise thoroughly what you are about to do,' and could think of little to say
when he was with her. A certain paralysis still affected his tongue
when he attempted to pronounce the word 'love' in her presence.
He was looking forward to the effect the news of his and Nora's
departure would cause in his circle.

Joyce began the familiar dunning process once more, first writing
to Yeats to ask the return of his translations of Hauptman, unless
Yeats had decided to use them. And could he have some money?
Yeats replied that the plays were badly translated, the theatre had
no money to pay authors, and in any case it was not their policy
to put on foreign plays. 'We must get the ear of our public with

Irish work.' As for money, he was unable to help. He had done his best to get Joyce work and that was all he could do.

The Gilford agency telegraphed him on 2 October. There was a job in Switzerland. He must be ready to leave immediately.

Skeffington too refused him money. 'You have my best wishes for your welfare, and for that of your companion, which is probably much more doubtful than your own.' Lady Gregory demanded assurances of a serious intention, and when she got them, sent him £5.

'I'm not like Jesus Christ,' he informed Colum, whom he ambushed in the National Library. 'I can't walk on the water.' He was, said Colum, putting on the air of a desperado.

From George Roberts, whose sample bag he had so recently plundered, he demanded fare money. 'I am counting on £1 between you and [Frederick] Ryan. That is not exorbitant, I think, as it is my last. May I count on you for this *early* on Friday? Answer kindly. I may call.'

Russell too, he touched.

The boat was leaving the Dublin quays at nine o'clock on the evening of 9 October. That was a day of last-minute panic. Since Starkey was unable to provide money, Joyce left a note at his father's chemist shop. He would be back in twenty minutes and expected to find a parcel containing:

1 toothbrush and powder
1 nail brush
I pair of black boots and any coat and vest you have to spare

If Starkey wasn't there when Joyce got back then he was to meet him without fail outside Davy Byrne's pub at ten past seven. Roberts had not coughed up either. 'For God's sake give me that 10/- to bearer or meet me at North Wall boat at 9 o'clock.'

He managed it onto the boat with barely enough money to get to Paris. Nora proceeded onto the boat separately. John Joyce was on the dock and was not supposed to know his son was running off with a servant girl. Unlike Eveline of *Dubliners*, she had no qualms. They sailed off into exile. 'There is no doubt,' said Colum, 'that Joyce looked forward to a return to Ireland with Nora when he would be recognised and honoured.' That was not to happen, but the thought of it made the play *Exiles*. They never lived in Ireland again, but stayed together until death separated them. That would have surprised most they left behind. Of all Joyce's friends, only Francis Byrne had said, 'Don't wait and don't hesitate. Ask Nora, and if she agrees to go away with you, take her.'

And he did.

Chapter Eight
A Dull Place Full of Slavs

To journey overland from Dublin to London, or Paris, took no longer in 1904 than it does now. The day after leaving Dublin Joyce and his companion were in London. He called on Symons in the hope of extracting a loan, without success. Symons was away.

The morning following they were in Paris with enough money to take an open carriage, hopefully, to the Gare de l'Est. But there was not enough money to go on to Zurich. Joyce left Nora in a park while he went off in search of Douce, the ex-pupil who had lent him the money eighteen months previous to return to Dublin (That was one debt John Joyce repaid, considering it a matter of honour). Douce was away in Spain on holiday but Joyce had more luck with Dr Joseph Rivière, who had fed him and assisted in his abortive attempt to study medicine at the Sorbonne. Rivière lent him sixty francs and offered to introduce him to the son of a Zurich banker. Joyce had to decline. Nora was waiting in the park, penniless and lonely, and suffering from the curse. That, at least, was one inconvenience she would not have to suffer again for ten months. Joyce met Constantine Curran and another ex-student from UCD, but kept Nora out of their way. The secret was blown anyway. A crony of John Joyce's had gone on board the boat before it left Dublin and seen them together. Old Joyce, informed of Nora's surname, said, 'She'll never leave him,' a witticism which stood as prophecy. His son was still anxious that Nora's family might seek to cause trouble. 'Has she been advertised for in the papers in Dublin?' he asked Stanislaus in a note written, very quickly, from the Gasthaus Hoffnung, Zurich, on the morning of 11 October.

It seems to have been a busy day. Joyce arrived on the morning train and booked into the hotel (*Hoffnung* means hope, which must have appealed to him), getting down immediately to an operation which had been on his mind for some months. The remains of Nora's innocence were put behind her before Joyce sat down to write to his brother an appeal for money. At the end of the note, on a part to be detached so the rest could be shown to the family, he inscribed: 'Finalement, elle n'est pas encore vierge; elle est *touchée*.' Leaving Nora to recover from the experience, Joyce presented himself to the director of the Zurich Berlitz school, Herr Malacrida, and was told there was no job for him. Malacrida had no knowledge of any transaction with Miss Gilford but addressed her a letter of remonstration which did not strike Joyce as a communication passing between people who did not know one another. He decided he had been swindled, but there was nothing to do but wait, and hope that Malacrida came up with something. Joyce managed to survive for a week in Zurich, growing to like that city, before Malacrida sent him on to Trieste, that mainly Italian city on the Adriatic which was the principal port of the Austrian empire. It was thought there was a job there, so Joyce and Nora set off on a journey not without incident. While in Zurich he had written a new chapter of *Stephen Hero* (a part of the manuscript which is lost) and begun a new short story called 'Christmas Eve'. This last was intended for the *Irish Homestead*, which had no intention of printing any more of his stories. He never finished it.

The two arrived in Trieste on 20 October with nowhere to stay. Attempting to extract information from some drunken British sailors, Joyce managed to get himself arrested along with them, and released from custody only with the reluctant intercession of the British consul whom, naturally, Joyce resented. Joyce was promptly informed by Bertelli, sub-director at the Berlitz school, that he was misinformed about any vacancy there, so set to borrowing money 'right left and centre', no mean feat in a strange city, and looking for employment. He looked unsuccessfully for a post as English correspondent in a commercial house and got himself one private pupil. He thought he might have done well with private pupils but had no money to live on while he accumulated them.

Almidano Artifoni,[1] proprietor and director of the Berlitz school, came to his rescue with the offer of a job at his second school, in Pola, an Austrian naval station fifty miles down the Istrian peninsula. Joyce, having little alternative, accepted and spent the next four months there, not liking it much. 'Istria is a long boring place

[1] Joyce borrowed his name for the Jesuit teacher of Italian in *Stephen Hero*, *A Portrait* and *Ulysses*.

wedged into the Adriatic peopled by ignorant Slavs who wear little red caps and colossal breeches.' Artifoni found those naval officers and ignorant Slavs who wished to learn English a source of profit and hired Joyce in spite of having one English teacher in Pola already. Good socialist that he was, he advised Joyce, who still professed that faith himself, to sign all papers as if he and Nora were married, and took care to cheat his new employee when it came to the signing of contracts. Joyce and Nora arrived on the boat with dirty laundry protruding from a battered suitcase, having left their trunk behind in Zurich to be sent on. The key to it, in spite of entreaties sent to Stanislaus along with the pleas for money, was still in Dublin. Joyce's correspondence was complicated, he complained, since he had got through four addresses during his brief stay in Trieste, and he was desperate for news of Ireland. Nora too was anxious to discover what stir her decampment had made (None. Stanislaus was told at Finn's Hotel merely that 'Miss Barnacle had gone away').

Stanislaus was able to report a satisfactory encounter with George Russell who had remarked unkindly that a touch of starvation would do Joyce good, thinking it wicked of him to run off with Nora. Getting the news of Joyce's appointment in Pola, Stanislaus waited until long past midnight before going to inform Russell of his brother's triumph. 'I am very glad to hear it,' said Russell. 'I am sure you are,' said Stanislaus maliciously, 'that's why I came to tell you. I knew you'd be delighted, but I'm afraid that "touch of starvation" must wait a little while longer.' Exit Stannie, with Russell, vanquished, protesting.

Joyce was being paid about £2 a week for sixteen hours work, most of his pupils being naval officers. He and Nora had got themselves a small furnished room and kitchen near the school. Private pupils were forbidden to Berlitz teachers for fear of their setting up on their own, so Joyce had time on his hands and used it for writing, getting through some pages of his projected 'Esthetic Philosophy' most of which later he incorporated in *A Portrait* in a highly unrealistic manner.[2] This writing was done either in cafés or on the

---

[2] – Aristotle has not defined pity and terror. I have. I say – Lynch halted and said bluntly :
– Stop! I won't listen! I am sick. I was out last night on a yellow drunk with Horan and Goggins.

bed in their tiny room as Nora, sometimes, entertained visitors. She made him cigarettes on a machine to save money – seventy for tenpence – and cooked their meals (or so Joyce claimed). By way of luxury they went in the evenings to a local café where Joyce read *Le Figaro* and sometimes got up music with Eyers, the other English teacher, who played the piano well. Both were bitten by unseasonal mosquitos, since the weather was still fine. Joyce put on weight and attended a dentist every week, it being his ambition to get all his teeth in order in six months time with the aid of proceeds from his poetry. Other amusements: Joyce ends a letter to Stanislaus in November:

> I really can't write. Nora is trying on a pair of drawers at the wardrobe.
> Excuse me.   Jim.

A couple of weeks later the consequence of such amusements made itself obvious. Nora had no more idea of the mechanics of pregnancy than Joyce. He asked his brother to embark, with the aid of Cosgrave, on the study of midwifery and embryology (as if that would be any use). Perhaps Skeffington, being a feminist, would know about these things. From his Aunt Josephine, more sensibly, he requested a 'Don't-be-alarmed-my-dear' letter for Nora. In the event, he and Nora, despite the best gynaecological advice, miscalculated the birth of their first child by a month.

They appeared to be happy in the discovery of one another. Nora, Joyce noted, cared nothing for his art, but 'though I am quickly disillusioned I have not been able to discover any falsehood in this nature which had the courage to trust me. It was this night three months ago that we left the North Wall. Strange to say I have not yet left her on the street, as many wise men said I would.' He was able to prise more of her history out of her, and the admission that she played with herself, which he found satisfactory since it was an

---

Stephen went on :
– Pity is the feeling which arrests the mind in the presence of whatsoever is grave and constant in human sufferings and unites it with the human sufferer. Terror is the feeling which arrests the mind in the presence of whatsoever is grave and constant in human sufferings and unites it with the secret cause.
[Therefore an accidental death is not tragic because it is remote from terror and pity according to the terms of Stephen's definitions.]

art he practised himself. She told the story of the curate who put his hand up her dress and of being thrashed with a walking-stick by her uncle for consorting with her Protestant.

There were the normal complement of quarrels and makings-up afterwards in their now freezing room. He passes her a note under the table in the Café Miramar: 'Nothing you can do will annoy me tonight. I will not be made unhappy by anything. When we go home I will kiss you a hundred times. Has this fellow [probably Eyers] annoyed you or did I annoy you by stopping away?' Nora says he has a saint's face. He thinks it is a debauchee's face, but a retired debauchee's. He has a bad cramp in his stomach and Nora prays, 'O my God, take away Jim's pain.' They go to see a film at the Bioscope. Lothario throws Gretchen into the river and runs away. 'O, policeman, catch him!' says Nora. She calls him 'Simple-minded Jim,' and curls his hair for him with tongs. He thinks he looks fine in his new brown suit.

Nora tried, unsuccessfully, to learn French, having more than enough trouble with the Istrian dialect (not to mention Serbo-Croat and German, the other two local languages). Joyce exchanged English lessons with another teacher for German and was taught a more accurately modern Italian by Alessandro Francini Bruni, Artifoni's deputy at the school. He said loftily he had learnt his Italian from Dante and was supposed to teach Francini Dublin English in return for his own lessons, but managed not to. Francini gave the pair a room in his house, which had the luxuries of a stove and a desk, and the pleasant distraction of an Austrian officer and his mistress, who lived next door and chased one another laughing about the room at night.

The Joyces (Nora had taken to calling herself Nora Joyce) made friends of the Francini Brunis. Francini, a Florentine four years older than Joyce, was newly eloped with his young wife, whose name, like Sheehy-Skeffington, he added to his own, though not for feminist reasons. The four got up musical parties. Joyce soon mastered modern Italian. 'At that time,' said Francini Bruni, 'he spoke a rather odd Italian, an Italian covered with wounds and scabs. It was, in fact, a dead language, come to join the babel of living tongues.' Nora's progress was slower, it taking her many months to manage as many as thirty words of dialect.

Stephen Hero began to progress again. By the end of December

Joyce was on Chapter XV, the end of which is the first part to survive. In his writing the twenty-two-year-old author was immersing himself in his university life of only three or four years before. He sent four chapters off to Stanislaus in January with a demand for a long critical letter and all documents, including relevant portions of his brother's diary, dealing with the years at University College. His intention was to continue his novel through to the episode at the Martello Tower, thereby revenging himself on Gogarty, and his final exile from Ireland – that island he now called mockingly *'L'isola di santi e savi'.* He was engaged with Francini Bruni in the translation of George Moore's *Celibates* into Italian, from which, vainly, they hoped to make money. When he showed the first story of *Celibates* to Nora she remarked that Moore didn't know how to finish a story, and when she saw Joyce copy parts of his Epiphanies into *Stephen Hero* she asked, 'Will all that paper be wasted?' Joyce was not yet above trying to play Pygmalion. 'Nora, of course, doesn't care a rambling damn about art.'

He sent too to Stanislaus the story which appears in *Dubliners* as 'Clay' with instructions to offer it to the *Irish Homestead.* Enclosed was a receipt for the fee, should there be one. He was being too optimistic. The *Irish Homestead* did not want any more Joyce, He blamed Russell. '*What* is wrong with all these Irish writers – what the blazes are they always snivelling about? Isn't it funny to read Roberts's poem about a mother pressing a baby to her breast? O, blind, snivelling, nose-dropping, calumniated Christ wherefore were these young men begotten?'

More treachery. *The Speaker* he discovered, had sent a cheque for a poem of his to Dublin in November. What happened to it? 'Examine Charlie.' On his twenty-third birthday he takes Nora on a steamer to the island of Brioni and declares that he admires and loves and trusts her, how much he cannot say. But at the same time is contemplating leaving her – hence his anxiety to round up some money. He has got himself pince-nez spectacles for reading and reports that the prescription is very strong. 'As soon as I get money I shall have my teeth set right by a very good dentist here. I shall then feel better able for my adventures.' He is sure that individual passion is the motive power of everything. 'The whole structure of heroism is, and always was, a damned lie.'

Charlie had in fact pinched his five shillings – or else his father had, endorsing the cheque 'James A. Joyce'. His luck was out with *Chamber Music* too. Hearing from Symons that Grant Richards was bankrupt, Joyce sent a request for the return of the manuscript, unless Richards intended publishing. Richards answered that he very much admired the verses and would like to hold on a while. Meanwhile, he was prevented from returning them because they had been locked up in a warehouse with other of his effects.

Still no key from Stanislaus, Joyce having a keen desire to get at the poetry he had locked in the trunk, thinking to sell it. *Harpers* turned down a poem, 'Bid Adieu', which cannot have surprised him since he described it himself as obscene. It is, by the standards of 1905. Joyce decided, for reasons which had as much to do with his own welfare as his brother's, that Stanislaus would be better off as a language teacher on the continent. He began a campaign to that end, sending Stanislaus copious information and detailed instructions on how to go about it – what examinations to pass, what certificates to collect. Final advice: grow a moustache, pretend to know everything, and dress magnificently. Joyce himself was transferred to Trieste at the end of February and certainly did not dress magnificently, moustache or otherwise. He and Nora had one suit and one dress between them, the rest of their wardrobe, such as it was, being incarcerated in the trunk. 'I often notice that eccentric people have very little taste,' said the other English teacher in Trieste, regarding Joyce's clothes. 'They wear anything. If you have no taste you go in for grey. Stick to grey. Doesn't matter what kind – always looks gentlemanly.' Joyce was pained by this impertinence.

The move to Trieste was precipitated in best comic-opera fashion. Istria, like Ireland its separatists, had its share of irridentists – in this case Italians who wished to throw off the Austrian yoke and join the motherland. Some spent their time watching the comings and going of warships at Pola. The Austrians taking exception to this expelled all foreigners, Artifoni included. Joyce did not mind at all leaving Pola – so long as he had a job elsewhere. 'I hate this Catholic country with its hundred races and thousand languages,' he said, and wanted a move to Italy. Trieste was an improvement, being predominantly Italian and, like Dublin, a seaport with its own distinctive speech, a town big enough to support opera

and theatre but not so big that everyone was ignorant of everyone else's business. In later life Joyce looked back fondly on what
had been the Austrian empire, a ramshackle institution certainly,
but whose government was so inefficient beside those twentieth
century governments that followed that it could for the most part
be conveniently ignored. Joyce's pretence to Socialism was soon
discarded: he no more wanted his life interfered with by the state
than by the church. 'But why should I have brought Nora to a
priest or a lawyer to make her swear her life away to me? And why
should I superimpose on my child the very troublesome burden
which my father and mother superimposed on me? Some people
would answer that while professing to be a socialist I am trying to
make money: but this is not quite true at least as they mean it. If
I made a fortune it is by no means certain that I would keep it.
What I wish to do is to secure a competence on which I can rely,
and why I expect to have this is because I cannot believe that any
State requires my energy for the work I am at present engaged
in.'

A fine speech, addressed to Stanislaus. Artists who embrace
socialism generally wind up kicking at state interference and the
amount of income tax they are required to pay to finance it. Joyce,
no exception, did not want to be bothered by priest, lawyer or
tax-man. As for Nora, whom he was so ready to defend against
their intrusion, she only wished he would get on with the book so
they could get rich and go to live in Paris.

At first she liked Trieste, even with language the formidable
problem it was. Pregnancy seemed to agree with her. Joyce reported
back to Dublin that she looked very well and very pretty. 'Just now
she came in and said "The landlady has her hen laying out there.
O, *he's* after laying a lovely egg." Jaysus! O Jaysus!' But landladies did not like the sight of pregnant Nora and neither did
Artifoni's wife, or the wife of Bertelli, his deputy. It now occurred
to Nora that her late maternal grandmother was bound to have left
her money in her will, since she had been so fond of her. Joyce,
more than willing to believe it, sent off instructions to the brother:
'Proceed to the Four Courts as a matter of urgency and get a copy
of the will of Catherine Healy, born Mortimer, deceased Abbeygate
Street, Galway in the year 1895, 6 or 7. Send a copy at once, and
Nora's birth certificate.' The latter would be necessary to claim the

bounty. '*And* send the key to the trunk.' Alas, Mrs Healy had been careless enough to die intestate.

A second source of bonanza was to be the winning of a puzzle competition in an English magazine called *Ideas*. The prize was £250, to be won by whomever deciphered 48 words, served up in batches of six. Joyce puzzled away and solved 42 before he broke the news to Stanislaus, to whom he would send in a sealed, registered envelope, his complete entry, the idea being to sue the magazine if for some reason they failed to award Joyce the prize. This scheme, which might have changed the history of modern literature, failed on account of the slowness of the mails between Trieste and London. Joyce had by early May got as far as Chapter XXII of *Stephen Hero* which prepares the death of Stephen's sister Isabel (modelled on the death of George) but was slowed down by his puzzle-solving. He had given up the idea of seriously writing more verse but in an introduction to English Literature written for the school gave the highest palms to Shakespeare, Wordsworth and Shelley. He offered *Chamber Music* to John Lane, who declined but was thirty years later to publish *Ulysses*. For the time being another, more remote, literary production engrossed his energies.

Joyce did not want Dublin to forget him. One way to alert the burghers of that town to his still lively existence was a broadside (in both senses of that word) he had written before leaving Dublin. Indeed he had gone so far as to get *The Holy Office* printed before he got on the boat, but had not then the money to take delivery of the sheets. He now had fifty copies of this scatological diatribe printed in Trieste and sent the copies to Stanislaus with instructions to deliver them in envelopes with flaps closed and names of the victims clearly written on the outside. The victims were those writers in Dublin who had displeased him. That is to say, nearly all the writers in Dublin. The conscience of the race is also to be its sewer:

> *Myself unto myself will give*
> *This name, Katharsis-Purgative.*
> *I, who dishevelled ways forsook*
> *To hold the poets' grammar-book,*
> *Bringing to tavern and to brothel*
> *The mind of witty Aristotle,*
> *Lest bards in the attempt should err*
> *Must here be my interpreter . . .*

119

There followed individual blasts at the bards – Colum, Cousins, Russell ('. . . Or him who once when snug abed/Saw Jesus Christ without his head').

> *But all these men of whom I speak*
> *Make me the sewer of their clique.*
> *That they may dream their dreamy dreams*
> *I carry off their filthy streams . . .*
> *Thus I relieve their timid arses,*
> *Perform my office of Katharsis.*
> *My scarlet leaves them white as wool:*
> *Through me they purge a bellyful.*

(Joyce is certainly the first writer to find that rhyme for Katharsis.) He finishes his trans-continental fart with that image of defiance which is familiar from the first version of *A Portrait of the Artist* so peremptorily dismissed by Russell and Eglington:

> *So distantly I turn to view,*
> *The shamblings of that motley crew,*
> *Those souls that hate the strength that mine has*
> *Steeled in the school of old Aquinas.*
> *Where they have crouched and crawled and prayed*
> *I stand, the self-doomed, unafraid,*
> *Unfellowed, friendless and alone,*
> *Indifferent as the herring-bone,*
> *Firm as the mountain-ridges where*
> *I flash my antlers on the air . . .*
> *And though they spurn me from their door*
> *My soul shall spurn them evermore.*

This broadside was dismissed in Dublin as typical Joycean excess. 'Who, in Heaven's name,' as Colum was to ask, 'betrayed him?' No one, but Paranoia *is* a muse among others. Joyce *was* to be Katharsis and not for Ireland, or Irish Literature, only. He was neither self-doomed, friendless nor alone, but indifferent certainly he could be, and indifference is a form of strength.

That old possibility of a new career appeared to present itself again, which would have been good news to Nora. She always did say Jim would have done better if he'd only stuck to singing. Giuseppe Sinico (another Triestine whose name he borrowed for his fictions – this time for the unfortunate lady who ends up under a train in 'A Painful Case'), a composer of operas and voice teacher, told him that after two years study he might apply his voice with its 'very beautiful timbre' to the theatre. That Joyce did not wind up in La Scala we do not find cause for regret. A lack of application may have had something to do with it.

All was not sweetness and light at the school, Signore Artifoni and Bertelli expressing horror at the size of Nora's belly, both having avoided procreation themselves. Signora Bertelli thought it unnecessary to pay Joyce his salary in advance (Joyce thought it necessary to eat and pay for what he ate) and Bertelli himself, when he detected Nora's condition remarked to Joyce that he must be raving mad. This gentleman did not increase Joyce's fondness for him by being a vegetarian, a German and a foul poet. He had printed at his own expense:

> O, can there be for a mother's heart
> A fairer poem
> Than when her child after many an effort
> Lisps the first word?

Joyce vented his irritation on some students.
'Good morning, sar,' says a 'vulgar little Hungarian'.
'The devil bite your bottom,' answers Joyce.

Nora, as the summer got under way, lay prostrate from the heat in their single room, given them, after countless refusals from child-hating Triestines, by a kindly Jewess, Signora Canarutto. Nora did not like the sloppy Italian food and complained of heartburn, which she and Joyce diagnosed as sinister pains in the chest. There were kitchen utensils in their room but Nora declined to use them, advancing as excuse that she did not like other people's kitchens. The eating out which this made necessary imposed an intolerable strain on a salary which Joyce, who had been content with it a few months previous, now decided was fit only for a navvy or a stoker. The English teacher accused Joyce of thinking of nothing but eating. The Triestines, who had a Mediterranean devotion to costume, sniggered at Nora's short dress when she appeared bulging in the streets. She could not make clothes for the child, though Aunt Josephine sent her patterns, and Joyce resented the waste of the materials he had bought. She cried continually. She said to Joyce she could not live that life with him much longer. These strange symptoms he was inclined to put down to the weather, the temperature in July hovering around 100 degrees Fahrenheit.

'I asked her today [12 July 1905] would she like to rear a child for me and she said very convincingly that she would, but, in my present uncertain position I would not like to encumber her with a family.' A little late for second thoughts. It did occur to Joyce to dump Nora on her family but there was the problem that she did not want to have anything to do with them, nor were they likely to welcome her back 'encumbered.' Joyce, in any case, was about to be lumbered with a family, ready or not.

He was now attempting energetically to get Stanislaus to Trieste, in spite of the desperate state of affairs he described so graphically, ostensibly to discuss a new and more than usually ludicrous plan: if he could save £20 by Easter (if pigs had wings) *and* sell his verses, *and* dispose of the completed *Dubliners*, as yet unfinished, to Heinemann who, he was sure, would take it, *and* have the prospect of his novel selling, *then* the three of them (Joyce had forgotten for the moment the new Joyce that was about to enter the world) could take a modest cottage outside Dublin, pay six months rent in advance and live happily on his savings and Stanislaus's earnings. This proposal did not set Stanislaus on fire and was superseded a little later by another, a good deal more practical and of considerable benefit to James Joyce if not immediately his brother. He would be asking Stanislaus to join him in Trieste, at the Berlitz school. That Stanislaus decided to come was an index of his courage, considering the descriptions of life there Joyce had sent.

'. . . you can understand that the regime of these schools is a reign of terror and that I should be in a more terrorized position were it not that many of my pupils (noblemen and *signori* and editors and rich people) have praised me highly to the director who being a socialist is very sensible of my deservingness in consequence.' Artifoni took Joyce aside and warned him against looking for a position elsewhere. It was policy immediately to dismiss any teacher who had the temerity to do so. He locked Joyce's BA certificate in his safe and mentioned in passing that Joyce's copy of his contract of employment was legally invalid, not having been stamped, whereas his, Artifoni's, was. The slightest annoyance from Joyce and he would find himself on the street. And who, with his notorious immorality, would give him employment?

Joyce had come across some genuine treachery. In these auspicious circumstances, Georgio Joyce was born.

Chapter Nine

Arseless in Rome

'The Boarding House' and 'Counterparts', two of the more frigid stories of *Dubliners* were written, said Joyce, with the sweat streaming down his face. He did not like a sun which turned men to butter and longed for the temperate climate of Ireland. The baths were so far out of town he had been swimming only twice, but decided to make another excursion on 27 July. Returning to their room from a café at three in the afternoon, he found Nora in pain. They were under the impression she was suffering a particularly malignant form of indigestion until Signora Canarutto informed them otherwise. Nora, not expecting the birth for another month, had made little preparation for it, but the landlady was kind and helped them with the essentials. Joyce ran off to summon Dr Gilberto Sinigaglia, one of his pupils, who attended to Nora while Joyce was given dinner by the landlady and her family. At nine in the evening an aunt of the family came in smiling and nodding, 'Xe un bel maschio, Signora,' so Joyce knew he had an heir. Nora was very brave during the birth and clapped her hands when told it was a boy. Georgio had dark blue eyes and a fine voice, as one would expect of a male Joyce. He appeared to enjoy the operatic arias his father whistled for him.

Back in Dublin the rest of the tribe were woken up a little past midnight by Joyce's economical telegram: 'Son born Jim.' Stanislaus read the telegram reverently by candlelight and took it then to his father at the top of the stairs, conscious of dynastic duty. John Joyce said nothing but wept privately, and went to some trouble rounding up enough money to send a return telegram. Aunt Josephine said, 'Bravo, Nora!' Stanislaus wondered if his brother's 'Ingenuous dignity, nobility and amiability' would affect his relationship with his son, thinking perhaps hopefully that those qualities would keep him from the temptation he had felt to abandon responsibility.

Vincent Cosgrave, who had been allowed the privilege of reading the finished parts of *Stephen Hero*, expressed his delight at both book and child and spread the news about Dublin. Gogarty, who did not understand Joyce's annoyance at his 'betrayal' of him, became quite sentimental, hoping that Joyce, made mellow, would now agree to reconciliation. Cosgrave, knowing Joyce better, remarked nervously: 'Thanks be to God I never kicked his arse or anything.' He had reason to be nervous, having attempted a betrayal of which Joyce was so far ignorant and not the sort of betrayal he could ever be expected to forgive (Stanislaus did know of it but kept quiet). Gogarty, they were all certain, would get a right royal comeuppance when Joyce got to the tower scene. Cosgrave did object to the name 'Lynch' and to being described as poor by 'the arseless Joyce' a reference to a certain occasion when Joyce was supposed to have been seen in O'Connell Street minus the seat of his trousers after climbing some railing to make advances to a strange girl.[1] Constantine Curran too, was authorized to inspect the book, but had not yet pronounced on it. No one, least of all Stanislaus, doubted that it would be 'one of the novels of the century'.

As for money, Joyce had of course made the birth of his son the occasions of new demands, but his father felt a fitter use for his monthly cheque was to devote it to celebration. Stanislaus confessed his lack of talent at cadging money but sent instead detailed criticisms of Joyce's chapters, in his assessment of his brother's talents comparing him favourably with some of the great names of modern European literature, Turgenieff, Maupassant, Tolstoy. Joyce approved of Maupassant but would not take Tolstoy seriously as a Christian saint. 'I suspect that he speaks the very best Russian with a St Petersburg accent and remembers the Christian name of his great-great-grandfather – this, I find, is at the bottom of the essentially feudal art of Russia.'

The Bora, that fierce wind of the northern Adriatic, roared over Joyce's head and knocked down Triestines in the street. Joyce, ever hypersensitive to the weather, particularly when it appeared as manifestation of Something Up There, sat in a wood, sniffing the fragrance of the earth (so he said) and offered up a prayer to the Vague Something Behind Everything! 'For the love of the Lord Christ change my curse-o'-God state of affairs. Give me for Christ'

---

[1] See p. 307.

sake a pen and an ink-bottle and some peace of mind and then, by the crucified Jaysus, if I don't sharpen that little pen and dip it into fermented ink and write little sentences about the people who betrayed me send me to hell. After all, there are many ways of betraying people. It wasn't only the Galilean suffered that. Whoever the hell you are, I inform you that this is a poor comedy you expect me to play and I'm damned to hell if I'll play it for you. What do you mean by urging me to be forebearing? ...'

He pondered the degrading and unsatisfactory nature of his exile and dreamt of eating again a slice of boiled leg of mutton with turnips and carrots, a grilled beefsteak and some corned beef and cabbage. Would his talent, he wondered, be equal to writing under such deprivation? Grant Richards did not oblige his appetite by publishing *Chamber Music*, nor Heinemann by publishing *Dubliners*. Apart from the longed-for victuals, Joyce desired also the sight of his brother's long face across the table from him. Correspondence was not a satisfactory substitute. He was missing his whetstone, but that at least he might have.

Artifoni had lost his second English teacher and wanted a new one now that the summer was over and the commercial classes felt able once again to get down to the work of bettering themselves. Joyce suggested Stanislaus and Artifoni agreed. The salary was to be forty crowns a week which, taken with Joyce's forty-five, made £3/11/0d, a sum which could with care support a small family. It was of course Joyce's intention that he should arrange Stanislaus's money, and that Stanislaus should share the same house, the better to be able to take up the burden. What scruples Stanislaus felt about abandoning his sisters in Dublin he was advised to forget. What could he do for them anyway?

Stanislaus asked his father for money to help him on his journey. He was at first told to go to hell. At the end of October he managed to set out for Trieste (which was, from time to time, to be on the hellish side) fortified with reams of advice from James, and a little money. The brother, anxious that Stanislaus should not squander too much substance on feeding himself on the long, third-class, journey, advised him to take with him a can of tinned meat and a knife, and to turn up well dressed because he was coming to a respectable position. Passing through Berlin Stanislaus picked up some money wired by Artifoni, which was just as well since he was to arrive to a predictably penniless household. He moved into a spare room in the same house as James and Nora and was immediately dumped into their quarrels.

Joyce had hit the bottle again and Nora was no better able to manage a household with a baby to look after than she had been without one. She at least ate in, with the Canarutto family. Joyce ate out in cafés and bistros, staying on after his meals to consume large quantities of wine, sing drinking songs and engage in political argument in the rougher bars of the town. To Stanislaus fell the duty, once assumed by the slight figure of Francini, of retrieving him from the gutter.

I am an artist, Joyce complained, not a domestic animal – and ought therefore to be able to lead a free and happy life. To Aunt Josephine he confided that relations between himself and Nora were about to suffer some alteration. But the alteration was dependent on getting his hands on some money and that possibility was remote. Stanislaus attempted to improve his behaviour by applying fists, but without effect. Drunks are inclined to take blows lightly. Francini told him he was wasting his time.

Existence was not totally grim. Francini was not beyond drinking a little wine himself. He, his wife and the Joyce entourage took a flat together and spent some evenings clowning and singing. Francini entertained with an imitation of the infant Georgio, gurgling at his milk-bottle while Joyce wheeled him about in the pram and Nora watched in amusement, commenting humorously on their antics in her Galway brogue.

At the school Stanislaus settled down to become a proper professor while James spiced his English lessons with speeches against Artifoni, Berlitz, the Austrian Government, women, the Church and the tax-collector. 'That woman has a nice small breast, but her conscience is wide as a sewer,' Francini reports one of his lessons. 'Her husband is happy because her boyfriends are helping to develop her good points. I am developing myself too. Go you and do likewise. Sop up fourteen shots of absinthe on an empty stomach and you'll see. If this cure doesn't develop you, why, you're hopeless. You may as well give up trying to learn English according to this method . . .'

'This morning – strange to say, for it never happens to me – I hadn't a cent. I went to the director and told him how things were.

I asked him for an advance on my pay. This time the keys of the safe weren't rusted (as they usually are), but the director refused, calling me a bottomless well. I told him to go and drown himself in it, and took myself off. Now what am I to do? Wretch that I am. My wife is no good at anything except producing babies and blowing bubbles. If I'm not careful she'll follow up George the First by unloading a second male successor for the dynasty. No, no, Nora, this game doesn't suit me. So long as there are bistros in Trieste, I'm afraid your man will have to pass his nights away from home, flapping around like a rag in the breeze . . .' How much this contributed to his pupils' mastery of commercial English is problematic.

Nora threatened to go back to her family in Galway and got around to writing letters announcing her return without actually posting them, but exercised the sharp edge of her tongue on Jim and declined her household duties. He, like many another writer, discovered the difficulty of holding the baby and at the same time communing with the Muse. Stanislaus regretted leaving the relative peace of the Murray household in Dublin and confided his agonies in his aunt. 'I am sorry to hear Liquor is cheap,' she answered, but 'there is some excuse for Jim drinking it is the old story of finding forgetfulness.' She counselled him against sending money home since Pappie was making very bad use of it. How he managed to do any such thing strains the imagination.

To these petty frustrations were added a greater: Joyce now entered into his first momentous struggle against censorship (if we leave aside his quarrels with the college authorities as prophetic but minor). Grant Richards agreed in February 1906 to publish *Dubliners*, not without reservations. He thought very highly of it but did not detect in it very many of those selling qualities which publishers look for. Indeed, it suffered from two notable disabilities – it was about Ireland, a subject which tended even then to depress people, and it was a collection of short stories. Nevertheless he offered terms which were not ungenerous by the standards of the time: a ten percent royalty on copies sold, thirteen counting as twelve, no royalty on the first five hundred, and first refusal of all Joyce's work completed in the next five years. These terms Joyce accepted, remarking that any future work of his was largely dependent on his getting money, and promising a thirteenth story to add to the twelve completed, 'unless perhaps you have as superstitious an objection to the number thirteen as you seem to have with regard to Ireland and short stories in general.'

The thirteenth story, 'Two Gallants', was indeed to cause trouble, by outraging Richards' printer's moral sensibility.[2] Joyce, requested to do so by Richards, sent him a description of his present state and prospects, confident of early publication, no storm having yet broken: 'I am an English teacher here in a Berlitz school. I have been here for sixteen months during which time I have achieved the delicate task of living and of supporting two other trusting souls on a salary of £80 a year. I am employed to teach young men of this city the English language as quickly as possible with no delays for elegance and receive in turn tenpence for every sixty minutes so spent. I must not omit to mention that I teach also a baroness.

'My prospects are the chance of getting money enough from my book or books to enable me to resume my interrupted life. I hope these details will not bore you as much as they bore me. In any case I give them to you only because you have asked me for them.'

He signed the contract and promised a fourteenth story 'A Little Cloud'. Richards suggested an autobiographical novel. Joyce replied that he was engaged on one and had finished 914 pages, but was stalled because of anxiety about his condition.

Now began the hiatus which prevented publication of *Dubliners* for eight years. In April, the printer to whom Richards had sent 'Two Gallants' without reading it himself, demanded suppression or alteration. Joyce declined either operation and referred belligerently to certain blue pencil markings made on manuscripts returned to him by Richards. The word 'bloody' in particular seemed to cause offence.[3] Richards, who had only renewed publishing by setting up a company in his wife's name, was not eager to take on the whole apparatus of Edwardian puritanism. 'I don't want the critics to come down on your book like a cart load of bricks,' he told Joyce. 'I want

[2] The gallants are Lenehan and Corley. Both are penniless, having spent the afternoon in a public house. Lenehan is a hanger-on. Corley, his hero, 'a gay Lothario', speaks in an advanced manner for 1906 publication, of his amours. Lenehan spends an evening waiting while Corley extracts a gold coin from his latest conquest, a serving-girl. 'I know the way to get around her, man,' says Corley. 'She's a bit gone on me.'
[3] As it did when Shaw's *Pygmalion* was first performed six years later.

you to give me a word that we can use instead of "bloody" in the story *Grace*.'

Three passages in 'Counterparts' also caused annoyance :

'a man with two establishments to keep up, of course he couldn't . . .'

'Farrington said he wouldn't mind having the far one and began to smile at her . . .'

'She continued to cast bold glances at him and changed the position of her legs often; and when she was going out she brushed against his chair and said "Pardon !" in a Cockney accent.'

Joyce chose to attack the printer. 'In no other civilized country in Europe, I think, is a printer allowed to open his mouth' – ignoring the fact certainly known to him, that in England a printer is as liable for what he prints as a writer for what he writes and a publisher for what he publishes (Thus, ingeniously, the English were for so long spared the trouble and expense of setting up a censor's office, letting their printers do it for them).

Finding the word 'bloody' neither indecent nor blasphemous, Joyce at first refused to excise it anywhere it appeared, but was incautious enough to mention that it did in fact appear more often than Richards, or his printer, had noticed. And if they were looking for offences to propriety, why not object to the episode in 'An Encounter', where the old pederast leaves the two boys in a field to perform, within their sight, a distinctly immoral act? Joyce then agreed to alter passages in three stories, but too late. Richards, alerted now to the 'enormity' of 'An Encounter' wanted the story removed from the book.

More letters were exchanged. Joyce, increasingly irritated, agreed to delete the offending word in six places, and to cut out a passage in 'Counterparts'. The objection to 'An Encounter' turned out to have been more or less a bargaining counter from Richards, but he maintained his objection to 'Two Gallants'. Joyce stuck by the story, suggesting that Richard 'buy two critics' if he was afraid of critical reaction. 'The points on which I have not yet yielded are the points which rivet the book together. If I eliminate them what becomes of the chapter of the moral history of my country? I fight to retain them because I believe that in composing my chapter of moral history in exactly the way I have composed it I have taken the first step towards the spiritual liberation of my country. Reflect for a moment on the history of the literature of Ireland as it stands at present written in the English language before you condemn this genial illusion of mine which, after all, has at least served me in the office of a candlestick during the writing of this book.'

In another letter, at the end of June: 'It is not my fault that the odour of ashpits and old weeds and offal hangs round my stories. I seriously believe you will retard the course of civilization in Ireland by preventing the Irish people for having one good look at themselves in my nicely polished looking-glass.'

But Richards was not so much concerned with the moral regeneration of Ireland as with making a living at publishing and keeping out of trouble. Filson Young, an Irish writer of little importance, read *Dubliners* for him and he too counselled against publication. 'Unfortunately as things stand at present,' Richards told Joyce 'you cannot buy one critic of importance, to say nothing of two; sometimes I wish one could.' The writer stood by his guns, listing the concessions he had made and hoping that the publisher would acquire the courage of his, Joyce's, convictions. He had a long time to wait.

Bored with Trieste, unable to get on with his novel and fed up with his poverty-stricken state, Joyce contemplated a move, spurred on by a scandal at the Berlitz school. Bertelli, Artifoni's manager, appears to have helped himself to such of the school's funds as he could lay hands on and disappeared, leaving Artifoni in parlous circumstances and for the time being unable to afford the luxury of two English teachers. The banking firm of Nast-Kolb and Schumaker advertised the position of clerk, who must be fluent in English and Italian, for their branch in Rome. On the theory that Rome could scarcely be worse than Trieste, Joyce wrote off an application, enclosing testimonials to his commercial competence and social standing, including the one extracted from Timothy Harrington, Lord Mayor of Dublin, four years before, and carefully preserved. He was offered a position at £150 a year, half-again his Trieste income, and a two-month trial, subject to a satisfactory interview with the bank manager. On 30 July 1906, Joyce, Nora and the infant Georgio crossed the Adriatic on the deck of the night boat to Ancona (leaving Stanislaus to deal with debts left behind) and proceeded on by train to Rome in the hopes of better things to come – Joyce arguing bitterly with cabmen, railway officials and moneychangers along the route. Frightened by the sight of the Tiber and terrified of the prospect of failing in his interview with the bank manager, Joyce did not take well to the Eternal City but survived his interview and celebrated by listening to an outdoor band play selections from *Siegfried*.

Rome was a mistake. Joyce did not like it at all, neither the city, her citizens nor the work he was subjected to. He began his clerking at half past eight in the morning and continued at the bank until half past seven in the evening, with a two-hour Italian lunchbreak. The work was damnably boring and he was expected to maintain a higher standard of visible respectability than with Berlitz. This he found a little difficult with the seat soon out of his trousers (appropriated from Stanislaus). He did not appreciate sitting wrapped up in his coat through the August heat. His eyes hurt him, his glasses annoyed him. They were cheap and flawed in both lenses. 'Diritto, Signor Joyce. Non è bello cosi,' said the banker, seeing him slumped over a letter he was writing back to Stanislaus. 'Sit up, Mr Joyce. That doesn't look good.'

At first he indulged in some *turismo*. The dome of St Peter's seemed to him less impressive than St Paul's in London and he was disappointed in the quality of the music sung at a minor mass. The Colosseum was full of touts and tourists and Rome had not a decent café. (Georgio at least enjoyed the ancient monuments, finding them splendid places to echo the inherited Joyce tones – even St Peter's).

In no time flat there were desperate appeals to Trieste for money. True, his new employers had given him an advance of 100 lire, but within two weeks of his arrival back went a list of expenses to long-suffering Stanislaus.

skirt (Nora)	9	Lire
blouse "	8	"
" " "	9.50	"
combs	2.0	"
shirt (self)	3.50	"
hat "	5.0	"
hand. and collars	2.0	"

I have paid the rent here in full and have 52 lire left but it will not last me till the end of the month.

Nor did it. A few days later:

'Dear Stannie: The substance of the present is financial. It is Thursday morning the 16th and I have 25 lire. In my list I forgot to include bonnet for Georgio 3 lire but the real reason the money goes so quickly is that we eat enormously. Nora is getting much healthier looking. Here is her usual dinner – two slices of roast beef, 2 polpetti, a tomato stuffed with rice, part of a salad and a half-litre of wine. We buy the meat cooked and then take it to a little wine-shop where we are supplied with plates etc. I think the only thing to be done is this: to ask A [Artifoni] for a week's salary in advance and to send it to me. Remember that on Monday morning I shall have *no* money so that if you have not sent on some already you must telegraph it.'

His own appetite was not so bad. 'Last night,' he tells his brother, thanking him for prompt sending of funds, 'we ate an entire roast chicken and a plateful of ham, bread and wine – and went to bed hungry.' Explicit instructions went back to Trieste. The two tailors whom Joyce had swindled were to be told he had emigrated to Glasgow or Edinburgh. Artifoni was to be paid back the sum he had loaned Joyce but Francini might beg for the rent owing since Stanislaus could claim not to be responsible for his brother's debt (He was sleeping on the floor at the time, the furniture having been repossessed, convinced, quite rightly, that a good deal of James's expenditure of *his* money went on drink). Stannie sent money by telegram, an expensive process. Joyce spent it. Georgio developed a precocious taste for eating in restaurants, Nora a prodigious talent for blowing soap bubbles the size of footballs. Joyce wrote nothing beyond a few paragraphs.

He was engrossed still in Ireland. Gogarty provided a diversion, the Dublin theatre-going rabblement another, Gogarty by marrying Miss Martha Duane of a landed family from Galway on 1 August 1906. 'Guess the latest,' said Nora, meeting Joyce in the street, 'guess who's married!' Gogarty? Joyce took it badly. A new betrayal. Gogarty was not supposed to be in Dublin. He was supposed to be en route to Italy to see Joyce, having written from New York in June to promise a meeting in three months' time. 'I suppose I will be gladder to see you than you to see me but I miss the touch of a vanished hand and the sound of a voice that is still.' Instead he had the nerve to get married.

133

Because your voice was at my side
I gave him pain,
Because within my hand I held
Your hand again.
There is no word nor any sign
Can make amend —
He is a stranger to me now
Who was my friend.

This piece of slush, included in *Chamber Music*, had been addressed to Nora during Joyce's courtship of her. 'A stranger to me now' is Gogarty and it requires wilful effort not to detect homosexual overtones. Perhaps more important, Joyce was hoping to extract sponsorship from Gogarty particularly when, soon after, his mother died and left him considerable money. Joyce had agreed to bury the hatchet. He scanned the *Tribune* of Rome for a promised announcement of Gogarty's arrival, but Gogarty was blissfully unaware of this latest affront to the arseless Joyce eking out his poverty on a clerk's stool and pondering revenge. William Butler Yeats might boost Mister Gogarty's (now Fellow of the Royal College of Surgeons of Ireland) literary reputation by putting some of his poems, years hence, into the *Oxford Book of Modern Verse*, but Joyce would mark his true niche in literary history by making him Buck Mulligan. Cosgrave sent him this, and Joyce remembered— *The Song of the Cheerful Jaysus*:

I'm the queerest young fellow that ever was heard
My mother's a Jew; my father's a Bird
With Joseph the Joiner I cannot agree
So here's to Disciples and Calvary.

If anyone thinks that I amn't divine,
He gets no free drinks when I'm making the wine
But have to drink water and wish it were plain
That I make when the wine becomes water again.

My methods are new and are causing surprise:
To make the blind see I throw dust in their eyes
To signify merely there must be a cod
If the Commons will enter the Kingdom of God.

Now you know I don't swim and you know I don't skate
I came down to the ferry one day and was late
So I walked on the water and all cried, in faith!
For a Jewman it's better than having to bathe.

If Gogarty had preferred to forget the authorship of this tedious blasphemy, he was not allowed to. It is trotted out in *Ulysses*, slightly improved. Gogarty's fashionable anti-Semitism Joyce regarded as 'stupid drivel'. It was part of current Irish nationalism to deride England as a country crippled by Jewry. Joyce saw a lengthy exposition of this inspired point of view written by Gogarty in a November issue of *Sinn Fein*, organ of the separatists, and remembered with anger. Who were the cultureless Irish to despise the 'oldest race on earth?' The vague memory of one Hunter, a Dublin Jew, stirred in his mind and he began to contemplate a story he might call 'Ulysses'.

The Irish, in Yeats's memorable phrase, were disgracing themselves once again and Joyce heartily wished he were present to take part in the fun. The occasion was the first presentation of Synge's masterpiece *The Playboy of the Western World*, at the Abbey Theatre. The rabblement, roused to fury at Synge's portrayal of the Irish peasantry as something other than Christian gentlefolk, howled down the performances with such success that Yeats and Lady Gregory were obliged to put the play on for an extra week. Joyce, devouring accounts in the *Daily Mail* and *Freeman's Journal*, could not be certain at that distance who had made the greater fool of himself – Sheehy-Skeffington (as usual, on the side of the angels), his brother-in-law Richard Sheehy, or Yeats, who appealed to the non-existent sensibilities of the barrackers as the author of those seven and a half pages of patriotism, *Cathleen ni Houlihan*. Silly Willy (as Maud Gonne called him) got short shrift. 'The play was rightly condemned as a slander on Irishmen and Irishwomen,' pronounced Sheehy. 'An audience of self-respecting Irishmen had a perfect right to proceed to any extremity.' The police thought otherwise and broke a few heads. Colum's father was had up for disorderly conduct and Joyce, thinking it was Colum himself, was delighted, but frustrated. 'I feel like a man in a house who hears a row in the street and voices he knows shouting but can't get out to see what the hell is going on. It has put me off the story I was "going to write" to wit, *The Dead*.'

'The Dead' would have to wait. So too 'Ulysses', which 'never got forrader than the title.'

Anarchists set Joyce's teeth on edge by rudely exploding bombs in his hearing. A cart-driver careening through the streets missed running down Nora and Georgio but caught the little boy under his eye with the whip and raised a weal, not waiting to apologize. The matter of the trousers became urgent, a question of finding ten lire to buy new ones. Stanislaus prudently refused to share their misery in Rome. Nora stubbornly declined to improve herself. Taking a rest from bubble-blowing she pondered theology. 'Is Jesus and God the same?' she asked.

> Dear Stannie:
> I hope you are very well I am sure you would be glad to see Georgie now he is well able to run about he is able to say a lot he has a good appetite and he has eight teeth and also sings when we ask him where is Stannie he beats his chest and says non c'e piu
>
> Nora.

'Do you notice how women when they write disregard stops and capital letters?' remarked Joyce. (Here comes Molly Bloom.)

The happy pair were evicted and had trouble finding a new room. The Romans, apparently, did not approve of children. 'The old Bethlehemites must have been like these Italian bastards,' said Joyce. 'I feel for poor old Joseph.' Georgie whined and Nora got pregnant again. Joyce managed to put pen to paper only to write letters of complaint to Stannie. The eviction, and consequent stay in an hotel cost a pile of money. Henry James, said Joyce, deserved a running kick in the arse for writing his 'teaslop' about beautiful Italy. Rome reminded him of a man who lived by exhibiting his grandmother's corpse. 'I have seen a lot of Romans now and if anyone asks you what I think of them you may say that so far as I can see their chief preoccupation in life is the condition (to judge from their speech) broken, swollen etc of their *coglioni* and their chief pastime and joke the breaking of wind rereward. This kind of mechanical obscenity is damnably tiresome. However, it is an expletive which I am reserving for the day when I leave the eternal city as my farewell and adieu to it.'

This day was not far off. Nora got fed up with the new room and took another. Double rent to pay. 'No pen, no ink, no table, no room, no time, no quiet, no inclination,' reported the writer.

Attempting to cash in some money wired by Stanislaus he ran up against an 'ignorant whore' of an official, who questioned his papers.

Joyce got annoyed and said 'By Jesus, Rossini was right when he took off his hat to the Spaniard, saying "You save me from the shame of being the last in Europe",' which the official invited him to repeat on neutral ground. He declined.

Elkin Mathews in London agreed to publish *Chamber Music*: no royalties on the first 300 copies then fifteen per cent, selling price one shilling and sixpence. Joyce no longer cared for the verses, nor did he contemplate (wisely) making more than a few shillings from them but supposed they might as well be published. He was working appallingly hard to keep above the breadline. After the long stint at the bank he took pupils for private lessons. For a time he took ten one-hour lessons a week at an Ecole de Langues for the sum of 10 lire a week, noting with annoyance that his dim-witted students paid half a lire each for their hour, a dozen at a time. In the bank he paid out £10 to a female descendant of Shelley and 200 lire to the Roman correspondent of the *Freeman's Journal*, resenting it. Some customers complained to the management of his appearance. He decided he was not meant to be a model bank clerk.

Diversions: he attended church services, even one conducted by an English evangelist. The choir in St Peter's wasn't bad but a ticket to *Götterdämmerung* in Italian was a poor investment. 'Here comes Siegfried', confided his somnolent, and garlicky, neighbour every time he heard the horn motif, and the highlight of the performance was that Brunhilde's horse shat on the stage. Joyce's own colonic tract was not always so obliging. Purgatives cost him one lira a time. More money was wasted on the law. Joyce, succumbing to the national temptation to litigation, contemplated suing Grant Richards for breach of contract but took a barrister's advice not to do so. That cost 10 lire. He offered instead to agree to the suppression of 'Two Gallants' and the offending passage in 'Counterparts', but that was all. Richards regretfully declined to publish without further cuts. Joyce had by now lost enthusiasm for *Dubliners* in any case. The stories seemed to him dull and two of them, 'After the Race' and 'A Painful Case' downright bad. When and if he could return to his novel he wished to adhere scrupulously to sexual truth, fortified by his tilting against a censorship he had not thought existed:

> . . . my opinion is that if I put down a bucket into my own soul's well, sexual department, I draw up Griffith's[4] and Ibsen's

[4] Arthur Griffith, leader of *Sinn Fein*.

and Skeffington's and Bernard Vaughan's[5] and St Aloysius' and Shelley's and Renan's water along with my own. And I am going to do that in my novel (inter alia) and plank down the bucket before the shades and substances above mentioned to see how they like it: and if they don't like it I can't help them. I am nauseated by their lying drivel about pure men and pure women and spiritual love for ever: blatant lying in the face of the truth. I don't know much about the 'saince' of the subject but I presume there are very few mortals in Europe who are not in danger of waking some morning and finding themselves syphilitic . . . Perhaps my view of life is too cynical but it seems to me that a lot of this talk about love is nonsense. A woman's love is always maternal and egoistic. A man, on the contrary, side by side with his extraordinary cerebral sexualism and bodily fervour (from which women are normally free) possesses a fund of genuine affection for the 'beloved' or 'once beloved' object . . .

The beloved was as fed up as he was. Christmas 1906 brought an appeal from John Joyce in Dublin for a pound, which his son had not got. The bank generously granted its employees a day off. Joyce ate pasta for Christmas dinner in the hope of surviving until the end of the month.

By February he had had enough. He handed in his notice and only then began looking for a job elsewhere, unsuccessfully canvassing Marseilles. At the very last possible moment, nothing having turned up, Joyce retreated back to Trieste. Artifoni had promised a job if and when he chose to go back. Seven months of Rome was more than enough. Joyce had not saved any money—that was an ambition he clung to a long time. He had nothing to show for his stay, except a new bulge in Nora's belly. But there was in his head now the idea of a story which might be written about the one-day's odyssey through Dublin of a rather ordinary man. (Here comes Leopold Bloom.)

'My mouth is full of decayed teeth,' he mourned, 'and my soul of decayed ambitions.'

[5] Popular Catholic preacher.

Chapter Ten
Writing with Lugubrious Intention

In Rome Joyce had made no friends, saved no money, written little – and not even found a decent café to pass the time in. True, while he was there Matthews had agreed to publish *Chamber Music* but Joyce was so little interested in his verses that he preferred to leave their arrangement and the proof-reading to Stanislaus. The Romans did him the final honour of mugging him before he left. It was not an episode about which he was particularly communicative but it appears he celebrated his imminent departure from the eternal city, which at least does boast some decent local wines, to the point of near-stupor and while doing so exhibited the contents of his last pay packet to two gentlemen with whom he had been drinking. They followed him into the street and relieved him of his burden, 200 crowns. Acquaintances picked him up, preserved him from arrest and took him home, where no doubt he got a friendly reception from Nora.

On 7 March 1907 the three arrived back precipitously, and penniless. Trieste was at least that 'warm port by the sea' and Joyce had friends there. Francini was inclined to be forgiving about the unpaid rent and put them up for a few days while Stanislaus was delegated to find new quarters. Artifoni at first flatly refused to re-employ Joyce, in spite of his promise, but did not like the idea of his setting up as a private teacher either. Joyce was too popular with some of the richer and influential pupils. When Stanislaus pointed to his brother's parlous situation James laughed and said 'Well, then, I have you.' Stanislaus was not amused and was kept from returning to Dublin only by the sure knowledge that Dublin was worse.

Artifoni was induced to offer Joyce a pittance in return for six hours' tuition a week. This Joyce accepted, hoping to make up the income by giving private lessons. He succeeded well enough and one of his pupils, Roberto Prezioso, editor of the *Piccolo della*

139

Serra, the principal newspaper of Trieste (so called because it had begun as a one-page sheet), commissioned him to write three articles on the supposed colonial relations between England and Ireland, the idea being that Italian irredentists would be able to detect the analogy with their own situation. Prezioso may have hoped in this manner to avoid annoying the Austrian authorities while still delivering a denunciation of the oppression of small nations by larger neighbours. That was not precisely how Joyce saw it and in the explanation of his country's situation which he provided he declined to adopt the conventional Irish bombast. His attitude to his own nationality was thoroughly nineteenth-century, as if politics had ceased with the death of Parnell. Nor did he present his people as in any way deserving of independence or the respect of the world. In Ireland there would always be a traitor at the right moment, therefore the organisation of militant resistance to the English in secret societies was one 'eminently suited to the Irish character because it reduces to a minimum the possibility of betrayal.'

The villain of the piece was the Church, which first betrayed Ireland to the English King Henry II (a fiction much cherished by the Irish) and never gave an ear to their complaints.

> Already weakened by their long journey, the cries are nearly spent when they arrive at the bronze door. The messengers of the people who never in the past have renounced the Holy See, the only Catholic people to whom faith also means the exercise of faith, are rejected in favour of messengers of a monarch, descended from apostates, who solemnly apostasized himself on the day of his coronation, declaring in the presence of his nobles and commons that the rites of the Roman Catholic Church are 'superstition and idolatry'.[1]

This intriguing addition to the conspiracy theory of history brought Joyce some acclamation in Trieste. What was the answer to be to Ireland's troubles? Joyce suggested hope lay with Sinn Fein's separatist policies of boycott and passive resistance but must have done so with tongue in cheek since he had been sarcastic about that policy when he was still in Ireland. In any case it was Sinn Fein that brought Ireland eventually to that bloody confrontation which

---

[1] Joyce refers to that declaration, now dropped, then made, as of law, by English monarchs at their coronation, as Head of the Chuch of England.

horrified Joyce. Still, the artist could not be expected to be political prophet as well.

Joyce presented three lectures also at the Universita del Popolo at the invitation of another pupil. The first, another celebration of the woes of Ireland, which he called 'Ireland, Island of Saints and Sages,' contained the statement 'No one who has any self-respect stays in Ireland, but flees afar as though from a country that has undergone the visitation of an angered Jove.' The last was on the Irish Literary Renaissance, which will have contained more abuse than the title would lead one to expect, but is lost. In between was a lecture on James Clarence Mangan to which those worthy Triestines wishing to improve themselves will have gone asking 'Who?' but must have come away asking 'So what?' It is not that Italian library shelves are full of translations of Mangan, but Joyce did have the material left over.

As for his own work, in April he suffered a fit of revulsion for the poems and set off to the post office to telegraph Elkin Mathews withdrawing them. But Stanislaus, who set high store by them, walked the streets with him for hours, arguing for publication. Joyce insisted he was neither lover nor 'pote' and therefore had no business publishing 'love pomes', but Stanislaus won.

Chamber Music was duly published, in May, and Arthur Symons greeted its appearance in the *Nation* with a highly favourable review as he had promised ('There is no substance at all in these songs, which hardly hint at a story; but they are like a whispering clavichord that someone plays in the evening, when it is getting dark.'). Thomas Kettle, friend from University College and newly elected Nationalist MP, later to lose his life fighting in the British Army in 1916 against the Germans, noticed it in a friendly manner in the *Freeman's Journal* but complained: 'There is no trace of the folklore, folk dialect, or even the national feeling that have coloured the work of practically every writer in contemporary Ireland. Neither is there any sense of that modern point of view which consumes all life in the language of problems.'

No, Joyce had problems enough of his own with which to consume life. From Dublin arrived a pathetic missive from his father, now once again at the end of his tether and with the Workhouse staring him in the face. Five girls, Charlie (old Joyce almost calls him 'one man' but changes his mind) and himself, and the dog Nigger,

141

had all to live on an income of two shillings and threepence a day:
'If I had some permanent position, however small and if the
aforesaid ex-ecclesiastic had the ability and inclination to get some
employment to enable him to live, *off my hands*, things would be
different. Now, I must break up house (by the way, that won't
entail much energy, as everything is broken up quite sufficiently
already) and go into lodgings *by myself*. I have been for the past
fortnight trying to get the 3 little ones fixed and have so far succeeded that I could get them into a convent (Glasnevin) through
the influence of Mr James Kavanagh for £24 a year.'

There follows a plea for regular money from James and Stanislaus,
to take care of the little girls, and a more heartfelt plea to get
some position for Charlie, *any* position – '*do*, for I can't stand it
any longer, and for many reasons *I must* get rid of *him*. Well, Poppie
is so insolent and my life has been made so unendurable by her
that she must go.' Perhaps then he would at last be able to return
to Cork. 'For the few, very few I sincerely hope, years I have yet
to live I'll try if I can't find some of my old friends of long ago
who may be glad to see me again, and even amongst strangers I
may receive respect and perhaps even affection, refused me by my
children . . . Perhaps in years to come, long after my release from
this world, you may learn to feel some of the pangs I have endured,
and then you will appreciate the feelings of a Father who loved
his children and had high ambitions for them, and spared no
money when he could afford it, to educate and make them what
they should be, but who when adversity came and he could no
longer gratify all those wants, was despised, disrespected, jeered at,
scoffed at and set at defiance. Well, remembering, *as I do*, the fond
love I had for you as child, boy *and man*, I pray God you may be
spared such ingratitude. I should very much wish to have your
Photo and Georgie's, also a full account of the Rome affair, and
what are your present prospects. As I said, this may be my last
letter to you, so don't treat as usually, but reply fully, and *by
return.*

'If Stannie, too, has not *quite* lost the *little affection* he *may* have
had for me, I should also be glad to hear from him, with Photo
also. Goodbye, Jim, and may God protect you, is the prayer of your
still fond and loving, though broken hearted, FATHER.'

Scarcely the bonhomous Simon Dedalus of *Ulysses*. The letter contained also a long whine about Joyce's miserable mistake (Nora) but got John Joyce some sympathy and a very little money. James himself had now to face a new affliction, a rheumatic fever, the consequence of one of his sojourns in the gutter, which landed him in the city hospital during July and August. He was joined in the hospital by Nora, who gave birth in the pauper's ward on 26 July, to a daughter, Anna Lucia. She was given twenty crowns in charity.

Joyce did not get the few shillings he hoped for from *Chamber Music.* It took Elkin Mathews six years to unload 200 copies, never mind the 300 required before Joyce could make any royalty. The poems did particularly interest musicians and over the years several (including Joyce himself) set the lyrics to music. The first was the English composer Geoffrey Molyneux Palmer who wrote requesting permission to set some of the verses while Joyce was still in hospital. He was happy to grant it, and to other composers, though Mathews was not always co-operative.

In hospital he finished the last story of *Dubliners,* the delicate and miraculously-wrought 'The Dead'. He sent the book of fifteen stories off to Elkin Mathews who, perhaps with one eye on the limping sales of *Chamber Music,* declined the honour of publishing it.

'The Dead' is Joyce's first long exploration of the theme of sexual jealousy and frustration, later to be spread across so many pages of *Exiles, Ulysses* and *Finnegans Wake.* In this case it is not the living Blazes Boylan who provokes jealousy but that dead Michael Bodkin (became Michael Furey) in the graveyard in Galway, who had died for Nora, or so she liked to think. Since it is Joyce who is writing, rather than a storyteller like Maupassant, there is more to it than simple sexual tension, but sexual jealousy was rooted deep enough in Joyce for him to resent even a dead lover who had done no more than go walking with his love.

> He tried to keep up his tone of cold interrogation, but his voice when he spoke was humble and indifferent. 'I suppose you were in love with this Michael Furey, Gretta,' he said.
> 'I was great with him at that time,' she said. Her voice was veiled and sad. Gabriel, feeling now how vain it would be to try to lead her whither he had purposed, caressed one of her hands and said, also sadly :

143

'And what did he die of so young, Gretta? Consumption was it?'

'I think he died for me,' she answered . . .

. . . He did not like to say even to himself that her face was no longer beautiful, but he knew that it was no longer the face for which Michael Furey had braved death.

Joyce was no longer sure of his own love for Nora, as he told Stanislaus. It would take a jolt of jealousy to reassert itself, and that was not long in coming.

The South Africa Colonization Society declined his application for a position and the *Corriere della Sera* decided to do without a piece from him on a Dublin exposition. He would have liked to return to Dublin in the role of successful reporter, as does Ignatius Gallaher in 'A Little Cloud'. 'I may not be the Jesus Christ I once fondly imagined myself,' he told Stanislaus, 'but I think I must have a talent for journalism.'

The arrangement with Artifoni came to an end when the school was leased out to two of the teachers there, Joyce's socialist bene- factor going back on his word and turning over the debts of both Joyces to the new lessees. Stanislaus struggled on at the Sculoa Berlitz but James decided to go freelance, charging ten crowns a lesson, and managed to attract a few pupils, but not enough to remove the burden of support from his increasingly disgruntled brother. One of these was a sea-captain of invincible stupidity who insisted on receiving his fortnightly lesson on board his ship. A more promising pupil was Ettore Schmitz, the middle-aged owner of factories manufacturing a marine anti-corrosive paint which made him a good deal of money. A lapsed Jew of amiable, self-effacing character he was, for the time being, a failed writer. Years previously he had published two novels, one under the name of Italo Svevo, which had sunk without trace. He had given up writing but under Joyce's encouragement was to start again and produce in time that satirical onslaught on psycho-analysis, *The Confessions of Zeno*, a wry account of a man who spends the better part of his days having 'one last cigarette' and writing down the circumstances of each successive last gasp, usually on cigarette packets. (Schmitz carried the joke a little too far. After a bad motor accident in 1928, as he lay dying, he asked his wife for 'one last cigarette'.) He writes his autobiography principally in order to annoy his psycho-analyst who is attempting unsuccessfully to cure his addiction. Like most assaults on the principal twentieth century religion, it is written by a Jew, a member of the race which invented that religion, but it surpasses in wit any other assault on psycho-analysis. It would not have been written without Joyce's encouragement. Schmitz had come to him to learn enough English to conduct his English business (he had a factory at Deptford) and revealed modestly that he had written two novels. Joyce read them and enthused, 'Do you know that you are a neglected writer?' Schmitz in turn was given Joyce's work to read, the first three chapters of what had now become *A Portrait of the Artist as a Young Man.*

During his stay in hospital Joyce had had leisure to think, and thought out the plan of his novel. *Stephen Hero* was to be reduced from a projected sixty-three chapters to five and the childhood experiences were to be much condensed. Instead of being a straightforward narrative related from a detached, if not unsympathetic stand-point, the book would in its style reflect the development of the hero's consciousness. *A Portrait* would be the history of Stephen Dedalus's soul (At first he wished to change the name Dedalus to Daly, but quickly changed his mind).

With his book now firmly planned Joyce left hospital and in eight months had managed to finish the first three chapters, more than half the book. The third chapter contains accounts of whores, of the guilty soot-covered packet hidden up the chimney, of the hell-fire sermons and of Stephen's repentance and reconciliation with the BVM. After his experience with the relatively innocent stories of *Dubliners* he had little hope of seeing it published. 'What I write with the most lugubrious intentions would probably be prosecuted in England as pornographical.' He abandoned *A Portrait* until Schmitz was to return the favour of enthusiasm.

He decided that *Ulysses*, when he wrote it, would be a short book instead of a short story and with an Italian friend translated Synge's *Riders to the Sea* which he had read in Paris and not much liked. After Synge had taken on Irish philistinism (or rather, after Irish philistinism had taken on Synge) Joyce decided he was a writer of considerable quality.

Fits of creative energy alternated with fits of non-productive lassitude. 'I have retired from public life,' announces Joyce to his brother, reclining on the sofa of their mean quarters. 'For the

145

present I am going to devote my attention to getting rid of my rheumatism, having my voice trained, and fattening myself.' The voice-training proceeded no farther than a few lessons before being abandoned, like all the previous attempts to make his fortune that way.[2] The 'fattening' was sought through the ends of bottles. 'Do you want to go blind,' asked Stanislaus, applying fists as a cure. 'Do you want to go about with a little dog?' Nora added to this litany. 'Yes, go now and get drunk. That's all you're good for. Faith I tell you I'll have the children baptized tomorrow.'

Another threat, also not carried out, was to burn his manuscripts.

His eyes, which had never been good, began to give serious trouble, aggravated by heavy drinking and by the unfelicitous atmosphere of the gutters where occasionally he lay. The pince-nez to be used for reading had been changed for a pair of spectacles and his short-sightedness gave the impression that he did not know where he was going or what he might meet. 'He wears glasses and really he uses them without interruption from the early morning until late in the night when he wakes up,' wrote Ettore Schmitz in an exercise set by Joyce. 'Perhaps he may see less than it is to suppose from his appearance but he looks like a being who moves in order to see. Surely he cannot fight and does not want to. He is going through life hoping not to meet bad men. I wish him heartily not to meet them.'

The months between his return to Trieste in March 1907 and his next, momentous, excursion in July 1909 were unrelieved by any major crisis. Joyce made half-hearted attempts to get teaching jobs elsewhere, resurrected, and then abandoned an earlier plan to establish an agency for Irish tweeds in Trieste (very patriotic, but

---

[2] As a consequence of these lessons Joyce sang in a concert performance of the quintet from Act III of *Die Meistersinger*. 'Do you understand the infatuation of people for this opera?' he asked Molyneux Palmer. 'I think it is pretentious stuff.' One almost despairs at the inability of the author of the greatest comic novel of the twentieth century to enjoy the greatest comic opera of the nineteenth. But Joyce may have been irritated by the words he had to sing, probably these, in the lesser tenor part of David:

> *dass ich Meister bald heiss'*!
> *Meister, Meister bald, gar bald ich heiss'*!
> *(that I soon shall be a Master*!
> *A master quite soon I shall be*!)

When Joyce was firmly established a Master himself, his objection to *Die Meistersinger* seems to have evaporated.

tweed is not really suited to the Mediterranean climate), tried a few more publishers with *Dubliners*, and in December 1908 conceived a plan, partly intended to reconcile his father with his mésalliance, to send Georgio to Dublin the following summer in charge of Stanislaus. Where the money was to be found was not explained but Georgio demonstrated inherited optimism by asking all he met for the loan of a valise to carry his clothes to 'Dubirino'. Nora suffered a miscarriage after three months and Joyce examined the foetus 'whose truncated existence I am probably the only one to regret.' Maunsel and Co, new Dublin publishers, expressed an interest in *Dubliners*, having heard of it from Elkin Mathews. Joyce, preferring an English publisher if he could get one, waited a year, then sent the book in April 1909. He determined to renew work on *A Portrait* after Schmitz's favourable account of it, rendered in fractured English, but perceptive:

> . . . I like very much your second and third chapters and I think you made a great mistake doubting whether you would find a reader who could take pleasure at the sermons of the third chapter. I have read them with a very strong feeling and I know in my own little town a lot of people who would be certainly stroke by the same feeling . . . I think that I have at last also discovered the reason why these two [the second and third] chapters are for me so beautiful while the first one which surely is of the same construction, by the same writer who has surely not changed his ways, written evidently with the same artistic aims, fails to impress me as deeply. I think it deals with events devoid of importance and your rigid method of observation and description does not allow you to enrich a fact which is not rich by itself. You should write only about strong things. In your skilled hands they may become still stronger . . .
>
> Excuse me, dear Mr Joyce, these remarks which prove only my conceitedness . . .

Schmitz, having read only three chapters, could not know Joyce's whole intention of presenting the embryonic growth of Stephen's soul. The idea of embryonic growth deeply interested him (which may explain what would seem to be the ghoulish inspection of the aborted foetus) and is in one chapter of *Ulysses* laid on with a trowel. Joyce could begin with a description of the growth of a

147

soul and insist a few years later on constructing a complete and detailed map of the growth of language itself, all within the framework of fiction.

More cries of misery proceeded from John Joyce in Dublin, drenched in self-pity ('my health is fast breaking up and I feel certain I have seen my last Xmas' – he had another twenty-two years to go) but also a certain tenderness from memories of James as a child, provoked by photographs of Georgio. James decided to go to Dublin himself, instead of sending Stanislaus, as Stanislaus had all along known he would, borrowed a year's tuition in advance from Schmitz, set off with Georgio, in July 1909, and walked right into a ferocious emotional storm.

Chapter Eleven
The Poor Fellow that I Love

The visit of Joyce's to Dublin after nearly a five year absence becomes the framework of his only play, *Exiles*, written between *A Portrait* and *Ulysses*, dismissed by some as having the brilliance of neither and made the subject of critical flannel even by its admirers.[1] That it is a brilliant play in performance was proved by Harold Pinter's London production in 1970. It goes without saying that the structure is Ibsenesque, even to the title.

Richard Rowan, a writer, returns to Dublin after nine years' exile in Rome, where he had made a name for himself, bringing with him Bertha, an intelligent but uneducate woman who had followed him into exile and born him a son, Archie, now eight years old. Rowan's old friend Robert Hand, with whom he had spent his youth drinking, chasing women and sharing a cottage, is now a successful journalist and wishes to aid Rowan by procuring for him the chair of romance literature at the university. He wishes also to achieve the sexual conquest of Bertha while Richard's back is turned. Robert Hand bears a striking resemblance to Oliver St John Gogarty. Bertha notices, as they land at Kingstown pier and catch a glimpse of Hand in the crowd, that he has put on weight.

Act 1. Robert calls on Richard to announce that he has arranged a dinner that evening for Richard at eight o'clock at the home of the vice-chancellor, who will offer him the chair he wants. Robert wants credit for having defended his absent friend against his critics in Dublin during his exile.

> ROBERT: I will fight for you still because I have faith in you, the faith of a disciple in his master. I cannot say more than that. It may seem strange to you . . . Give me a match.

[1] Padraic Colum: '*Exiles* is not a play about adultery, actual or suspected; the writer of *A Portrait of the Artist* is not going to lay before us anything so banal.' As if the writer of *Ulysses* thought the subject banal.

RICHARD: (*Lights and offers him a match*) There is a faith
still stranger than the faith of a disciple in his
master.

ROBERT: And that is?

RICHARD: The faith of a master in the disciple who will
betray him.

(Note resemblance to Jesus Christ.)

ROBERT: Good afternoon, Richard. We shall meet tonight.

RICHARD: (*Touches his hand*) At Philippi.

(And Julius Caesar.) 'When you have a thing it can be taken from
you,' Richard explains to young Archie. 'But when you give it, you
have given it. No robber can take it from you.'

Robert having retired, Bertha tells Richard that she has received
an invitation from Robert to pay a call at his cottage in the sub-
urbs that very evening, at eight o'clock. She asks him to forbid her
to go. He refuses. Her soul is her own business. She is free to do
as she likes.

Act II. Twenty past eight, at the cottage where Robert and
Richard had caroused in their youth. Robert answers the door,
expecting Bertha but . . . it is Richard, who explains he has known
Robert's intention all along. Then why won't he do something about
it, Robert asks? 'Because in the very core of my ignoble heart I
longed to be betrayed by you and by her – in the dark, in the
night – secretly, meanly, craftily. I longed for that passionately and
ignobly, to be dishonoured for ever in love and in lust, to be . . .
To be for ever a shameful creature and to build up my soul out of
the ruins of its shame.'

(We shall later see that this was in fact one of Joyce's own
fancies.)

Robert naturally assumes that his little adventure is over and hides
in the garden when he hears Bertha knock at the door, wishing to
avoid the embarrassment of seeing her. Bertha is not at all flustered
to see Richard but gets annoyed when he announces he is going
off, leaving her alone with Robert. She assumes he wishes to spend
the evening with Robert's cousin, Beatrice Justice, a fragile Protestant intellectual with whom he can discuss things beyond Bertha's
ken – and perhaps more than merely discuss things. Not so, he
says. 'You may be his and mine. I will trust you, Bertha, and him
too. I must . . . Bertha, love him, be his, give yourself to him if you

150

desire – or if you can.' Exit Richard, enter Robert, who is soon busily resuming his former intention. 'Do not go, Bertha! There is still time. Do you love me too? I have waited a long time. Do you love us both – him and also me? Do you, Bertha? The truth! Tell me. Tell me with your eyes. Or speak!' Curtain.

What hapens next? We can be forgiven for asking the question since Joyce invites it. Does she or doesn't she? No answer.

Act III. The morning after, back at the Rowan residence. Bertha is discovered moping by the maid, having been up since the dawn, unable to sleep. Richard has been in his study all night and has gone for a walk. The maid makes Bertha a nice cup of tea. Arrival of Beatrice Justice, bearing a copy of the morning newspaper. Robert has stayed up all night to write a leading article, 'A Distinguished Irishman'. 'Not the least vital of the problems which confront our country is the problem of her attitude towards those of her children who, having left her in her hour of need, have been called back to her now on the eve of her long-awaited victory, to her whom in loneliness and exile they have at last learned to love.' And so on. Richard Rowan's hour has arrived, if he wants it. Exchange of words between Bertha and Richard. She calls him womankiller. Enter Robert in answer to Bertha's summons. He is going away for a couple of weeks in Surrey.

ROBERT: (*Catching her hands*) Bertha! What happened last night? What is the truth that I am to tell [to Richard]? (*He gazes earnestly into her eyes*). Were you mine in that sacred night of love? Or have I dreamed it?

BERTHA: (*Smiles faintly*) Remember your dream of me. You dreamed that I was yours last night.

ROBERT: And that is the truth – a dream? That is what I am to tell?

BERTHA: Yes.

ROBERT: (*Kisses both her hands*) Bertha! (*In a softer voice*) In all my life only that dream is real. I forget the rest. (*He kisses her hands again*) And now I can tell him the truth. Call him.

Robert informs Richard that he failed – Bertha is still his – and that after his failure he dined with the vice-chancellor, wrote his article, picked up a divorced lady and had her in a cab, then went home and packed his bags for Surrey. Last scene between Richard and Bertha.

RICHARD: *(Still gazing at her and speaking as if to an absent person)* I have wounded my soul for you – a deep wound of doubt which can never be healed. I can never know, never in this world. I do not wish to know or to believe. I do not care. It is not in the darkness of belief that I desire you. But in restless living wounding doubt. To hold you by no bonds, even of love, to be united with you in body and soul in utter nakedness – for this I longed. And now I am tired for a while Bertha. My wound tires me. *(He stretches himself out wearily along the lounge. Bertha holds his hand, still speaking very softly)*

BERTHA: Forget me, Dick. Forget me and love me again as you did the first time. I want my lover. To meet him, to go to him, to give myself to him. You, Dick. O, my strange wild lover, come back to me again!

Why the title *Exiles*? Joyce answered the question in notes he wrote while writing the play – or half answered it. 'A nation exacts a penance from those who dared to leave her payable on their return.' Richard notes the phrase in the editorial praising him, *'those who left her in her hour of need,'* looking searchingly at Bertha. Gogarty appears also in *Ulysses* as Ireland's gay betrayer, so we may accept the comparison. The play is to be a 'rough and tumble between the Marquis de Sade and Frieherr v Sacher Masoch' with Richard (like Joyce) the masochist who extracts fine details of his rival's love-making. Did he kiss you on the lips? Did he kiss you the other way? But the principal themes are friendship between men, and sexual jealousy. 'A battle of your soul against the spectre of fidelity,' says Robert, 'of mine against the spectre of friendship.'

'As a contribution to the study of jealousy,' Joyce reminds himself, 'Shakespeare's *Othello* is incomplete.' During the first trip to Dublin of 1909 Joyce was to have ample opportunity to study jealousy at first hand.

The trip began well. 'The first thing I saw on the pier at Kingstown was Gogarty's fat back but I avoided him.' At Westland Row railway station the whole of the Joyce family was waiting to inspect Georgio, who delighted them by his high spirits. John

Joyce was particularly pleased and expressed his satisfaction in characteristic manner some days later. John and James stopped at an inn during a walk in the country. The old man sat down at the piano to play a tune from the third act of *La Traviata*.

'Did you recognize the aria I just played?'

'Yes, it belongs to Armand's father in Verdi's opera.'

The words are an expression of regret. 'Ah, foolish old man. Now I see the harm I did.' Joyce knew his father had forgiven his indiscretion and himself asked forgiveness of his intolerance.

Within a few days he had met most of the old crowd. Cosgrave noted his splendid health but Gogarty, the medical man, commented 'Jaysus, man, you're in phthisis.'[2] Russell and John Eglington met him in the street, and were cordial, Russell saying he looked like a man of business. 'Very ecclesiastical,' said Eglington. Sheehy-Skeffington said he looked very blasé. Everybody said he looked melancholy.

Gogarty was exceptionally civil, as he had been ever since Joyce had left Dublin. He had even invited Joyce to join him during a stay in Vienna, promised him pupils and sent him a pound (intercepted en route by the Joyce family). Now he asked him to lunch to discuss a plan or two, sending his chauffeur round to pick him up. Joyce declined. Gogarty ran into him later in Merrion Square. Joyce passed him by but Gogarty went after him and, holding him by the arm, made a long and confused speech professing friendship and bafflement. Joyce allowed himself to be taken to Gogarty's house, but declined refreshment of any sort. To every overture from the prosperous doctor Joyce replied, quiet and sober and no doubt highly exasperating. 'You have your life. Leave me to mine.'

This incivility extended even to declining an outing to Eniskerry in the Gogarty automobile. Finally, Gogarty, blushing says, 'Well do you really want me to go to hell and be damned?'

To which Joyce generously answered: 'I bear you no ill-will. I believe you have some points of good nature. You and I of six years ago are dead. But I must write as I have felt.'

'I don't care a damn what you say of me,' says Gogarty fearlessly, 'so long as it is literature.'

'Do you mean that?' says Joyce.

[2] i.e. Suffering the effect of too much drink.

'I do,' says Gogarty. 'Honest to Jaysus. Now will you shake hands with me at least?'

'I will,' says Joyce, 'on that understanding.'[3]

One cannot properly be the friend of the chief villain of one's fiction. Better to brood apart on his villainy.

A worse villain raised his head – Vincent Cosgrave, that idle companion of the kips and the bars and the failed medical examinations. On 6 August he threw Joyce into a fine spin by claiming that, on the nights when Nora had not seen Joyce at the time when she was still skivvying in Finn's Hotel, she had spent her time with the serpent Cosgrave. 'You stood with him: he put his arms around you and you lifted your face and kissed him. What else did you do together?'

His eyes full of tears of sorrow and mortification and his heart full of bitterness and despair, he wrote in wretched anger: 'O, Nora, pity me for what I suffer now. I shall cry for days. My faith in that face I loved is broken. O, Nora, Nora, have pity on my poor wretched love.'

That love of which he had been so unsure some months before seems to have returned in force once he thought *another* had been at it. He was mistaken. Cosgrave was lying, probably in a fit of jealousy and not realizing what a bomb he had put under Joyce. He had tried to 'get inside' Joyce with Nora in their courting days but had been rebuffed. Joyce did not know about it because Nora had not told him. But Stanislaus did know, hence his vague reference to Cosgrave's treachery and Joyce's denial that Cosgrave had ever betrayed him. It was that ignorance of Joyce's which allowed Cosgrave to say, 'thanks be to God I never kicked him in the arse.'

With time to brood Joyce fell to thinking of Georgio's paternity. 'The first time I slept with you in Zurich was 11th October and he

---

[3] Ulick O'Connor gives it as his opinion that this episode is a figment of Joyce's imagination, a story invented for the benefit of Stanislaus, who knew Gogarty did not like him and professed to regard Gogarty as a bad influence on his brother (The above account comes from a letter of Joyce's to Stanislaus). Mr O'Connor is probably right, as the stilted dialogue would indicate, but Joyce's version is worth having as an example of his tendency to embroidery. Gogarty's version was that Joyce came to his house, spent a long time gazing enigmatically out into the garden of his rich friend, said only 'Is this your revenge?' got up, and left.

was born 27th July. That is nine months and sixteen days. I re-member that there was very little blood that night . . .'

Was Nora lying down in 'that field near the Dodder (on the nights when I was not there)' when she kissed that 'friend' of his? 'Did you place your hand on him as you did on me in the dark and did you say to him as you did to me, "What is it, dear?" '

Joyce now proposed to throw up everything and return to Trieste, the agony of truth seeming to him preferable to the agony of doubt. He would not now go to Galway to see her mother or continue his efforts to foist *Dubliners* on Maunsel and Co (whom he now considered eminently suitable to publish his book), but would return immediately to Trieste, or at least as immediately as Stannie sent the money. 'I am speaking now to the girl I loved, who had red-brown hair and sauntered over to me and took me so easily into her arms and made me a man.'

Stanislaus he informed via an abrupt postcard on 8 August that 'my business here is ended. Send money.' On that tenth day in Dublin however, he first took his misery to the one friend he still considered both intimate and loyal, J. F. Byrne, living at the time at that most momentous address, No 7 Eccles Street, where Stephen Dedalus and Leopold Bloom are to end their odyssey. With much sobbing and groaning Joyce related his story. Byrne had never seen a person so shattered, but improvised immediately the one theory which could convince – conspiracy.

Gogarty must be in league with Cosgrave to destroy Joyce by breaking his spirit with lies as once he had tried with drink. Joyce accepted this explanation with relief and was able to get back to the business of being an artist, a writer in search of publication and an indigent looking for a job. Stanislaus in any case rapidly dis-abused him of the idea of Nora's betrayal by writing to inform him of Cosgrave's unsuccessful attempt on her. Nora, in distress, had kept her dignity and wrote to Joyce telling him he ought to disburden himself of her as a creature unworthy of him.

This little episode has in it the makings not only of *Exiles* but of parts of *Ulysses* too. In *Exiles* Cosgrave and Gogarty are fused. When Joyce, thoroughly ashamed of himself for doubting Nora, began the process of seeking forgiveness, he wrote : 'My sweet noble Nora, I ask you to forgive me for my contemptible conduct but they maddened me, darling between them. We will defeat their cowardly plot, love. Forgive me, sweetheart, won't you?' In *Ulysses* Ithaca is Eccles Street and the hero's circumstances are those of Alfred Hunter, the kindly Jew who had brushed Joyce down after a scuffle in June 1904, when he had attempted to pick up a lady other than Nora and been beaten up by her escort while Cosgrave looked on with his hands in his pockets. But it would be some years before that book properly took shape in Joyce's mind.

Thomas Kettle, Nationalist MP, tried to use his influence now to secure Joyce a lectureship at the new National University (an extension of the old Royal University which had granted Joyce his degree. The government had bowed to Catholic complaints that it was inadequate and agreed to expand its facilities, without changing its character), as Robert Hand similarly exerts himself for Richard Rowan in *Exiles*. Contemplating a successful return to Dublin, Joyce assembled credentials and presented himself to the university, only to be told that Catholic Ireland did not yet feel the need for an acquaintance with Italian literature. He was offered evening classes in commercial Italian at £100 a year. He refused this not very splendid post and made up his mind to return to Trieste.

He was disappointed also in his negotiations with the executors of the estate of the lately dead John Synge, from whom he wanted permission for an Italian performance of his translation of *Riders to the Sea.*

With Maunsel he appeared to have more success. George Roberts, the managing director, and Joseph Hone, who financed the house, offered him a contract for the publication of *Dubliners,* with royalties to run at five per cent more than those offered by Grant Richards when he had agreed to publish. Joyce signed and, tempting fate, blithely announced to Stanislaus 'It will appear next March.'

Caruso was in town to give a concert and Joyce thought to interview him for a Dublin newspaper, but none was interested. Another journalistic project which did come to fruition was a review of the première of *The Shewing-Up of Blanco Posnet* for the *Piccolo della Serra.* Shaw's one-act Western had been banned[4] from public performance in England by the Lord Chamberlain on the grounds of blasphemy (Blanco, a horse-thief, makes disparaging

---

[4] Shaw's preface, three times the length of his play, is an attack on censorship. Joyce's interest stems from his opposition to censorship.

references to God under the impression he is about to be hanged, but discovers at the curtain that he has found the Godhead, as do so many of Shaw's characters). Lady Gregory and Yeats were able to put it on in Dublin because the authority of the Lord Chamberlain did not extend there. Officials of the Viceroy's Office at Dublin Castle did try, unsuccessfully, to suppress it, but it had its première on 25 August, before the large audience which the would-be censors had guaranteed it. They did not repeat the behaviour of the première of *The Playboy* (blasphemy is a crime much less offensive to Irish sensibility than heresy, as Robert Hand points out to Richard Rowan).

Joyce, who at best regarded Shaw as a playwright incapable of the appropriate modern style, at worst a charlatan, predictably did not like *The Shewing-Up of Blanco Posnet* and said so in *Piccolo*: having abandoned God himself he did not like to see anyone else find Him. 'Mr Shaw, not unlike his latest protagonist, has behind him a profane and variegated past. Fabianism, vegetarianism, anti-alcoholism, music, painting and the drama – every progressive movement, whether in art or in politics, has had him for champion; and now, it may be, some divine finger has touched his brain, and at that touch he, like his own Blanco Posnet, unmasks himself.'

Joyce got free tickets off the manager of the Abbey Theatre by representing himself as a reporter from the *Piccolo*, only afterwards offering the piece to Prezioso, the editor, who accepted it. Armed with this acceptance Joyce felt free to have cards printed with the legend, James A. Joyce, *Piccolo della Serra*, Trieste. These he used as an entrée to the Dublin *Evening Telegraph*, whose editor showed him round the building, providing thereby more material for *Ulysses*, the Aeolus episode.

The *Telegraph* ran a modest little paragraph, without offering any prize to the first reader to guess who had written it: 'Mr George Bernard Shaw's censored play, *The Shewing-Up of Blanco Posnet*, seems to have attracted attention even so far away as in Italy. It is a curious fact that the principal Italian criticism of 'Blanco Posnet' should have been written for the *Piccolo della Serra* by Mr James Joyce, who is, it is interesting to note, a fellow-citizen of Mr Shaw's and one of the few Irishmen on the Italian Press.'

Having established himself with the aid of a few bits of pasteboard as a leading member of the Italian Press, Joyce paid a visit to the manager of the Midland Railway in the hope of scrounging a Press pass to Galway: it was necessary for him to go there to write articles for the *Piccolo* encouraging Italian tourists to visit the place, he said. The manager parted with a first-class pass.

The day after *Blanco Posnet* he took Georgio to Galway, a little apprehensive of his welcome. He need not have worried. Michael Healy, Nora's uncle, put them up and Joyce spent pleasant hours talking to Mrs Barnacle, in whom he recognized Nora. He got her to sing *The Lass of Aughrim*, that song which makes Gretta cry in 'The Dead', to think of Michael Furey.

Joyce explored Galway, visiting the house where Nora had lived as a child with her grandmother, pretending to be a prospective buyer in order to see the room where she had slept. He had hoped that he and Nora would visit the place again next year. 'You will take me from place to place and the image of your girlhood will purify again my life.'

Galway is a town of inscriptions. 'From the fury of the O'Flaherties, Good Lord, deliver us,' decorates the western gate. Continuing the process of exorcizing 'that common dishonourable wretch' Joyce visited the memorial to Mayor Lynch: 'This memorial of the stern and unbending justice of the Chief Magistrate of this city, James Lynch Fitzstephen, elected Mayor, AD 1493, who condemned and executed his own guilty son, Walter, on this spot, has been restored to its ancient site AD 1854, with the approval of the Town Commissioners, by their Chairman, Very Rev. Peter Daly PP, and Vicar of Saint Nicholas.' Young Lynch, while drunk, is supposed to have stabbed to death a sexual rival. With mixed feelings Joyce must have pondered his fate in that town which was the ancestral homeland of the Joyces and from where they and the other 'native' Irish had once been barred: 'that neither O nor Mac shall strutte nor swaggere through the street of Gallway.'

Nora's mother noticed him sighing deeply and warned he would break his heart at it. He was pining away for his love and longing for that next meeting which, apart from its especial importance as dénouement to the unfortunate fit of jealousy, would bring blessed sexual relief. 'Do you remember' he wrote to Nora 'the day I asked you indifferently "where will I meet you this evening?" and you said without thinking "Where will you meet me, is it? You'll meet me in bed, I suppose".' He wished it were so.

He was heartily sick of Dublin and less than pleased at keeping his own company in bed. Images tormented him there of Nora in every kind of pose, 'grotesque, shameful, virginal, languorous'. He was to be Lord of her body and soul when he got back and for the time being wished she would send him a certain sort of letter which might help calm what he called the anguish of his longing. 'How I would love to surprise you sleeping now!! There is a place I would like to kiss you now, a *strange* place, Nora. *Not* on the lips, Nora. Do you know where?'

No doubt she did, but did not on this trip oblige him with the sort of relieving letter he had in mind, or if she did, those letters have not surfaced.

'Jim,' Nora was to say to herself, 'that poor fellow that I love, is coming back. He is a poor weak impulsive man and he prays to me to defend him and make him strong.' He did pray to her. She had been to his young manhood, he said, what the idea of the Virgin Mary had been to his boyhood. One minute he saw her as virgin and madonna and the next as shameless, insolent, half-naked and obscene. He remembered moments of passion, such as the first love-making in Pola, with her on top of him, pronouncing a certain word of provocation and with a madness in *her* eyes: 'Tonight I have an idea madder than usual. I feel I would like to be flogged by you. I would like to see your eyes blazing with anger.'

That would have to wait. Stanislaus had not yet rounded up the return fare. Besides James and Georgio there was to be a new addition. Margaret Joyce, the eldest sister, was departing to the peace of a convent in New Zealand, where she was to give piano lessons and send up prayers for the soul of her errant brother. Charlie too had departed the Joyce household into the deeper water of matrimony. Now James proposed, for the usual plethora of perfectly good reasons, the new plan of bringing back to Trieste his eighteen-year-old sister, Eva. She would keep Nora company and save the expense of hiring a servant-girl, Joyce having decided that luxury was now indispensable. She claimed some skill at dressmaking, so could save them huge sums that way, and could be induced to take typewriting lessons. Her voice also could be developed and to this end James went to some trouble to have obstructing tonsils removed before he left Dublin.

Another essential expenditure was on a present for Nora,

designed by Joyce himself, an arangement of brown leather case, gold chain and cubes of old ivory. Inside the case was a card inscribed in gold *Nora 1904-1909*, and the ornament itself. The principal feature was a piece of ivory inscribed, on one side, *Love is unhappy*, and on the other, *When Love is away*, a quotation from *Chamber Music*. Joyce wrote Nora a letter describing it on 3 September, apparently drunk, since he repeats himself and the tone could best be described as one of lugubrious confusion. 'Save me, my *true* love! Save me from the badness of the world and of my own heart!'

More practically, to Stannie, 'For Jesus Christ sake send money unless you want to send me into a madhouse.' Every day spent in Dublin, he claimed, was money lost. His health, he mentioned in passing, was much improved. This would be due to his giving up the bad habit of consuming alcoholic beverages and restricting himself instead to lithia water (just why Joyce – temporarily – had to give up drink may be surmised from the next chapter). Taking these protestations with a pinch of salt, Stanislaus nevertheless exerted himself to raise the money.

James himself raised £3 from his new publishers and once again swindled the railways out of a first class pass to London. Even so, the last telegram he sent his brother was 'Domattina otto Pennilesse,' 'Tomorrow at eight, penniless,' the last word being less than impeccable Italian and not a joke which succeeded in putting Stanislaus into a good mood.

Thomas Kettle, newly married, promised to spend two days of his honeymoon in Trieste (he did not). Joyce had by now decided he was his best friend in Ireland. With that other best friend Byrne he spent a farewell evening. Byrne lost his key and was forced to climb the railing at No 7 Eccles Street. Few details of the evening escaped Joyce and those he could recall and did not mind recording, became material for *Ulysses*.

Kettle introduced him to some people at the Gresham Hotel as the great national writer of the future. Joyce thought for a moment he heard his country calling him, but heard a voice louder still: '*Everything* that is noble and exalted and deep and true and moving in what I write comes, I believe, from you. O take me into your soul of souls and then I will become indeed the poet of my race. I feel this, Nora, as I write it. My body soon will penetrate into

10　César Amin's caricature of Joyce, drawn according to his own prescription, cobwebs, patches, shiny nose and all, and the Hibernocentric universe comes in for a bad quarter of an hour.

11 James Stephens, Joyce and John Sullivan in Paris in the 'thirties. Sullivan wrote charmingly about leprechauns. 'He wouldn't have far to look for his material', unkindly commented a Dublin wit.

yours. O that my soul could too! O that I could nestle in your womb like a child born of your flesh and blood, be fed by your blood, sleep in the warm secret gloom of your body!'

Less exalted, he hoped her breasts were growing from the regular ingestion of some cocoa he had sent her and that she would take to wearing black underwear to please him. 'Love is a cursed nuisance especially when coupled with lust also.' Amen.

The lustful lover arrived at Trieste with entourage on 13 September praying, for Jesus' sake, that nobody would attack him with bills. In this hope he was disappointed, and it was not long before he was back on another trip to Dublin, once again skidding penniless along a rainbow that ended in a mess of pottage, this time as the Man of Business.

Chapter Twelve

The Artist as Entrepreneur

As soon as he was back, the two of them, Jim and Nora, fell upon one another with honeymoon fervour. Unhappily, such fervour does not last. 'You have no right to be ugly and slovenly at your age,' he forewarned from Dublin, 'and I hope now you will pay me the compliment of looking well.' He was not disappointed. Her hair was not full of cinders. She looked young and girlish and, standing in the corridor, gave him a strange cry of welcome which engraved itself in his memory as did the image of her as she came to him that night with her hair loose to wake him up. Tired from the long journey, the lustful lover had gone straight to bed.

Their rapture did not please Stanislaus. 'Love is unhappy when love is away. So is Love's brother,' he commented sourly. And did anyone in Dublin ask after him? 'Oh yes, everybody,' said James blithely. 'I got a whole lot of messages for you but I've forgotten them.'

Jim and Nora attended a performance of the recently-composed *Madame Butterfly*. But when the Butterfly sang *'Un bel dì'* : 'One day, one day we shall see a spire of smoke rising on the furthest verge of the sea, and then the ship appears,' Nora's soul did not sway with the same languor and longing as her companion's. Quite the reverse; she was positively rude.

And when he came home to her bed in the small hours after an evening in the café, to tell her of all he hoped to achieve and all the work he would do, she announced that she was too tired to listen and bluntly went to sleep.

And as they walked through Trieste after buying a glass jar for home-made marmalade, and Joyce's jaundiced eye chanced on a priest, and he said 'Do you not find a kind of repulsion or disgust at the sight of one of those men?', Nora said, shortly and dryly, 'No, I don't.' Worst blow of all! Was she with him or against him?

Now what could induce Nora to be so surly? The answer is less than romantic. Joyce had not been so faithful to his newly redis-covered love as those lyrical protestations from Dublin might have suggested to her. He had fallen back on that sexual convenience he had used since he was fourteen, and once again paid the penalty. As soon as the symptoms manifested themselves it naturally occurred to Nora to wonder if she might in turn suffer from the passion of their reunion.

'Poor little Nora, how bad I am to you!' But that was little consolation until time could reassure her that she was not clapped.

Sister Eva was the occasion of the next excursion. She did not take to Trieste but noticed with gratitude that it contained two cinemas (as she told Richard Ellmann in an interview in 1953). Dublin had no permanent cinema. The commercial opportunity immediately occurred to Joyce. It might take a little longer to forge the uncreated conscience of his race, but in the meantime he could earn a little profit by providing it with its first cinemas.

Accordingly, he appealed to Nicolo Vidacovich, a lawyer and one of his pupils, to intercede for him with the proprietors, and the intercession was successful. Joyce signed a contract to travel to Ireland on expenses of ten crowns a day, there to find sites for cinemas in Dublin, Cork and Belfast, and if authorised, to proceed with their establishment. He would receive one-tenth of the profit. Unfortunately for Joyce none of his partners were on the level of Sam Goldwyn.

There were four of them: Antonio Machnich, an upholsterer who had invented a new type of sofa which was also a bed, a leather merchant called Giovanni Rebez, a draper called Giuseppe Caris, and Francesco Novak, who ran a bicycle shop.

He left Trieste a little over a month after he arrived, unloading his pupils on Stanislaus until such time as he should get back. Nora's farewell was to call him an imbecile. She was rewarded by a curt, businesslike note as he passed through Paris, and then a week's silence. After a bad crossing via Dieppe (he was fussy how he crossed the Channel) another railway company was prevailed upon to furnish a free ticket. On his first day in Dublin he flung himself into his business with remarkable energy and kept up the pace while he was there. But no matter how hard he worked the fates had decreed that James Joyce was not to be a successful businessman. Nor is the climate in Dublin congenial to enterprise.

'I loathe Ireland and the Irish,' he declares when he gets around to writing to Nora. 'They themselves stare at me in the street though I was born among them. Perhaps they read my hatred of them in my eyes[1] . . . I felt proud to think that my son – mine and yours, that handsome dear little boy you gave me, Nora – will always be a foreigner in Ireland, a man speaking another language and bred in a different tradition.' The same sentiment he repeated to Padraic Colum, exhibiting Georgio speaking Italian.

The Irish repaid the compliment. Joyce found premises in Mary Street but found also an indifference on the part of the Irish to his plans to provide them with entertainment (He could hardly have chosen a worse site – no doubt he chose it as the first available, in order to get out of Dublin as quickly as possible. Though Mary Street is close to the principal street of Dublin it is in a neighbourhood of street markets and slum-dwellers, hardly likely to attract the quality). A licence was necessary. One was supposed to be forthcoming once the Dublin Corporation had approved his plans, but was not. Only the Recorder could grant one, but he was not sitting.

Machnich and Co were slow in forwarding money from Trieste. The owner of the Mary Street property became suspicious. After appeals to Trieste, £50 was sent to serve as a deposit. Where was Joyce's expense money? Why had Machnich not turned up to approve the premises?

Joyce hired an electrician and spent time supervising him among the wires in the basement. Machnich and Rebez appeared in November (with Novak following later) and Joyce, the burden of unrequited lust on him again, put them up in Finn's Hotel to be able to take them to dinner in the dining room where once Nora had served. There were abortive trips to Belfast and Cork to find premises. The projector was unaccountably delayed in transit. The electrician quit and Joyce's partners blamed him for hiring him in the first place. An advertisement for staff brought 200 replies and Joyce complained of having to interview fifty of them, though probably he enjoyed wielding authority: when Padraic Colum was invited to inspect the new cinema, to be called the Volta, he mistook Messrs Machnich, Novak and Rebez for imported work-

[1] It could on the other hand have been the novelty of his 'Austrian yellow' suit.

164

men because of the imperious manner in which Joyce addressed them in Italian.

The affair dragged itself on into December until the necessary licenses were got, the apparatus installed, benches and kitchen chairs provided for the patrons, and musicians hired. Half an hour before the delayed opening, on the 20th, another electrician quit, but Joyce scoured Dublin and found a replacement in the nick of time. He managed to get a favourable mention inserted in the *Evening Telegraph*, carefully omitting mention of anyone but himself:

> Yesterday at 45 Mary Street a most interesting cinematograph exhibition was opened before a large number of invited visitors. The hall in which the display takes place is most admirably equipped for the purpose, and has been admirably laid out. Indeed, no expense would appear to have been spared in making the entertainment one deserving of the patronage of the public. Perhaps its special feature is that it is of Italian origin, and is in that respect somewhat out of the ordinary and more conventional forms of such displays. For an initial experiment it was remarkably good, remembering how difficult it is to produce with absolute completeness a series of pictures at the first stage of their location in new surroundings the occasion may be described as having been particularly successful. The chief pictures shown were 'The First Paris Orphanage,' 'La Pourponniere,' and 'The Tragic Story of Beatrice Cenci.' The latter, although very excellent, was hardly as exhilarating a subject as one would desire on the eve of the festive season. An excellent little string orchestra played charmingly during the afternoon. Mr James Joyce, who is in charge of the exhibition, has worked apparently indefatigably in its production and deserves to be congratulated on the success of the inaugural exhibition.

Joyce sent this plug back to Stanislaus with instructions to get it into *Piccolo*, and sent also advertising posters, wishing to create in Trieste the image of a successful businessman.

This image may have been somewhat lacking. Both Dublin and Trieste branches of the Joyces were in trouble. John Joyce had gone into hospital suffering from conjunctivitis and iritis, leaving James with the task of supporting that household (Charlie, too, was desperately appealing for funds from Boston. He had attempted emigration as a solution to his problems, but the solution had turned out to be no more successful than any other so far dreamed up by any member of the Joyce family). On 17 November Joyce got a telegram from Trieste: 'Wire £4 writ landlord.' Their landlord Scholtz, impatient for two months rent, was suing. Joyce sent a few crowns and a demand note which Stanislaus could present to Vidacovich – almost enough for one month's rent. If that did not work, then 'A notice to quit has been served on this house (the Dublin branch) for the 1st December so that, thank God, we will all be on the pavement together for Xmas.'

It cannot be said that Joyce had been careful with the little paid him by his partners. Some he had lent to a cadging friend of his father's and almost his first thought in Dublin had been to buy a splendid set of sable furs, cape, stole and muff for his Venus in Trieste (like him a reader of Sacher-Masoch). He was not able to manage such extravagance, sable being inconveniently expensive, but sent her gloves which pleased her, and some yards of Donegal tweed to make a dress, these the product of an agency to sell tweed in Trieste granted him by a Dublin company, that old idea of his which he hoped would now succeed (not so his idea to export fireworks: he was told they did not travel well or safely).

His business-like air at least impressed Padraic Colum. 'This was a friendly Joyce, a more mellow Joyce!' 'I am not a poet,' he told Colum, like someone resigned to his own disability, but exhibited the copy he was making of *Chamber Music* as a present for Nora, inscribed in India ink on sheets of parchment and intended to be specially bound in covers decorated with their intertwined initials. Instructions were sent to Trieste to burn all other manuscript copies and to take the Joyce family crest from its frame and despatch it to Dublin to be bound into the cover.

Joyce was in a fever of impatience to get back to Trieste, partly compounded of his renewed detestation of the Irish but aggravated beyond bearing, in spite of medical complaint, by an intolerable lust. This found expression in a series of remarkable letters exchanged between himself and Nora – the sort of letters he had wanted at the last separation but had been, according to his own account, too shy to initiate. They have, on his part, considerable literary quality which is reflected in the more rapturous part of his pub-

lished work, but their principal function was to stimulate the re-
cipient to masturbation – both parties being anxious that sexual
energies not so released might find more unfortunate expression.[2]

First there was a row to be got over. An appeal first to his 'bad-
tempered bad-mannered splendid little girl' to be only a *little* more
polite in the future, and exert herself to help him in his work. If he
could write anything fine or noble in the future he could do so
only by listening at the doors of her heart (which turned out to be
truer than she could have guessed).

This jealous, lonely, dissatisfied and proud man (his own description) confessed to her that his love was a kind of adoration. He
ached to smother her in furs, prayed for her as once to the Virgin,
and when he had done putting on his front to Dublin, retired to
agonize, sobbing over the paper he wrote on. (Meanwhile, would she
please eat as much as possible so as more to resemble a woman).

The present of gloves and promise of furs (by 1 November no
longer sable but a more modest squirrel muff on steel chain but
lined with velvet satin) reminded her of a similar gift received at
Finn's Hotel a little more than five years before, so she sent him a
coquettish note, as from that address :

> I hope you are quite well, and will be very pleased to see you
> I hope you will write to me and let me know when I am to
> meet you again at present I am rather busy and cant get out
> for some time I hope you will excuse me and accept many
> thanks
>
> Nora Barnacle.

Alas, three weeks later the threat of imminent eviction had
changed her feelings and she wrote to inform him she had had
enough of poverty and degradation. This lash across the eyes, he
said, made him wander the streets like a filthy cur whose mistress
had cut him with her whip. Very well then, vile beast that he was,
he would sink back into the mire where he belonged, no longer
defiling her children with his loathsome touch. She had given him
the finest things of the world but had been only casting pearls

---

[2] The trustees of the Joyce estate insist, because of their explicit sexual
content, that two letters, of 8 and 9 December, may not be published,
nor certain sentences from eight other letters of the same year. The avid
student of Joyce's sex life must consult the originals in the Cornell University
Library, but will find them precisely according to the description given here.

before swine. The swine would allow her two-thirds of his income and pray always to her name and her memory, holier than God to him.

This moving epistle turned out to be a wasted effort, since she had already repented before she got it. Appraised of this he was able to write:

> Her soul! Her name! Her eyes! They seem to me like strange beautiful blue wild-flowers growing in some tangled, rain-drenched hedge. And I have felt her soul tremble beside mine, and have spoken her name softly to the night, and have wept to see the beauty of the world passing like a dream behind her eyes.

He still felt bashful, however, about a certain matter. Nora informed him in her 'old familiar roguish way' that she would punish him if he did not write. She sent also a request for some underlinen, whose urgency did not strike Joyce as it was intended. On 1 December he obliged her with an erotic letter, stimulated by her inclusion in a letter of hers of the word 'fuck'. The sound of the word he found like the act itself, 'brief, brutal, irresistible and devilish' but kept his eyes glued to the writing of it while he did what he was told to do. '. . . side by side and inside this spiritual love I have for you there is also a wild beast-like craving for every inch of your body, for every secret and shameful part of it, for every odour and act of it. My love for you allows me to pray to the spirit of eternal beauty and tenderness mirrored in your eyes or to fling you down under me . . . [Censored]'

That letter, of 2 December, may not be quoted in full, but since an explicit paraphrase of it has already appeared in an academic work it is presumably permissible to follow suit: Joyce, in his letter, expresses, in the crudest and most effective language, his desire to have intercourse with Nora, to make oral love to Nora, to have her do the same to him, and then to penetrate her anus; and to absorb all possible pleasures from these activities; to watch what he is doing and is being done to him, to feel it, (and since it is Joyce) to smell it.[3] He mentions also his excitement when she had

---

[3] I regret that this stilted language cannot be replaced by Joyce's lively original.

lifted up her clothes to let him watch her masturbating and, at some point in the composition of a highly skilful and evocative piece of pornography, manages to achieve orgasm himself, so that the letter is able to end on a suitably lyrical note . . . 'you are always my beautiful flower of the hedges, my dark-blue rain-drenched flower'. None of this may now seem exceptional but it was certainly Joyce's wish and Nora's that what was intensely private should remain so. Nora burnt many of his letters to her but those in Cornell survive because they were left in Trieste when he and she moved to Paris in 1920 (Her erotic letters to him may be among those papers deposited under seal in the National Library of Ireland. See last chapter). They certainly demonstrate that there was no deficiency of sexual passion between them.

The day afterwards he was at it again, but still apprehensive that what he wrote must 'read awful' in the cold light of day. His youthful habits had changed, and as those discovered who used loose language in his presence, he was fastidiousness itself in his own speech and severely disapproving of those who were not (Yes, the author who introduced that terrible quintet[4] of four-letter words into modern English literature with *Ulysses* and *A Portrait of the Artist as a Young Man* did not pronounce them himself even though he could write them to his wife).

'Nora, I am panting with eagerness to get your replies to these filthy letters of mine . . . If this filth I have written insults you bring me to my senses again with the lash as you have done before. God help me!'[5]

While Jim rhapsodised over the exotic underwear Nora would shortly be wearing in order to please him, she was wandering Trieste without any drawers at all, not in order to excite anyone, but because those she had had worn out. He sent her a banknote when he heard of her drawerless condition, then worked himself into a fine state of excitement describing what she would wear when he could

---

[4] The curious may save themselves the trouble of working it out. They are 'fuck, cunt, piss, shit and arse'.

[5] *Ulysses* :

THE HONOURABLE MRS MERVYN TALBOYS : (*Stamps her jingling spurs in a sudden paroxysm of sudden fury*) I will, by the God above me. I'll scourge the pigeon-livered cur as long as I can stand over him. I'll flay him alive.

BLOOM: (*His eyes closing, quails expectantly*) Here? (*He squirms*) Again! (*He pants cringing*) I love the danger.

169

afford it, renewing also his request for precise details of the liberties she had allowed previous suitors, cautioning her meanwhile to keep his 'filthy' letters to herself, once by telegram when he realized the enormity of what he had written. *'How on God's earth* can you possibly love a thing like me?'

He need not have worried. Nora put his letters to the same use as he put hers. A habit she had adopted herself in adolescence, and the thoughts necessarily attendant to it, did not shock her. Nora, alternatively Joyce's 'Fuckbird' and his 'proud blue-eyed queen', did not mind her lover's curious excitement and, though neither of them knew it, was contributing mightily to that comprehensive understanding of women (as, at least, it seems to men) which James Joyce achieved. Sexologists were few and far between in 1909, not that Joyce's interest was scientific, and women did not publish books detailing their sexual functions, needs and fantasies. There was no way for a man to know what it was like to be a woman but to ask one of those strange creatures.

Joyce's telegram to Nora read *Be careful.* He meant her not only to be careful to keep the letters out of anyone else's sight but to be careful not to get so *hot* after reading them that she would seek satisfaction through an agency other than her middle finger. He got hot too. 'I got your hot letter last night' says one (censored) letter, 'and did as you told me.' But 'the only thing I hope is that I haven't brought on that cursed thing again by what I did. *Pray* for me, dearest.' Lest Nora fear a recurrence of the occasion of his malady, he assures her that he will keep clear of whores. The symptoms do not appear to have disappeared as rapidly as he wished. Along with a request that Nora get in a comfortable chair (with what?) he asks that she ensure a comfortable bed for the two of them but feels it necessary to add (20 December) 'I have no great wish to do anything to you, dear. All I want is your company.' The next paragraph of that letter belies it. He says he is hungry for stracotto di maccheroni, a mixed salad, stewed prunes, torroni, tea and presnitz and . . . something censored.

'Excuse me, dear, I am *hungry* tonight.'

A few days later, another threat to leave him. 'I will not ask you to remember the children,' says Joyce, in effect asking her to remember the children. She was aware that that threat was her principal weapon. He scraped together enough to get her, by a round-about route, the best part of £1 for Christmas day.

When the partners left Finn's Hotel to live for a while over the cinema, Joyce took advantage of paying the £20 bill to ask the waitress to let him see the room where Nora had slept. He did and was excited at the thought of her undressing 'her fair young body' there. Another acquaintance with her past was the young Galway constable on special duty at the opening of the cinema. Joyce had given him a drink and pumped him. *Of course* he remembered Nora Barnacle! Joyce suffered another fit of jealousy, knowing perfectly well it was irrational. But Nora *could* once have turned her eyes towards that fine young man.

So there is Joyce, aged twenty-seven, once again back in Dublin, not yet decided he has no part to play in the life of that city, hoping even to see *Dubliners* printed there (the proofs were supposed to be ready by the time he left, but were not); in love with his wife (she might as well now be called his wife, though still he resisted the idea of marriage. She had put up with him for five years), to the point of dementia whenever he thought it possible to lose her, and unable to impress her with his poses as so easily he impressed others; author of some verses, a book of short stories and three-fifths of a novel; founder of Dublin's first (short-lived) cinema; suffering from VD and torn apart by a sexual energy entirely unremarkable at his age; suffering also from the inherited delusion that he could make money out of business; above all, longing for peace, even for the peace of the womb, the protective peace of a mother's arms.

'I am your child as I told you and you must be severe with me, my little mother. Punish me as much as you would like. I would be delighted to feel my flesh tingling under your hand. Do you know what I mean, Nora dear? I wish you would smack me or flog me even. Not in play, dear, in earnest and on my naked flesh. I wish you were strong, *strong*, dear, and had a big full proud bosom and big fat thighs. I would love to be whipped by you, Nora love!'

And there is Nora back in Trieste, twenty-four, mother of two small children and awaiting the return of a grown-up child so far displaying little sign of improving his bad behaviour; poverty-stricken and fed up with poverty; fed up with Jim but with nowhere else to go; dreaming of Paris and furs galore, and of being the wife of the greatest writer in the world, if only he would get on with it;

171

but above all in love with that man even when, at the same time, he told her he loved looking at 'the brown stain that came behind on her girlish white drawers', and told her he was ashamed to admit it.

On 29 December Joyce appeared before the Recorder at last and got the necessary music licence. Leaving Novak behind to run the cinema he got on the boat for home on 2 January 1910. He took with him his sister Eileen, almost twenty-one. She too, would make a welcome and economical addition to the household and Joyce would see to it that she too had her voice trained. That was the plan.

Chapter Thirteen
The Writer's Foul Intent

Finnegans Wake and the slim *Pomes Penyeach* were the only of Joyce's books to be published without protracted warfare with publishers, censors or both; the volume of poetry because it was such a slight business, *Finnegans Wake* because none but a handful had the faintest idea what was in it even after reading it. *Dubliners* was all too accessible and accumulated self-appointed censors with the force of an avalanche.

And so long as *Dubliners* was not settled, Joyce did not feel able to proceed with *A Portrait*. The imminent publication of his stories would once again release some creative spring in him, but that was not to be until 1914. He was to spend the intervening four years fighting his several demons – publishers, drink, failing eyesight, poverty (or, to be more accurate, the inability to reconcile his appetites and an income of less than £200 a year) and the stubborn and inexplicable disloyalty of certain persons to himself, the two principal demons in this department being his wife and his brother.

Stanislaus having snapped under the strain of Joycean domesticity had left to find a room of his own but was still far from immune from demands on his pocket. He was required even to pay instalments on the piano his brother was buying on a hire purchase system because of the insistance of the rental company on being paid; required also to lend out his room to his brother in order that he might give lessons away from the turbulence of his own household; required now to feed his sisters as well as his brother's dependents; required to pay for meals eaten at his brother's house (paid for but not always supplied); and thoroughly fed up with his role of brother's keeper.

A serious breach occurred one day in June of 1910. The evening had come and gone and Stanislaus had not been fed. James and Nora were out on the town and appeared very late. Stanislaus, exploding in anger, swore he had had enough. James was inclined to be conciliatory but Nora thought money, the fabulous sum of 1,000 crowns, was arriving the day following. 'Ah, let him go out of that,' she said. So he did.

That money did not arrive. Georgio, meeting Stanislaus a few days later in the street, displayed another inherited trait – nerve. 'We had no dinner today,' the child, who had yet to celebrate his fifth birthday, informed his uncle. 'Keep that in your head.'

When, on one occasion, Joyce was given money for a lesson, he set out to get food for the family but returned instead with a hand-painted silk scarf for Nora.[1] She sat down promptly to write yet another (unsent) letter to her mother announcing her return to Galway. Joyce, looking over her shoulder, said, 'If you're going home at least write "I" with a capital letter.'

'What difference does it make?' said Nora, who ranked a full belly ahead of calligraphic orthodoxy.

The bonanza which did not turn up was Joyce's share of the 'profits' from the sale of the Volta cinema. His partners had lost forty percent of their capital and Novak in particular had lost nearly everything, as the one deputed to stay behind in Dublin and run the business. Joyce, although quite aware of the company's losses, with his usual optimism still expected a share of the sale price when the partners decided to sell out. Indeed, he had tried to augment his presumed share by getting his father to arrange the transaction, thereby entitling himself to a commission on the sale of his own property (as he saw it). John Joyce, in any case, was too slow off the mark, and it was Novak who arranged the sale. Joyce got nothing. His partners had cheated him and the whole of Dublin had united in a malicious determination to ruin him by staying away from his cinema. The new tenants were English 'and, of course, will make it pay for of course Dublin will give support to Englishmen, but not to Irish or Italians.' (Perhaps the Englishmen did not persevere in the policy of entertaining Dublin with Italian movies.)

Schmitz, in London looking after his own rather more successful enterprise, wrote Joyce a letter of consolation. 'Your surprise at being cheated proves that you are a pure literary man. To be cheated proves not yet enough. But to be cheated and to present a great surprise over that and not to consider it as a matter of course is

[1] Richard Ellmann : Interview with Eileen Joyce.

really literary. I hope you are now correcting your proofs and not frightened to be cheated by your publisher.'

Alas, yes. George Roberts promised to publish on 20 January, but Joyce was not so sure he would, there having been a good deal of squabbling over what was to be cut out of *Dubliners*, what was to be changed and what was to be left in.

> 22 January 1911 [to the absent Stanislaus]
> It may interest you to hear that *Dubliners*, announced for publication for the third time yesterday 20 January, is again postponed *sine die* and without a word of explanation. I know the name and tradition of my country too well to be surprised at receiving three scrawled lines in return for five years of constant service to my art and constant waiting and indifference and disloyalty in return for the 150,000 francs[2] of continental money which I have deflected into the pockets of hungry Irishmen and women since they drove me out of their hospitable bog six years ago.

Joyce announced that month his intention of leaving Trieste, after another fight with Stanislaus, who appears to have entered into some sort of partnership with a 'Cockney virgin', one Miss O'Brien, over pupils. 'I intend to do what Parnell was advised to do on a similar occasion: clear out, the conflict being beneath my dignity, and leave you and the *cattolicissime*[3] to make what you can of the city discovered by my courage (and Nora's) seven years ago, whither you and they came in obedience to my summons, from your ignorant and famine-stricken and treacherous country.'

But he stayed, choosing to fight his demons for the time being from Trieste. Roberts asked him to omit from 'Ivy Day in the Committee Room', certain references to the late Edward VII, these apparently being Roberts's only objection to the book. Joyce answered that Grant Richards had not objected when Edward was alive and he could not see why Roberts should object when Edward was dead. He attempted once more a legal remedy but was told by a Dublin solicitor that no Dublin jury would uphold his case if he had made obnoxious reference to His late Majesty (This was

---

[2] Presumably a reference to the cinema and to his efforts to sell Irish tweed in Trieste. He did in fact arrange the sale of a few suits.

[3] Eva and Eileen attended mass. Joyce and Nora did not, except when there was liturgical or musical spectacle he wished to enjoy. But when there was he stood quietly in a corner and did not participate in the ceremony.

nonsense. Dubliners did not feel any strong attachment to the crown. They might, on the other hand, object to reference to Edward's loose habits with women. But the pretence was otherwise). It would be necessary also to lodge a bond for £100 with the court, Joyce being a non-resident.

This course of action being blocked, Joyce decided to go to the top and accordingly wrote to Edward's son, George V, enquiring if he took exception to the passage concerning his father. Buckingham Palace replied, in August 1911, that literary criticism was not within the king's province. Very well then, there was public opinion to apply to. Joyce did so, with a long letter addressed to the principal Irish newspapers, setting forth the history of his book and conceding sorrowfully in the last paragraph permission to Messrs Maunsel the right to publish 'Ivy Day' in whatsoever form they chose. 'Their attitude as an Irish publishing firm may be judged by Irish public opinion. I, as a writer, protest against the systems (legal, social and ceremonious) which have brought me to this pass.'

Two papers published the letter, *Sinn Fein* and the *Northern Whig,* the latter omitting the controversial passage which Joyce had thoughtfully included. Irish public opinion did not take notice, and neither did George Roberts. It was about then that Joyce took the manuscript of *A Portrait* and flung it on the fire. It happened that Eileen entered the room at that moment and was able to fish it out for him. He thanked her with three bars of soap, a pair of mittens and the acknowledgement there were pages in it he could never have rewritten.

In Dublin his youngest sister, Mabel, had died at the age of seventeen of typhus brought on as John Joyce said by life in 'this accursed hole', her exit from this world attended by Doctor Macnamara of the South Dublin Workhouse. John Joyce felt more broken than ever by the loss of one child whom he felt had loved him and talked again of the desirability of a quick death, lending credence to his sorrow by his anxiety to pass on to his eldest son those family portraits he had carried around all his life. The death of his sister added more fuel to Joyce's bitterness towards his own country. Ireland had lived up to his description of her. She *was* the sow that eats her own farrow.

In April of 1912 Joyce made another attempt to better his

circumstances, this time by attempting to qualify himself to teach in one of the better Italian state schools. In the examinations, spread over three days, and taking place in the city of Padua, he demonstrated his modest skills in the Italian language and not so modest skills in English (in spite of being asked to contribute an essay, in English, on the uncongenial theme of Charles Dickens. He got fifty marks out of fifty for that particular effort). His examiners decided that he was competent but the Ministry of Education at Rome chose to question his degree from the Royal University and, having done so, discovered that no reciprocity existed between the respective ministries, Italian and British, in the matter of recognising one another's degrees. Joyce was therefore officially an ignoramus and unfit, as he put it later under slightly different circumstances, 'to teach the sons of bitches broken English.'

The Universita Popolare, however, allowed the ignoramus to address them in two more lectures, on William Blake and Daniel Defoe. He had taken the trouble to read *Robinson Crusoe* carefully and enlightened his audience on that score, labelling the castaway for reasons both flattering and unflattering ('manly independence . . . unconscious cruelty . . . persistence . . . slow but effective intelligence . . . sexual apathy . . . practical and well-balanced religiosity . . . calculating silence') the archetypal English mind.

As for Blake, Joyce did not saddle him with those windy mysticisms inflicted on his memory by Yeats. He felt a natural affinity with an artist who had chosen for his life's companion a woman as ignorant as Nora: 'In his [Blake's] unlimited egoism,' Joyce said, 'he wanted the soul of his beloved to be entirely a slow and painful creation of his own, freeing and purifying daily under his very eyes, the demon (as he says) hidden in the cloud.' (It would be enlightening to discover if Nora heard this remark and, if so, what she thought of it.)

Nora's soul might not be freeing and purifying at the rate Joyce desired but one test she did pass with flying colours, that supremely important one of fidelity, and in the process gave her husband the necessary remaining material for *Exiles*. The villain this time was Roberto Prezioso, who provided not only Robert Hand's first name in the play but also his method of attempted seduction, if not his character and nationality. Prezioso had been close friend as well as benefactor to Joyce, publishing articles which really the citizens of Trieste might have done quite well without, but his admiration for Nora's ripening beauty led him to betray that friendship and this time Joyce had a *real* betrayal to ponder, not an imaginary one. Prezioso had fallen into the habit of visiting Nora in the afternoons to pay his compliments and express his admiration. 'The sun shines for you,' he told her (it sounds more impressive in Italian), a remark which duly appears in *Exiles* and *Ulysses*. Nora preened herself, even to the extent of getting her hair done, but reported all details of Prezioso's overtures to Joyce. He did not mind, indeed, was flattered that other men should find her as desirable as he did, until, some time in 1911 or 1912[4] Prezioso attempted to make love to her. Like any normally jealous male, Joyce decided that things had gone far enough and took the matter up with Prezioso, not however with the near insufferable nobility of Richard Rowan (who behaves as one ought to behave rather than as one does behave) but with the offended dignity of the self-righteous betrayed. He accosted Prezioso in the street to deliver his reprimand. Tullio Silvestri, the painter, who observed the confrontation as he passed by, saw tears of humiliation stream down Prezioso's cheeks.

The rift lasted until the summer of 1912, when articles by Joyce began to appear again in the *Piccolo* after an absence of a year and a half. Joyce remembered, of course, and used what he remembered, but was not inclined to be vindictive. Prezioso had had the grace to cry. Besides, one feels a curious affinity with, and compassion for those who choose the same loved object as oneself, at the same time – so long as they do not succeed.

In June 1912 it was the virtuous Nora's turn to visit Ireland, whence she had not been for eight years. On her way through Dublin to Galway she might stop and intercede on behalf of *Dubliners* with Roberts. Such was Joyce's bizarre idea. Whatever chance there was of Nora's charm working on that slippery gentleman was ruined by her taking along with her both John Joyce and brother Charlie, newly retreated from Boston with a brood of three children, unemployed and roofless. 'Well Jim and I am sure you

[4] Richard Ellmann's chronology. Professor Ellmann's astute detective work and interviewing of Francini Bruni, Eileen Joyce and the painter Tullio Silvestri uncovered this episode. But he gets at least one date wrong in his account of it (Richard Ellmann, *James Joyce*, OUP 1959). Nevertheless, this account depends on his, since no witnesses survive and none left a record.

would like to know something about your publisher,' Nora guesses three days after arriving in Dublin, 'well on Tuesday your Father Charley and myself went in and just pinned that charming gentleman well I asked what he meant by treating you in such a manner but your Father then began to speak so that Roberts took no further notice of me only spoke to your father he made some excuse saying he was very busy and said to call again and so Charley and myself called twice the next day but I am sorry to say he kept out of our way but Charley will do all he can he says he will watch him every day then he will write to you.'

Joyce left Trieste for Dublin before he got that letter, in a state of dull anger because he had had only a scrawled postcard in five days (five days!) since Nora had left. He had a bad pain in his side, which he was sure was the symptom of the onset of some fatal disease, and had to wake Georgie three times in the night for fear of being left alone to face death. And why wasn't Nora in raptures at the sight of the places of their courtship? She had in fact stayed in Finn's Hotel for two nights but that was more likely to exhibit herself to former workmates as a person who *stayed* in hotels these days instead of working in them.

She had gone on ahead with Lucia, the idea being that she might wheedle from her Uncle Michael enough money to send the fare for James and Georgio. Michael Healy, unfortunately, had squandered all his available cash ('a buckett full of money' said Nora) on getting a superfluous bone removed from his nose. Joyce had already presented himself to Schmitz with a request for payment in advance. As usual, he obliged, and Joyce set out for Dublin in a bad temper, for the third time in three years, and for the last time in his life.

Passing through London he called on Yeats, who was polite, which surprised him, and handed out tea and fruit. Joyce had decided the Italians would appreciate *Countess Cathleen* and broached to Yeats the production possibilities of a translation he had written with the assistance of Vidacovic. Yeats, who had completed a revised version of the play, was amenable so long as his new version was used. This was despatched to Trieste (Nothing came of this project. Vidacovic disliked the new version and refused to work on it. Yeats refused to allow performance of the old. It is a safe bet the Italians would have flocked to neither).

179

On this trip he made the acquaintance for the first time of James Stephens, whose work he had enjoyed (Stephens, unlike Yeats, was to succeed in writing well about the Gaelic past). His humour was quite different from Joyce's but after this first, rather unfortunate, meeting, they got on so well that Joyce felt able, twenty years later, to make the quite ridiculous suggestion that if he died, Stephens might complete *Finnegans Wake* for him.

'Come and have a drink,' said Stephens at their first meeting in Dawson Street. Joyce was in a bad mood. En route, Stephens, at a loss for conversation, told bad jokes but Joyce responded to nothing until he had ingested one third of a 'tailor' of malt (whiskey), an Irish measure. 'It takes seven tailors to make a man,' remarked Stephens brightly, 'but two of these tailors make a twin. Seven of them make a clan.' Stephens was on the right track: that sort of thing interested Joyce. He spoke, but the conversation did not proceed happily. Stephens, said Joyce, did not know the difference between a colon and a semicolon. His knowledge of Irish life was non-Catholic (Stephens being disabled by Protestanism from any proper knowledge of it) and so, non-existent. He would be better at a good job like shoe-shining. Stephens confided in turn that he had never read a word of Joyce's and never would, unless asked to review it destructively. Parting words: 'You should engrave on your banner and on your notebook the slogan "Rejoice and be exceedingly bad",' said Stephens.

'Ah,' said Joyce.

The first interview with Roberts went not very well. 'The Giant's Causeway is soft putty compared to you,' complained the Ulsterman, thinking of his own geography. Roberts suggested two possibilities by way of compromise. Either the offending passages from 'Ivy Day' and 'An Encounter' might be replaced with asterisks, with an explanatory preface from Joyce, or he might buy the sheets and publish the book himself, using a London firm to distribute it.

Departing Roberts to ponder this choice, Joyce set off for Galway, where he settled down to have a good time, brushing aside cries of anguish from Stanislaus, who had to deal with yet another threat of eviction on his brother's behalf. James, months previous, had been served with notice of eviction after paying the rent late. This had been suspended, according to him, by the agent involved, who had 'prevented' him from seeing a new apartment by assuring him, *in the presence of witnesses*, that the landlord, Picciola, was really quite fond of him and intended taking English lessons from him. Joyce found it easy enough to bluster from Galway. 'Whoever tries to eject me from that flat will pass a damn bad quarter of an hour.' He would sue the pig Picciola and the lying thief of an agent for 2,000 crowns damages. Stanislaus, with a distraught Eileen about to be thrown on the streets (Eva had gone back to Dublin homesick) found it easier to give up the fight and secure his brother a new flat.

Several projects engrossed Joyce in Galway, one of them a grandiose scheme to construct in Galway City a vast transatlantic port. This appeared to be of particular interest to Romeo Bartoli, a Triestine, who was qualified for such enterprises by his expertise in the singing of old music. More modestly Joyce set off for Clifden in the hope of interviewing Marconi, who had established a radio station there, but failed to find him. He took Nora to the Galway races and also to the Aran Islands, contributing an article to the *Piccolo* on these charming fishing outposts, describing them in a riot of political imagination as 'England's Safety Valve in Case of War'.

He made too a pilgrimage to the graveyard at Oughterard where Michael Bodkin, who had loved Nora and maybe lost his life for her, lay buried (In his writing Oughterard becomes Rahoon for reasons of sonority: the first syllable of 'Oughterard' makes a near rhyme with that word in Nora's letters which was 'brief, brutal, irresistible and devilish'). In that graveyard he found a headstone inscribed J. Joyce to which, naturally, he attached great significance (an inscription as rare in a Galway cemetery as J. Jarvis is in a Welsh one). He took up his father's pastime of rowing, and cycled a good deal. Michael Healy was not so lacking in funds that he could not feed his guests 'in great style'. Nora, to her husband's satisfaction (they were passing themselves off to Mrs Barnacle as properly married) was getting plumper. 'O, you are getting a show,' said the relatives. 'You are so fat!'

'Well what have you to say to Jim now,' Nora boasted to Eileen back in Trieste, 'after all our little squabble he could not live without me for a month.'

Joyce now earned for himself Stephen's title in *Ulysses*, 'bullock-befriending bard,' by concerning himself, at the urging of an Ulster friend in Trieste, Henry Blackwood Price, with foot-and-mouth disease, the only cure for which had been, in Britain and Ireland (and still is), slaughtering and burning of the infected beasts. Blackwood Price had heard of a serum cure developed in Austria and was in a fever to communicate this news to Ireland. Joyce obligingly put him in touch with William Field MP, president of the Irish Cattle Traders' Society, but Blackwood Price urged that Joyce might advance his career by taking up the question himself. 'You will get your name up if you write this up.' So Joyce, somewhat to the surprise of those who knew him, contributed an article on the dread agricultural scourge to the *Freeman's Journal*, without, however, finding new career opportunities in that direction. He parodies his own, and Price's, concern for the health of Irish beeves in the schoolmaster scene of *Ulysses*.

Still in Galway, he heard from Roberts, who now proposed to turn the printed sheets of *Dubliners* over to him. He could then offer them to Grant Richards. Since Richards's only objection had been that he could not get a printer to touch the book, that problem would be obviated. Joyce, knowing that Richards had other reasons for fearing publication, decided to get a lawyer and unwisely chose John Lidwell, a drinking companion of his father's.

On 17 August he set out from Galway to do battle, leaving Nora behind with the children. 'Courage Angelo Mio,' she encouraged by telegram. After a two-hour interview with Roberts the decision was reached that the book should be sent to Lidwell for his opinion. Meanwhile Joyce busied himself trying to find employment for Charlie. Offered the post of tenor at Sandymount Church for the magnificent sum of £10 a year, he arranged an audition instead for Charlie whom he now found a 'decent poor fellow'. Decent he may have been but his habits still landed him in trouble with the police. He had been fired from a job with the telephone company and was living on the dole. His elder brother, while blaming him for his poor condition, found him useful for the running of errands.

Lidwell's opinion, when Joyce at length succeeded in dragging it out of him, was far from helpful. He took it upon himself to pronounce on the moral question, bringing to the author's attention the fact that Dublin was blessed with a Vigilance Committee whose object was energetically to seek out and suppress all writings of immoral tendencies. Concerning 'An Encounter' he had this to say:

It has been well said that some errors would never have thriven were it not for learned refutation, there are some vices, and that which the paragraphs refer to is one of them, which in its prosecution and punishment should receive as little publicity as possible. Magistrates are directed to hear such cases in private and the Executive as much as possible endeavours to prevent its even being brought before the public – and I might quote Gibbon's *Decline and Fall* to show how much the subject is loathed 'I touch with reluctance and dispatch with impatience this most odious vice of which modesty rejects the name and nature abominates the idea.'

So much for the Love That Dare Not Speak Its Name: hardly calculated to persuade Roberts to publish. Joyce demanded a more satisfactory note, chasing Lidwell from his office to the bar of the Ormonde Hotel, where he was engaged in swapping dirty stories about country priests with John Joyce. Eventually he was persuaded to admit in writing, 'As the passages you have shown me are not likely to be taken serious notice of by the Advisers of the Crown, they would not interfere with the publication, nor do I consider a conviction could be easily obtained.' Lidwell gave it to Joyce as his private opinion that 'An Encounter' was disgusting and suggested he give it up and write a nice clean story about Ringsend instead. That distinctly noisome but otherwise unremarkable district had historical associations, he said, which Joyce had apparently overlooked.

Roberts was not impressed with Joyce's bit of paper, advancing as excuse that it was not addressed to him. Joyce asked Lidwell to readdress it – to Roberts. Lidwell refused on the ground that Roberts was not his client. Joyce offered to sign an agreement to indemnify the firm for £60, the approximate cost of bringing out the book in case it were seized. Roberts countered with a request for securities amounting to £2,000. Joyce declining, Roberts announced that the matter was at an end: he would take legal advice and not publish. Joyce would still not give up, ignoring all the indications that Roberts plainly did not *want* to publish the book. He wrote down his next proposal, which was that the book be published, without 'An Encounter' but with a note signed by Joyce to the effect that the book was incomplete. No other changes would be made.

To this proposal Roberts made the excuse that he must submit it to his solicitor, who happened to be in London. While this process took place Joyce complained to Stanislaus that the whole business was costing him a lot in standing drinks for everyone. Stanislaus reminded him rather urgently that his earning capacity was required immediately in Trieste. That hair-shirt of his was itching.

Joyce, suffering from another kind of itch, got himself a double-bedded room and wrote summoning Nora from Galway, hoping she was as plump as she had been and that her naughty tight lilac blouse was clean. 'The Abbey Theatre will be open and they will give plays of Yeats and Synge. You have a right to be there because you are my bride: and I am one of the writers of this generation who are perhaps creating at last a conscience in the soul of this wretched race.'

Roberts's solicitors now produced a new red herring: the book was full of libels, so many there was no point in instancing them. Litigation being the national pastime of Ireland, publication would produce a shoal of suits.[5] Even if all detectable libels were struck out there would remain the danger that some had been overlooked. To provide against that danger the author would be required to deposit a surety of £1,000 in Maunsel's bank account. Since that was scarcely possible, the only alternative was that Roberts should take his solicitors' advice and proceed against Joyce to recover costs and expenses for time, labour and materials expended on the book, Joyce having broken his contract by submitting a manuscript which he clearly knew to be libellous.

This latest piece of treachery[6] made some impression on Joyce. Roberts contrived to be absent from his office when Joyce called to collect the letter, so Joyce went off to show it to Lidwell, who agreed it was a pity but said Roberts was quite right. Joyce sat in his office for a while contemplating the purchase of a revolver with which to 'put some daylight into my publisher' (a common fantasy of authors). Instead he went back in the afternoon to resume the argument. This time he offered to take Roberts around Dublin in a car and get signed releases from each of the publicans mentioned

---

[5] When eventually *Dubliners* was published there were no libel suits.
[6] Joyce was not the only writer to suffer at Roberts's hands. 'I don't know why [Liam] O'Flaherty cuts me,' Roberts once remarked. 'After all, I never published him.'

in *Dubliners,* and from the secretary of the railway company mentioned (who, presumably, might object to the idea that someone might commit suicide under one of their trains). Roberts refused, saying he would write again to London. Joyce continued to waste his time: as any experienced author could have told him, civility is wasted on publishers.

Another interview took place a few days later. This time Joyce had Colum with him to lend support. He consented to omit 'An Encounter', delete or change parts of 'Ivy Day' and change the names of all public houses mentioned to fictitious ones, on condition that the book was published before 6 October. Colum asked innocently if the book was about public houses. Roberts left the room twice in a rage. When his bad temper took possession of him, remarked Colum 'one could see his narrowed eyes looking round for the carving knife.' It seemed to Colum neither an interview nor a consultation but an argument that could get nowhere. He had asked Thomas Kettle, who was a lawyer, for his opinion and Kettle had answered that Maunsel would indeed be liable to libel suits (Kettle himself took particular exception to 'An Encounter'. He told Joyce 'I'll slate that book'. Joyce did not mind).

It was plain to Colum as it was not to Joyce that Roberts would not publish under any circumstance, but he told Joyce to come back again in another few days. So the affair dragged on without that merciful ending which Colum thought would have been best, if Roberts had only said to Joyce, 'I'm bloody sorry but I did not know what I was letting myself in for when I passed your manuscript for publication. No matter what you cut off it now there will be actions that would ruin Maunsels.'

But Roberts did not say that. At the end of August he requested new and larger changes and excisions. Joyce flatly refused. Roberts made a generous offer: he would sell Joyce the sheets for £30, the true cost being £57. The idea dawned on Joyce of setting up his own publishing company, the only snag being the usual one. Colum incautiously mentioned that he had had an advance of £40 from a London publisher. 'Joyce looked significantly at the one whom I took to be his brother [Colum was of course mistaken. Stanislaus was in Trieste], as if to say that forty pounds would be the crock of gold.' But Colum held on to his gold.

Looking for premises for his new publishing house, Joyce found two unfurnished rooms in Jervis Street, around the corner from his last Irish business venture, the Volta. The rent was five shillings a week. The business could be conducted in one room while Charlie and his brood were accommodated in the other.

A new obstacle appeared: Roberts's printer, John Falconer, had apparently got around to reading what he had printed, and refused to release the sheets. Joyce had changed lawyers and now consulted his new solicitor, one Dixon. Dixon told him Falconer was bound to hand over the sheets to Maunsel but that he, Dixon, no longer wished to have anything to do with *Dubliners*. 'Why do you not use your talents for the betterment of your country and people?' he asked. Joyce, instead of answering as rudely as he was entitled to, made the peculiar reply that he did, by writing articles about Ireland for the Italian Press, and by selling Irish tweed though that was not at all in his line.

There was haggling about money with Roberts: it was eventually agreed that Joyce would pay him £15 within fifteen days and get 104 copies, the other 896 to be handed over on receipt of another £15, Joyce to sign a document releasing Maunsel from all possibility of being tainted by association with *Dubliners*. Nor could he call his publishing house *The Jervis Press*. Maunsel had works in Jervis Street. Joyce agreed to call it *The Liffey Press*. Falconer was equally shy of any association, so a cloak-and-dagger operation was arranged. An anonymous caller, unknown either to Falconer or Maunsel, would pick up the 104 copies and take them to No 2 Jervis Street and present them to Charlie, without revealing his identity. Charlie would then employ another mysterious messenger to bring the books to the binder.

This fine plan collapsed on 10 September with an absolute refusal from Falconer to part with the sheets. Roberts and Joyce called on Dixon, who told them that the only legal remedy was for Joyce to sue Maunsel and for Roberts in turn to sue Falconer. Such a process would be long and expensive. Dixon did mention that Roberts need not bother paying the printer, who would thereby lose his £57. Joyce decided that was something to work on. He went alone to Falconer to offer to buy the sheets. He would publish it anywhere they liked, Dublin, London, Trieste – with his own name on it as publisher and printer. Nothing doing, said Falconer. They did not mind the loss of £57. They had learned their lesson and would never again be fooled into printing that sort of thing.

And what would they do with the sheets, Joyce asked? They would burn them, they said.

Joyce went back to the Murray's, where he and Nora and the children were staying, ready at last to give up and go back to Trieste. He had managed to get hold of only one set of sheets and in the morning that book 'the child which I have carried for years and years in the womb of the imagination . . . [and fed] . . . day after day out of my brain and my memory' would go up in flames.

He ignored the steak waiting for him and went upstairs to the piano to sing a love song. Nora stayed where she was, thinking him rude.

'Ah! Do go up to him,' said Aunt Josephine. 'Can't you see, all that is for *you*.'

Colum gave him a letter of introduction to his London publisher and Joyce set out from Dublin for the last time on 11 September, never again to set foot in Ireland. That morning the 1,000 copies of *Dubliners* were destroyed. The route home was via London (where he called on Boon, Colum's publishers, to leave him *Dubliners*. He did not like it), Flushing (in Holland) and Munich. Waiting for the train at Flushing, he began to compose another of his doggerel broadsides, which he called *Gas from a Burner*. In it the entire personnel of Irish literature gets savaged. The words are put into the mouth of a character who is a combination of Roberts and Falconer. 'I printed the great John Milicent Synge / Who soars above on an angel's wing / In the playboy shift that he pinched as swag / From Maunsel's manager's travelling-bag.' Cousins's verse 'would give you a heart-burn on your arse.' Colum, Moore and 'Gregory of the Golden Mouth' (and purse) were equally lambasted.

Ladies and gents, you are here assembled
To hear why earth and heaven trembled
Because of the black and sinister arts
Of an Irish writer in foreign parts.
He sent me a book ten years ago:
I read it a hundred times or so,
Backwards and forwards, down and up,
Through both ends of a telescope.
I printed it all to the very last word
But by the mercy of the Lord

The darkness of my mind was rent
And I saw the writer's foul intent.
But I owe a duty to Ireland:
I hold her honour in my hand,
This lovely land that always sent
Her writers and artists to banishment
And in a spirit of Irish fun
Betrayed her own leaders, one by one.
'Twas Irish humour, wet and dry,
Flung quicklime into Parnell's eye;
'Tis Irish brains that save from doom
The leaky barge of the Bishop of Rome
For everyone knows the Pope can't belch
Without the consent of Billy Walsh.
O Ireland my first and only love
Where Christ and Caesar are hand and glove!
O lovely land where the shamrock grows!
(Allow me, ladies, to blow my nose) ...

Who was it said: Resist not evil?
I'll burn that book, so help me devil.
I'll sing a psalm as I watch it burn
And the ashes I'll keep in a one-handled urn.
I'll penance do with farts and groans
Kneeling upon my marrowbones.
This very next lent I will unbare
My penitent buttocks to the air
And sobbing beside my printing press
My awful sin I will confess.
My Irish foreman from Bannockburn
Shall dip his right hand in the urn
And sign crisscross with reverent thumb
Memento homo *upon my bum.*

Joyce had it printed and sent it back to Charlie to distribute. 'He's an out and out ruffian without the spark of a gentleman in him,' said John Joyce when he saw it, but Charlie handed it out anyway. John Joyce had already decided that *Dubliners* was a 'blackguardly' production.

Colum said, before he left, 'If you are in London and want somebody to help you with publishers, see a man named Ezra Pound.' 'Pound took me out of the gutter,' said Joyce. But not for the time being. He let Pound make the overture.

'It is dangerous to leave one's country,' Joyce told Schmitz, who asked him why *Exiles* was so named, 'but still more dangerous to go back to it, for then your fellow-countrymen, if they can, will drive a knife into your heart.'

They had burnt his book.

Chapter Fourteen
An Epic of Two Races

Well, at least he always *thought* they had burnt his book. Roberts afterwards swore it had merely been guillotined into shreds, which would no doubt have been great consolation to the author. Armed with one set of sheets he allowed Martin Secker the opportunity of adding his distinguished name to the list of publishers who refused it and got down again to 'teaching the sons of bitches broken English,' this time a little more securely, in Scuola Revoltella Superiore di Commercio of Trieste, devoting the afternoons to private pupils. In February of 1913 he proposed to Elkin Mathews, from whom he had bought twenty-four copies of *Chamber Music* at trade price for sale in Trieste, that he publish *Dubliners* with Joyce sharing the expenses if it were printed in London or totally assuming them if it were printed in Trieste. Mathews would then be left only with the cost of bringing out the book. Where precisely the author was to get the money was not explained. Mathews promptly declined, in spite of an offer of Joyce's to write a preface explaining 'the deliberate conspiracy of certain forces in Ireland to silence me.' This he wrote anyway, in November, and remained puzzled that it should not strike publishers as a first-rate advertisement for his book.

He decided to try Grant Richards again, thinking that recent events in Ireland (posturings in north and south threatened an apparently imminent civil war) might have rekindled interest in his country. This time Richards agreed to proceed, in March. By then Joyce had heard from that Ezra Pound whom Colum had recommended to him eighteen months before. Pound, one of the strangest Americans ever to inflict himself on literary London, was adept at finding patrons, bullying editors and writers, and making 'discoveries,' two others being Robert Frost and T. S. Eliot. Rebecca West, then a literary editor (no function was precise) of *The New Freewoman,* a journal which had not yet made up its mind between feminism and individualism, had asked him to contribute one page of a literary nature per fortnightly issue. Pound in time bullied his way to domination of five and more pages. Miss West, despairing of the loose organization, left the paper, to be replaced by Richard Aldington, with Pound's approval. Shortly after, the paper, accused of selling 'aeolian harps under the name of tin whistles' changed its name to *The Egoist*.

In December 1913 Pound, in spite of having no formal connection with *The Egoist* and no funds to dispense, wrote to Joyce suggesting he contribute as a way of keeping his name familiar. He mentioned also two American outlets which did pay, H. L. Mencken and George Jean Nathan's the *Smart Set*, and *Poetry*. Pound had heard of Joyce from Yeats. 'From what W.B.Y. says I imagine we have a hate or two in common.'

In that supposition Pound was mistaken. Joyce was not so extravagantly talented in that direction as himself, nor did their hates always coincide. Pound, however, displayed one trait which immediately endeared him to Joyce, who had obligingly sent him his work. He pronounced *A Portrait* to be 'damn fine stuff' and passed it on to *The Egoist*, hoping they would not jibe at 'one or two' of Joyce's phrases. He supposed also that the stories of *Dubliners* were good, though 'An Encounter' would not do for any magazine, and sent three of them on to the *Smart Set*.

Miss Dora Marsden, editor of *The Egoist*, glanced at the part of *A Portrait* given her and decided, without taking the trouble to read more than a little, that it would do. She was short of copy. The first, entirely unalarming instalment duly appeared in the issue dated 2 February which, sheerly by coincidence, happened to be Joyce's thirty-second birthday. 1914, he might suspect now, could be his year of miracles.

In June that year Dora Marsden departed her responsibility as editor of *The Egoist* to devote her time to philosophical work and the mantle fell to Harriet Shaw Weaver, a spinster lady approaching middle age, daughter of a pious, and rich, country doctor. Miss Weaver, apparently devoid of sexual instinct, unless repressed, made up the deficiency with a strong passion for social betterment. As a young woman she had been refused permission by her mother to read *Adam Bede*, on the grounds that novels were at least frivolous, if not perfidious, but managed to cultivate a taste for literature anyway, a circumstance which turned out fortuitous for the poverty-stricken writer in Trieste. Miss Weaver had money, even if she felt ashamed of it as 'unearned income' and after some years devoted to the Whitechapel Committee of the Society for Organising Charitable Relief and Repressing Mendicity (appropriate training for the future benefactress of James Joyce), turned her attentions, and her cheque-book, to the problems of Feminism and Individualism.

Miss Weaver's first step on the road to eventual publication of *A Portrait* had been the sending of money to a rescue fund for *The Freewoman*, Precursor of *The New Freewoman*, in turn ancestor (or ancestress) of *The Egoist*. By the time she assumed the editorship, nearly two years later, she had assumed also the burden of most of the finance. But she preferred to keep her generosity to herself. She was able to, since she was business manager, and concealed her help under the entry 'anonymous donation' when she did the bookkeeping. By the time she (unwillingly) became editor she was convinced of Joyce's worth and determined to help him. Her generosity to Joyce was to be of enormous importance to him, particularly once the war got going. No doubt, with his considerable talent for landing on his feet, he would have found some alternative means of survival, but Harriet Weaver was to save him the trouble.

Not only did Miss Weaver intend publishing Joyce, even though she had to keep *The Egoist* afloat to do it, she intended also protecting the text of his work against 'anyone who threatened, by chance or by choice, to corrupt it'. Her printer, usually regarded as an enlightened man, did threaten just that. The second paragraph of Chapter III would have to come out, that passage concerning the whores of Nightown:

— Hello, Bertie, any good in your mind?
— Is that you, pigeon?
— Number ten. Fresh Nelly is waiting on you.
— Good night, husband! Coming in to have a short time?[1]

Miss Weaver protested, to no avail. The printers insisted on the cut and since the alternative was to hold up publication, the issue

[1] Miss Weaver's printers, who had begun with the eleventh instalment, taking over from another firm, had substituted inverted commas for the dashes Joyce preferred to use to indicate dialogue. Miss Weaver soon put that right. Joyce thought inverted commas an offence to the eye and an unnecessary alienation.

12   Joyce and Philippe Soupault going over the 'French' 'Translation' of 'Anna Livia
Plurabelle'. Note the ruined condition of Joyce's left eye after repeated iridectomy.

13 Jim and Nora with Herbert Gorman,
his elusive biographer. Note tennis shoes
and the ubiquitous ashplant, that trademark
which came in useful for warding off canine
threats.

14 Zurich, 1938. Joyce at the meeting of
the waters. 'Beside the rivering waters of,
hitherandthithering waters of. Night!'

duly appeared, with the paragraph missing, on 1 August, three days before another interesting event, the outbreak of the First World War.

In Trieste Joyce had resumed the composition of the two remaining chapters of *A Portrait*, possibly spurred on by the necessity of finishing it in time to conform to Miss Weaver's schedule of serialization. *Dubliners* had finally been launched upon the world on 15 June, under Grant Richards's imprint, in an edition of 1,250 copies, 120 of them contracted by the author. The sales limped, but the reviews were generally favourable. Public morality did not collapse and nobody sued. Pound reviewed the stories enthusiastically in *The Egoist*, and the *New Statesman* suspected the possibility of genius.

The form of *Exiles* was now more or less firmly fixed in Joyce's mind. The previous November he had completed copious notes on characterization:

N.(B.) – 13 Nov. 1913
Garter, precious, Prezioso, Bodkin, music, pale green, bracelet, cream sweets, lily of the valley, convent garden (Galway), sea.

The notes extend to ten pages. But even if Joyce had the play fully worked out, he could not bring himself to write until *A Portrait* was out of the way. *Ulysses* would have to wait too. To the end of *A Portrait* is appended:

Dublin 1904
Trieste 1914

But Miss Weaver had to leave instalments out of *The Egoist*, pending delivery from Trieste, the ostensible reason being that the author was in Austria, from whence postal delivery had been suspended due to the existence of a state of war between that country and Britain. By a strange chance the last instalment to appear for the time being, on 1 September, was the concluding part of Chapter III. Perhaps Miss Weaver overestimated the distance between Trieste and neutral Italy, and overestimated the difficulty of getting mail over that rather loose border.

Joyce got on with it and finished the last two chapters by November, transmitting them to London via Italy and Switzerland. Miss Weaver had a little more censorship trouble. Her printer cut

Stephen's musing on the seashore in Chapter IV but found nothing objectionable in Chapter V, apart from the words 'farted' and 'ballocks' (neither word known to Miss Weaver), whose publication was completed by September 1915, with Joyce spending several months of his creative energies on revising the last chapter.

1914 had most likely seen also the compilation, if not the complete composition, of an unfinished work, *Giacomo Joyce*, which, like the epiphanies, is somewhere beween prose and poetry and provided material plundered for later work.

'When will you write an Italian work about our town? Why not?' Schmitz enquired in June of 1914 after reading his presentation copy of *Dubliners*. Joyce began to do so, using as material his infatuation for a young pupil of his, Amalia Popper. It was an unrequited passion, but a powerful one.

Miss Popper's family was rich, her father a Jewish businessman of the town. She accepted with amused condescension her teacher's admiration which, in the nature of things, he could only express clumsily:

> I rush out of the tobacco-shop and call her name. She turns and halts to hear my jumbled words of lessons, hours, lessons, hours: and slowly her pale cheeks are flushed with a kindling opal light. Nay, nay, be not afraid!

Joyce mocks himself:

> Easy now, Jamesy! Did you never walk the streets of Dublin at night sobbing another name?

But dreams in lust:

> She raises her arms in an effort to hook at the nape of her neck a gown of black veiling. She cannot: no, she cannot. She moves backwards towards me mutely. I raise my arms to help her: her arms fall. I hold the websoft edges of her gown and drawing them out to hook them I see through the opening of the black veil her lithe body sheathed in an orange shift. It slips its ribbons of moorings at her shoulders and falls slowly: a lithe smooth naked body shimmering with silvery scales. It slips slowly over the slender buttocks of smooth polished silver and over their furrow, a tarnished silver shadow . . . Fingers, cold and calm and moving . . . A touch, a touch.

194

Joyce did not get a touch, and did not elaborate the document called *Giacomo* (after that other comic lover, Casanova). Perhaps he had decided to confine all his writing to Howth Castle and Environs. Perhaps, prudently, he thought that Nora would be less than pleased with this love story. He contented himself with making a fair copy, as he had made a fair copy of *Chamber Music*, and abandoned that in Trieste, where it was rescued by his brother. Miss Popper, a young person of quality who never blows her nose, who is 'rounded by the lathe of intermarriage and ripened in the forcing-house of the seclusion of her race,' becomes a fragrant memory but a dangerous one. Giacomo may remember sitting high among the stinks and farts of the cheap seats at the opera, looking down at her all night, sitting in the stalls, wondering have her pure fingers ever erred, but he fears that he is past dreams of young love:

> Youth has an end: the end is here. It will never be. You know that well. What then? Write it, damn you, write it! What else are you good for?

Joyce was able to take his own advice, at least so far as writing was concerned.

He was able to recognize that Amalia was a dangerous passion, and even if he had not been able to, then her father was there gently to hint to him – 'My daughter has a great admiration for her English teacher' – an admiration which her English teacher would be better advised not to take advantage of. Joyce got the message, and appropriated the first name of this courteous Jew, Leopoldo Popper, for Leopold Bloom in *Ulysses*.

He had been forming the character of his strange hero for some years, since the idea of a short story about the one-day's wanderings of a Dublin Jew first occurred to him in 1906. He was curious about Alfred Hunter, who was a Jew, a Dubliner and burdened with an unfaithful wife. More important, Hunter may have been that kindly gentleman who assisted Joyce after the fracas in Stephen's Green in 1904 as Leopold Bloom is also to dust down and take home Stephen Dedalus after the drunken fight of the Nighttown episodes of *Ulysses*. One could see why his Ulysses was a Jew, but why was he the son of a Hungarian? Joyce was asked. 'Because he was,' said Joyce, indicating Teodoro Mayer as another Bloom prototype. Mayer was the proprietor of *Piccolo della Serra*, and his father had been a Hungarian peddler of postcards. Schmitz, who did not practice Judaism (his wife was a Christian) provided elementary instruction in his abandoned religion, and lent Bloom his quality of self-deprecating humour.

Bloom was invested also with some characteristics of his creator, as he saw himself – kindliness, tolerance, non-violence, curiosity, a fly-trap memory, an ability to detect mythological and historical echoes in mundane affairs – above all, middle age and sadness at the passing of youth. After his thirtieth birthday Joyce bored his friends with frequent reminders that the Romans had set that day as the end of adolescence.

Joyce had his Ulysses. Penelope was not far to seek. She slept with him every night, and if she was not an entirely satisfactory model, well, others would appear in time. As for Telemachus, son of the wanderer, Stephen Dedalus would do very well. There was material left which had not been used in *A Portrait*. Gogarty and the tower episode had not yet been dealt with. For other characters, there was the whole of Dublin. Circe turned men into swine: Joyce was well acquainted with the madame who did that every night in Mecklenburgh Street. Cyclops? Who better to stand in for a one-eyed savage than an obsessional Irish Nationalist? Joyce had known several in Dublin. Michael Cusack, for instance, blackthorn-wielding founder of the Gaelic Athletic Association and hater of all English and all Protestants. Citizen Cusack became Polyphemus.

To his friend Frank Budgen Joyce would explain his choice of Ulysses for hero: 'No-age Faust isn't a man. But you mentioned Hamlet. Hamlet is a human being, but he is a son only.[2] Ulysses is son to Laertes, but he is father to Telemachus, husband to Penelope, lover of Calypso, companion in arms of the Greek warriors around Troy, and King of Ithaca. He was subjected to many trials, but with wisdom and courage came through them all.' He was also draft-dodger, war-hero, 'first gentleman of Europe' because he hid his genitals from maidenly gaze, and inventor of the tank. 'Wooden horse or iron box – it doesn't matter. They are both shells containing armed warriors.'

[2] Joyce would also object to Jesus as a complete man on the grounds he had not, so far as we are told, known sexual love.

Ulysses eventually turned out to be the epic of two races (Israel and Ireland), Joyce explained to Carlo Linati, a translator of his, in 1920, 'and at the same time the cycle of the human body as well as a little story of a day (life) . . . It is also a kind of encyclopaedia.' Each of the eighteen sections, named for a character or an episode of the *Odyssey* (Telemachus, Nestor, Proteus, Calypso, Lotus-Eaters, Hades, Aeolus, Lestrygonians, Scylla and Charybdis, Wandering Rocks, Sirens, Cyclops, Nausicaa, Oxen of the Sun, Circe, Eumaeus, Ithaca, Penelope) would correspond only in a loose and arbitrary manner to the Greek epic. Joyce was not using Homer as a crib. These correspondences were unnecessary to an appreciation of the novel, and when it was published as a book (after serialization) Joyce dropped them.

Each section had also a colour, several techniques, an Homeric cast, a science or an art, a hidden sense, an associated organ of the body and several symbols. So, in Lestrygonians (where Bloom has his lunch) the symbols are 'Bloody sacrifice: foods: shame', the bodily organ the esophagus, the sense or meaning 'dejection,' the art architecture, the technique 'peristaltic prose,' the Homeric persons Antiphates, the Seductive Daughter and Ulysses, and the colour – blood.

These schemes of Joyce's were elastic, and changed when it suited him. A knowledge of them adds little or nothing to a first reading of *Ulysses*. Indeed, it may be that the worst way to go about reading that book is to read first one of the shoal of critical interpretations based on those schema. For many years those allowed access to them were prohibited publication, until Joyce allowed it in Stuart Gilbert's exegesis, *James Joyce's 'Ulysses'*.

Joyce was not playing intellectual games to amuse himself (the same cannot be said for some of his critical commentators[3]). His

---

[3] In *Ulysses on the Liffey*, under the heading 'Why Stephen Dedalus Picks His Nose', Professor Richard Ellmann offers this gem: '. . . Not having found a handkerchief in his pocket, he is obliged to proceed bravely without one, and announces, "For the rest let look who will". But to belie his nonchalance, he suddenly says, "Perhaps there is someone," and looks quickly behind him. This backward glance is a parting denial of the subjectivist universe which briefly attracted him at the beginning of the episode, as well as of the universe of moribund gloom which has filled his thoughts. Since Stephen is an artist, Joyce implies that art is not self-isolation, that it depends upon recognition of other existences as well as one's own.' Perhaps, also, his nose itched.

mind required a rigorous framework in which to work, heritage of scholastic discipline.

The framework of *Ulysses* was far from complete when he began it in 1914, breaking off in any case to complete *Exiles*. In the middle of that composition the ramshackle Austrian Empire disobliged him by declaring war on Serbia on 28 July. Within a few days, other European powers had joined in, and Joyce was in the embarrassing position of being an enemy alien. The Austrian authorities, however, failed to detect in him any threat to their realm. He was allowed to continue his employment unmolested for the best part of a year and to receive mail from London. His affairs were scarcely of a seditious nature. Not so with Stanislaus. Pugnacious as ever, he made no effort to conceal his sympathy for the Italian Irredentists of Trieste and was promptly shipped off to an internment camp for the duration of the war.

Joyce himself had no preference among the warring nations. An Irishman, he felt no allegiance to the British Empire even if he had been disposed to approve of war for any reason, but regretted that France and Germany, the principal artistic forces of Europe, should be embarked on the destruction of one another.

'Avanti, Cagoia!' ('Forward, slugs!') encouraged the sarcastic Triestines, mocking the Italian battle-cry, 'Forward, Savoy!' and Joyce was amused. The Italians had reneged on their treaty obligations to the Central Powers, preferring to await the right moment to switch sides and get their hands on some Austrian territory. It was plainly a matter of time only before the war came to Trieste but Joyce, for the time being, made no effort to move.

He had taken over some of Stanislaus's pupils, but many of his own had vanished, either conscripted into the Austrian armies or fled to Italy. The Commercial School remained functioning until the Italians got around to declaring war, in May 1915. Meanwhile Joyce was assisted with money from Michael Healy in Galway.

Through the serialization of *A Portrait*, Joyce had acquired another influential admirer, H. G. Wells, who suggested he might find it profitable to use his agent, J. B. Pinker. Joyce agreed, though Pinker was not going to be much of a success at pushing him. H. L. Mencken published 'The Boarding House' and 'A Little Cloud' in the May issue of *Smart Set* on the recommendation of B. W. Huebsch, whom he took to be the American publisher of *Dubliners*.

Joyce, hearing of this, wrote to Huebsch politely requesting a copy of the American edition of his book. But it was a false alarm. Huebsch, who had been acting disinterestedly, saw no commercial possibilities in a book of short stories, however fine.

Grant Richards, who had an option on *A Portrait*, objected to its having appeared as a serial, though the serialization had begun some time before Joyce signed the contract (the second) for *Dubliners*. Richards had turned the novel down anyway and Pinker set about hawking it around. Martin Secker was prompt in his refusal, Duckworth took until January 1916 before pronouncing that the book needed 'time and trouble spent on it to make it a more finished piece of work.'[4]

In June 1915, flight took precedence before all other matters. Joyce applied at the United States Consulate for a visa, managing to annoy the official there by his air of boredom. 'I am proud to feel that I am acting for the British Consul, who is the representative of the King of England,' said that uncharacteristic American.

'The British Consul is not the representative of the King of England,' said Joyce, always ready for a scrap with officialdom. 'He is an official paid by my father for the protection of my person.'

He got the visa. The Austrian authorities allowed him to use it to pass through to neutral Switzerland, on condition he took no active part in the war. That was scarcely likely. Joyce made the promise and left without difficulty, leaving his possessions behind him. He had intended going to Lausanne, but wound up in Zurich.

---

[4] Pound: 'As for altering Joyce to suit Duckworth's readers – I would like trying to fit the Venus de Milo into a piss-pot.'

Chapter Fifteen
Private Carr's Swank Hose

The Gasthof Hoffnung, scene of Nora's deflowering eleven years before, was an irresistible place of pilgrimage. Joyce found the proprietor's name was Doebliner, another of those correspondences which so delighted him. He stayed there two weeks before finding a flat.

The city in which Joyce, Nora and the children (Eileen had married a Czech, Frantisek Schaurek, and gone to live in Prague) were to spend the war was physically beautiful and even intellectually satisfying, being well-populated with artistic and other refugees from the turmoil beyond the mountains, the first category including August Suter, the sculptor, and Tristan Tzara, who launched the surrealist movement from the Café Voltaire while Lenin plotted a more evil turmoil in the Café Odéon.

The scenery was impressive, had Joyce chosen to appreciate it, but he found mountains boring, and walking them tedious.

> *There is a keen climber called Sykes*
> *Who goes scrambling o'er ditches and dikes,*
> *But to skate on his scalp*
> *Down the side of an Alp*
> *Is the kind of enjoyment he likes.*

Joyce's comment on the enthusiasm of a friend.

There were rivers and a lake and visitations, as in Trieste, of a manic-depressive wind. When the Föhn blew, sufferers were by turns exhilarated or downcast. Joyce, prize hypochondriac, enrolled.

There were refugees from every class and nationality of Europe, many Jews, rich and poor, among them, and a virulent propaganda battle raged between the Allied and Central powers for the affections of the Swiss, who remained steadfastly and comfortably neutral. Every April the Zurichers joyfully burnt the winter demon they called the Bögg and in the autumn got joyously drunk on the new vintage from the hills. The patron saints were Felix and Regula. A comforting degree of Prosperity and Order was to settle on Joyce during his stay there.

The going was rough for a few months. Michael Healy contributed £15 to tide them over, while Joyce advertised for students. From London Pound prevailed upon Yeats to get Joyce a grant from the Royal Literary Fund. The approach was made through Edmund Gosse, poet and critic and an official of the Fund. Gosse, persuaded by Yeats that Joyce was a man of genius, recommended him for a grant.[1] Satisfied that Joyce was indeed mendicant and deserving, the Fund awarded him a grant of £75, in three quarterly instalments of £25. The patronage was more than welcome. Joyce had still to make a penny in royalties out of any of his books. He was wandering Zurich in the second-hand cast-off coat of a departed German, bought from his landlady for eleven francs.

Nora, who was destined to speak dialect in all languages but French (as a consequence of learning them in Galway, Trieste and Zurich) began reluctantly to conquer Switzer-Deutsch, cheered up by a new hat bought with Uncle Michael's money. The family spoke the Triestine dialect at home and gathered Triestine friends in Zurich. One was Ottocara Weiss, a musical young man who had come to study political economy at the University. Weiss photographed Joyce strumming the guitar, no doubt wincing as he did so. Joyce played it very badly, accompanying himself in scraps of Verdi or Bellini (his operatic taste never was up to much. 'Wagner,' he announced about this time, 'reeks of sex.'). Anecdotes and puns were exchanged. Joyce's anecdotes were principally sexual, but decorously so: two Belgian diplomats try to embarrass the future Pope Leo XIII, when Papal Nuncio in Belgium, by asking his opinion of the carved figure of a nude woman. '*Vous aimez les objets d'art, Monseigneur. Regardez cela!*' The future Pope does so. '*O, c'est tres beau. C'est Madame, sans doute?*'[2]

Weiss soon departed for the army. Joyce acquired some wellheeled students who did not mind paying for lessons they had no intention of taking. He turned down the opportunity of explaining Ireland's woes in the *Journal de Genève* but undertook translation

[1] Gosse changed his mind after seeing *Ulysses*. 'It is an anarchical production, infamous in taste, in style, in everything. Mr Joyce is unable to publish or sell his books in England, on account of their obscenity . . . He is not, as I say, without talent, but he has prostituted it to the most vulgar uses . . .'
[2] Richard Ellmann : *James Joyce.*

work for the *International Review*, a paper dedicated to ending the war by persuading the Germans and the English that neither were really bad fellows. The publisher was Sigmund Feilbogen, ex-professor of commerce in Vienna and wielder of an ear-trumpet, according to Budgen, ever ready to detect the first whisper of peace.

Rumbles of war reached Joyce from Ireland. Sheehy-Skeffington was shot during the Easter Rising of 1916 for urging British troops to refrain from looting, tragic end for a stubborn pacifist. Joyce was asked if he looked forward to an independent Ireland. 'So that I might declare myself its first enemy?' he answered.

Dubliners sold twenty-three copies in the whole of 1915 and *A Portrait* seemed no nearer publication. Nor did *Exiles* seem nearer performance. Yeats could not put it on even if he had wished (he did not). 'Our players have had to go to the music halls to keep in existence until the war is over.' Pound read it and gave as his opinion that it would not do for the stage. 1915, year of discomfort, non-achievement and a new exile, ended encouragingly. Miss Weaver, distressed at Joyce's failure to find a publisher, offered to bring out *A Portrait* herself, so long as her 'staff' (of one, as a matter of fact – Richard Aldington. Miss Weaver had not wished to discourage Joyce by letting him know the size of the operation. *The Egoist* had a nucleus of not more than 200 regular readers) and fellow directors (ie Dora Marsden) agreed to this daring venture. Dora was told that Mr Joyce had a friend who would indemnify *The New Freewoman Ltd* against loss. Financially dependent on Harriet Weaver herself, she thought it better not to object, though suspecting, rightly, that this 'friend' was Miss Weaver.

Having somewhat lost faith with 'regular publishers' Joyce was pleased to accept the offer, once sure that no regular publisher could be found. He was to receive the very generous royalty of twenty-five per cent on every copy sold at six shillings. Miss Weaver did not care who published *A Portrait* so long as it was published, and did not at all mind her own paying for it. At the same time she took elaborate pains to ensure that no one, least of all Joyce, thought it was anything but a perfectly ordinary publishing venture, intended to make a profit.

Her immediate anxiety, reinforced by Pound's reports (sometimes twice daily) was that Joyce was in dire straits. She sent him £50, under the pretence that 'stringent economies' made possible payment for serialization rights. When Joyce wrote to thank her she answered 'I feel wretched and ashamed to think we had had your wonderful book and made you no return whatever. The kindness is entirely yours in never having drawn attention to the fact . . . May I send you good wishes for your birthday?' His thirty-fourth. Joyce instructed Pinker to cease his efforts to sell the book and pass it on immediately to *The Egoist*. 'Too much time has been lost already.'

More was to be lost. Miss Weaver applied in turn to seven printers. All refused, in varying tones of shock and horror, to touch the book. 'We return the manuscript which you left with us and beg to say that we could not for one moment entertain any idea of publishing such a production . . . It may be true to life but there are expressions therein which, to record in print seems to me to serve no useful purpose . . . Out standing is such that we are very particular as to what we put our name to, and we would not knowingly undertake any work of a doubtful character even though it may be a classic.'

But *A Portrait* did after all achieve publication in 1916, just barely. After hiatus with two American publishers, one of them the Yale University Press, Ben Huebsch decided to publish *A Portrait* and *Dubliners* too. Miss Weaver agreed to buy sufficient sheets from Huebsch to publish 750 copies in England. Pinker proving ineffectual, she doubled as Joyce's agent, forwarding all mail between Zurich and New York by express post, paying for the sheets the day after she got them, negotiating with Elkin Mathews on Joyce's (and Huebsch's) behalf for American rights to *Chamber Music*. So great was the American's enthusiasm he had decided to bring that out too.

On 30 December, Heubsch was able to cable 'published', a polite fiction. Joyce had decided that *A Portrait* must bear the date 1916 to allow publication of *Exiles* in 1917. 'I got just enough copies from the bindery,' the obliging Huebsch wrote Miss Weaver, 'to make it possible for me truthfully to say that the book was published. The distribution to the bookshops and to the reviewers will be made this month (January).' Joyce always maintained with superstitious certainty that he knew the propitious moment for publication of his books.

The Egoist Limited (so renamed from *New Freewoman Limited* to save Joyce appearing under that embarrassing imprint — another

203

of Harriet Weaver's favours) were equally quick off the mark. Miss Weaver got the sheets of *A Portrait* on 22 January 1917, after their hazardous journey through the U-boats, whipped them off to the binder, and published the first English edition of *A Portrait of the Artist as a Young Man* on 12 February 1917. She had missed Joyce's birthday this time by only ten days.

With these publications Mr Joyce may be said to have arrived for good and all, so far as the world of literature was concerned. The claim of *A Portrait* to be literature, heralded H. G. Wells in *The Nation*, 'is as good as the last book of *Gulliver's Travels*'. 'One conversation in the book is a superb success, the one in which Mr. Dedalus carves the Christmas turkey; I write with all due deliberation that Sterne himself could not have done it better.' Nevertheless, Mr Wells did object to Mr Joyce's 'cloacal obsession'.[3] But Swift had that obsession too.

In August 1916 Joyce had had another windfall, thanks once again to the energies of Pound and Yeats, this time proceeding from the Civil List dispensed personally by the British Prime Minister, Asquith. His secretary, Edward Marsh, was prevailed upon to read Joyce's work, and found it to his liking. He asked for the opinions of Yeats and George Moore. Yeats replied with straightforward praise. Moore, thinking perhaps of the political overtones of giving money to an Irishman when Ireland was in a state of smouldering rebellion, answered with a letter which was principally a declaration of distaste for the Irish:

> The Irish like priests and believe in the power of priests to forgive them their sins and to change God into a biscuit . . . I am an admirer of Mr Asquith and regret that he cannot bring himself to believe that there can be no settlement, and that all attempts at settlement will fail. The Irish like discipline, and if Mr Asquith would treat the Irish as the Pope does he would be the most popular man in Ireland.
> Yours sincerely,
> George Moore
> P.S. I am sure that from a literary point of view Joyce is deserving of help.

[3] 'It is Wells's countrymen who build water-closets wherever they go,' Joyce protested.

He got the help anyway, £100, and in February, after publishing *A Portrait*, Miss Weaver, anonymously, removed the possibility of serious destitution, at least for the next year. Joyce was suffering a particularly bad and prolonged bout of eye trouble, this time the serious diseases of glaucoma and synecchia, which prevented his doing any work and obliged him to pass the time in a darkened room. He was talking to his friend Felix Beran, poet and fellow-toiler at the now defunct *International Review* when the post arrived with a registered letter from a London firm of solicitors: an anonymous admirer would forward through them four sums of £50 each on 1 May, August, November and February. Joyce was naturally curious to know where the money came from but would have to wait.

John Quinn, Irish-American lawyer and bibliophile, added to his bank balance by buying the manuscript of *Exiles*. He did not like the play when he got around to reading it but was happy to part with £20 for the corrected proofs of the American edition of *A Portrait*.

If these gestures were a relief to Joyce's poverty they were also measures of recognition which he felt long overdue. What fame he had achieved on his own territory, in Zurich, had been chiefly confined to the coffee houses and bars, but now his growing reputation entitled him to be introduced to other celebrities as a celebrity in his own right. He was introduced to Feruccio Busoni, composer, adapter of Bach and formidable piano virtuoso, whose music, being instrumental rather than vocal, did not please him (he did not like Bach either). The meeting was not fortunate. Joyce informed Busoni that Shakespeare, whatever his poetic powers, was no dramatist (meaning that he was insufficiently steeled in the school of Aristotle). 'You deny him the main thing and grant him the lesser,' protested Busoni.

This introduction of celebrities was affected by Philipp Jarnach, Busoni's secretary and a composer himself. Jarnach had the misfortune to live close by Joyce and to have a sense of pitch more finely tuned than his neighbour's. A compromise was reached: Joyce would sing and play his abominably out-of-tune piano only at certain hours when Jarnach was out of the vicinity.

Before he was safely out of the red Joyce had a strange encounter with a Dutchman calling himself Jules Martin, who interested him in the possibility of 'improving' a screen scenario. Joyce examined carefully the material put before him. Martin intended producing a film called *Wine, Women, and Song*. 'We'll get wealthy women into it,' explained the astute impresario, 'women in fur pelts. We'll teach them how to walk and then charge them a fee for being in the film.' It would not be necessary to have any film in the camera. Joyce decided not to lend his name to this project, despite his interest in the cinema, but felt kindly disposed towards Martin. He might be destined for the prison cell but at least he proceeded in that direction with style.

Exiles had yet to appear on the stage anywhere. Martin proposed putting it on in Zurich. He would play Richard Rowan and Mrs Harold McCormick, student of psycho-analysis and Rockefeller heiress, would make a fine Bertha, being qualified for the part by her money, her furs and diamonds (Bertha would look better in furs and diamonds) and her imposing *embonpoint*. Mrs McCormick, however, failed to be persuaded to throw in her lot with Jules Martin.

Exiles was at least published, in May 1918, by Grant Richards in London and by Huebsch in America. In London the Stage Society, whose aim was to put on worthwhile plays, as opposed to what the commercial theatres of the day dished up, considered producing it on and off from January 1916, but did not get around to it until February 1926. Joyce imagined that Bernard Shaw had objected on the grounds of obscenity, but was probably mistaken.

Miss Weaver's money enabled him to take his doctor's advice and leave the unhappy climate of Zurich for Locarno for the duration of the winter. Nora and the children were sent ahead. The condition of Joyce's eyes had prevented his doing much work on *Ulysses* but he was understandably reluctant to undergo the operation prescribed. 'I dislike the idea of cutting out pieces of the iris at intervals.'

The choice was removed from him by an attack of glaucoma so severe that he could not move for twenty minutes from pain. His ophthalmologist insisted on an iridectomy on his right eye. It was necessary, but it permanently reduced his vision. By October he was well enough to proceed to Locarno. Nora found the place pleasant, the locals being 'just like Italians lively and dirty and disorderly.' (In Zurich she had been apprehended in the street for discarding a piece of paper.) There Joyce put the finishing touches to the first three episodes of *Ulysses*, broken off when he left Trieste. Harriet Weaver undertook to publish *Ulysses* as she had done *A Portrait*, in serial form, and Pound found American publishers in the *Little Review*, another journal run by literary ladies, Margaret Anderson and Jane Heap.

Joyce was able to work well enough at the Pension Daheim but found the absence of distraction in that placid town rather annoying. Martin provided diversion by getting himself locked up in prison in Lausanne for some minor but unsuccessful embezzlement and Joyce undertook a rescue mission to the Dutch Consul in Zurich. Martin was transferred to a hospital and from Amsterdam came a letter revealing to Joyce that 'Martin' was in fact Juda de Vries, fugitive son of a distinguished gynaecologist, who thanked Joyce for looking after 'the black sheep of the family'. During his incarceration he displayed his gratitude by fashioning a present for Joyce. It was a wooden box, the size of a family bible, inscribed 'My First Success! by James Joyce.'

'When you make money,' said Martin, 'you can conceal it in the box. Everybody will think it's a book.' Martin reformed well enough to become a dentist. Joyce caught up with him in Ostend in 1926 and discovered him 'pulling all the teeth and legs he can.'

The Joyces returned to Zurich in January, the head of the family no longer able to tolerate the boredom of the place, urged on his way by an unlikely earthquake. Nora too was relieved. 'Jim never spoke a word to me at the Pension Daheim,' she said, 'and the rest of the family were tubercular.' (They were not tubercular, just ill-tempered. Child discipline was not one of Joyce's strong points. 'Children should be educated by love,' he said, 'not punishment'. This precept meant in practice that Nora was left to discipline them. Georgio and Lucia were both turbulent children.)

Nora did not much appreciate the new book, objecting to the bad language when her husband read parts to her. 'My husband is writing a book,' she announced to Paul Suter, younger brother of the sculptor. 'I tell you, *das Buch ist ein Schwein.*'

'Do you know how to tell whether a woman is any good or not?' Joyce asked Suter.

'No,' said Suter.

'Well,' said Joyce, 'take her to a picture gallery and explain the pictures to her. If she breaks wind, she's all right.'

Nora would have passed that test. So, for that matter, would her husband. His execrable taste was often commented.

In February Joyce acquired another patroness, that same Mrs McCormick who had turned down the opportunity of creating the part of Bertha. She too wished to remain anonymous but Joyce managed to extract her identity from a common acquaintance, Charlotte Sauermann, soprano at the Zurich opera, admirer of Joyce's voice and probably the person who suggested the idea of a gift to Mrs McCormick. It was substantial – 12,000 francs to be paid at the rate of 1,000 francs a month. Joyce was now comfortably well off, or would have been with less expensive tastes or a frugal wife. Nora was as fond as he of spending money and no sum was too large to leave as a tip for waiters, or spend on a new hat.

Claud Sykes, unemployed actor earning a living by teaching English, suggested a new way of getting rid of this largesse. He had met Joyce at the time of Martin's film project and was eager, like all resting actors, to get back on the stage. Why not form a troupe to put on plays in English? The Swiss were being bombarded with German, French and Italian culture. Max Reinhardt's company had come to Zurich and so had Frank Wedekind, to produce his own plays. The British Consulate would be pleased, and *Exiles* could be one of the plays presented.

The author of *Exiles* fell in happily with this suggestion. Calling on Percy Bennett, British Consul-General, Joyce managed to rub him up the wrong way, but got official blessing for the company, to be called The English Players. The first play was to be Irish, *The Importance of Being Earnest.* Sykes and Joyce recruited the cast where they could find them, turning up a few professional actors, Joyce, acting as paymaster, agreeing to give the professionals thirty francs for one performance, on 29 April, and the amateurs ten francs to reimburse them for tram fares. This arrangement was satisfactory to all but one member of the cast, Henry Carr, a young man who took the part of Algernon Moncrieff and played it well. But he was an employee of the Consulate and shared the official (hostile) view of Joyce, that he was less than devoted to the British cause and had committed semi-treason by working for a neutralist paper after taking British Government money.

For his role Carr equipped himself with a new wardrobe, the principal item of expense being a pair of trousers.

The performance went down well, the house was full and the company made a modest profit. 'Hurrah for Ireland!' Joyce called out during the applause, in case anyone was under the misapprehension they had seen an *English* play. 'Poor Wilde was Irish and so am I!'

Carr was annoyed when he found only ten francs in his envelope, though he had earlier offered to forego any payment at all. He went off in a sulk instead of attending the cast dinner. Carr demanded 150 francs of Sykes to pay for the clothes, and Joyce lost his temper when he heard of the demand. Two days after the performance he appeared at the Consulate to demand money owing for twenty tickets Carr had sold. Carr gave him fifteen francs, all he had been paid for the tickets, and asked for his own 150. Joyce told him his sense of honour as a British subject should have obliged him to play without though of payment.

'You're a cad,' screamed Carr, whose nerves had suffered from the war (he had been taken prisoner by the Germans and handed over in an exchange), 'You've cheated me and pocketed the proceeds. You're a swindler. If you don't get out I'll throw you downstairs. Next time I catch you outside I'll wring your neck!'

'I don't think,' said Joyce, taken aback at the vehemence of Carr's reaction, 'that this is fit language to be used in a Government office.' Exit Joyce, preserving a dignified restraint, but not without difficulty.

In a fury he fired off two letters, one to Percy Bennett, demanding Carr's dismissal, the second to the police, demanding protection. Bennett's answer was to inform Sykes that official approval would be withdrawn from the English Players if Joyce remained associated with them. Sykes, finding Joyce's efforts (and temporary solvency) more useful than official sanction, preferred to stick with him.

The usual remedy occurred to Joyce. He filed two suits, the first alleging non-payment of twenty-five francs due for tickets; the second an action for libel based on what Carr had said at the Consulate. He won the first, with Carr obliged to pay court costs and pay Joyce sixty francs damages. He celebrated with a song, to the tune of *Tipperary*:

> *Up to rheumy Zurich came an Irishman one day,*
> *And as the town was rather dull he thought he'd give a play,*

So the German propagandists might be rightly riled,
But the bully British Philistine once more drove Oscar Wilde
CHORUS : *Oh, the C.G. is not literary,*
           And his handymen are rogues.
           The C.G.'s about as literary
           As an Irish kish of brogues.
           We have paid up all expenses
           As the good Swiss Public knows,
           But we'll be damned well damned before we pay for
           Private Carr's swank hose . . .

Carr gets it in the neck in *Ulysses* too, becoming the drunken British soldier who assaults Stephen in the Circe episode.

The second case went less well. It was not heard until February. Joyce could produce no witness to the libel since the only others present had been two colleagues of Carr's, neither of whom was willing to tell the truth as Joyce saw it. He was forced to withdraw the suit, pay court costs and damages of 120 francs. This he refused, forcing the court to proceed by distraint. A court officer duly appeared at the Joyce apartment but could remove none of the furniture since it was not Joyce's. Nor could he take away books (essential to the practice of his profession) or his typewriter (necessary for a writer with bad eyes).

'Then,' said the official, 'I am afraid, Herr Doktor, that I must ask you to show me what money you have on you.'

Joyce exhibited the contents of his wallet, one hundred francs, which he claimed as essential to feed his family. The official was obliged reluctantly to remove forty.

The family was in no danger of starving. Padraic and Mary Colum had successfully put it about in America that a great Irish artist was being hounded by agents of the British Government and was in danger of having no less than 10,000 francs taken from him. Scofield Thayer, millionaire philanthropist, sent seven hundred dollars and a friend of his, equally alarmed, added another three hundred. But Joyce gave more than twice that to the Players, and vented his annoyance further on the British Empire by taking to reading the *Zürcher Post*, known to the locals, because of its pro-German sentiments, as the *Züri Boche*. A restrained response to provocation (apart from the occasional litigation) was normal to him. The strongest term of abuse he allowed himself now was 'lout'.

Pound, less restrained, stuck his oar in from London, offering some gratuitous advice, and the threat of exposing all to the readers of the *Little Review*, to Sir Horace Rumbold, British Minister to Berne: 'Dear Sir, If it be not already too late, I should like to caution you that you can find no surer means of making a few converts to Bolshevism or to the more violent revolutionary factions than by continuing or permitting to continue the persecution of James Joyce by the Zurich officials within the sphere of your influence.' The Ambassador remained blithely unalarmed by the spectre of Bolshevism. (He got slammed too: Joyce casts him as a hangman in *Ulysses*. It seems not to have affected his subsequent career. He became Ambassador to Berlin.)

Nora, at her husband's persuasion, lent unsuspected talents to the Players. In the summer of 1918, despite official disapproval, the company put on a triple bill of Barrie, Shaw and Synge. The Synge was *Riders to the Sea* and Nora took the part of the bereaved mother, Maurya, with some fine, if risible in the wrong mouth, lines to speak. ('There does be a power of young men floating round in the sea and what way would they know if it was Michael they had, or another man like him, for when a man is nine days in the sea, and a wind blowing, it's hard set his own mother would be to say what man was in it.') This went down well with Nora's fine Galway brogue and imposing figure, and the other actors copied her with more success than is usual when the English attempt Irish accents.

Joyce continued his assistance to the English Players (who seem mostly to have staged Irish plays) until he left Zurich, though they never put on *Exiles*. The fiasco over Henry Carr's trousers had one unfortunate long-term effect: it provided material for the fiction that Joyce was anti-British (and for a play by Tom Stoppard).

Chapter Sixteen

A Dolorous Passion

'No doubt Joyce has a grievance,' remarked Horace Taylor, apropos the Consulate affair, 'but what he doesn't understand is that all these people are out for a quiet life.' Taylor met Joyce while on a cultural mission to Zurich. He had been sent to escort a collection of modern British paintings intended to compete with German and French exhibitions. Being an employee of the Ministry of Information he was only indirectly concerned with the Consulate so that Joyce felt able to accept his invitation to dinner. Taylor brought with him another employee of the same Ministry, Frank Budgen, thinking he and Joyce would get on. Ex-seaman and self-taught painter, Bugden had been stranded by the war and found employment in the commercial department of the Consulate, remote from Bennett, Carr and the others. He was a bluff and forthright character who never quite comprehended just why Joyce liked him so much, but they got on famously as soon as Joyce overcame an initial suspicion. As he explained:

'You remember that evening at Taylor's pension on the Zurich-berg?'

'Yes, of course I do,' said Budgen.

'Well, I went up to Taylor's to dinner with a mind completely made up that you were to be a spy sent by the British Consulate to report on me in connection with my dispute with them.'

'And what good reason had you for coming to the conclusion that I wasn't a spy?'

'Because,' said Joyce, 'you looked like an English cricketer out of the W. G. Grace period. Yes, Arthur Shrewsbury. He was a great bat, but an awkward looking tradesman at the wicket.'

Budgen was soon introduced to Joyce's work, which he found much to his taste. The painterly care which the writer lavished on words particularly impressed him: Joyce announces that he has been working hard all day. Budgen assumes that means he has written a great deal. No, says Joyce quite seriously, two sentences. Has he been seeking the *mot juste*?

'No,' says Joyce. 'I have the words already. What I am seeking is the perfect order of words in the sentence. There is an order in every way appropriate. I think I have it.'

The words describe Bloom, on his way to lunch, struck by the sight of women's silk petticoats hanging in a window: 'Perfume of embraces all him assailed. With hungered flesh obscurely, he mutely craved to adore.'

Budgen asked him how long he had been working on *Ulysses*.

'About five years,' said Joyce, 'but in a sense, all my life.'

'Some of your contemporaries think two books a year an average output.'

'Yes, but how do they do it? They talk them into a typewriter. I feel quite capable of doing that if I wanted to do it. But what's the use? It isn't worth doing.'

Budgen's closest friend was Paul Suter. Conversations were droll at the Café Pfauen, though Nora did not approve of the quantity of Fendant de Sion drunk. 'A German lady called to see me today,' Joyce told Suter and Budgen there one evening. 'She is a writer and wanted me to give an opinion on her work, but she told me she had already shown it to the porter of the hotel where she stays. So I said to her: "What did your hotel porter think of your work?" She said: "He objected to a scene in my novel where my hero goes out into the forest, finds a locket of the girl he loves, picks it up and kisses it passionately." "But," I said, "that seems to me to be a very pleasing and touching incident. What did your hotel porter find wrong with it?" And she tells me he said: "It's all right for the hero to find the locket and then pick it up and kiss it, but before he kissed it you should have made him wipe the dirt off it with his coat sleeve."'

'And what did you tell her?' asked Budgen and Suter together.

'I told her,' said Joyce, 'and I meant it too – to go back to that hotel porter and always take his advice. "That man," I said, "is a critical genius. There is nothing I can tell you that he can't tell you".'

An occasional amusement after these evenings was to 'pay a visit to Budgen.' August Suter had executed six monumental statues for the municipal offices of Zurich. Budgen sat for one of them and was plainly recognisable even if immobile and over-lifesize. Joyce performed before it a sort of ritual dance, 'a thing of whirling arms,' as Budgen described it, 'high-kicking legs, grotesque capers and coy grimaces.' A little wine was poured at these times, as salute to the frozen Budgen.

White wine, said Joyce, is like electricity. 'Red wine looks and tastes like liquefied beefsteak.' The speciality of the Pfauen was Fendant, pale greenish amber in colour and tasting a little of earth rich in copper ore. 'Er schmeckt nach Erz,' commented Suter ('It tastes like ore.'). Joyce, staring at the yellow-tinted carafe, said: 'Erzherzogin' ('Archduchess'). So it was called henceforward. Joyce repeated this joke in Italian asking Ottocaro Weiss: 'What does this remind you of?' 'Orina,' said Weiss. 'Si,' said Joyce, 'ma di un' archiduchessa.'

A Greek restaurant claimed their allegiance for a while, Joyce being as compulsive a collector of Greeks as of Jews. One, who was illiterate, could nevertheless recite long passages of the Odyssey, learnt by heart. Another had written a book proving that Athens was the gravitational centre of the world and that the Greeks should on that account receive special consideration at the peace conference in such matters as the re-apportioning of Bulgarian and Turkish territory. Budgen thought they talked too much. 'Aren't they strangely like Jews? They look like Jews and they all talk at once and nobody listens.'

'Not so strangely,' said Joyce. 'Anyway, they are Greeks. And there's a lot to be said for the theory that the Odyssey is a Semitic poem.'

(So, in Ulysses, jewgreek meets greekjew.)

Budgen, introduced to the family, found Nora 'a stately presence' but sometimes formidable and sharp-tongued, dismissive of her husband's work. 'Some people were up at our flat last night,' Joyce related in amusement, 'and we were talking about Irish wit and humour. And this morning my wife said to me, "What is all this about Irish wit and humour? Have we any book in the house with any of it in? I'd like to read a page or two."'

Nora seemed to Budgen, judging her as a painter, a very good-looking woman but to some extent 'a daughter of anguish,' perhaps because he saw her at times when her husband had caused her a little anguish. She was not beyond handing out some Fendant herself and joining, after her fashion, into the conversation:

'Now that's too bad. And is he talking to you again about that old book of his, Mr Budgen? I don't know how you stand it. Jim, you ought not to do it. You'll bore Mr Budgen stiff.'

'If I bore Budgen,' said Joyce, 'he must tell me. But he has the advantage of me. He can understand and talk about my book. But I don't understand and can't talk about painting.'

Nora was not to be persuaded. 'What do you think, Mr Budgen, of a book with a big, fat, horrible married woman as the heroine? Mollie Bloom!'

Budgen painted both of them. The trouble with Joyce, he found, was getting him to sit still. Mrs Joyce reminded him, artist or not, that she was solid bourgeoise. 'Now Mr Budgen,' said Nora firmly, when it was necessary that she should change her clothes, 'leave the room, please.'

Taste in women was the topic of conversation (Nora being absent) one evening at the Pfauen. Budgen dredged from his memory the story of the king of a cannibal island who chose his consort by lining all the women of the tribe up against a horizontal pole, then picked the one whose posterior protruded to the greatest extent. Joyce, he recalled, said 'without the ghost of a smile' – 'I sincerely hope that when Bolshevism finally sweeps the world it will spare that enlightened potentate.'

Budgen was in the way of knowing Joyce's tastes intimately, being made the confessor of a new infatuation. Joyce's eye had lighted in the street on a near neighbour, one Marthe Fleischmann. He was struck by her resemblance to the girl he had seen wading in the sea, the same who had turned him finally away from the Virgin. Fraulein Fleischmann noticed his agitation but felt unable at first to return his attentions, being the mistress of a gentleman called Rudolf Hiltpold whose vigilance, however, was not perfect.

Fraulein Fleischmann had her own flat, having an independent income augmented by Hiltpold, and passed her time there adjusting her appearance and reading novels. Her education had been cursory: she had only a passing acquaintance with French, the language in which the amorous Joyce first wrote to her, sneaking around the corner to post the letters through her door himself, then staring through her windows in the evening in the hope of seeing her read them.

215

He mistook her at first for a Jewess, on account of the softness and
regularity of her features and the gentleness of her eyes. She was
not. He explained that he was thirty-five (like Yeats knocking a
year off), the age at which Shakespeare 'conceived his dolorous
passion for the "dark lady".' He sent her an inscribed copy of
Chamber Music once he knew her name.[1] She did not read English,
in fact never took the trouble to read any of his work, even in
translation, in spite of being convinced he was in love with her. But
once she had determined, in her snobbish way, that he was a person
of some consequence, she allowed an affair of a sort.

The first time Budgen heard any recital of this business he was
disinclined to pay attention. 'How weary, stale, flat and unprofitable
to bachelor ears are married men's tales of their extra-marital
amours!' he said. 'And what married man doesn't have his Marthe
Fleischmann?' He had already heard complaints from Nora about
Joyce's behaviour: 'Leaving the Pfauen one night I walked in
company with Nora Joyce. She became tearful and through her
tears she told me that Jim wanted her to go with other men so
that he would have something to write about.' Joyce, pretending
to be more drunk than he was, was shuffling up the rear, hoping,
presumably, to catch some helpful words . . . 'That Nora would or
could have co-operated in any way is out of the question. She was
a respectable married woman with all that implies and any such
enterprise lay outside her will and means.'

Next time Joyce mentioned Marthe he was calm, sober and per-
suasive. Budgen was to be roped in whether he liked it or not. 'I
think, Budgen, that in this matter you have only one woman in
mind.' He meant Nora, and he was quite right. Budgen was fond
of her. 'But you know,' Joyce insisted, 'if I permitted myself to be
under any restraint in this matter it would be spiritual death to
me.' Fraulein Fleischmann, Joyce disclosed, had been quite co-operative in the matter of his sexual inclinations, discussing at length the
sort of feminine undergarments preferred by him. 'First I saw of her,'
said Joyce, pointing out her house, 'was at the back of the house.
She was in a small but well-lit room in the act of pulling a chain.'

He decided to celebrate his thirty-seventh birthday, 2 February

[1] This, and four letters, came to light when Fraulein Fleischmann, in reduced circumstances, went to Heinrich Straumann, Professor of English at
Zurich University, after Joyce's death, seeking advice on how to sell them.

1919, which happened to be Candlemas, in her presence, but needed a suitable venue. Budgen was in temporary possession of August Suter's studio. Joyce decided that would do. 'She's coming later this afternoon,' Joyce announced, taking it for granted that Budgen would co-operate. The decor seemed to his taste except for one omission: 'Those pictures of yours, Budgen, are very good. I know they are. But the general impression is too chaste. Haven't you got something with a nude woman on it. You know what I mean.'

Budgen had no such picture but offered to get one up in charcoal while Joyce departed for an hour to borrow a Jewish candelabra, as he described it, from a friend (What for? The friend inquired afterwards. 'For a black mass,' said Joyce).

Budgen describes his efforts: 'I did the best I could with the idea of an earth goddess in mind, and for Joyce's benefit and to simplify matters for myself I chose a recumbent position and a rear aspect, to which I accorded as much bulk as I reasonably could. Try to please the customers. I finished with a few outlines of mountains in the background to add literary point to the motive. It was a bad drawing, resembling in its characteristics contour drawings I have seen colleagues piss in the snow with half their attention taken up by talking over their shoulders to a waiting companion.'

'Splendid,' said Joyce enthusiastically. 'The very thing.' He left to pick up the lady, returning in a few minutes. Budgen found her no great beauty. 'As an old shipmate of mine would have described her, she was high up in the focsle and fairly broad in the beam.' Banalities were exchanged for half an hour and Fraulein Fleischmann duly smirked when Joyce pointed out the width of the posterior depicted in Budgen's drawing. Budgen put the drawing in the stove when Joyce left to escort Fleischmann home, but it seemed to have had the desired effect. Later that evening he came across Joyce, who said in an aside, 'I have explored this evening the coldest and hottest parts of a woman's body.' The coldest part, one presumes, is feet.

The affair ended in June, when discovered by Hiltpold, who threatened violence. Fraulein Fleischmann had been so upset by Herr Joyce's attentions she had been driven to the point of suicide, she told her protector. Joyce, who had not seen her since 'the feast of candles', paid a visit to the lion's den, expressed proper contrition and handed over to Hiltpold all Marthe's communications to him.

So, for the time being, ended that comic episode, though Fraulein Fleischmann claimed that Joyce paid her occasional visits in later years. Joyce had signed a postcard to Marthe 'Odysseus' and addressed her as 'Nausikaa.' No other trace of her appears in his work except that Gerty MacDowell, the Nausicaa of *Ulysses*, inherits Fleischmann's limp. But 'she was no sex kitten,' as Budgen said.

Joyce was certainly aware of the comic content of this attachment but liked, every now and then, to indulge in some ridiculous fever, be it love or litigation. He would not have entered into a liaison which might have endangered his marriage.

In May of 1919 Joyce set off with Budgen for a few days near Locarno and there made the acquaintance of a baroness who owned two islands in Lago Maggiore and whose reputation as a (retired) orgiast had earned her the name of Circe. On one of these islands she had established a doll factory and decorated the salon of her house with Odyssean motifs and a painting of herself as a beautiful young woman. Joyce and Budgen, quite fascinated, paid the island a visit at her invitation and Joyce was presented before he left with some relics of her youth – a packet of erotic letters and a valise of books on the subject of sexual perversions. These he found useful when he began the composition of the Circe episode. He was at the time finishing The Sirens, one of the least successful in the sense that it did not achieve the effect which Joyce hoped for. Pound found it disappointing and even Miss Weaver allowed that it seemed to her to reach less than Joyce's usual pitch of intensity. He was annoyed. The technique of the episode was that of a *fuga per canonem* in eight parts. 'I did not know in what other way to describe the seduction of music beyond which Ulysses travels.' A reader ignorant of the technique Joyce was employing could be forgiven for wondering at the abrupt change of style. And, appraised of the technique, might justifiably comment that it does not work. The fugue is not a technique intended for prose – not even Joyce could bring it off and retain sense. But he was determined to resist criticism: 'I confess that it is an extremely tiresome book but it is the only book which I am able to write at present . . .' Writing the Sirens made him unreceptive to other music. At a performance of *Die Walküre* he asked Weiss in the interval, 'don't you find the musical effects of my Sirens better than Wagner's?' 'No,' said Weiss bluntly, and Joyce stalked off.

218

The war by now being more or less over, apart from side-shows (the haste of the Italians to seize Trieste had annoyed him) Joyce determined to leave Zurich. Budgen asked him why he didn't go back to Ireland and got the simple answer, 'Because I'm a coward and afraid of being shot.' Joyce's exile from his country was not so rooted in betrayal as he claimed. Prudence had a good deal to do with it. Stanislaus was released from internment, battling with his brother's landlord in Trieste and pleading for relief. 'I have just emerged from four years of hunger and squalor. Do you think you can give me a rest?'

James determined to go back to Trieste, possibly because he had now decided it was necessary to augment his income by teaching again. Miss Weaver had interrupted the stay in Locarno with a message passed through her solicitors. She was settling on him the sum of £5,000 of five per cent War Loan. Nora danced a jig on the steps of a tram and Joyce rushed back to Zurich without informing Budgen.

But the bounty, on sober examination, was not so huge. Five per cent of £5,000 amounted to £250 a year, only £50 more than Miss Weaver's customary remittance. Joyce suspected, thanks to the prompting of Pound, that the donor was John Quinn. He wrote to the solicitors hinting he knew who their client was, without saying whom. Miss Weaver transmitted further clues: 'Briefly, the qualities of your writing which most interest her are your searching piercing spirit, your scorching truth, the power and startling penetration of your "intense instants of imagination".' But still Joyce would not hazard a guess.

Next time she wrote, principally to announce that *The Egoist* had lost their printers, mainly on account of objections to *Ulysses*, Miss Weaver carped against the Sirens episode, and then revealed all in the last paragraph: 'Perhaps I had better add that it was I who sent the message through Messrs Monro and Co and that I am sorry I sent it in the way and in the form I did. It is rather paralyzing to communicate through solicitors. I fear you will have to withdraw all words about delicacy and self-effacement. I can only beg you to forgive my lack of them.' Spared the pains of delicacy and self-effacement he offered her the manuscript of *A Portrait*, as soon as he was able to retrieve it from his desk in Trieste.

The Egoist had nearly reached its end as a magazine. Harriet

219

Weaver was tired of fighting printers. The Cyclops episode, which reached her in November, filled her with enthusiasm and she determined to devote her energies to seeing the whole book properly published. 'I have read it through, but too hastily to venture on any comment – except the passing remark that on finishing the chapter it was difficult to speak straight and to avoid interlarding one's words with the favourite and quite unladylike adjective so constantly employed by the figure who is the narrator.'[2]

Exiles had its first production in August, at Munich, in German. Joyce hoped to attend the production, instructed Stanislaus to get his dinner jacket out of mothballs in Trieste and send it on in time for the first night, and dropped a hint to Mrs McCormick that she could usefully finance the trip. Visa problems prevented his attending, but it was as well. One Munich paper suggested the play was a little rarefied for the general public; another, more rudely, dismissed it as 'Irish stew.' 'Flop' and 'fiasco' were the words Joyce attached to the production, which was immediately withdrawn.

Joyce began to pack up in September for the return to Trieste, but had an unpleasant surprise before he set off. Calling at the bank on 1 October to pick up his 1,000 francs from Mrs McCormick he was abruptly informed his credit was cut off. Appeals to Mrs McCormick failed, even the offer of the manuscript of *Ulysses*. It appeared the lady was annoyed at his refusal to be psycho-analysed by the revered Professor Jung (Joyce thought little of this particular pastime. 'Why all this fuss and bother about the mystery of the unconscious? What about the mystery of the conscious? What do they know about that?'). A scapegoat being necessary Joyce picked on Ottacaro Weiss, who knew both Jung and Mrs McCormick but was entirely innocent of any conspiracy to

---

2 Virginia Woolf had found incongruous the conjunction of the spinsterly, woollen-gloved Miss Weaver, when in April 1918 she brought the Woolfs part of the manuscript of *Ulysses*, hoping they might print it on their press. 'Her neat mauve suit fitted both soul and body,' wrote Mrs Woolf in her diary, '. . . her table manners were those of a well-bred hen. We could get no talk to go. Possibly the poor woman was impeded by her sense that what she had in the brown paper parcel was quite out of keeping with her own contents. But then how did she ever come in contact with Joyce and the rest? Why does their filth seek exit from her mouth?' Miss Weaver learnt of a similar passage from the diary accusing her, among other crimes, of wearing woollen gloves, after Mrs Woolf's death. 'What is wrong with woollen gloves?' was her plaintive, but only comment.

deprive Joyce of his income. It is possible that Mrs McCormick had come to the conclusion that Joyce spent too much of her money in the Pfauen or thought, now that the war was over, that indigent artists could get on very well without her largesse. At any rate, she withdrew it.

And so Joyce was deposited back in Trieste on 16 October 1919 in that familiar old situation – down at heel and waiting for something to turn up. This time the stay would not be so long or the circumstances so dire, but he had had more than a year of comparative ease, and he was itching for fame and comfort.

Chapter Seventeen

'It Will Keep the Professors Busy for Centuries...'

'If all goes well,' Joyce informed Miss Weaver in May 1918, 'the book should be finished by the summer of 1919.' Writers tend to be optimistic about such matters – Joyce was out by more than two years in his estimate. Fits of literally blinding pain prevented his working for weeks at a time. For nine weeks from May to the end of July 1918, for instance, he was unable to read or write. Money worries were another distraction and so were quarrels.

The actual writing of several episodes, too, gave him more trouble than he had anticipated. To embark on the invention of new styles and new language with every episode was not a light task, even for genius. Nausicaa, begun before he left Zurich, was not finished until February or March 1920 (Joyce had gone to the trouble of reading pulp fiction, some supplied from Dublin by his Aunt Josephine, to get the style of Gerty MacDowell right: 'Passionate nature though he was Gerty could see that he had enormous control over himself. One moment he had been there, fascinated by a loveliness that made him gaze, and the next moment it was a quiet grave-faced gentleman, self control expressed in every line of his distinguishd figure.' Bloom has in fact been playing with himself until interrupted.)

Circe, model for a thousand attempts at phantasmagorical imitations, required eight drafts before Joyce was able to declare it finished in December 1920. There remained still to be written the concluding three chapters, Eumaeus, Ithaca and Penelope, simpler in style than those preceding, but nevertheless requiring the best part of a year's effort.

The path of serial publication was not strewn with rose petals. In London, Harriet Weaver sought in vain a printer willing to risk all that Joyce produced. Only four episodes out of the first ten proved acceptable. Miss Weaver, feeling the expense of energy and time a waste, wound up *The Egoist* in December 1919.

> ... We have in working practice in England a printer's censor-
> ship much more drastic than that of the official censorship
> itself. So it comes about that an intelligence abnormally acute
> and observant, an accomplished literary craftsman who sets down
> no phrase or line without its meaning for the creation as a
> whole, is faced with a situation in which the very possibility
> of existence for his work lies at the mercy and limitations of
> intelligence of – let us say – the printing-works foreman!

Miss Weaver still thought she had a printer who would undertake
Ulysses in book form, but in this supposition turned out to be
mistaken.

The novel ran into trouble in America too. There were no sanc-
tions on printers producing obscenity, but there was the vigilant
US Post Office, entrusted with the purity of what was sent through
the mails, and there were privately appointed watchdogs of public
morality. Miss Anderson and Miss Heap began *Ulysses* in the March
1918 issue of their *Little Review*. In 1919-1920 three issues were
confiscated by the Post Office and burnt, without deterring the
ladies: 'This is the second time I have had the pleasure of being
burnt while on earth,' said Joyce, thinking of the fate of that first
printing of *Dubliners,* 'so that I hope I shall pass through the
fires of purgatory as quickly as my patron S. Aloysius.' He was
remote from prosecution but Margaret Anderson and Jane Heap
were not. The issue of July-August 1920, containing part of Nausicaa
landed them in court after a complaint from the secretary of the
New York Society for the Prevention of Vice, John Quinn acting as
attorney for, and intermittently quarrelling with, the literary ladies
from Chicago. The trial began in February 1921. Two of the
judges finding the passages objected to incomprehensible, there was
a delay of a week to enable them to attack the whole episode. John
Cowper Powys, witness for the defence, testified that the passages
were in no way capable of corrupting young girls, but the judges,
after struggling manfully to detect obscenity, decided they had found
it and fined Anderson and Heap $50 each on the understanding that
they avoided prison only by undertaking to publish no more Joyce.

The harrying of the *Little Review* had a serious effect: Ben
Huebsch came to the conclusion it would be imprudent to publish
Ulysses. Joyce, by then in Paris, was able to get on without him.
The last sojourn in Trieste had lasted barely eight months.

That city, no longer the thriving port of a polygot empire, had degenerated into a rather boring little Italian town, large enough to satisfy Stanislaus (who spent the rest of his life there) after four years in internment, but lacking those stimuli his brother had become used to in Zurich. The flat abandoned in 1915 had enjoyed the visitations of bombs and, according to Joyce, thieves. He expected to find everything as he had left it, neatly transported by Stanislaus to some place of safe keeping. Where, for instance, was his dinner-jacket? Stanislaus had no longer any patience for such questions, nor were Frantisek and Eileen Schaurek, returned to Trieste with children of their own, delighted to have Joyce, Nora and their adolescent offspring added to an already overcrowded household, total population now nine.

Quinn and Huebsch provided some funds, Huebsch from royalties, Quinn in return for the manuscript of *Ulysses*, sent to him piece by piece. Joyce sulked for six weeks. *Ulysses* – he told Budgen – like himself, was on the rocks. There was not even 'the Archduchess's most excellent piss' to cheer him up. Appeals to Mrs McCormick to renew her subsidy were fruitless. Appeals also to Budgen to join him in Trieste were unavailing. Joyce had nobody to talk to about *Ulysses*, which may explain his initial difficulty in getting back to writing. Stanislaus now had interests of his own to pursue and Budgen can hardly have been tempted by Joyce's descriptions of Trieste: but Joyce had always a difficulty in understanding the desire of other people to get on with their own lives.

He resumed teaching, but only his few hours a day, at the Commercial School, in January, and by then had found renewed enthusiasm for writing. Nausicaa was finished and Oxen of the Sun. On this episode, which he considered the most difficult in the book until he began the next one, he expended by his own calculation 1,000 hours. The sin of Ulysses's companions in making a meal of the sacred beasts was to be represented by 'the crime committed against fecundity by sterilizing the act of coition'. Technique (with frequent reference to a chart of the development of the child in the womb), a nine-part illustration of the history of the English language, starting with 'a Sallustian-Tacitean prelude' and proceeding via Anglo-Saxon, Mandeville, Malory, Milton, Bunyan, Pepys-Evelyn, Defoe-Swift, Steele-Addison-Sterne and Landor-Pater-Newman to 'a frightful jumble of pidgin English, nigger English, Cockney, Irish, Bowery slang and broken doggerel'. Stanislaus being profoundly uninterested in such technicalities, Joyce was obliged to expound them on paper to Budgen. In an attempt to get him to Trieste he offered him a livelihood teaching English, a room which he had not got, and Tullio Silvestri's studio. Budgen preferred to return to England.

Feeling in the need of a holiday, Joyce contemplated transporting himself and his family to England for a month or two, or even Ireland. He needed clothes too, and where better to buy clothes than Dublin? 'I wear my son's boots (which are two sizes too large),' he wrote Pound, 'and his cast-off suit which is too narrow in the shoulders, other articles belong or belonged to my brother and to my brother-in-law.' Nora he thought could proceed to Galway with the children while he remained in Dublin to finish the book. But the fact somehow impressed itself on him that there was a considerable war waging in Ireland, and he would not in Dublin be able so blithely to ignore that war as he had another in Trieste and Zurich. He was aware that he must leave that dead town Trieste ('*de mortuis nil nisi bonum*') but uncertain where to go and what to live on when he got there.

Pound resolved this difficulty for him by urging him to visit Paris for a few days. The suggestion came during Pound's visit to Italy in May and June 1920. Mrs Pound was ill, so her husband took her to Sirmione on Lago di Garda, suggesting Joyce join them there. He set out to do so on 5 June but found on arrival at the railway station that a passenger train which had left some hours before had been in a collision. Another had been cancelled owing to a strike. Neither these omens nor the news that there had been a terrific storm at Sirmione prevented his making a further effort. He arrived there three days later, 'bringing my son with me to act as a lightning conductor'. The meeting was happy enough, Pound finding Joyce pleasing 'after the first shell of cantankerous Irishman'. He gave him a pair of boots and a suit (both too small, but no worse than what he was wearing) and offered to put him up in Paris for a few days. Joyce returned to Trieste after two days, determined to clear out, if only for a few months.

The family left for Paris two weeks later, via Venice and Milan. Joyce resigned his position at the Commercial School, now upgraded to become the University of Trieste, and asked that his brother be appointed (Stanislaus got the job after waiting a year). He was sufficiently irritated with his brother to avoid turning up at the station to say goodbye. He made the last mistake of collecting enough money to buy a Burberry coat, entrusting his brother with the purchase. He never got it (brother James called once at Burberry's branch in Paris to have a look at the stock, then forgot his commission. In December of the following year he promised to return the money and managed it finally in March 1922 by which time, Stanislaus complained, it had lost much of its value through fluctuation in exchange rates. He ought to have known better than give it to James in the first place). At least he was no longer his brother's keeper.

Paris seemed immediately pleasing. Joyce decided to stay there three months to finish the book, and was there most of the rest of his life. It is hardly surprising he found the city congenial: there was hardly an artist, musician or writer of consequence who did not find his way there some time in the 'twenties.

The first port of call was a private hotel in the rue de l'Université, recommended by Pound for its cheapness. Pound had been busy, urging Jenny Serruys, a literary agent, to undertake the translation of *A Portrait* into French. When she decided she had not the time, Pound took it to Madame Ludmilla Bloch-Savitsky, whose immediate intention was to begin work on another translation. Pound removed the volume from her hands in his best bullying manner, replacing it with *A Portrait*: 'You must translate Joyce's book, and right away. There's nothing in the literature of the world today, and not much in the literature of the past, that is up to it.' Madame Bloch-Savitsky agreed. Her version, entitled *Dedalus* with Joyce's consent, was published in Paris in 1924. She was of more immediate assistance in lending him a small flat close to the Bois de Boulogne until the beginning of November. Jenny Serruys contributed a bed for Georgio, a table to write on and various small sums of money. Her fiancé, William Aspenwall Bradley, contributed an old army overcoat. Mlle Serruys undertook, at her own suggestion, the less onerous translation of *Exiles*. She hoped to induce Aurélien-Marie Lugné-Poë, who had introduced the works of Maeterlinck, Paul Claudel, Ibsen, Björnsen, Strindberg, Hauptmann *et al* to the French, similarly to introduce Joyce at his celebrated Théâtre de l'Oeuvre.

226

Invitations were forthcoming to literary and theatrical soirées but Joyce did not adapt well to the new milieu. He was conscious of his poverty and his poverty-stricken appearance and his, so far, comparative lack of fame. In any case he had always preferred a circle which revolved around him and him alone, a normal conversational gambit being immediately to dismiss from consideration all subjects which failed to interest him.

That was not yet possible. He took instead to absenting himself from conversations which bored him. Sylvia Beach found him doing just that at a party of the poet, André Spire's, on 11 July. Joyce had refused drink all afternoon, turning his glass down when it was offered. Pound, amused by this unaccustomed abstinence, teased Joyce by ranging all the bottles on the table in front of him. Joyce got 'very red' and retired annoyed to the adjoining library. Sylvia Beach, a young admirer. 'so frightened I wanted to run away' got up the courage to follow him.

'Is this the great James Joyce?' she asked, trembling.

'James Joyce,' he answered, offering a limp hand. She was to be the publisher of *Ulysses*.

Miss Beach was a courageous woman, the daughter of a Presbyterian Minister from Princetown, New Jersey. Introduced to Paris at the age of fourteen, when her father travelled there to impart moral instruction to American students, she conceived a passion for France and French literature. Her first ambition had been to open a French bookshop in New York and she had called on Ben Huebsch to ask his advice. It would cost a lot of money which she had not got. In 1917 she had returned to Paris and there struck up a friendship with Adrienne Monnier, forceful proprietress of La Maison des Amis des Livres, to whom were attracted such figures as Gertrude Stein, her companion Alice B. Toklas, Louis Aragon and André Gide.

Under the influence of Monnier, Miss Beach opened an English bookshop and lending library around the corner from La Maison, borrowing her mother's life-savings to do so. She called it Shakespeare and Company and attracted subscriptions from all of Adrienne Monnier's regular clients (Gertrude Stein withdrew hers in protest at *Ulysses*, but not for long).

Miss Beach explained her trade to Joyce, whose works she had in her bookshop, noting that his eyes, 'a deep blue, with the light of

227

genius in them', were 'extremely beautiful,' but saddened to see him hold the notebook so close to them as he wrote down her address. In the middle of this operation a dog barked in the street. Joyce turned pale and trembled. 'Is it coming in?' he asked. 'Is it fierce?'

Miss Beach assured him it was merely chasing a ball in the street.

The next day he appeared at Shakespeare and Company, dressed in a dark blue serge suit, a black felt hat, dirty tennis shoes and twirling an ashplant, the gift of an Irish officer from a British man-of-war which had visited Trieste. He sought Miss Beach's help in finding a permanent flat and some language pupils, and treated her to a slightly blarnified version of his history: he had narrowly escaped arrest in Trieste in 1915, for instance, as a British spy. On the other hand she found him, as geniuses go, very easy to talk to. He became known to her and Monnier by the nicknames he gave himself, 'Melancholy Jesus 'and 'Crooked Jesus'.[1]

The hunt for a patron continued. 'Pound wanted the Duchess of Marlborough to apply for the position vacated by Mrs M [McCormick],' Joyce wrote to Stanislaus, 25 July, 'but her bloody old father W. K. Vanderbilt died here in the next street to us the day before yesterday, very inconsiderately, I think.'

£10 was extracted by Pinker from Huebsch in royalties and a few pounds at a time borrowed from new acquaintances, one substantial loan of £4 being drawn at the first meeting from Fritz Vanderpyl, a good-natured Belgian art critic.

Pound had gone back to London. In August T. S. Eliot appeared as emissary from him, bringing with him Wyndham Lewis, whose work Joyce to some extent admired (*The Egoist Press* had published his novel *Tarr*). He was bearing a brown paper parcel given him by Pound for Joyce, containing yet another pair of shoes to replace the tennis gear. Eliot was not aware of the contents, and first became so when Joyce opened the packet in the lounge of the Hôtel Elysée. Joyce let the battered contents sit on the table while resuming conversation. Eliot asked him to dinner. Consenting, he told Georgio,

---

[1] Miss Beach, too, had a nickname, as Arthur Power informs me. Having a somewhat quarrelsome disposition, she was known as 'Miss Bitch'. Mr Power without any claim to historical accuracy adds a story current in his days in Paris, to the effect that she and Adrienne Monnier, in a fit of strenuous love-making, broke the bed they shared.

who was present, to go home and tell Nora. Georgio protested. Joyce insisted, handing him the undone packet to take with him. 'Having exchanged a good number of stormy words,' Lewis wrote, 'in a series of passionate asides – in a good imitation of an altercation between a couple of neapolitan touts – Joyce, père et fils, separated, the latter rushing away with the shoes beneath his arm, his face crimson and his eyes blazing with a truly southern ferocity – first having mastered himself for a moment sufficiently to bow to me from the hips, and to shake hands with heroic punctilio.'

Following this scene the three repaired to an expensive restaurant of Joyce's nomination and there wined and dined rather well. Joyce picked up the bill and added lavish tips. Both Lewis and Eliot found Joyce arrogant and excessively Irish. 'What provincials they are,' moaned Lewis, 'bless their beastly brogues!'

Eliot agreed. 'I never succeeded in getting out of the door *behind* him, have you?' asked Lewis. 'He is very *You First*. He is very *After you*!'

'Oh yes. He is polite, he is polite enough,' agreed the unctuous Eliot. 'But he is exceedingly arrogant. Underneath. That is why he is so polite. I should be better pleased if he were less polite.'

Some of this seeming arrogance proceeded from Joyce's distaste for Eliot's so-far published work, as Eliot no doubt was aware.

Shortly after this visit Miss Weaver, who had finally given up hope of finding an English printer for *Ulysses*, came once more to the relief of Joyce's mendicity (which did not stop his buying expensive meals) with a further gift of £2,000, money which her aunts were settling on her and for which she felt no personal need. This time the gift was to be entirely in Joyce's control so that he might draw on the capital during his 'best, most creative years'. The money was a little slow in finding its way through the Bank of England, so Miss Weaver sent £200 in October, thinking it might be useful. With this bounty Joyce felt able to take an expensive flat on the Boulevard Raspail, at a rent of £300 a year.

A case of books essential for the finishing of Circe arrived in Paris that month after spending three months en route from Trieste. It was finally retrieved from a station on the German border. *Circe*, the last episode of the middle part of *Ulysses* could now be disposed of. It was finished by Christmas, in spite of a further eye attack, and Joyce proceeded on to Eumaeus, Ithaca and Penelope, introducing Budgen into the first episode as a lying drunken sailor. (When Budgen protested that it was uncharacteristic of Englishmen to tell lies, Joyce merely laughed.)

On Christmas Eve Sylvia Beach and Adrienne Monnier arranged a meeting with Valéry Larbaud, esteemed novelist, critic, poet and collector of toy soldiers. The two were civil to one another and Larbaud expressed a polite interest in *Ulysses,* having already read *A Portrait* at Miss Beach's suggestion and liked it. Two months later when he was ill in bed with 'the grippe' Miss Beach sent him the sections of *Ulysses* printed in the *Little Review* and the next day had a letter from him saying he was 'raving mad' over *Ulysses.* 'It is wonderful! As great as Rabelais!' Full of enthusiasm, he determined to help Joyce however he could. He would contribute an article to the *Nouvelle Revue Française* and give a 'séance' at La Maison des Amis as soon as the book was finished. In early summer he left Paris on holiday and lent Joyce his flat, relieving him of the expense of the Boulevard Raspail.

In March 1921, Huebsch, following the successful prosecution of the *Little Review,* decided that he could not publish *Ulysses* without cuts. John Quinn, acting for Joyce, withdrew the book and he, despondent and overworked after many long nights' writing went to pour out his despair to Sylvia Beach: 'My book will never come out now.' But Miss Beach had a brainwave. 'Would you let Shakespeare and Company have the honour of bringing out your *Ulysses?*' He accepted 'immediately and joyfully', and Miss Beach, after consultation with Adrienne Monnier, went ahead, undeterred, in her own words, 'by lack of capital, experience, and all the other requisites of a publisher'.

Monnier's printer, Maurice Darantière of Dijon, unusually devoted to literature for one of his calling, agreed to take on the work, knowing that he could not be paid until the subscriptions came in, *if* they came in. He displayed, too, great patience in the matter of proofs. It was explained to him that Joyce would need at least three sets for revision as he went along. Darantière pointed out that resetting type involved considerable extra expense, but Miss Beach insisted that Mr Joyce must have as many proofs, with wide margins, as he liked. Sometimes he required as many as five consecutive settings and claimed he wrote at least one third of *Ulysses* on the proofs.

Miss Beach decided on an edition of 1,000 altogether – 100 copies to be printed on Holland paper and signed by the author, price 350 francs – 150 on *vergé d'arche* selling at 250, and the remaining 750 on cheaper linen paper at 150 francs, still a very great sum to pay for a book (The French expected to buy novels for about 3.50 francs). Joyce would get sixty-six per cent of the profit. Miss Weaver announced that she would be glad to issue an edition of her own, printed in France from Darantière's plates, to be sold in England while Miss Beach concentrated on Europe and America. She sent him a contract offering twenty-five per cent of the price of the English edition until expenses had been covered, and ninety per cent of the profits thereafter. If that arrangement was acceptable to him she would send an advance of £200.

He cabled acceptance.

The day publication arrangements were agreed with Sylvia Beach, she, Adrienne Monnier and others decided to celebrate with a visit to the Bal Bullier, a Montparnasse dance-hall less decorous than the cafés usually frequented by intellectuals. There Joyce met Arthur Power, a young artist and hopeful writer from Dublin. Power had gone to the Bullier to meet a young laundress in the hope of completing her seduction that evening and had no desire to engage in intellectual chat. But the laundress did not turn up and he was drawn to the Beach/Joyce table and sat next to Joyce, who engaged him in long conversation about Dublin, Ireland and literature. When the party broke up the two went on for a final drink to the Closérie des Lilas.

A few days later Power called on Joyce to ask him to a party, but made the mistake of turning up at the Joyce flat with a pocket all too obviously full of bottles. He got a cold reception from the family. He felt glad to escape as quickly as possible, with Joyce seeing him to the door.

'You know I am an intelligent man,' Joyce said ruefully, 'but I have to put up with this sort of thing . . . However, we will meet again soon.' Arthur Power was to assume importance to future students of James Joyce. He developed the habit of writing down his recollections of Joyce's conversation after spending evenings with him. As Frank Budgen pointed out, Joyce was continually taking notes during conversation himself but froze if he saw anyone else do it.

Power realized that, given the state of Joyce's eyes, Nora's vigilance was entirely for his own good. Sylvia Beach noted too that he actually enjoyed being called a 'good-for-nothing' by Nora, as a relief from the adulation he got from admirers. He never knew what time it was, Nora chafed. And how could she keep a servant with his irregular hours?! 'Look at him now! Leeching on the bed and scribbling away!' These outbursts usually ended in general mirth and Nora would regret she hadn't married a farmer or a banker or even a ragpicker.

Throughout 1921 *Ulysses* moved more or less steadily towards completion, with occasional hitches, as in the typing of Circe. The handwriting of Joyce's original manuscript was so appalling that several typists gave up in despair. One of them turned up at the flat, rang the doorbell, and when the door was opened simply threw the bundle of papers on the floor and walked away. Another typist turned out to have an excessively moral husband, an employee of the British Embassy. He was so enraged by what he could read of Circe that he tore part of it up and threw it in the fire. Fortunately, his wife had hidden most of it and was able to sneak it back to Joyce. The missing part presented a slight problem. Joyce had no copy himself but had made a fair copy to send to John Quinn in return for money. But when Quinn was asked for the loan of the relevant pages he rudely refused (thus reinforcing the opinion of patrons which Joyce shared with Dr Johnson) and would not allow them even to be copied (thus giving credence to that widespread opinion of bibliophiles which holds that they are more interested in bits of paper than what is written on them). Eventually he relented and sent photocopies.

In May there was a meeting with Marcel Proust, concerning which there were several versions. 'I observe,' Joyce had written to Budgen, 'a furtive attempt to run a certain Mr Marcel Proust of here against the signatory of this letter. I have read some pages of his. I cannot see any special talent but I am a bad critic.' The portents were not good.

The two met at a supper party for Stravinsky and Diaghilev, which was much more Proust's style than Joyce's. He had not even the appropriate evening clothes. Accounts agree that Proust arrived late and that the two were introduced, then diverge wildly. Padraic Colum's version:

PROUST: Ah, Monsieur Joyce ... You know the Princess ..
JOYCE: No, Monsieur.
PROUST: Ah, you know the Countess ...
JOYCE: No, Monsieur.
PROUST: Then you know Madame ...
JOYCE: No, Monsieur.

Which may be taken as Joyce's own joke at Proust's expense, the French master by that time being in the grave and unable to answer back. William Carlos Williams had a version in which Joyce complained to Proust of a headache and Proust to Joyce of a bad stomach, and both went home. Margaret Anderson had it that each confessed ignorance of the other's work and that was that. Most unlikely. Joyce would not have been so rude.[2]

The version of the meeting which Power recorded was this: 'I met him once at a literary dinner (said Joyce) and when we were introduced all he said to me was "Do you like truffles?" "Yes," I replied, "I am very fond of truffles." And that was the only conversation which took place between the two most famous writers of their time.'

Finally, Budgen's version: 'Our talk consisted solely of the word "no". Proust asked me if I knew the duc so-and-so. I said, "No". Our hostess asked Proust if he had read such and such a piece of *Ulysses*. Proust said "No". And so on. Of course the situation was impossible. Proust's day was just beginning. Mine was at an end.'

The hostess, Mrs Violet Schiff, was able to provide Richard Ellmann with the sequel to the story, which has Joyce 'drifting' into Proust's taxi along with the Schiffs, a little tipsy and anxious to continue the acquaintance – and Proust, equally anxious to get rid of him – leaving the ditching operation to Mrs Schiff.

News of Joyce's adventures with the bottle reached Harriet Weaver in London, and greatly upset her. Wyndham Lewis called on her and let slip that he had had several 'uproarious all night sittings (and dancings)' – as the culprit described them to Budgen – with Joyce, that Joyce entertained lavishly (which he did) and was frequently drunk (which he was).

[2] Joyce was very seldom rude to anyone *in public*, except to his wife, a rudeness which is generally acceptable even in the politest society, and to publishers, another permissible lapse where writers are concerned.

It did not at first occur to Miss Weaver that Joyce got his work done whatever his frailties. She had been brought up to regard drink as a great evil and had been reinforced in that view by the damage she had seen it do in her experience as a social worker. In a state of considerable agitation she wrote him a stern letter of reproval. It came as an unpleasant shock to him – he would be in a bad way if he lost Miss Weaver's support – and wrote in panic to Budgen asking his advice. Budgen advised him to play the whole thing down, but he decided on a frontal attack. On 24 June he addressed her a letter, a long rambling unsubstantial apologia which he called, with deprecating charm, his speech from the dock.

> . . . as for myself having been asked to say why sentence of death should not be passed upon me – I would like to rectify a few mistakes.
>
> A nice collection could be made of legends about me. Here are some. My family in Dublin believe that I enriched myself in Switzerland during the war by espionage work for one or both combatants. Triestines . . . circulated the rumour, now firmly believed, that I am a cocaine victim. The general consensus in Dublin was (till the prospectus of *Ulysses* stopped it) that I could write no more, had broken down, and was dying in New York. A man from Liverpool told me he had heard that I was the owner of several cinema theatres all over Switzerland . . . Mr Pound describes me as a dour Aberdeen minister. Mr Lewis told me he was told that I was a crazy fellow who always carried four watches and rarely spoke except to ask my neighbour what o'clock it was. Mr Yeats seems to have described me to Mr Pound as a kind of Dick Sniveller.[3] My habit of addressing people whom I have just met for the first time as 'monsieur' earned me the reputation of a *tout petit*

[3] This is my attempt to decipher Joyce's handwriting. The form of this letter published in the *Letters* is a censored version. Miss Weaver insisted that certain passages she considered embarrassing be cut from Joyce's letters to her, before allowing publication. These mostly concerned Joyce's indigence, her own generosity to him, his rude remarks about certain eminences (such as Shaw, Yeats), his drinking habits, and Lucia Joyce's illness. But Miss Weaver left his letters to the British Museum Library under a ten-year seal and these became available for inspection in 1971. In the letter above I have restored some of the cuts relating to the drink problem (or lack of problem as Joyce saw it). It must be said that most of Miss Weaver's *cuts* were extremely innocuous. Unfortunately, she wholly destroyed any letters she considered too private ever to be published.

bourgeois while others consider what I intend for politeness as most offensive. I suppose I now have the reputation of being, an incurable dipsomaniac. One woman here circulated [?] the rumour that I am extremely lazy and will never finish anything (I calculate that I must have spent nearly 20,000 hours in writing *Ulysses*). A batch of people in Zurich persuaded themselves that I was gradually going mad and actually endeavoured to induce me to enter a sanatorium where a certain Dr Jung (the Swiss Tweedeldum who is not to be confused with the Vienesse Tweedledee, Dr Freud) amuses himself at the expense (in every sense of the word) of ladies and gentlemen who are troubled with bees in their bonnets.

And so on. He denies that he is keeping bad company (another accusation of Miss Weaver's, apparently) and returns to the principal charge against him (this passage is one of those excised by Miss Weaver):

To return to the indictment. What Mr Lewis and Mr McAlmon told you is, I am sure right but at the same time you may have misunderstood what they said. I do not attach as much importance to the 'excess' mentioned as you do and as Mr Lewis does, apparently. And yet you are both probably right. This is another reason why your letters relieved me. I suppose you will think me an indifferent kind of rascal. Perhaps I am ...

This letter begins to remind me of a preface by George Bernard Shaw. It does not seem to be a reply to your letter after all. I hate pose of any kind and so I could not [words missing] highflown epistle about nervous tension and relaxation, or asceticism, the cause and the effect of excess etc etc. You already have one proof of my imbecile stupidity. Here now is an example of my emptiness. I have not read a work of literature for several years. My head is full of pebbles and rubbish and broken watches and lots of glass picked up 'most everywhere. The task I set myself technically in writing a book from eighteen different points of view and in as many styles, all apparently unknown or undiscovered by my fellow tradesmen, that and the nature of the legend chosen would be enough to upset anyone's mental balance. I want to finish with the book and try to settle my entangled material affairs definitely one way or the other. (Somebody here said of me. 'They call him a poet. He appears to be chiefly interested in matresses.').

And so on. In admission of some guilt, he confesses ignorance of ancient Greek, then:

> Now I end this long rambling shambling speech, having said nothing of the darker aspects of my execrable character. I suppose the law should now take its course with me because it must now seem to you a waste of rope to accomplish the dissolution of a person who has now dissolved visibly and possesses scarcely as much 'pendibility' as an uninhabited dressing-gown.

Another friend and drinking companion of Joyce's and Lewis's, Robert McAlmon, American poet, writer and dilettante publisher, had come to the defence, assuring Miss Weaver that Joyce drank in moderation and always behaved like a gentleman. Miss Weaver, well aware that McAlmon drank himself, disbelieved him, but came to decide, over the months, that Joyce's drinking habits were no concern of hers so long as he continued to work. McAlmon did come in useful for loans. He was married to Winifred Ellerman, daughter of a shipping magnate, who wrote under the name of 'Bryher' and supported Harriet Weaver's projects with her own money. The McAlmon marriage was for convenience's sake only[4] but Robert had access to his wife's money, hence his soubriquet, after they divorced, 'McAlimony'. He struck some people, including Nora, as an odious creature. Arthur Power could not stand him and wondered how Joyce could. After observing a quarrel between Power and McAlmon, Joyce remarked to Power, with some overtones of self-satisfaction, 'I'm sorry that people are always fighting over me.' Joyce did not mind borrowing $150 a month from McAlmon until the publication of *Ulysses*, and was careless about paying it back, so perhaps it did not matter who liked him and who did not.

That summer Lugné-Poë announced he had no desire to lose 15,000 francs on *Exiles*, and Joyce did not seem terribly distressed. *Ulysses* went well until he had another bad eye attack. He was drinking one evening with McAlmon when the American pointed to a rat running down the stairs. 'Where, where?' said Joyce in a panic, 'that's bad luck,' and lost consciousness. The following even-

---

[4] McAlmon said his wife married him in order to be able to travel without a chaperone.

ing, this time with Nora, he collapsed in pain from another attack of iritis and this time was disabled for five weeks. It may have been at this time that he discovered Miss Beach's own oculist, Dr Louis Borsch, an American, but the date is uncertain.[5]

Joyce's own specialist had advised an immediate operation. He disagreed, on the grounds that it was unwise to operate during an attack. He wanted to see Dr Borsch. Miss Beach flew to get him, but the doctor could not go to the bedside of another doctor's patient, so he said. Joyce must come to him. So Miss Beach flew back across the town, got the patient into a taxi and bundled him over to Borsch, who gave him the diagnosis he wanted: the operation could wait.

Subscriptions rolled in from Gide, Yeats, Hemingway, T. E. Lawrence, even from French friends of Adrienne Monnier's who were told *Ulysses* would be a good English primer, and from several who had no idea what they were subscribing to, being drunk when McAlmon, diligent for his friend, got them to sign. A prospectus had been sent out extolling the virtues of the book, but one who failed to succumb to its blandishments was Bernard Shaw:

> Dear Madam, [he wrote Miss Beach] I have read several fragments of *Ulysses* in its serial form. It is a revolting record of a disgusting phase of civilization; but it is a truthful one; and I should like to put a cordon round Dublin; round up every male person in it between the ages of 15 and 30; force them to read it; and ask them whether on reflection they could see anything amusing in that foul mouthed, foul minded derision and obscenity ... It is, however, some consolation to find that at least somebody has felt deeply enough about it to face the horror of writing it all down and using his literary genius to force people to face it ... I must add, as the prospectus implies an invitation to purchase, that I am an elderly Irish gentleman, and that if you imagine that any Irishman, much less an elderly one, would pay 150 francs for a book, you little know my countrymen. Faithfully,
>
> G. Bernard Shaw

Joyce was delighted with the letter. It won him a bet with Miss

---

[5] Richard Ellmann, in *James Joyce* dates the first meeting with Dr Borsch on July-August 1922, but Sylvia Beach in *Shakespeare and Company* (Faber, 1960) dates it after the completion of Circe and while Joyce was still working on the proofs of *Ulysses*. See p. 249.

Beach – a packet of cigars. He was convinced that Shaw would only buy the book (but would certainly buy the book) anonymously.

By October Penelope was at the printers and Joyce was able to announce with relief that the writing of *Ulysses* was over, bar, of course, a good deal of proof reading and revision. He was still sending to Dublin for information. On 2 November: 'Is it possible for an ordinary person to climb over the area railing of No 7 Eccles Street, either from the path or the steps, lower himself down from the lowest part of the railing till his feet are within 2 feet or 3 of the ground and drop unhurt. I saw it done myself by a man of rather athletic build.'[6]

He was heartily fed up with the occupant of No 7 Eccles Street and 'looking forward to the expiration of my seven years' sentence'. 'In the words of the Cyclops narrator the curse of my deaf and dumb arse light sideways on Bloom and all his blooms and blossoms.'

With the book finished, Larbaud could proceed with his promised séance. It was set for 7 December. Part of Penelope was to be read in French and the translator chosen was Jacques Benoît-Méchin, a very young composer from Sylvia Beach's bookshop. When he asked to see the scheme for the book in order to understand better what he was doing, Joyce was willing to give him only parts of it, though he had given Larbaud the whole. Joyce told Budgen that he detested critics who assumed he wrote with 'tongue in cheek' but the reason he gave Benoît-Méchin for keeping his intentions to himself does suggest a desire to indulge in private jokes on a vast scale. 'If I gave it [the scheme of *Ulysses*] all up immediately,' he

---

[6] (See p. 106.) A man would have to be reasonably agile to manage the descent, of about ten feet. No 7 Eccles Street, like many other Irish buildings of historical or architectural value, is no longer with us, but the facade of the ground floor remains and so do the well and the railings. The front door was removed to the Bailey pub in Duke Street in 1967, where it may still be inspected. When news of the imminent demolition leaked, a rescue party of three set out to retrieve the door, pushing a handcart through the streets. These three were Mr John Ryan, the writer, who then owned the Bailey; Patrick Kavanagh, the poet; and Mr Leslie Mallory, the journalist and film-maker. The building was the property of an order of nuns (who have so far built nothing on the empty site). Mr Mallory tells me that the Reverend Mother in charge was initially reluctant to part with the door on the grounds that it was associated with 'that pagan writer.' But her objections were overcome by a donation to the Foreign Missions. See photograph of myself engaged in Joycean research at No 7.

told Benoîst (as reported by Richard Ellmann), 'I'd lose my immortality. I've put in so many enigmas and puzzles that it will keep the professors busy for centuries arguing over what I meant, and that's the only way of insuring one's immortality.' Of course he did in the end release the key to *Ulysses*, but by then he was halfway through *Finnegans Wake,* and *that* is a production that could not be unravelled by a thousand professors in a thousand years.[7]

There was an audience of 250 for the séance. Larbaud was nervous and decided at the last moment to omit some risqué passages from his reading of Penelope, though the audience had already been warned that certain pages to be read were bolder than was common then in the land of Rabelais.

'The séance went very well,' Joyce reported to Harriet Weaver.

> In the middle of the Cyclops episode the light went out very much as it did for the Cyclops himself but the audience was very patient. Strange to say Mr Larbaud's biographical introduction also contained a number of mis-statements though I had answered many times the questions he asked me. Nobody seems to be inclined to present me to the world in my unadorned prosaicness.[8] At the last moment he decided to cut part of the Penelope fragment but as he told me so only when he was walking to the table I accepted it. I daresay what he read was bad enough in all conscience but there was no sign of any kind of protest and had he read the extra few lines the equilibrium of the solar system would not have been greatly disturbed ...

Joyce hid behind a screen during the performance, which also included a reading in English from the Sirens by a professional actor, but to his mortification was dragged out at the end by Larbaud and embraced Gallic fashion. The performance garnered many extra subscriptions.

Shakespeare and Company was now adorned with a Greek flag presented by Joyce. He regarded the cobalt blue and white as lucky for him and determined that the book cover should be in those colours. Darantière went to endless pains to find the right dye and

---

[7] I hear there is a gentleman attempting this Herculean task, on the theory that *Finnegans Wake* has only seven different layers of meaning. I wish the gentleman luck, this side of the asylum. Joyce himself forgot what stretches of *Finnegans Wake* 'meant'.

[8] Still protesting innocence of the drink charge.

the right way of reproducing the tone Joyce wanted, and achieved it with the aid of a painter friend of Joyce's, Myron Nutting.

On 1 February, a bad omen. A man bumped into him in the street and muttered some words. Joyce went the familiar shade of white. He had interpreted the words as 'You are an abominable writer'. It was a bad day to hear those words.

Appropriate date of publication was of course 2 February 1922, Joyce's fortieth birthday. Darantière protested in vain that it couldn't be done. Of course it could, said Miss Beach. She must have at least a few copies to present to the author on his birthday. Darantière managed to oblige. The guard on the Dijon-Paris express, seven a.m. on 2 February, would have two copies. Miss Beach turned up on time, the train pulled in and the guard got off with a parcel in his hand. A few minutes later she was at Joyce's door with copy Number 1 of *Ulysses*. That book had seen the light of day thanks to the unceasing efforts, in three countries, of as formidable a phalanx of literary ladies as ever was.

Chapter Eighteen
French Bottles and Irish Bullets

Copy Number 2 of *Ulysses* went immediately into the front window of Shakespeare and Company but had to be removed. Word spread that *Ulysses* was at last published and the place was besieged by subscribers anxious for their copy. Miss Beach was obliged to hide hers lest the eager customers divided the one copy between them. When more began to arrive from Darantière, the author lent assistance with the parcelling. Miss Beach, with a bottle of glue-remover, erased the traces of this operation from Joyce's hair and *Ulysses* was got safely into the hands of its subscribers in Europe. Getting it to America was to be a different matter.

The combined birthday and publication celebrations were not entirely to Joyce's taste. There was dinner first, with a circle of admirers, and then a visit to a café. But eventually the café closed. Joyce saw that as no good reason to terminate the evening, but Nora did. 'I must be saved from these scenes,' the celebrated author complained as his wife bundled him into a cab.

Nora had not changed her mind about 'that book', as she called it, finger pointed scornfully in Miss Beach's bookshop. She had read the last pages of Penelope and had a fair idea what they were about. 'I guess the man's a genius,' was her comment, 'but what a dirty mind he has, hasn't he?' She did not particularly relish the praise lavished on her as model.

'Go along with you!' she snorted at Robert McAlmon when he remarked that her husband had learnt a prodigious amount about women from her. 'People say I have helped him to be a genius. What they'll be saying next is that if it hadn't been for that ignoramus of a woman what a man he would have been! But never you mind. I could tell them a thing or two about him after twenty years of putting up with him. And the devil take him when he's off on one of his rampages.'

These rampages were not infrequent. McAlmon noted that there was at least one night a week when Joyce refused to take to his bed until he absolutely had to. A favourite hangout was the Gypsy Bar, where McAlmon danced with the whores to the bad jazz of a French orchestra while Joyce recited sonorous Dante. The girls were properly appreciative, if Mrs Joyce was not herself too happy at having McAlmon cart her husband home after dawn, he being in no great shape either. 'I say, McAlmon,' said Joyce solicitously, as the poet retched one night against a lamp-post, 'your health is rather delicate. Maybe they'll be saying I'm a bad example for you.'

Frank Budgen arrived to inspect his old friend in his new glory and was taken with McAlmon to the Gypsy Bar. The meeting was not happy. Mina Loy and Djuna Barnes, two good-looking, bright American writers then part of the Paris literary scene, did not conceal their impatience with Budgen's English dullness. Joyce did nothing to rescue Budgen from the brilliance engulfing him (according to McAlmon, who, by his own account, was suffering no such inadequacy), until Budgen, in despair, disappeared into the night, leaving Joyce to a period of guilty Celtic gloom which drove the two women away. The two remaining stayed until five in the morning, when thrown out by the *patron*. The *next* five hours were spent in a small bistro on the Boulevard St Germain, where the many products of the whole of French alcoholic genius were systematically sampled. By ten o'clock in the morning Joyce was so drunk that his taxi-driver refused to help him climb the stairs of the hotel where, once again, he and Nora were ensconced. McAlmon did so, though he was little capable himself. Nora was waiting.

'Jim, you've been doin' this for twenty years, and I'm tellin' you it's the end,' she began, in best wifely style. 'Do you understand? You've been bringin' your drunken companions to me too long, and now you've started McAlmon in the same way.'[1]

This speech was more futile than usual, since Joyce could not hear it. McAlmon dumped him on the bed and explained it was all Budgen's fault: he had upset Joyce's sensitive nature. Nora then turned tender. 'I always told him that man would do him no good.'

McAlmon staggered home, and received illustration of Joyce's

[1] This story is McAlmon's and the detail is consequently suspect. It seems in retrospect unlikely Nora would blame Joyce for setting a bad example to McAlmon, whom she detested, except as a way of scoring off her husband.

cunning (that one-third part of his motto – the other two parts being silence and exile) only a few hours later, and before he had got to sleep himself. A telegram arrived demanding his presence at half-past four in the afternoon. Somehow he managed to drag himself back to Joyce's hotel. As soon as he walked through the door Joyce, looking 'owl-like and earnest' said: 'And, McAlmon, what have you been hearing today about the apartment the man said we were to have?'

Considering his condition, McAlmon was remarkably quick off the mark. 'Oh, he's seeing about it now. I'm to meet him at six o'clock.' Nora was anxious to move into a proper apartment again. Joyce had devised a plausible alibi.

A new drinking companion had arrived sometime in late 1921. Ernest Hemingway, not yet a novelist himself, but a fervent admirer of Joyce's work, turned up one morning at Shakespeare and Company without bringing either his letter of introduction from Sherwood Anderson or his wallet. Miss Beach gave him a warm welcome anyway. Hemingway melted enough to take off his shoe and sock to show off war wounds.

'When does Joyce come in?' he asked.

'If he comes in, it's usually very late in the afternoon,' said Miss Beach. 'Haven't you ever seen him?'

'We've seen him eating at Michaud's with his family,' said Hemingway, who could very rarely afford a restaurant meal – he was living in dire poverty with his first wife, Hadley, and baby son, 'but it's not polite to look at people when they are eating, and Michaud's is expensive.'

'Do you eat at home?' inquired Miss Beach.

'Mostly now,' said Hemingway, being brave and proud, and turning down an immediate dinner invitation. 'We have a good cook.'

Miss Beach insisted he take away as many books as he pleased. Shakespeare and Company became for Hemingway, as for other writers, mailing-box, office, and meeting-place as well as library and bookshop, and Miss Beach was rewarded for her kindness by being taken with Adrienne Monnier to six-day cycling events and boxing matches.

'Joyce came here with me a few times,' Hemingway told A. E. Hotchner in 1950, passing the bar called the Closérie Lilas. 'I knew him from 1921 till his death. In Paris he was always surrounded by professional friends and sycophants. We'd have discussions which would get very heated and sooner or later Joyce would get in some really rough insults; he was a nice man but nasty, especially if anyone started to talk about writing, nasty as hell, and when he really had everything in an uproar, he would suddenly depart and expect me to handle the characters in his wake who were demanding satisfaction. Joyce was very proud and very rude – especially to jerks.

'He really enjoyed drinking, and those nights when I'd bring him home after a protracted drinking bout, his wife, Nora, would open the door and say, "well, here comes James Joyce the author, drunk again with Ernest Hemingway!"'

Hemingway had not yet taken to assaulting literary antagonists (McAlmon, his first publisher, once received in thanks a split lip), but he was proud of his fists and his size and was teaching Ezra Pound, who was not very well adapted to the pursuit, the manly art (Wyndham Lewis observed one of these lessons with sardonic amusement. Hemingway said Lewis had 'the eyes of an unsuccessful rapist' and Lewis was equally rude about Hemingway, but too clever to get in the way of a fist). Joyce was not fooled by Hemingway's tough-guy act and if there were bar-room brawls in Joyce's wake they were likely Hemingway's idea. 'Joyce remarked to me one day,' Sylvia Beach wrote, 'that he thought it was a mistake, Hemingway's thinking himself such a tough fellow and McAlmon trying to pass himself off as the sensitive type. It was the other way round.'

Ulysses was attracting many other, sometimes quite strange, visitors to Shakespeare and Company. The work appeared in catalogues of erotica alongside *Fanny Hill* and *The Perfumed Garden*. An Irish priest, buying his copy, asked Miss Beach, 'Any other spicy books?' Jack Kahane, publisher and author of 'dirty books'[2] envied Miss Beach on account of her discovery of a really 'obscene' book, as he described it, and begged to be allowed to take over the rights. Frank Harris appeared in a horse-drawn carriage, especially hired for the occasion to impress Miss Beach, and offered her *My Life and Loves*, that immensely long and mendacious account of bogus conquests and non-existent friendships with the great. It

[2] Or 'DBs' as his son, Maurice Girodias, calls them.

went much further than Joyce, he assured her. Miss Beach sent him on to Kahane, but could not resist a little joke. When Harris, running once to catch a train, asked for an 'exciting' book she gave him Louisa May Alcott's *Little Women*. One writer she was sorry to turn down was D. H. Lawrence, whose *Lady Chatterley's Lover*, so far published only in Italy, was without copyright protection. Miss Beach understood his merit as a writer, and pitied him for his illness, but did not want a name as a publisher of erotica and, besides, had no money to bring out another book, not Lawrence's, nor Harris's, nor even Aleister Crowley's. 'The Beast', too, turned up with the offer of his memoirs.

Recognition of a sort was forthcoming from the new Irish Free State, which Joyce, because of the civil war raging there, disparagingly called the 'Free Fight'. Desmond FitzGerald, Minister for External Affairs in the Free State Government, paid him a visit and suggested that the new state should nominate him for the Nobel Prize (being ignorant, obviously, of the nomination mechanisms as well as naïve about his fellow-countrymen's likely feelings towards Joyce). If FitzGerald put the question to the Irish cabinet, said Joyce, not only would he not get the prize, FitzGerald would lose his job. The minister asked him if he contemplated a return to Ireland. 'Not for the present,' said Joyce.

'It is to be safe from the rabid and soul-destroying political atmosphere in Ireland that I live here,' he told Arthur Power, 'for in such an atmosphere it is very difficult to create good work, while in the atmosphere which "Father Murphy" creates it is impossible. At a very early stage I came to the conclusion that to stay in Ireland would be to rot, and I never had any intention of rotting, or at least if I had to, I intended to rot in my own way, and I think most people will agree that I have done that.'

He was also afraid of having a bullet put through him. Parnell *had* had quicklime flung in his eye. He was out of sympathy with the new nationalism, though he said he did not wish to offend those of his countrymen who were devoting their lives to a cause they felt to be necessary and just. He never accepted an Irish passport, or any honour from the Irish state, though he could hardly be accused of having been a Unionist: many Irishmen have found convenient a formal attachment to the British state without being overcome with admiration for the British character. 'Ireland is what she is,' Joyce said to Budgen, 'and *therefore I am what I am* because of the relations that have existed between England and Ireland. Tell me why you think I ought to wish to change the conditions that gave Ireland and me a shape and a destiny?'

Joyce's addiction to theories of conspiracy led him to suspect there was one afoot in the British Press to prevent mention of his book, but in fact two reviews had appeared in England within a month of publication.[3] The first, in *The Observer*, acknowledged genius but objected to obscenity. The next appeared in an unexpected quarter, causing considerable amusement to Joyce, Harriet Weaver and Sylvia Beach. The *Sporting Times*, popularly known as the *'Pink 'Un'*, got hold of a copy and thought it deserved front page treatment: 'SCANDAL OF JAMES JOYCE'S ULYSSES . . .' 'James Joyce is a writer of talent, but . . . he had ruled out all the elementary decencies of life and dwells appreciatively on things that sniggering louts of schoolboys guffaw about.' *Ulysses*, they concluded judiciously, would 'make a Hottentot sick'.

Stanislaus seemed to agree to some extent: 'I suppose *Circe* will stand as the most horrible thing in literature, unless you have something worse on your chest than this "Agony in the Kips". Isn't your art in danger of becoming a sanitary science. I wish you would write verse again . . . Everything dirty seems to have the same irresistible attraction for you that cow-dung has for flies.'

But fine reviews were forthcoming from Middleton Murray, in the *Nation and Athenaeum*, Arnold Bennett in *The Outlook* ('The best portions of the novel – unfortunately they constitute only a fraction of the whole – are superb. I single out the long orgiastic scene, and the long unspoken monologue of Mrs Bloom which closes the book . . . The former will easily bear comparison with Rabelais at his fantastical finest . . . The latter . . . might in its utterly convincing realism be an actual document, the magical record of inmost thoughts thought by a woman that existed.'), Djuna Barnes in *Vanity Fair* ('One wonders if at last Ireland has created her man.'), T. S. Eliot in the *Dial*.

The *Dublin Review* said reading the book constituted the commission of a sin against the Holy Ghost, which scarcely mattered.

[3] He was apt also to judge the worth of a review of *Ulysses* according to whether or not it included the name and address of the publisher. Critical praise does not directly pay anyone's rent or grocery bill.

Paul Claudel, a devoted Roman Catholic, must have felt the same way. He returned his inscribed copy. A more damaging criticism appeared in the *Sunday Express*, damaging because it might (and probably did) provoke the authorities to act against the book. 'I say deliberately,' wrote James Douglas in that paper, 'that it is the most infamously obscene book in ancient or modern literature. The obscenity of Rabelais is innocent compared with its leprous and scabrous horrors. All the secret sewers of vice are canalized in its flood of unimaginable thoughts, images and pornographic words. And its unclean lunacies are larded with appalling and revolting blasphemies directed against the Christian religion and against the name of Christ . . . The book is already the bible of beings who are exiles and outcasts in this and in every civilized country. It is also adopted by the Freudians as the supreme glory of their dirty and degraded cult.'

At Joyce's insistence, this garland of abuse was included in the list of press notices to be used as advertising. The 'cheap' first edition was sold out in a little over a month, and the more expensive editions not long after, with the author carping at the drudgery of having to sign his name in the 350 franc copies. The last three copies sold by Miss Beach fetched £22. £50 was the asking price for second-hand copies in London, so great was the book's notoriety (thanks in part to the *Sunday Express* and the *'Pink 'Un'*). Miss Weaver, whose appearance was unlikely to attract the attentions of Scotland Yard, carted some copies around to booksellers, smuggling three into Bumpus, where one of the partners objected to having such incendiary material on the premises. Her generosity was unflagging. She sent him 'royalties' without taking into account advances she had already paid, and in March made him another gift of £1,500, making a total so far of £8,500.

Nora decided this bounty could be put to good use with a trip to Ireland. Joyce argued with her and lost. There were ferocious rows, but on 1 April she left with the children. He bombarded her with telegrams as she passed through London, but she was determined. He was so anxious for their safety, McAlmon noted, that he went off drink. 'And do you think they're safe then, really? You don't understand, McAlmon, how this is affecting me. I am worried all the day, and it does my eye no good. Ah well,' and Joyce would heave a great sigh and write her another heart-rending letter.

247

My darling, my love, my queen. I jump out of bed to send you this. Your wire is postmarked 18 hours later than your letter which I have just received. A cheque for your fur will follow in a few hours, and also money for yourself. If you wish to live there (as you ask me to send two pounds a week) I will send that amount (£8 and £4 rent) on the first of every month. But you also ask me if I would go to London with you. I would go anywhere in the world if I could be sure that I would be alone with your dear self without family and without friends. Either this must occur or we must part forever, though it will break my heart. Evidently it is impossible to describe to you the despair I have been in since you left. Yesterday I got a fainting fit in Miss Beach's shop and she had to run and get me some kind of a drug. Your image is always in my heart. How glad I am to hear you are looking younger! O my dearest, if you would only turn to me even now and read that terrible book which has now broken in my breast and take me to yourself alone to do with me what you will! I have only 10 minutes to write this so forgive me. Will write again before noon and also wire. These few words for the moment and my undying unhappy love. Jim.

But the prospect of living in Ireland soon palled for Nora. Those former comrades of the war of independence, the Free-Staters who accepted the Treaty with Britain, and the remnants of the IRA who did not, were energetically slaughtering one another. The lodging-house where Nora was staying in Galway became part of the battle-field. The IRA occupied a warehouse opposite and the Free State Army answered by opening up with machine-guns through the Joyce family's bedroom windows. The three of them ran through the town and got on the Dublin train, but found they still had front-seat tickets for the war. The train being of strategic importance obviously had to be protected by armed troops and since there were armed troops on it it was equally imperative for the rebels to send bullets whistling through the passenger compartments. Nora and Lucia wisely spent the journey lying flat on the floor while Georgio sat scowling defiantly out the window. This time they did not pause in Dublin, but fled precipitously back to Paris. 'No doubt you will see Nora some other time when she goes to revisit her native dunghill though it is doubtful if Georgio or Lucia will go,' Joyce wrote in an ill-tempered letter to his Aunt Josephine. 'The air in Galway is very good but dear at the present price. The only enlivening feature of their journey seems to have been their interview with my father who amused them vastly by the virulence, variety and incandescence of curses which he bestowed on his native country and all in it – a litany to which his eldest son says *Amen* from the bottom, that is to say, the nethermost or lowest part of his heart.'

Once Nora was back Joyce determined to travel to London to discuss with Harriet Weaver her projected English edition. He thought a meeting was overdue. Miss Weaver looked forward to meeting him, but with some feeling of apprehension. She was frightened of drunks and unused to Joyce's sort of drunk: to her a man who drank was a man who beat his wife and children and wound up in the police courts. A new onset of eye trouble delayed the visit. His left eye, previously unaffected, was invaded by iritis and he was panic-stricken at the thought of going blind in both eyes. His doctors advised an operation but Joyce was reluctant: the last, no doubt unavoidably, had permanently impaired the vision of his right eye.

Miss Beach was summoned urgently to the hotel during a severe bout of pain. She found Nora renewing the compresses on his eyes from a bucket of ice-water. 'When the pain is unbearable he gets up and walks the floor,' she said. Dr Borsch, Sylvia Beach's oculist had obliged him by advising the operation be put off until the attack died down. Now he obliged him again. He agreed that the operation might be put off until Joyce had been to London. Yet another doctor insisted on the removal of all Joyce's teeth, so he had that to look forward to as well when he set out for London in August.

Miss Weaver's fears proved unfounded. She found Joyce utterly charming in the Irish manner, though her instinct for thrift was a little offended by his insistence on travelling everywhere by taxi and tipping hugely. It was her money he was spending – but Miss Weaver was able to suppress such unworthy thoughts. She could see no way of producing her edition of *Ulysses* for at least eight months but was so moved by Joyce's obvious depression at this prospect that she tried again. John Rodker, a small London publisher used to producing limited editions on hand-presses, but familiar with Paris, agreed to act as her agent in France. Darantière would do the printing – an edition of 2,000 to sell at £2 2s each – and the

249

title page would read: *Published for the Egoist Press, London by John Rodker, Paris 1922.*

Joyce was not in any condition to behave extravagantly during that trip. He was felled by an attack of conjunctivitis and spent most of the time counting the brass knobs on his hotel bed. The weather was foul and he was forced to give up his plans to visit an English seaside resort – to which dismal places he felt a strange attraction – and made a miserable trip back to France in a howling gale. Miss Weaver asked him before he went what he would write next, and he answered, 'I think I will write a history of the world'. It was going to be a peculiar history of the world.

His cousin, Kathleen Murray, had met him in London, and he had asked her what her mother, who had provided so much of the material for *Ulysses*, thought of the book. She was embarrassed.

'Well, Jim, Mother said it was not fit to read.'

'If *Ulysses* isn't fit to read,' said Joyce, 'life isn't fit to live.'

Chapter Nineteen

Here Comes Everybody

Getting *Ulysses* to subscribers in America presented problems – the US postal authorities were determined to preserve their country from corruption and succeeded in intercepting most copies. Some were sent piece by piece, wrapped in newspaper, to be re-bound on Columbia's shore. Forty copies were smuggled across the Ontario border by Barnet Braverman, a friend of Hemingway's (the Canadians had unaccountably failed to ban *Ulysses*). Mr Braverman crossed by ferry from Windsor to Detroit once a day with two copies making an alarming bulge front and rear of him, eyed suspiciously by US Customs. But they, as it happened, were more eager in those days to suppress booze than literature.

Miss Weaver's edition of 2,000 was subscribed in four days. Joyce, attempting to rest at Nice, got several welcome royalty cheques but was soon driven back to a new furnished flat in Paris by foul weather. Nora made a slight effort to read 'that book'.

'She has got as far as page 27 counting the cover,' her husband reported, noting balefully that even the weather conspired against him : it had not rained in Nice for nine months before his arrival. Leeches had to be applied again to his eye to relieve congestion but he noted hopefully that by raising his head he could achieve partial vision through the bad eye. 'This means that there is a clear space in the lower part of the nebula on the lens.' Dr Louis Colin, an oculist in Nice, dosed the nebula with a strong and painful solution, and part of it disappeared. Major operations for the removal of teeth, and on the eyes, were still necessary but might be put off a few weeks.

Four hundred of Miss Weaver's copies were seized going through New York, this necessitating a new small edition of another 500. Miss Weaver did not want to undertake a larger edition until Joyce had finished his correction. But all 500 of these were seized by British customs at Folkestone and most likely burnt.[1] Miss Weaver had been advised by lawyers that court action would be futile and expensive. One copy of *Ulysses,* sent by air from Paris had been seized at Croydon Airport in December, and found its way to the Director of Public Prosecutions. That gentleman, deciding that the book was *prima facie* obscene, so instructed HM Customs and Excise. *Those* gentlemen, duly warned, were waiting to pounce when *Ulysses* sailed into Folkestone harbour.

With the book running into such opposition in England and America it seemed clear, at least to Joyce, that Miss Beach should get on with a third edition in Paris. She did in the end produce many editions, but for the time being announced a little huffily that she did not feel like 'hustling to boom the book'. She had scarcely any time left for Shakespeare and Company, which was her livelihood. 'Possibly the fault is partly mine,' a chastened Joyce wrote to Miss Weaver 'I, my eye, my needs and my troublesome books are always there. There is no feast or celebration or meeting of shareholders but at the fatal hour I appear at the door in dubious habiliments, with impediments of baggage, a mute expectant family, a patch over one eye howling dismally for aid.'

The eye operation took place in April 1923, after the removal of seventeen infected teeth, Borsch presiding. Joyce was conscious and the knife seemed to him to loom over him like a great axe. The one-tenth vision in the bad eye had been improved by dosing it in a dionine solution to one-seventh or one-eighth and the operation improved it still further to about one-half. The artist could at least see to write, even if his handwriting resembled 'that of the late Napoleon Bonaparte when irritated by reverses'.[2]

'Yesterday,' Joyce announced to Miss Weaver, on 11 March, 'I wrote two pages – the first I have written since the final *Yes* of *Ulysses.* Having found a pen, with some difficulty I copied them out in a large handwriting [this being pre-operation] on a double sheet of foolscap so that I could read them. *Il lupo perde il pelo ma non il vizio,* as the Italians say. The wolf may lose his skin but not his vice or the leopard cannot change his spots.'

---

[1] A few survived, no doubt appropriated for their own use by Customs officials, and later sold.
[2] The morning after Waterloo, from the look of it.

These two pages, a sketch on the Irish King Roderick O'Connor, were the first of that terrible epic *Finnegans Wake*, which was to be sixteen years in the completion.

Finnegans Wake is not a book which can be picked up and read. Indeed it is debatable it can be read at all, or even that its author intended it to be read. It can be *listened* to with pleasure, and there exist recordings of readings by Joyce, and others (a certain courageous lady has made a film of it too). It is 628 pages long and not a single page is comprehensible without the assistance of at least one book of exegesis. Whether its author intended it to be entirely comprehensible is another debatable question (if you read it aloud, he claimed, it becomes clear. It does not) but he was certainly aware from the beginning that any attempt to read his *Work in Progress* (the real title was kept a secret from everyone but Nora) would have a distinctly soporific effect on the reader. 'The dentist is to make me a new set for nothing as with this one I can neither sing, laugh, shave nor (what is more important to my style of writing) yawn . . .' he wrote to Harriet Weaver, who was puzzled at this new 'style' of his and nervously expressed misgivings to intimates. Was Mr Joyce unhinged? Miss Weaver was able to convince herself otherwise. In July 1923 she made over to him the bequest of her recently deceased Aunt Emily, the sum of £12,000. She had given him £20,500 apart from incidentals.[3]

'The task I have set myself is dreadfully difficult,' said Joyce, 'but I believe it can be done.' This task was the creation of a new language (insofar as sounds which do not make sense can be said to constitute language), a *night* language. From epiphanies of dreams Joyce progressed to an entire book which is a dream, and if *Finnegans Wake* sounds like someone mumbling in their sleep that is because the hero is asleep. That hero is the Finnegan of the Irish bar room song:

> *Mickey Maloney raised his head,*
> *When a gallon of whiskey flew at him;*
> *It missed, and falling on the bed*
> *The liquor scattered over Tim.*

[3] These gifts by no means made Joyce rich. The combined income from capital and royalties never went much above £1,000 a year. Miss Weaver's latest gift was not delivered until the following May. In the interval he signed one more begging letter 'Job Joyce'.

'Och, he revives! See how he raises!'
And Timothy, jumping up from the bed,
Sez, 'Whirl your liquor round like blazes –
Souls to the devil! D'ye think I'm dead?'

But the philosophy is not the amiable saloon bar philosophy of, say, a John Joyce, but that of Giovanni Battista Vico (1668–1744), whose *Scienza Nuova* had long interested Joyce, quite apart from the significant coincidences that Vico was afraid of thunderstorms and that there is a coastal road outside Dublin called the Vico Road. Vico's work had been the enunciation of a new cyclical theory of history. The cycle was Theocracy, Aristocracy, Democracy, followed by a *ricorso*: the Gods speak in a clap of thunder and we are back to the first stage again. The whole history of the world could therefore be enacted in and around Dublin and take place entirely in the dream of a Chapelizod innkeeper, one Porter, who is also HCE, and variously Humphrey Chimpden Earwicker (thence, via the French for earwig, *perce-oreille*, to Persse O'Reilly), Brian Boru, Napoleon Bonaparte, Finn MacCool, Parnell, Swift, Here Comes Everybody, Haveth Childers Everywhere, 'our Human Conger Eel', 'Hecech', and so on, through innumerable variants, many, no doubt, as yet undetected by Joycean scholars. To state that HCE has many identities does not make the detection of them easy. His wife, his daughter, and his two sons have also many roles to play. Chapelizod means 'the chapel of Iseult', for instance, so the innkeeper's daughter becomes Isolde and Joyce is able to indulge a horrendous pun by calling her also 'Mildew Lisa'. The appreciation of that joke requires the knowledge that the first words of Isolde's aria over the dead body of Tristan, in *Tristan und Isolde* are 'Mild und Leise' (gentle and soft). *Finnegans Wake* is a gigantic multilingual crossword puzzle, the theme Resurrection (either by whiskey or divine agency) and the language built on puns. Normal response to a pun is to wince. *Finnegans Wake* is a very winceable book, even to the title, which refers not only to the song, but to the world awakening,[4] and to the Viconian cycle – French *fin* and English *again* – 'End again'. As Joyce pointed out, the Church was founded upon a pun (Latin *petrus* – rock. 'Upon this rock I found my

---

[4] This explains Joyce's fury whenever an apostrophe was intruded into the title of his book. The point is that Finnegans are waking, whomever they may be.

Church'). Why should he not found a new language upon puns? The difficulty is that mastering that language is comparable in difficulty to mastering simultaneously Sanskrit and Mandarin Chinese and there are those, admirers of the rest of Joyce's work, who would prefer to expend what energy they have for serious study grappling with something more rewarding. *Finnegans Wake* has of course numerous admirers.

'*Ulysses* and *Finnegans Wake*,' wrote Anthony Burgess, that fine (and usually comprehensible) novelist, in his foreword to *A Shorter Finnegans Wake*, 'are highly idiosyncratic and "difficult" books, admired more often than read, when read rarely read through to the end, when read through to the end not often fully, or even partially, understood. This, of course, is especially true of *Finnegans Wake*. And yet there are people who not only claim to understand a great deal of these books but affirm great love for them – love of an intensity more commonly accorded to Shakespeare or Jane Austen or Dickens. Such people feel impelled to take on the task of advocacy, so that others should not miss what the devotees consider to be a profound literary pleasure...'

It is this writer's opinion that *Ulysses* does not need advocacy, is indeed damaged by much of it. But *Finnegans Wake* most certainly does and potential readers of it could well start with Mr Burgess's boiling-down of the text, and his helpful explanations. 'Boildoyle and rawhoney on me,' says a character called Jute in the Wake, 'when I can beuraly forsstand a weird from sturk to finnic in such a patwhat as your rutterdamrotter. Onheard of and um-scene! Gut aftermeal! See you doomed.' Few will understand many weirds from sturk to finnic even with Mr Burgess's help. There is still the music to be enjoyed by those who are not allergic to puns.

'If ever I try to explain to people now what I am supposed to be writing,' Joyce said, 'I see stupefaction freezing them into silence.' Undoubted stupefaction did not freeze Stanislaus into silence. He refused to be 'whirled around in the mad dance by a literary dervish...'

I have received one instalment of your yet unnamed novel in the transatlantic review. I don't know whether the drivelling rigmarole about half a tall hat and ladies' modern toilet chambers (practically the only things I understand in this nightmare production) is written with the deliberate intention of pulling the reader's leg or not. You began this fooling in the Holles Street episode in *Ulysses* [Oxen of the Sun] and I see that Wyndham Lewis (the designer of that other piece of impudent fooling 'The Portrait of an Englishwoman') imitates it with heavy-hoofed capering in the columns of the *Daily Mail*. Or perhaps – a sadder supposition – it is the beginning of softening of the brain. The first instalment faintly suggests the Book of the Four Masters [it was indeed intended to suggest this old Irish history] and a kind of Biddy in Blunderland and a satire on the supposed matriarchal system. It has certain characteristics of a beginning of something, is nebulous, chaotic but contains certain elements. That is absolutely all I can make of it. But! It is unspeakably wearisome.

Stanislaus never reconciled himself to the *Wake*, even turning down a presentation copy of it when it was finally published sixteen years later. He regarded those years as a waste of his brother's talents. Valery Larbaud, on the other hand, was enthusiastic, as an extract appeared in Ford Madox Ford's *Transatlantic Review*. Larbaud, said Joyce modestly, 'is in a trance about it'. Miss Weaver, as more of the production appeared was not. She was able to appreciate the poetry, 'but I am made in such a way that I do not care much for the output from your Wholesale Safety Pun Factory nor for the darkness and unintelligibilities of your deliberately entangled language system. It seems to me you are wasting your genius. But I daresay I am wrong and in any case you will go on with what you are doing, so why thus stupidly say anything to discourage you? I hope I shall not do so again.'

This rebuke prostrated Joyce for a while, but he kept stubbornly to his chosen course. 'Why don't you write sensible books that people can understand?' asked Nora, but got no answer that made sense to her. For every person asking Nora's eminently reasonable question there were several urging Joyce on. Two such were Eugene and Maria Jolas. Eugene Jolas, Franco-American publisher of the review *transition* was as obsessed as Joyce with words and went so far as to draw up a manifesto declaring resoundingly that 'the revolution in the English language is an accomplished fact' and going on to pronounce, with lardings of William Blake, that 'Time is a tyranny to be conquered', 'The writers expresses. He does not communicate', and, finally, 'The plain reader be damned.' Joyce was a natural hero to such as signed, but was not himself a manifesto-signer nor even a revolutionary. The English-speaking world, he declared, could have its language back when he had finished with it.

'Do you think I may be on the wrong track with my *Work in Progress?*' Joyce anxiously asked McAlmon. 'Miss Weaver says she finds me a madman. Tell me frankly, McAlmon. No man can say for himself.' McAlmon, whose opinion of the merits of *Work in Progress* was distinctly sceptical, assured him he was not technically mad. Rude remarks were forthcoming from Gertrude Stein and Picasso. Stein was convinced that the only reason her own genius had not been universally recognized was that Joyce had stolen her thunder : Picasso remarked that Joyce was one of the great incomprehensibles who could be understood by anybody. Hemingway was impressed by Joyce's reading of the 'Anna Livia Plurabelle' passage which contains the names of hundreds of rivers and the words for 'peace' in dozens of languages. McAlmon liked it too (it is very mellifluous) but said he did not care how many languages were represented. Jolas undertook to publish each episode in *transition* as Joyce produced it.

Joyce got down properly to writing *Finnegans Wake* in the summer of 1923, on holiday in Bognor Regis, that bleak Sussex resort, home of retired newagents and tyrannical landladies. Appropriately, the author of thunderclaps was promptly visited by a terrific thunderstorm. London, Joyce reported, was terrified. Alexandra House, Clarence Road, Bognor, was not much to his taste. '... it is rather queer the way they serve the meals for you when you once let the fork out of your hand you have to wrestle with the girl for your plate and they put out all the electric lights at 11 in the bedrooms.' Kathleen Barnacle, Nora's youngest sister, accompanied them. 'He's a weakling, Kathleen,' Nora said (as reported by Kathleen to Richard Ellmann). 'I always have to be after his tail. I wish I was married to a man like my father. Being married to a writer is a very hard life.'

'He's on another book again,' she told Kathleen gloomily, but in Bognor took advantage of his profession, in the only recorded instance during their thirty-five years together. Wishing to exchange a pair of suede shoes which had split, she threatened the manager, 'My husband is a writer and if you don't change them I'll have it published in the paper.'

In August the family were back in Paris, staying in a slightly superior hotel but busily flat-hunting. Joyce had little idea so far of the eventual shape to be assumed by *Work in Progress*. He was tunnelling into it via several mineshafts, he told Harriet Weaver, and hoped they would meet at the centre.

Some diversions presented themslves, like Lincoln Gillespie, an ex-teacher of mathematics, who had discovered himself to be able to understand modern literature after being knocked unconscious by a truck. He grew a Joycean goatee and lectured on the master. 'And mind you,' he confessed to the stupefied American Women's Club in Paris, 'I did not understand their [Joyce's and Stein's] work myself until after my accident.' Ezra Pound contributed to the general air of artistic lunacy by writing an opera on Villon in spite of being virtually tone-deaf, extracting the notes painfully from banjo, mandolin, or from the instrument he appeared most at home with, the bassoon. The opera had a mildly successful performance but Georgio Joyce did not sing in it as his father had hoped.

Another composer literally making a lot of noise in Paris was George Antheil, a young American who had a flat above Sylvia Beach's bookshop and used the frontage of Shakespeare and Company as a ladder when he forgot his keys. Pound 'helped' him by writing a pamphlet called *George Antheil and the Treatise on Harmony*, which was an exposition of Pound's own ill-informed musicology, not Antheil's, as Antheil sharply pointed out.

Antheil's style of playing the piano was to use the keyboard as a punching-bag, and he used piano-rolls in performance, he said, because the pianistic contortions of his music were beyond the capacity of human hands. Joyce attended several of his concerts, including the very rowdy première of his *Ballet Mécanique*. Loud as the music was it was drowned by energetic catcalls from the partisan audience, with pro- and anti-Antheil factions matching the composer's energy by enthusiastically punching one another in the face while Ezra Pound roared out a defence of Antheil from the top gallery. The protagonists were eventually silenced when a huge wind-machine went into operation, freezing the heckler's into submission and scattering wigs and toupées like leaves before a storm. Joyce's peculiar comment on Antheil's noisy productions was that some of his music reminded him of Mozart. When Antheil proposed that he compose an opera based on the Cyclops episode of *Ulysses* Joyce was delighted. Antheil intended an orchestra consisting of a battery of thirteen roll-operated pianos, a phalanx of percussion and various noise-making machines. The soloists would sing the words through amplifying microphones while dancers presented the action in mime. Unfortunately, Antheil never got around to writing this masterwork.

Patrick Tuohy, the young Irish painter who had completed a very witty portrait of John Joyce the year before, turned up in May 1924 with a request that Joyce sit for him. Joyce consented after argument, declaring that he felt no particular affection for his face: he had seen its reflection too many times in battered, hungry, ill or hung-over condition. During the sittings, Tuohy, who talked too much for Joyce's taste, expounded on the difficult art of catching the sitter's soul. 'Never mind my soul,' said the sitter. 'Just be sure you have my tie right.' Tuohy got his tie right, but the picture, now at the University of Buffalo, is not as good as the one of John Joyce. Tuohy, who wound up a suicide, was probably intimidated by his subject.

After the sittings Joyce had to submit to another iridectomy, his fifth eye operation. It was followed by a holiday in Saint-Malo (with Joyce irritated by Breton bagpipes but interested enough in the (Celtic) Breton language to pronounce on its inferiority to Irish Gaelic. Any new language would come in handy in the overlarding of obscurities in *Work in Progress. De la Gaule à la France* was on his reading list.

In Paris, where Joyce was pleased not to be, there were squabbles over the French translation of *Ulysses*. A coalition had been established of Auguste Morel, French poet and translator, Stuart Gilbert, who had retired as a colonial judge in Burma (Joyce picked up some Burmese words off him) and Valery Larbaud, with Joyce as overseer. The partnership was not entirely harmonious. Larbaud was finally nominated ultimate arbiter in 1928 according to the terms of what Joyce ironically called the 'Treaty of Trianons' after the restaurant where it was thrashed out. Meanwhile, Larbaud was for a time under injunction to keep away from the rue de l'Odéon, where Adrienne Monnier was fuming over his part in another literary imbroglio.

259

Yeats wrote from Dublin with a renewed request for Joyce's presence. He was lobbying to have him awarded a new literary prize set up by the Free State government, but for which Joyce was ineligible by reason of non-residence. He refused these invitations and indicated his opinion of the new régime by remarking their impudence in displaying the whole island of Ireland on their postage stamps when the territory of the state as established by treaty specifically excluded Northern Ireland. A link with Dublin snapped in November 1924 with the death of Josephine Murray. Joyce's grief was intense.

An operation in that month to remove a secondary cataract was not a spectacular success. Dr Borsch apparently had a bet on with Joyce about the promised improvement to his sight. In January Joyce reported two conversations to Harriet Weaver.

DR BORSCH : How are you?
   J.J. : Inclined to pessimism.
DR BORSCH : You don't think etc.
   J.J. : Well . . .
DR BORSCH : What will you bet?
   J.J. : Fixing a date.
DR BORSCH : A month. How much will you bet?
   J.J. : O well . . .
     (later)
   J.J. : You removed the front wall of the capsule and the lens?
DR BORSCH : Yes.
   J.J. : Can a cataract form on the back wall?
DR BORSCH : Sure.
   J.J. : Is it likely in my case?
DR BORSCH : No. If it did I'd win my bet quicker.
   J.J. : (Prolonged smile).

Borsch was as eager to use the knife as most surgeons.

More eye operations were necessary. In February Joyce wrote: 'On Friday night I really thought I was as near unreason as my worst critics think me but they gave me some morphine which gave me relief.' Visiting the theatre at Fécamp on a summer trip to the south of France, he could not see the actor's faces from the ninth row of the stalls and had to abandon a walk on the beach when his sight clouded over. He displayed the usual resistance to operations, holding out until November, when he had to undergo two, which left him for a time completely blind in the left eye. 'Twice a day they flash a light before my eyes and say, "You see nothing? Not anything?" I am tired of it all. This has gone on so long.' In June 1926 he had a tenth operation on the left eye. The eleventh would come after an interval of four years. During those years he wrote painfully, in large characters, and could barely see what he had written.

Chapter Twenty

A Future Inside Literature?

That constituent of the Joycean motto which was cunning (the other two being silence and exile) is not to be underestimated. If Miss Weaver was not wholly enthusiastic for *Work in Progress* could she not in some way be drawn closer to it? Joyce encouraged her to guess at the intended title, but gave that up when she got too close. Another device had occurred to him earlier in 1926. 'A rather funny idea struck me that you might "order" a piece and I would do it. The gentlemen of the brush and hammer seem to have worked that way.' She obliged in appropriate language.

> Sirs: Kindly supply the undersigned with one full length grave account of his esteemed Highness Rhaggrick O'Hoggnor's Hogg Tomb as per photos enclosed and oblige.
>
> Yours faithfully, Henriette Véavère

The Joyce word game could be infectious, though Miss Weaver, like other admirers, still wished he would tire of it. The photographs were of an alleged giant's grave.

The result was the following.

> brings us back to Howth Castle & Environs. Sir Tristram, violer d'amores, had passencore rearrived on the scraggy isthmus from North Armorica to wielderfight his penisolate war; nor had stream rocks by the Oconee exaggerated themselves to Laurens County, Ga, doublin all the time; nor avoice from afire bellowsed mishe to tauftauf thuartpeatrick; nor yet, though venisoon after, had a kidscad buttended a bland old issac; not yet, though all's fair in vanessy, were sosie sesthers wroth with twone jonathan. Rot a peck of pa's malt had Shem or Shen brewed by arclight and rory end to the regginbrow was to be seen ringsome on the waterface.

. . . accompanied by a key explaining that Sir Amory Tristram, first Earl of Howth, who changed his name to St Lawrence, was born in Brittany, called (North) Armorica; that there was a Dublin Co., Georgia, founded by a Dubliner called Peter Sawyer and that its motto was 'Doubling all the time'. A further page of explanation followed, mentioning Aramaic puns, local Dublin geography, the affairs of Parnell and Swift, and further wordplay in German, Middle English, Italian, Latin, French and Gaelic. What precisely all this has to do with a giant's grave might not at first strike a casual reader, but apparently Joyce had in mind 'the topographical aspect' of HCE as he stretched in death-slumber from Howth Head to the Phoenix Park.

Ezra Pound's comment on another part of the manuscript, sent to Joyce on the same day he posted Miss Weaver's 'order' to her seems apposite. 'I will have another go at it, but up to the present I make nothing of it whatever. Nothing so far as I make out, nothing short of divine vision or a new cure for the clapp can possibly be worth all the circumambient peripherization.

'Doubtless there are patient souls, who will wade through anything for the sake of the possible joke . . .'

Harriet Weaver was not much pleased with her order either. Joyce announced it would have pride of place, on the first page, and that she would like the finished piece better. 'One great part of every human existence is passed in a state which cannot be rendered sensible by the use of wideawake language, cutanddry grammar and goahead plot,' he explained.

He strove always to find new layers of puzzles so that the piece, as is appears in *Finnegans Wake*, is in fact blessed with new ones. (The first sentence, by the way, to conform with Viconian theory, is a continuation of the last in the book which begins: 'A way a lone at last a loved a long the . . .' Joyce, having ended *Ulysses* with the strongest word in the language, wished to end *Finnegans Wake* with the weakest.)

> riverrun, past Eve and Adam's, from swerve of shore to bend of bay, brings us by a commodius vicus of recirculation back to Howth Castle and Environs.
> Sir Tristram, violer d'amores, fr'over the short sea, had passencore rearrived from North Armorica on this side the scraggy isthmus of Europe Minor to wielderfight his penisolate war nor had topsawyer's rocks by the stream Oconee exaggerated themselse to Laurens County's gorgios while they went doublin their mumper all the time: nor avoice from afire bellowsed mishe mishe to

tauftauf thuarpeatrick: nor yet, though venissoon after, had a
kidscad buttended a bland old issac: not yet, though all's fair in
vanessy, were sosie sesthers wroth with twone nathandjoe. Rot a
peck of pa's malt had Jhem or Shen brewed by arclight and rory
end to the regginbrow was to be seen ringsome on the aquaface.[1]

The burden of the piece is that we are in early history (or possibly
prehistory) and Sir Tristram had not yet rearrived (passencore –
pas encore) from Brittany, Saywer had not yet founded Dublin, Ga.,
St Patrick not yet confronted paganism nor Issac Butt tangled
with Parnell, nor Vanessa and Stella with Swift, nor John Jameson
distilled whiskey nor Arthur Guinness brewed beer. And 'at the
rainbow's end are dew and the colour red . . . When all vegetation
is covered by the flood there are no eyebrows on the face of the
waterworld.' Very simple really. Apart from certain other subtleties,
that takes care of one half of the first page of *Finnegans Wake* and
there are only 624½ to go.

Part of the summer of 1926 was spent in Belgium. Joyce liked
touring in spite of the fact that no place he was able to find had
weather to suit him: wintry weather was cold and summer weather
was stormy. His tours were not holidays. He continued to work. In
Belgium he learnt Flemish which, inevitably found its way into
the mosaic of *Work in Progress*, and paid a visit to Waterloo to
expand his knowledge of Bonaparte, who could hardly be left out of
a universal history.

The unwelcome news arrived from America that one Samuel
Roth, who had praised *Ulysses* to the skies, was giving expression
to his admiration by pirating it in a magazine called *Two Worlds
Monthly* which had previously run parts of *Work in Progress*,
also without permission, but had paid for them. Roth told Hemingway that he had used Joyce's name really only as a draw and thought
his readers would prefer more amusing fare, but continued his
piracy until he suspended publication with the last of Oxen of the
Sun and was subsequently admonished by the New York Supreme
Court but not required to pay damages. Joyce made the piracy the
occasion of drawing up a grand International Protest, addressed to
the American public 'in the name of that security of works of the
intellect and the imagination without which art cannot live'. An

---

[1] Faber and Faber edition, London, 1950, 1960.

impressive list of signatories was appended, but the protest did no good at all, except possibly to gain the victim a little publicity, which Pound, refusing to sign, guessed was the prime motive. Bernard Shaw, also refusing (he had just won the Nobel Prize for Literature) sensibly pointed out: 'The protest is all poppycock: nobody that the pirate cares about will blame him for taking advantage of the law. But Mr Joyce can point out that the law has produced an absurd situation. Instead of suppressing the book, which is its object, it is inviting every bookseller to rush out an edition of it.' As to Pound's complaint, it had a certain justice. Joyce was never averse to publicity so long as he could manage it himself, and avoided journalists principally on account of their habit of inaccuracy.

(One Basil Woon, a member of that profession, increased his distaste for it by calling on him to request, on behalf of his employers, an article on what it felt like to be going blind.)

Joyce counted in thousands the hours of work he invested in each episode of *Work in Progress* and in hundreds the number of abusive press cuttings referring to it. The bizarre idea occurred to him of getting James Stephens to take up the burden, under his direction, though their encounter in Dublin in 1912 had not been entirely fortunate. Stephens had achieved recognition in the Free State for his novel *Deirdre*, receiving for it that Tailteann Prize which Yeats had wanted bestowed on Joyce. *Deirdre* favourably impressed him but could scarcely have been remoter from his own work. It is a tragic tale of ancient Irish love-jealousy and murder which had already been worked by George Russell, Yeats and Synge. Dissimilarities in style, however, meant nothing to Joyce beside the fact that Stephens shared the same birthday – so he was told – 2 February 1882,[2] and had a name which was a combination of his own (James) and his hero's (Stephen). He paid a visit to Stephens, who was living in Paris at the time, but did not yet spring on him the project of taking over *Work in Progress*.

A trip to Holland in May 1927 was slightly spoilt by one of

[2] Stephens was secretive about his bitter childhood and his ancestry. He was probably abandoned as a child. Almost certainly he did not know his true birthday and may have picked 2 February because it was Saint Brigid's Day and traditionally supposed to be the first day of the Irish spring. He chose it long before there was any friendship with Joyce (*Letters of James Stephens* ed. Richard J. Finneran, Macmillan 1974).

265

Joyce's two principal phobias – dogs (he had been driven out of Paris by the other one – thunderstorms. He blamed their increasing frequency on the number of radio transmissions disturbing the atmosphere). Normally, his friends and family took great pains to protect him from these animals. Many of them seem to have understood that the tall myopic gentleman did not like them, and reacted accordingly. He was reclining alone on the beach at Scheveningen when the animal attacked him, broke his glasses and resisted the attempts of its owner to restrain it for a quarter of an hour, preferring repeated forays on Joyce. Otherwise he liked Holland, the Dutch temperament and Dutch cuisine but was forced back to Paris by . . . thunderstorms. But he managed to learn some Dutch.

Pomes Penyeach was published in June. Joyce hoped that this slight collection of verse would demonstrate that he could still write 'sanely' and therefore lessen the criticism of *Work in Progress*. But it was scarcely noticed. One at least of the thirteen short poems, the whole of his output since *Chamber Music*, is very fine:

A Flower Given To My Daughter

Frail the white rose and frail are
Her hands that gave
Whose soul is sere and paler
Than time's wan wave.

Rosefrail and fair – yet frailest
A wonder wild
In gentle eyes thou veilest,
My blueveined child.

It was Amalia Popper who had given the flower to Lucia more than a decade before.

The German translation of *Ulysses* also appeared that year, 1927. Joyce had gone through the manuscript with the translator, explaining to him such difficult English as the sexual connotations of 'crab' and 'Toby Tostoff'. 'Anna Livia Plurabelle', the labour of 1,200 hours by the author's count, was finished to his satisfaction in October and read to friends. Well aware of the melodic power of his voice, he enjoyed reading it. McAlmon describes one reading when also present were the Colums, Hemingway, Sylvia Beach, Stuart Gilbert and others. McAlmon, in honour of the occasion and acknowledgement of his well-known thirst, was given a glass of whiskey.

> ... And now he read this passage of his work in progress in a way that gave it its full emotional value. It was night, night, night, life haunting me with wonder and despair, and the mystery of birth and life and death and twilight and the dark river ever flowing and Joyce-Hamlet delving into the mystic and eternal chaos questing – Stephen Dedalus a little less precious, a little less the aesthete, intent upon the incarnate spirit. But, I, listening, saw only those grimly determined faces which *would* look intense and intent. Mary Colum now and then forced herself to acknowledge a comic touch with a smile, but her position as an intellectual also forced her to 'understand'. The others looked at space or at Joyce, and nodded their heads as Joyce's melodious voice continued. Sometimes his lovely tenor broke as he chuckled, a real live chuckle, at his own wit in the script. Then strained smiles broke on the faces of the assembled listeners. But they had set their faces into what they believed the proper expression for listening, and it was cruel to ask them to break the wax or break the mask with a natural grin.

McAlmon was not, as is obvious from internal evidence, the best and most reliable witness. When Mary Colum complained to Joyce of McAlmon's slur on her (which appeared in his book *Being Geniuses Together*) he said with a smile: 'But you were the only one present who frankly said you did not understand it. I remember how you laughed at passages that were humorous – that was more than any of the others did.'

Joyce frequently surprised hostile critics by declaring he thought it the motive of all artists to give pleasure but was genuinely delighted when anyone detected the jokes in *Work in Progress,* even without expressing approval of the whole. Mary Colum, for instance, had committed a grave impertinence after the reading. When Joyce asked his audience's opinion, she screwed up her courage and answered: 'Joyce, I think it is outside literature.' His answer was reserved for her husband. 'Your wife,' he said gravely, 'said that what I read was outside literature. Tell her it may be outside literature now, but its future is inside literature.'

Frank O'Connor, another Irish writer who paid him a visit,

was not terribly impressed with the Joycean wordplay either. He was passing through the hallway when he noticed a print of the River Lee on the wall, in a strange frame.

'That's nice,' said O'Connor. 'What is it?'

'That's cork,' said Joyce, deadpan.

'I know it's Cork,' said O'Connor, a Corkman, 'but what's the frame made of?'

'That's cork,' said Joyce. 'I had great trouble getting the French frame-makers to make it.'

O'Connor felt a little dizzy. 'I felt,' he said, during a BBC broadcast after Joyce's death, 'that the man was suffering from association mania, a thing I knew quite well due to a young lady I was quite familiar with who had an awful tendency whenever I was speaking of George Moore to turn the conversation onto Dartmoor.'

J. F. Byrne, who had reassured Joyce in 1909 that Vincent Cosgrave's claim to have seduced Nora was false, turned up in November for a few days' visit. He brought the news that Cosgrave's corpse a few months previous had been fished out of the Thames. Joyce's grief was not conspicuous. Byrne, 'the latest Irishman to ring my bell', was persuaded to stay on for a few days' conversation. Another old friend, Frank Budgen, made a peace overture[3] after an interval of three years, and Joyce accepted.

An attack of inflammation of the intestines, brought on, Joyce said, by overwork and worry, sent Miss Weaver across the Channel to him in January 1928. She asked him to stop wasting his time trying to justify *Work in Progress* to her but he insisted on going through it with her part by part, and awakened some enthusiasm (if it were not for Joyce's agonized explanations to her we would have a good deal less idea what *Finnegans Wake* is about). She stayed on for his forty-sixth birthday, by which time he had recovered sufficiently to dance at his party with Robert McAlmon while Antheil provided the musical accompaniment. 'Look at that Joyce!' said Adrienne Monnier, watching him caper. 'It's the satyr on a Greek vase.'

[3] Joyce had filched Budgen's wallet after getting him drunk. The point of this exercise, according to Richard Ellmann, was to retrieve an excessively candid letter Joyce had written to Budgen about his own situation, afterwards repenting his honesty and not trusting Budgen to keep it to himself. Budgen quite rightly took offence at this scurrilous behaviour. Joyce was inclined to treat his friends as doormats.

Lucia, who had been studying dancing for two years, took the part of a wild vine in a 'ballet Faunesque' and Miss Weaver attended a rehearsal during her trip. Always willing to worry about anyone but herself, she hoped that Joyce's daughter could make a career of her own and so escape the emotional insecurity she felt in the shadow of her father. That was not to be. Lucia's emotional illness, dismissed at first by her father as 'absentmindedness' got worse rather than better. Her dancing career would soon cease and her illness (it became clear that it was a form of schizophrenia) would become, of all griefs that James Joyce had to endure, perhaps the most intense, because he would allow himself to blame himself for it. The chemical origins of schizophrenia were unknown in his day and the fashionable explanation of most mental illness, reinforced by Freudian claptrap, was to blame it on persons close to the patient, preferably the father or mother. Lucia's life had certainly been unsettled: she had been twice required to learn a new language (besides English) and had struggled physically (so had her brother) against the prospect of going to school for the first time in Zurich. To blame her illness on her father (as Stanislaus did, and as Tom Gallacher, the Scottish playwright, has done, in *Mr. Joyce is Leaving Paris*) is grossly unjust.

George (as he now preferred to be called) was meanwhile training his voice and made his public debut in 1929. He had won one argument with his father. 'For ten years he *would* have me a tenor,' he told Kay Boyle, the Irish-American novelist. 'Baritone, bass, the voice teachers would tell him, and so he'd cart me off to somebody else. Tenor he *would* have me, and if you want to know the truth, that I couldn't comply was what drove him to drink and broke his heart.'

A good part of 1928 was spent in travelling. Ford Madox Ford lent a house in Toulon in April and later in the year Joyce travelled to Salzburg, Frankfurt, Munich and Le Havre. In March Eileen Joyce Schaurek and her children passed through Paris on the way to Ireland. Her husband, Frantisek Schaurek, had died a suicide eighteen months before and she thought a return to Ireland best. Her brothers contributed to her upkeep. (Eileen opened a boarding house in Bray called 'Ulysses'. It suffered the usual fate of Joyce enterprises: the demands of creditors shut it down.)

A happier family event was the marriage of Stanislaus, after forty-four years of celibacy, to Nellie Lichtensteiger. James met the newly-weds in Salzburg, where he was rebuked once again for *Work in Progress.* He assured his brother that a time would come when he would write comprehensible prose once more. *Work in Progress,* unfortunately, took up all the time he had left. There was to be no reawakening.

Another complainant was H. G. Wells, whose help Joyce wished to enlist in persuading a recalcitrant public of the book's merits. Wells duly took the trouble to read the episodes, then sent him a long, remarkable letter, first expressing his admiration for Joyce's past work, then explaining the differences between them: 'Your mental existence is obsessed by a monstrous system of contradictions. You may believe in chastity, purity and the personal God and that is why you are always breaking out into cries of cunt, shit and hell. As I don't believe in these things except as quite personal values my mind has never been shocked to outcries by the existence of waterclosets and menstrual bandages – and undeserved misfortunes.'

> Now with regard to this literary experiment of yours. It's a considerable thing because you are a very considerable man and you have in your crowded composition a mighty genius for expression which has escaped discipline. But I don't think it gets anywhere. You have turned your back on common men, on their elementary needs and their restricted time and intelligence and you have elaborated. What is the result? Vast riddles. Your last two works have been more amusing and exciting to write than they will ever be to read. Take me as a typical common reader. Do I get much pleasure from this work? No. Do I feel I am getting something new and illuminating as I do when I read Anrep's dreadful translation of Pavlov's badly written book on Conditioned Reflexes? No. So I ask: Who the hell is this Joyce who demands so many waking hours of the few thousand I have still to live for a proper appreciation of his quirks and fancies and flashes of rendering?
>
> All this from my point of view. Perhaps you are right and I am all wrong. Your work is an extraordinary experiment and I would go out of my way to save it from destructive or restrictive interruption. It has its believers and its following. Let them rejoice in it. To me it is a dead end.
>
> My warmest good wishes to you Joyce. I can't follow your

banner any more than you can follow mine. But the world is wide and there is room for both of us to be wrong.

Even after this very clear statement Joyce remained convinced that Wells could be brought round by a few well-aimed arguments, and felt the same about that other apostle of clear prose and non-admirer of *Work in Progress*, Arnold Bennett. There was to be a clear distinction between those who were to follow the Joyce banner and those who were not: those who were willing had to be willing also to give up the hundreds of hours Wells and Pound saw as necessary to get to 'the possible joke'.

An extravagant admirer who turned up in Paris in the summer of 1928 was Scott Fitzgerald, with his emasculating wife Zelda in tow. Fitzgerald worshipped Joyce (as may be seen from a caricature he drew of himself kneeling in prayer before a haloed 'St James'), though what he could have made of *Work in Progress* with his limited intellectual equipment remains a mystery. He was so much in awe of the master that he offered to jump out of the window to prove his adoration. Joyce feared for his sanity.

The year ended in near-tragedy. Nora's health, apart from imagined ailments during pregnancy, had been fairly robust. But now a cancer of the womb was detected. Nora was understandably frightened, and James insisted in sleeping by her side during an exploratory operation and a series of radium treatments at the American Hospital in November. Sylvia Beach had been told by the doctors that Nora's case was hopeless if the cancer spread, and confided in Harriet Weaver, but the news was kept from Joyce for fear of a complete collapse on his part. As it was, his eyes inflamed again.

Miss Weaver had her own worries, Dora Marsden being the principal,[4] but forgot them to rush once again to Paris to be with the Joyces. Nora had to go into hospital again in February to face the serious operation of hysterectomy. Sylvia broke the news to Joyce, who could not bring himself to sanction the operation until

[4] *The Egoist Press* had been revived to publish her long-awaited but unsaleable *The Definition of the Godhead*, dedicated to a female divinity. Miss Marsden had come to believe that the Holy Ghost was a she. Miss Weaver, while devoted to her, felt that she too was wasting her genius'. Her upkeep cost little but she made heavy emotional demands. Miss Marsden went so far in these as to insist that Harriet Weaver, gentle creature that she was, drown some superfluous kittens of hers.

after his birthday. Nora sat through the party looking frail and nervous. Joyce moved into the hospital with her and stayed until she was released. Miss Weaver prolonged her stay in Paris for two months afterwards to keep her company during her convalescence. Harriet Weaver seemed, as was often remarked, the nearest thing on earth to a saint and was entirely unaware of it.

Chapter Twenty-One
Mr Germ's Choice

'I am always making imaginary journeys,' said Joyce, but managed a great many real ones. After a *Déjeuner Ulysse* held ostensibly to celebrate the publication of that book in French, the Joyces went off in July 1929 to Torquay, realizing an old ambition to visit the West Country. Joyce, true Dubliner, was addicted to the seaside.

For the *déjeuner* a chartered bus carried a shoal of Bloomites beyond Versailles to a small village containing the Hôtel Léopold (Bloomsday, 16 June, had long since become a regular festival with bouquets of blue and white flowers and theatre invitations sent to Bloom's creator. Nora did not get the point. 'Why that particular day?' she asked).

One who distinguished himself at the *déjeuner* was the young Samuel Beckett, at the time engaged in the 'translation' of the last pages of 'Anna Livia Plurabelle' (or 'ALP') into 'French'. 'But there were two riotous young Irishmen[1] and one of them fell deeply under the influence of beer, wine, spirits, liqueurs, fresh air, movement and feminine society,' Joyce wrote to Larbaud, who was unable to be present, 'and was ingloriously abandoned by the Wagonette in one of those temporary palaces which are inseparably associated with the memory of the Emperor Vespasian.'[2]

Beckett was one of the contributors to *Our Exagmination round His Factification for Incamination of Work in Progress*, a title dictated by Joyce for a collection of essays (twelve. There must naturally be twelve disciples) intended to shed some light on the night book. Budgen, who had a painterly feeling for Joyce's word-play, was another contributor. McAlmon, less reverently, suspected Joyce's technique had something to do with glaucoma. Other contributors included William Carlos Williams, Eugene Jolas and Stuart Gilbert.

---

[1] *Not* Arthur Power, as it happens. He assured me he was not present on this adventure.

[2] *Pissoirs.* Vespasian was the first to tax them.

One of two 'protesting' letters appended at the end was signed Vladimir Dixon, this being Joyce himself at his most ponderously humorous. 'Dear Mister Germ's Choice, in gutter dispear I am taking up my pen toilet you know that, being Leyde up in bad with a pre-wailent distemper (I opened the window and in flew Enza), I have been reeding one half ter one the numboars of "transition" in witch are printed the severell instorments of your "Work in Progress".' And so on. This epistle, never acknowledged by Joyce, was delivered to Miss Beach's bookshop. She was publishing *Our Exagmination* and was instructed by Joyce to insert it.

The Joyces were accompanied to Torquay, where they stayed a month, in an expensive hotel, by Mr and Mrs Stuart Gilbert. Joyce spent some time assisting Gilbert with the revision of his book *James Joyce's ULYSSES.* Miss Weaver was induced to spend a week with them at the Imperial hotel, Joyce insisting that she stay there. It was against her instinct to spend money on herself, but he negotiated a reduced rate for her. She noticed that Nora, still weak after her operation, had fits of weeping over Lucia.

After a trip to Bristol Joyce went on to London to discuss with T. S. Eliot the publication by Faber and Faber of 'ALP', to finish a gramophone record of the piece and to visit friends. His eyes were so bad that he could not read the script, even in half-inch letters. Some passages of the recording are quite beautiful (Augustus John: 'I thought [it] the most terrific thing I had listened to for many a year'). Joyce sounds tired (as he should, since night is coming on) but also ill, and old beyond his forty-seven years. He adopts a strong and almost working-class Dublin accent. He has the range and tone of an accomplished actor.

He met George Moore again, to whom he offered a copy of the French edition of *Ulysses.* 'I shall be delighted to accept any book you choose to send me,' Moore answered frostily, 'but I hope you don't mind me reminding you that I can read English.'

Back in Paris, Joyce was visited by James Stephens, now apprised of Joyce's idea of transferring authorship to him. Stephens, reported Joyce, thought that 'ALP is the greatest prose ever written by man'. He was, however, well aware of the lunacy of Joyce's plan but promised to take it up if it became impossible for Joyce to continue.

A new enthusiasm which offered rich diversion from work was

John Sullivan, the Irish tenor, whose voice Joyce thought 'incomparably the greatest human voice I have ever heard, beside which Chaliapine is braggadocio and McCormack insignificant.' His comparative lack of success was of course to be blamed entirely on the conspiracy of Italian singers which had a stranglehold on the opera houses of London, New York and Chicago. Joyce set himself to get Sullivan through that ring, utilizing all the armoury of agitation he had built up in his own career – petitions, wire-pulling, letters to the press and rude publicity.

Sullivan owed his connection with Joyce to Stanislaus, who had found him in Trieste reading a copy of *A Portrait of the Artist* and recommended him to his brother. His voice was of the old-fashioned full-throated sort for which, as it happened, many of the more extravagant operatic parts of the nineteenth century had been written. Contemporary tenors, unwilling to tear their voices (and livelihoods) to pieces at an early age, were in the habit of doctoring such as Gounod and Bellini, omitting high passages, dropping to a lower key or otherwise butchering the score. Sullivan, on the other hand, was capable of the acrobatics as written. All he needed, declared Joyce, was a competent publicist – himself.

Sullivan was then a leading tenor at the Paris Opéra but had not the recognition he, and Joyce, believed he deserved. He had a wife, offspring and a mistress to support, eleven dependents in all, and he drank. Apart from being 'intractable, quarrelsome, disconnected, contemptuous, inclined to bullying, undiplomatic,' as Joyce reported to Miss Weaver, eager to demonstrate that he too could play at patronage, he was also 'good humoured, sociable, unaffected, amusing and well informed'. And he could sing high C sharps as no one else. (Music began and ended for James Joyce with tenors who could sing high notes, the more frequently hit and the longer held the better.)

For the time being Joyce contented himself with bullying friends into attending performances of Sullivan's and bullying journalists into writing about him. But considerable energy would be expended on his behalf over the next two or three years.

From time to time it was suggested to Joyce that he marry Nora. In the spring of 1930 he decided to do so 'for testamentary reasons' He wished to settle his estate and was told he could do so more easily if he and Nora were legally married and domiciled in England.

He wished to abandon the large flat in Square Robiac where he had lived for the unprecedented space of five years, put his belongings in store and take a small place in London for a few months 'to save hundreds of pounds I spend yearly in hotel bills there'. Joyce had realized, by the end of the year, nearly £2,000 of his capital, £100 at a time, in response to various emergencies. Miss Weaver was well aware of the depredations, sharing the same solicitor with Joyce, Fred Munro. Inclined to nervousness at any suggestion that Joyce contemplated 'economies' or moves of any sort she hastened to Paris in April. There she found that Joyce had been advised by friends from Zurich (including Marthe Fleischmann, still domiciled with Herr Hiltpold) that there was an eye surgeon in that city, Professor Alfred Vogt, who had a reputation as a miracle worker. She helped persuade him to shelve his plans for matrimony. Instead he travelled to Zurich to consult Professor Vogt. His eyesight was now so diminished that he had consented to learn to type. Suggestions that he should do so before had been met with contemptuous silence.

A series of operations began in Zurich in May. Professor Vogt's report, written a month later, gives in bald medical language, a fair picture of Joyce's sufferings.

> *Left eye.* A ninth operation was performed on this eye for tertiary cataract by Professor Alfred Vogt at Zurich on the 15th of May 1930. The growth was cut through horizontally, but proposed operation could not be completed as the vitreous body, most of which seems to have been lost during the last two operations, threatened to collapse completely by emergence or during the acute attack of Scopolamine poisoning which immediately followed the eighth operation. The dangers attendant on the ninth operation were successfully avoided as was an excessive haemorrhage. Ten days after the operation an attack of mechanical iritis due to the presence of blood occurred but lasted only ten hours and did not leave any exudate. A week later leeches were applied which successfully removed all blood from anterior chamber of the eye. On the 3rd June it became possible to make a microscopic examination. This revealed that the incision made, contrary to what happened in other operations, had remained open and unclogged by exudate but that blood had entered into the vitreous body, which a much operated eye would take some months to eliminate. It also revealed however that at the last operation the

276

back wall of the capsule of the lens had not been removed, possibly because its removal was too difficult and that in the time intervening between the eighth and ninth operation, 1½ years, it had been gradually overclouded so that it is now in a condition of almost *secondary cataract*, thereby occluding practical sight. At some future date which Professor Vogt cannot yet fix a tenth operation (capsulotomy) should be performed.

Right eye. This has not suffered appreciably in consequence of the operation on left eye, it still presents a complicated cataract on which an eleventh operation must ultimately be performed.

General Observations.
It has been decided to defer the tenth operation till middle of September 1930. The operation just performed will probably produce a slight amelioration of vision in the left eye, which before had a seeing power of 1/800 to 1/1000. On the other hand the seeing power of the right eye, estimated some months ago at 1/30, diminished constantly but slowly as the cataract developed. The most favourable factor in the case is, that, accord-to all medical opinions, in both eyes, optic nerve and periphery of the retina functioned perfectly normally. It is also, Professor Vogt believes, that the macula also is *normal* and that is, if the two operations still necessary are made with special instruments and when the eyes are in a non-glaucomatous condition, that there is every hope of obtaining ultimately a fair measure of clear and practical vision.

The next operations were comfortably remote and Joyce had back a measure of vision. Vogt prescribed new glasses and sent him back to Paris without presenting a bill.[3] Nora communicated this news joyfully to Harriet Weaver but asked her to suppress it until permission from Joyce: he had in mind a spectacular stunt for Sullivan's benefit which required the good news to be kept quiet for the time being. Joyce was no sooner back in Paris than Sullivan issued a letter to the editor of the *New York Herald*, copies to all principal newspapers, written in a style suspiciously reminiscent of that author of many protests, James Joyce:

[3] He did not extend the same favour to Eamonn de Valera, another Irish patient of his.

Théâtre National de l'Opéra

Your musical critic Mr Louis Schneider, in his notice of the recent performance at the Paris Opera of *Guillaume Tell*, with Mr Lauri-Volpi in the tenor role, informs the numerous readers of your journal that this was an exceptional performance, such as only a really great artist could have given. As I have, for many years, sustained this part, notably the most difficult ever written for the tenor voice, at the National Academy of Music here, where I am today *titulaire de rôle,* I claim the right, under your favour, to state publicly in these columns that Mr Lauri-Volpi, quite departing from the tradition upheld at this theatre for the past hundred years by all who have preceded him, cut out more than half of the singing part assigned to him by the composer. To be precise, all the arduous recitatives, without one exception, were suppressed. The duet with Tell in the first set was reduced to one-third of its length and vocal difficulty, as was the duet with the soprano in the second act and the celebrated and trying trio which immediately follows. As if this were not enough, Mr Lauri-Volpi most prudently avoided the perilous duel with the chorus which was written to form the climax of the whole Opera.

These being the facts, I courteously invite Mr Lauri-Volpi to sing this part in its entirety and as it was composed by his fellow countryman Rossini and as I myself have sung it over two hundred times throughout France, Belgium, Spain and North and South America, but especially in all the principal cities of Italy . . . If Mr Lauri-Volpi will sing this role, without transpositions or omissions at any Paris theatre or concert hall, where I may be allowed to sing it also, I am willing to accept Mr Louis Schneider as judge . . .

Et tout le reste est . . . publicité.

As it happened, Sullivan was due to sing Arnold in *Guillaume Tell* at the Opéra on 30 June. Joyce, sitting in one of the boxes, was ready for his grand gesture. Taking care that many eyes were on him, he leaned forward dramatically during a lull in the performance, recognized by all, removed his heavy spectacles and declared, with all the histrionic ability he could summon: 'Merci, mon Dieu, pour ce miracle. Après vingt ans, je revois la lumière.'[4] This had the stunning effect desired. A little later he added to the evening by

---

[4] 'Thank you, dear God, for this miracle. After twenty years I can see the light again.'

shouting out, 'Bravo Sullivan! Merde pour Lauri-Volpi!'[5] which some thought was going a little too far.

Et tout le reste est . . . publicité. The miracle of recovered sight was duly reported in the papers, with prominent mention of Sullivan (and Professor Vogt). As remarked elsewhere, Joyce had no objection to press publicity so long as he was able to control it.

In July and August Joyce and Nora travelled again to London and on to North Wales where he, naturally, studied a little Welsh. Most of the time in London was spent canvassing on Sullivan's behalf. He scarcely had time to see Harriet Weaver, except to secure a loan to cover the return to Paris.

Back in Paris he exerted himself to rope in George Antheil, who was supposed to be writing an *Anna Livia* symphony at the time, but was not (he had actually produced one Joycean work, a song for *The Joyce Book*, settings of *Pomes Penyeach* by thirteen different composers, edited by Herbert Hughes, an Ulster composer, and published in 1933). The idea was that Antheil write an opera based on Byron's *Cain*, designed specifically as a vehicle for Sullivan's voice. Antheil was as willing to embark on this work as any other, but wanted a 'peppy libretto' from Joyce as a draw. 'I would never have the bad manners,' answered Joyce, 'to rewrite the text of a great English poet. Somebody must curtail the text of the first and third acts and if it is to the advantage of the scheme in general my name may be used. I am quite content to go down to posterity as a scissors and paste man for that seems to me a harsh but not unjust description.'

Joyce got out the scissors with the assistance of Herbert Gorman, an American critic and historical novelist recently appointed by him as his official biographer. But Antheil would be satisfied with nothing less than a full-scale libretto by Joyce himself, suspecting shrewdly that that would get the opera produced. 'Antheil,' remarked Joyce sadly, 'missed the chance of a lifetime.' Joyce had managed, however, to pester Sir Thomas Beecham, via Lady Cunard, to hear Sullivan. Beecham admitted Sullivan had an amazing voice and promised to get him a hearing in London.

So Joyce got back to his own work, suspended for many months between eye trouble and the effort of boosting Sullivan. The new

[5] 'Bravo Sullivan! Shit on Lauri-Volpi!' This is his own account of the evening and may be slightly decorated.

section was based on children's games of all nationalities (and languages) and he thought it the lightest and gayest thing he had written.

From Zurich he got an unexpected compliment from Herr Professor Carl Jung, previously an antagonist. Paying tribute to *Ulysses*, which he had succeeded in reading after considerable mental effort, Jung particularly praised Molly Bloom's monologue. 'The 40 pages of non-stop run in the end is a string of veritable psychological peaches. I suppose the devil's grandmother knows so much about the real psychology of a woman. I didn't.' Joyce showed this tribute to Nora, who was unimpressed, as always.

In December George married Helen Kastor Fleischman, a handsome American divorcée ten years his senior with whom he had been having an affair for some years. His father dipped into his capital for another £100 to celebrate the union, provoking an angry reaction from Fred Munro. Nora at first disapproved of the match because of the age difference but very quickly reconciled herself to it. 'My wife and daughter-in-law,' Joyce wrote Harriet Weaver two weeks after the wedding, 'are at present on the most affectionate terms.' Joyce seized on the departure of George as another excuse for getting rid of the flat, disposed of the lease and moved into another hotel in April 1931, in preparation for a few months' removal to London.

Helen Joyce, according to Mr and Mrs Arthur Power was 'the smartest woman in Paris. You'd spot her coming a mile off in the street'. She patronized the couturière Schiaparelli, and for a time attempted to influence Nora in the direction of greater elegance, without much success. Nora relapsed quickly. 'Nora Joyce,' Mrs Power remembers, 'looked like she'd never left Galway. I remember her once wearing long black lace-up boots and a huge shapeless black dress.'

'Am leaving for England in a day or two when I recover from a nervous breakdown I had,' Joyce wrote Stanislaus on 14 April. He was worried about the attentions of a Triestine lunatic called Corti who had written accusing him of being his (Corti's) father's murderer and promising revenge. Joyce was anxious that Stanislaus should secure an accurate description of Corti and his brother (seemingly also a homicidal maniac) for circulation to the French frontier police to prevent their entry. Stanislaus seemed curiously indifferent to this threat to his brother's existence, and was equally dilatory in copying out his brother's letters for transmission to Gorman, not that Gorman was getting much co-operation out of the subject of his biography either.

'In 1909 it had been arranged that I was to take a trip to Dublin and bring Georgie with me,' Stanislaus wrote Gorman, dropping a not very gentle hint. 'At the last moment my brother wanted to go, as I had always inwardly suspected he would. He was met at the station of Westland Row in Dublin by a family group who asked him "Where's Stannie?" It's a question I have often asked myself.' Gorman might not therefore expect from Stanislaus that slavish devotion he had in the past lavished on his brother's interests. My Brother's Keeper had resigned the post.

The French version of 'ALP', begun by Samuel Beckett, and completed under Joyce's direction, was ready for publication by May and part of it was given an airing at a séance organized by Adrienne Monnier in late March, before the Joyces left for London. Mlle Monnier began with a speech about Joyce, followed by a talk from Philippe Soupault, one of the team of translators, about the difficulties of rendering it into French. The recording of Joyce reading it in English was played, followed at length by a recitation of the French version from Mlle Monnier.

Robert McAlmon, to whom the atmosphere of piety at these gatherings was suffocating, had unwisely allowed himself to attend. 'It is indeed a ghastly thing to observe the ghouls, the frustrated old maids of various sexes, the dandruffy young men, and the badly dressed women who clutter up literary gatherings,' he felt. 'They are too pathetic to be tragic, and they are too dumbly worshipful to know what is actually going on.' (On the other hand, it was Joyce's work that was being read, not McAlmon's, which may explain his pique.)

There were 200 present, many packed into a back-room, where McAlmon was. Also present was a distinguished looking old gentleman unknown to him. Adrienne Monnier read the passage fast, and few, even had they been capable of understanding a word, could hear her, according to McAlmon. In a moment of weakness he raised his hands to his face in a gesture of prayer and the old gentleman rushed across the room and slapped him in the face. This was Eduard Dujardin, whom Joyce always gave credit for having invented

the *monologue intérieur* in his novel *Les Lauriers sont Coupées.*
Joyce, by giving him that credit, had rescued him from obscurity.
Les Lauriers had been republished in France and Joyce had even
been able to arrange an English translation.

Now McAlmon was under the impression he had been slapped
for *lèse-majesté*, but it turned out that Dujardin had mistaken his
gesture for one of horror at the sight of Madame Dujardin's swollen
ankles. The mistake being explained, Dujardin later wished to
apologize.

After a month in the Hotel Belgravia in London (the economy
drive of a few weeks before, prompted by Fred Munro, had been
quickly forgotten) Joyce and Nora found a small flat in Kensington
and made preparations, after the interval of twenty-seven years, to
get married. This ceremony took place at Kensington Registry Office
on 4 July, well-attended by Press photographers (who are in the
habit of reading official announcements of forthcoming marriages,
even when that displeases those getting married). Joyce was certainly
not pleased to find their picture on the front page of the London
Evening Standard.

The clerk at first refused to marry them, on the grounds they
were married already. To save embarrassment and avoid the Press
Joyce had made up an elaborate story about a previous ceremony in
Trieste, invalid by reason of Nora's having given a false name.

Fred Munro had prepared a counter-argument. The clerk was
convinced. So they were married. Joyce was in a thoroughly bad
mood for days. He had not managed to arrange the Press very well
this time.

Chapter Twenty-Two
An Extravagant Licentious Disposition

'There's one thing I hate,' Nora complained to her sister, who paid her a visit after the marriage, 'going out to dinner and sitting with artists until one in the morning. They'd bore you stiff, Kathleen.' Her husband was pretty bored with London. Campden Grove, where the flat was, he christened Campden Grave. Putnams, the publishers, gave him a testimonial luncheon, but he was far from being a success. As usual he refused to be drawn into conversation unless the subject happened to be himself. All other overtures were met, said Harold Nicolson, 'with the gesture of a governess shutting the piano'.

Joyce's initial hostility to Nicolson may be explained by the fact that Nicolson had just taken up employment with Lord Beaverbrook as editor of the 'Londoner's Diary' in the *Evening Standard* (a job he detested). Nicolson wrote in his own diary, 30 July 1931:

To luncheon with the Huntingdons [Constant Huntingdon was Chairman of Putnams] to meet James Joyce. We await the arrival of this mysterious celebrity in a drawing-room heavy with the scent of Madonna lilies. There are the Huntingdons (Gladys a little nervous), Lady Gosford and Desmond MacCarthy [eminent critic]. We make conversation apprehensively. Suddenly a sound is heard on the staircase. We stop talking and rise. Mrs Joyce enters followed by her husband. A young-looking woman with the remains of beauty and an Irish accent so marked that she might have been a Belgian! Well dressed in the clothes of a young French bourgeoise: an art-nouveau brooch. Joyce himself, aloof and blind, follows her. My first impression is of a slightly bearded spinster: my second is of Willie King [art historian] made up like Philip II: my third of some thin little bird, peeking, crooked, reserved, violent and timid. Little claw hands. So blind that he stares away from one at a tangent, like a very thin owl.

The very thin owl turned out to be in a decidedly waspish mood. Mrs Huntingdon engaged him on the topic of Svevo: he dismissed this subject sharply. The conversation turned to a recent murder.

'Are you interested in murders?' Nicolson asked Joyce, hoping to draw him out (he was, in fact, interested in murders).

'Not in the very least,' said Joyce, with piano-closing gesture.

It was mentioned that Sir Richard Burton had once been British Consul in Trieste. Joyce displayed a flicker of interest at the mention of Trieste.

'Are you interested,' asked MacCarthy, 'in Burton?'

'Not,' said Joyce, 'in the very least.' The talk turned, inevitably, to *Ulysses* and Joyce listened with interest to Nicolson's story of his troubles with the BBC (see page 286). 'He is not a rude man,' was Nicolson's verdict. 'He manages to hide his dislike of the English in general and of the literary English in particular. But he is a difficult man to talk to.' MacCarthy also employed understatement. 'Joyce', he remarked, 'is not a very *convenient* guest at luncheon.'

Miss Weaver courted disaster by raising the subject of drink and diet. She had become enthusiastic about vegetables. Would it not be a good idea, she suggested, to begin meals with a glass of water and to alternate glasses of wine with glasses of water, if wine were really necessary? 'Raw vegetables,' Joyce told her, 'were created by the Lord to be thrown at Covent Garden tenors.' He was similarly enthusiastic about water.

His hopes of foisting Sullivan on Covent Garden came to nothing, so he switched his attentions to John Dulanty, Irish High Commissioner in London, hoping to arrange concert performances of *Guillaume Tell* under his patronage with Sir Thomas Beecham conducting, and taking care to keep Nora in the dark about these renewed exertions. Mrs Joyce thought Mr Joyce would be more profitably employed looking after his own affairs. '. . . He prefers not to write to you himself just now,' Miss Weaver wrote Sullivan, 'or his family would imagine he was launching another crusade on your behalf which would wear him to a shred several degrees more threadlike than even his present appearance makes.' Nothing came of this grand project.

A more promising *divertissement* was the appearance in the *Frankfurter Zeitung* of an 'impudent forgery', a story called 'Vielleicht ein Traum', signed James Joyce. The true author was Michael Joyce, a young writer then at the beginning of his career. The *Frankfurter Zeitung*, appraised of James Joyce's fury at this latest affront to genius, apologized, printed a correction under the heading 'Michael und James' and blamed the error on the translator, Irene Kafka. She in turn blamed her secretary. 'It has been translated from me out of the English typescript of *Michael Joyce*, whose short stories I translate and publish for some years already. Now my new secretary had been mistaken and she thought that there could exist only one sole Joyce, the author of Ulysses. So she wrote James instead of Michael, as I had dictated to her. And I did not remark that as I controlled her writing. And I got a terrible shock when the paper came out.'

Even Mr Michael Joyce, previously unaware of publication in Frankfurt, apologized to Mr James Joyce, but that eminent man of letters, sniffing the possibility of litigation, was unwilling to drop the matter. Miss Weaver, before the revelation of the real Michael Joyce, had been sent to scour the catalogues of the British Museum Library in search of him. All she found under that name was *An Exposure of the Haunts of Infamy and Dens of Vice in Bombay*, 1854. T. S. Eliot, by now a director of Faber and Faber, who were publishing sections of *Work in Progress* and considering *Ulysses*, was enlisted, along with Sean O'Casey (an extravant admirer), Professor Ernst Robert Curtius in Bonn, Dr Daniel Brody, publisher of the German *Ulysses*, and contingents of lawyers in Frankfurt and London. Stanislaus, who had by now lost all enthusiasm for his brother's battles, was instructed to get the affair ventilated in as many newspapers as possible. Joyce gave up after three months when it was pointed out to him that a lawsuit, besides appearing vindictive, could not get him more than £25 damages. The affair cost him £48 in legal fees.

These irritations proved a little too much for Joyce's nerves. An Irish friend, T. J. Kiernan, observed one outlet for his rage during this stay in England. During a trip to the lavatory he observed that Joyce, who was alone with him, put his hands to his head and let loose an agonized scream lasting half a minute. 'Look. That'll be enough now, do you mind?' said the sensible Kiernan, and Joyce immediately resumed his more normal taciturn manner.

At the end of September he returned with relief to Paris, in-

tending to get on with the neglected *Work in Progress*. Adrienne
Monnier gave a dinner in his honour in November, with guests
assembled to hear a radio talk on him by Harold Nicolson on the
BBC. But some eminence in the Corporation pushed the alarm
button at the last moment and the talk was not allowed to be broadcast. Nicolson protested and was allowed to give it two weeks later,
but only on condition that the corrupt *Ulysses* was not to be
mentioned by name. The BBC cancelled his contract anyway.

Ezra Pound, now living in Rapallo where he could better admire
the Fascist glories of Mussolini, brightened up Christmas with a
Joycean ditty to the tune of *The Wearing of the Green*:

> *O Paddy dear an' did you hear*
> *The news that's going round,*
> *The Censorship is on the land*
> *And sailors can be found*
> *Expurgating the stories*
> *That they used to tell wid ease*
> *And yeh can not find a prost'choot*
> *Will speak above her knees.*

*   *   *

> [Desmond FitzGerald, Irish Government Minister, speaks]
> *'They've had up the damn boible*
> *'To examine its part an' hole,*
> *'And now we know that Adam*
> *'Used to practice birt-control,*
> *'In accordance wid St Thomas*
> *'And dhe faders of the church,*
> *'And when pore Eve would waant to fuck*
> *'He'd lambaste her wid a birch.'*

*   *   *

> *Sure I thought of Mr Griffeth*
> *And of Nelson and Parnell*
> *And of all the howly rebels*
> *Now roastin' down in hell*
> *For havin't said 'Oh deary me!'*
> *Or 'blow' or even 'blawst'*
> *An' I says to Lowsy Esmond:*
> *'Shure owld Oireland's free at last.'*

286

This canto was appreciated in Paris, but when Joyce wrote to Pound on New Year's Day, 1932, he had sad news. John Joyce had died two days before. His son learnt the news of his last illness on 27 December and immediately telegraphed to Dublin to ensure the best possible medical treatment. For eleven years John Joyce's greatest desire had been that his son see him before it was too late, and now it was. His last thoughts had been of James. 'Tell Jim,' he gasped on his deathbed, 'he was born at six in the morning.' James Joyce, consulting an astrologer, had asked for this information.

'He had an intense love for me,' Joyce wrote Eliot, 'and it adds anew to my grief and remorse that I did not go to Dublin to see him for so many years. I kept him constantly under the illusion that I would come and was always in correspondence with him but an instinct which I believed in held me back from going, much as I longed to.'

The same note appears in a letter[1] to Herbert Hughes, an Irishman, but a Protestant Ulsterman who could be expected to understand. 'I could not go to see him,' Joyce wrote, 'because he lived among savages.'

Harriet Weaver sent money to pay for the funeral, a service she would be performing also for James Joyce himself nine years later. On 17 January, Joyce conveyed his despondency to Miss Weaver.

> . . . I am thinking of abandoning work altogether and leaving the thing unfinished with blanks. Worries and jealousies and my own mistakes. Why go on writing about a place I did not dare go to at such a moment, where not three persons know me or understand me (in the obituary notice the editor of the *Independent* raised objection to the allusion to me)? But after my experience with the blackmailers in England I had no wish to face the Irish [possibly a paranoiac reference to his marriage]. My father had an extraordinary affection for me. He was the silliest man I ever knew and yet cruelly shrewd. He thought and talked of me up to his last breath. I was very fond of him always, being a sinner myself, and even liked his faults. Hundreds of pages and scores of characters in my books came from him. His dry (or rather wet) wit and his expression of face convulsed me often with laughter. When he got the copy I sent him of *Tales Told*

[1] A series of thirteen unpublished letters, four postcards and four telegrams to Hughes were auctioned at Christie's (London) in April 1974 for £4,000 ($9,660).

etc.[2] (so they write me) he looked a long time at Brancusi's portrait of J. J.[3] and finally remarked: Jim has changed more than I thought. I got from him his portraits, a waistcoat, a good tenor voice, and an extravagant licentious disposition (out of which, however, the greater part of any talent I may have springs) but, apart from these, something else I cannot define. But if an observer thought of my father and myself and my son too physically, though we are all very different, he could perhaps define it. It is a great consolation to me to have such a good son. His grandfather was very fond of him and kept his photograph beside mine on the mantelpiece.

I knew he was old. But I thought he would live longer. It is not death that crushed me so much but self-accusation . . .

Trying to cheer him up, Miss Weaver announced that she was cancelling all his outstanding debts for his fiftieth birthday, 2 February, which was also the tenth anniversary of *Ulysses*. But that was not a cheerful day. During the afternoon Lucia, who directed many of her irrational rages at her mother, threw a chair at Nora and had to be taken off to a *maison de santé* for a few days by George who, of all the family, was firmest with her.

There was good news from America. Bennett Cerf, whose company, Random House, were publishing *A Portrait* and *Dubliners* under licence from Huebsch, proposed to publish *Ulysses*. Joyce, anticipating the usual delays over anything to do with that book, agreed readily, looking forward to an advance of £700. But it would take more than that to lift him out of his depression. Helen Joyce obliged, by giving birth on 15 February to a boy, named Stephen James Joyce in honour of his grandfather and his grandfather's creation. Joyce wrote that day his best and most moving poem, *Ecce Puer*, not forgetting his father but trying to bury him, and at the same time celebrating his grandson.

> *Of the dark past*
> *A child is born;*
> *With joy and grief*
> *My heart is torn.*

---

[2] 'Tales Told of Shem and Shaun' an episode of *Work in Progress*.
[3] An abstract representation of Joyce, consisting of a spiral and three straight lines.

Calm in his cradle
The living lies.
May love and mercy
Unclose his eyes!

Young life is breathed
On the glass;
The world that was not
Comes to pass

A child is sleeping:
An old man gone.
O, father forsaken,
Forgive your son!

'Je suis papa mais pas poète,' Joyce said about this poem, being strangely modest, but allowed its publication. Helen Joyce wanted her son baptized. George had no objection but thought it prudent to keep the ceremony a secret from his father. Padraic and Mary Colum assisted in the deception as godparents. Colum's French was imperfect, and when the priest asked him, on behalf of the infant Stephen Joyce, whether he renounced the Devil and all his works, he answered vehemently, 'Non!' So perhaps the child's grandfather was present in spirit. The priest asked if this were the grandchild of *l'écrivain célèbre* and the Colums were properly nervous that word would get out. But Joyce did not find out for years.

Grief was more frequent than joy, the chief cause of it Lucia's illness. Her father refused to accept that she was schizophrenic and that there was little hope of a cure, and reacted with horror to suggestions, even when they came from George, that she should be put in a home. As a form of therapy he encouraged her to a new interest in art-work, getting her to design wallpaper (which he sent to his German publisher with instructions that he should keep it out of the hands of 'unscrupulous persons') and lettrines (large initial letters) which could be used to decorate his own work. Another project was for an edition of Chaucer's *ABC Poem*, using Lucia's lettrines, publication to be subsidized by Joyce without his daughter's knowledge.

But Lucia's illness was worse than he would acknowledge. Some part of it seemed sexual in expression, if not in origin. Lucia had fallen in love with Samual Beckett but he did not return that passion, and found it necessary to tell her that he came to the flat to see her father, not herself. 'Mr Bird,' she told William Bird, publisher, writer and drinking companion of the father's, 'the trouble with me is that I'm sex-starved.'[4]

A fiancé was found for her – Alex Ponisovsky, a young emigré who had given Joyce lessons in Russian. He was persuaded to take an interest by his brother-in-law Paul Léon, also a Russian emigré, who had more or less become Joyce's unpaid secretary and Paris solicitor. Another inducement was the possibility of a dowry, which Joyce was willing to contemplate.

Ponisovsky proposed, Lucia accepted, neither of them with much enthusiasm, and an engagement party was held which ended in disaster. Lucia went after the party to the Léon's, lay down on their sofa and lapsed into a catatonic state. When she had recovered Joyce decided on a trip to London but Lucia suffered what he called, with understatement, a 'bad *crise de nerfs*' at the Gare du Nord and their luggage had to be taken off the train. Joyce wrote to Miss Weaver asking her to let the flat in Campden Grove and moved back into a hotel. Lucia spent nine days at the Léon's and then a week with the Colums. Padraic Colum recalls the stay :

> I remember her coming in. It was night, and she stood looking out of a window. 'That star,' she said in her strange, reflective way, 'means something.' Pathetically she remained there, looking out, for some time.
>
> There was a notion among Joyce's friends that it would be good for Lucia to have a routine job of some kind. A distinguished entomologist, an American, Dr Howard, was living nearby at the time, and he had mentioned that he wanted to have someone familiar with English to transcribe his notes for him. We thought the job might suit Lucia, and Dr Howard agreed to try her out; one morning I took her to the entomologist's workroom. In the late afternoon she came back to the apartment and, throwing herself down on a sofa, demanded, 'Is that the sort of work for me? Do you think it is? Why do I, an artist, have to waste myself on that kind of work?' She spoke as if she had a grievance. The kindly entomologist never saw Lucia again.
>
> My wife was afraid Lucia might do something to herself, and slept in the same bed with her at night, pinning the girl's

[4] Ellmann.

nightdress to her own with a safety pin. It was a difficult time for Mrs Colum, who, we were shortly to find, was going to have a dangerous operation. But she never ceased to show Lucia fondness and attention.

Sunday came, and as I was going to mass, Lucia said she would like to go with me. Joyce telephoned, while we were gone, to ask about her. When he was told she was at Mass he said, 'Now I know she is mad.' He did not know it, and it was the last thing he wanted to know, but Joyce often said things out of perversity.

What Joyce refused to admit his wife suspected, though not all of Lucia's animosity was directed at her mother. 'I saw him crying when he couldn't see to write,' Lucia told Padraic Colum, but she said it without sympathy.

A psychiatrist was smuggled into the Colum's, on the pretext of seeing Mrs Colum. 'Mademoiselle seems to have been hearing a good deal about sex,' he said. Mary Colum relayed this remark to Joyce. 'She never heard it from us,' he answered in horror.

Mr Ponisovsky called for dinner with Lucia and proposed to take her to the theatre afterwards. Colum, under Joyce's orders, forbade it. 'Have I left my father's to be ordered about by you?' Lucia said, and ran down the stairs. Colum pursued her and brought her back. Her suitor had taken the opportunity to disappear by the roof exit. Their engagement was soon forgotten.

Mary Colum escorted Lucia at the end of May to a clinic run by Dr G. Maillard at l'Hay-les-Roses, without telling her where they were going, and remained haunted always by Lucia's look of 'bewildered appeal' as she realized where she was. She stayed there some weeks and was diagnosed schizophrenic 'with serious prognosis'.

Maillard proposed that Lucia be kept at his clinic but Joyce had to go to Vogt again for an eye consultation and took Lucia with him. Vogt saw him on 10 July and berated him for staying away so long. After much probing Vogt decided in September that Joyce's right eye, now nearly blind, could not safely be operated on for two years. The postponing of operations was welcome enough news to him. He repaired with Nora for a holiday in Nice, keeping Lucia nearby, and worked again, after long absence, on *Work in Progress*. Lucia, too, worked on her lettrines.

W. B. Yeats wrote to inform him that he and Bernard Shaw were busy establishing an Irish Academy of Letters and that both considered Joyce the first essential member. Joyce answered courteously that he wished the Academy well but could not see what he had to do with it. That was the last chance of a formal link with Ireland. Joyce complained always that Ireland withheld recognition from him, and when Ireland offered it, declined.

Another form of recognition pleased him greatly. The scale of *The Joyce Book* surprised and delighted Joyce, demonstrating as it did the degree of admiration felt for his work by so many musicians. Composers who either set or attempted to set his verses included Arnold Bax, Eugene Goosens, Arthur Bliss, Edgardo Carducci, Gustav Holst (who tried and failed. Goosens remarked that his own verses 'A Memory of the Players in a Mirror at Midnight' were 'great fun to set, though extremely difficult'. An understatement), Herbert Howells, John Ireland, Philipp Jarnach, Albert Roussel and Darius Milhaud. Augustus John went to Paris to produce a drawing of Joyce for the cover. Joyce was 'most kind and patient' in sitting for him, but an oil John began was never finished. Darius Milhaud caused a little trouble, with some very Joycean complaints: he wanted a 20-guinea fee for the limited edition, 12 guineas for any subsequent edition, a contract, and the right to separate publication. If everything else had to be paid for, why not the music? And as for the suggestion that he would benefit from the publicity, why, it was *they* who would benefit from the inclusion of *his* name.

Joyce took considerable interest in the fortunes of *The Joyce Book*, even taking the trouble to advise Milhaud how to compose his piece properly, but was not able to attend a performance of the songs at a concert in London, on St Patrick's Eve, 16 March 1932, having accepted an invitation to a lunch in his honour given by the American Club in Paris. Of all the settings he preferred those best of Carducci and Hughes. *The Joyce Book* was published (naturally) on 2 February 1933.

His search for a 'cure' for Lucia was unrelenting and took him at one time or another to psychiatrists, physicians, gland specialists, quacks – even to Carl Jung. Back in Paris, he gave her 4,000 francs to buy a fur coat, which always seemed to him a sure specific for whatever ailed women, and installed two girls in relays to take the strain of looking after her off Nora. In March 1933, Lucia was subjected to a new 'cure', the ingestion of copious draughts of sea-water which, naturally, distressed her. Nor did it have any miraculous effect.

Joyce from time to time suspected he was suffering from alcoholic poisoning, 'colitis', or once, when he had a bad headache, meningitis. Miss Weaver made occasional allusion to drink in her letters. These, and other irritations and imagined betrayals (by Miss Weaver of all people) led him to suspend correspondence with her for more than a year, leaving it to Paul Léon, and when Miss Weaver came to Paris to enquire into his affairs, as she did every several months, she was excluded from invitations to the Joyce household. She excused his rudeness on the grounds that he was distracted by anxieties for Lucia. 'Dr Debray is resolutely and absolutely of the opinion that drink has nothing to do with his collapse,' Léon assured her in March 1933. 'It may have perhaps weakened Mr Joyce's resistance but it is in no way the cause of anything in his health. He examined his liver and digestive tubes and he emphatically says that they are in perfect order and absolutely not of the types he knows to be necessarily the consequences of an abuse of drinking. I was very glad that he was so emphatic about it as I had noticed that Mr Joyce of late had fallen under the influence of so many reproaches of too much drink that he was himself beginning to believe in the fact that he was under the influence of alcoholic poisoning. After the opinion of the doctor I can absolutely reassure you in this respect.' Baloney, Miss Weaver might have said, if her vocabulary had contained so strong an expression.

The year passed with Lucia in and out of sanatoria and Joyce in and out of sickbeds, with Vogt alternately pessimistic about the eyes and then more willing to take risks than his patient was. Frank Budgen finished his book, *James Joyce and the Making of 'Ulysses'* but Gorman, the biographer, had seemingly disappeared without trace. It ended in forensic triumph. Bennet Cerf's enthusiasm for *Ulysses* was not so violent that he was eager to take on the apparatus of American censorship, with attendant legal costs. But he was galvanized by an approach from Morris Ernst, a lawyer with a taste for prosecuting causes. Ernst offered to forgo his fee, *if he lost*. If, however, he won, as he had every intention of doing, then he would settle for a lifetime royalty on *Ulysses*. Cerf, feeling he had nothing to lose, agreed to this deal and with that accession of courage which comes from knowing there is something to be got for nothing, insisted on a test case for *Ulysses*. It was granted. The Honourable John Woolsey, Judge of the United States District Court in New York manfully undertook his duty and carefully spent several weeks reading not only *Ulysses*, particularly those passages of which the Government complained, but read as well 'a number of other books which have now become its satellites'.

'I am quite aware,' he decided, 'that owing to some of its scenes *Ulysses* is a rather strong draught to ask some sensitive, though normal persons to take. But my considered opinion, after long reflection, is that whilst in many places the effect of *Ulysses* on the reader undoubtedly is somewhat emetic, nowhere does it tend to be an aphrodisiac.

'*Ulysses* may, therefore, be admitted into the United States.'

'*En somme*,' said Joyce to Eliot, 'one half of the English-speaking world has given in. The other half, after a few terrifying bleats from Leo Britannicus, will follow – as it always does.'

Cerf published in February and in two months sold 33,000 copies.

But something had gone out of Joyce's life. 'James Joyce acted as so many of my clients have always acted,' Morris Ernst recalls. 'It is an axiom in my life that good people hate to win. They find no pleasure in giving up a Cause. I recall that Joyce was bereft when he was no longer pointed out as the one who had authored and undertaken the Cause of *Ulysses*.'

It is pleasant to be able to record that after a long and distinguished career Mr Ernst is still collecting royalties on *Ulysses*.

Chapter Twenty-Three

Lots of Fun at Finnegan's Wake

Lucia, after further tantrums, was sent for a long stay at the sanatorium at Nyon[1] where she had previously been diagnosed schizophrenic. 'She'll get all right they say,' Joyce wrote Budgen. 'One needs all Job's patience with Solomon's wisdom and the Queen of Sheba's pinmoney thrown in.'

In May 1934 George, Helen and Stephen Joyce sailed for America, Helen's homeland, where George hoped to score some success in his singing career. They were gone for a year, and much missed. James Joyce with fatherly concern sent his son streams of musical advice, recommending to him what to sing and how to sing it. Even Nora, who approached pen and paper with extreme dread, managed communication . . .

> Mrs Dyer invited us to an evening party I must say it was very smart she had the most wonderful buffet everything on the table was from the colonies I must tell you the funniest part of that was when I was getting into a new evening dress Jim thought the back was too décolleté so he decided he would have to stitch up the back of the dress can you imagine the result? Of course he stitched it all crooked so I had to undo the stitches again I decided it was better [to] have a bare back I wish you could have seen him stitching my skin back bone altogether.

Lucia did not improve. When her parents visited her in August they were reduced to despair. Flashes of violence had meant that she must be kept under constraint. Joyce found this imprisonment most distressing and secured permission to transfer her to Zurich (where Jung was on the staff), there to try a new cure. Jung's judgement was that a psychoanalytic intervention from him

---

[1] Zelda Fitzgerald was treated at the same place. Nancy Mitford describes it in her biography *Zelda* as luxurious.

might cause a deterioration. Lucia suffered also from the condition of having too many white corpuscles in her blood. Her father clung a while to this straw, thinking that might be the seat of mental infection, but when Harriet Weaver sent him a book recommending grapes as a cure for anaemia he answered irritably: 'Thanks for the book calling my attention to the excellence of the juice of the grape. The best-seller who wrote it never had a more ardent disciple than I. But alas not even scraped carrots can solve the dreaded problem which for years has involved me and now confronts me under a bewildering aspect.'

In October he was scarcely more sympathetic.

> It seems to me that the attempts made by more than one person to poison her mind against me have failed and that I am in such a position that whether I go or stay I shall be blamed as the culprit. Maybe I am an idiot but I attach the greatest importance to what Lucia says when she is talking about herself. Her intuitions are amazing. The people who have warped her kind and gentle nature are themselves failures and if they smile at her remarks as those of a spoilt bourgeoise child it is because they are stupid failures into the bargain.

He and Nora had taken to noting what they interpreted as instances of clairvoyance. She knew, for instance, that her aunt, Eileen Schaurek, had moved from Dublin to Bray. How? Joyce was convinced she could not have seen a letter from Dublin announcing the move, and convinced that he had not told her. He sent Harriet Weaver this dialogue, which indicates that Lucia was speculating, followed by a long account of his detective work designed to prove that she was not speculating.

> Lucia, turning to me abruptly: So it was all an invention of
>   yours about Eva's letter?
> I: No. I always tell you the truth. Did Dr Brunner not
>   give you the letter?
> Lucia: No.
> I: He forgot it then. I'll ring him up.
> Lucia: He is a bit *gaga* like all his psychiatrists. Eileen is a bit
>   loony. So am I, they say. I think it would do me good
>   to be with her, keeping house. Not necessarily in
>   Dublin. In Bray, say. It must be very pretty in Bray.

I: Yes. In summer.

Lucia had another reason for wishing to visit Ireland, as the dialogue
reveals a few days later:

Lucia: I have been thinking all day of John MacCormack. It
         is unjust. Why is he a count, a millionaire etc? I
         thought of writing to the pope.
I: Be careful of your grammar. He is a learned man.
Lucia: He's an old dotard. But it is unjust. How long will
         your country refuse to recognize what you have done.
I: How long indeed?
Lucia: I want to reconcile you. It is time for some great
         person of your country to come forward and hold out
         a hand to you and to us.
I: Hear. Hear.

And Lucia's clairvoyance was promptly demonstrated again. At
seven a.m. on the day following their conversation a helpful
telegram arrived from MacCormack and the day after that there
appeared in the *Irish Times* an article on *Work in Progress* which
Joyce found 'not unfriendly'. Grateful as he was for any symptom
which seemed to him to alleviate his daughter's suffering, Joyce
regarded these 'powers' of hers with suspicion. 'It is terrible to
think of a vessel of election as the prey of impulses beyond its
control and of natures beneath its comprehension,' he wrote C. P.
Curran, 'and, fervently as I deserve her cure, I ask myself what will
happen when and if she finally withdraws her regard from the
lightning-lit revery of her clairvoyance and turns it upon that
battered cabman's face, the world.'

Jung was inclined to put some of the blame for Lucia's condition on Joyce. It was his opinion, and the opinion of certain other
doctors, that Lucia should be certified. Joyce would not consent,
said Jung, because Lucia was his *'femme inspiratrice'*, and his own
psyche was so strongly identified with hers that to have her certified would be to admit his own 'latent psychosis'. His style, like
hers, was schizophrenic, with the difference that in him it was a
matter of choice and in Lucia of disease. Joyce did not go over the
border-line of lunacy because he had the strength of genius which
Lucia had not. This string of psychological peaches had fortunately

no affect on Joyce. He withdrew his daughter from 'the Reverend Doctor Jung's' care and returned to Paris, now accompanied by his sister, Eileen, brought over at Lucia's request.

Miss Weaver, wishing to help, invited Lucia to London. She travelled across with Eileen in February 1935 but took advantage of her aunt's temporary absence in Dublin to do a bolt. She stayed out all night and informed Miss Weaver when she got back in the morning that she was a grown-up woman and would be obliged if she was left alone. Miss Weaver got little sympathy from Joyce. 'Your letter expresses great sympathy for my sister,' he wrote in April, after Lucia had gone on to Ireland with Eileen. 'Possibly Lucia, not having been brought up as a slave and having neither Bolshevik[2] nor Hitlerite tendencies, made a very bad impression on you and she certainly does not flatter, but in my opinion the difference between my daughter and my sister is the difference between a knife and a corkscrew which any intelligent person can see by a glance at their faces.'

Lucia did not behave herself in Dublin. She sent a letter to her mother invoking gas ovens and threatening suicide. Michael Healy, by now an old man, travelled across Ireland to report on her condition and was at first reticent. What was wrong with her walking around Dublin, Joyce wanted to know? But then she vanished for six days, before being picked up by the Dublin police. Constantine Curran, then Registrar of the Appeal Court, had discreetly hinted to the police that if Miss Joyce were found wandering in a distressed condition, nothing was to be told to the Press. She was put in a nursing home for the time being but now expressed a desire to return to Miss Weaver. Joyce was not keen that she should, 'as it turns out that the latter [Miss Weaver] has been for months past in collusion with Eileen "not to write this to Paris etc.", keeping me in ignorance of all the sordid squalor of the case and of the warning of the authorities that their next step would be to commit her or intern her. I was told "she is getting on fine" and Miss Weaver, as with her other female charms, walked blue-eyed and prim-mouthed into my sister's booby-trap.'

[2] Miss Weaver's left-wing sympathies were driving her rapidly onto the bosom of the Communist Party. She who had subsidised *Ulysses, A Portrait of the Artist* and *Finnegans Wake* would come in time to subsidise the *Daily Worker* and shrug off the suppression of Hungary as good for the Hungarians.

He changed his mind when he heard of a doctor in London who was competent to administer a course of injections of a new bovine serum which had been to some extent successful with mental patients part of whose illness was glandular in origin. Joyce had seized on the possibility that Lucia's illness had that nature and in February had had his suspicion confirmed by a Parisian doctor who diagnosed a deficiency in adrenalin secretion. Now he seized on the news of this new cure. Miss Weaver was sent to Harley Street where the specialist, without seeing Lucia, agreed on a course of twenty-five injections. Miss Weaver's flat was prepared for Lucia's reception (the windows were nailed almost shut) and she got in a trained nurse (the nails did not stop Lucia throwing books out of the windows, to the annoyance of passers-by). The injections, which Lucia resisted, seemed to do some good, but not much. When Miss Weaver rented a summer cottage near Reigate she had to engage an especially large nurse. Lucia still had fits of violence.

Dr Macdonald, the specialist who had treated Lucia, suggested her removal to a clinic at Northampton for further treatment. She went there in December 1935, but the following month Macdonald announced that her certification was necessary, according to English practice, if she were to remain there. Joyce refused. Harriet Weaver unwittingly added to his agony. Visiting Northampton with a friend who was a trained nurse, she waited in a room where one of Lucia's medical papers was lying on the desk. The friend glanced down and caught the word '?carcinoma'. She told Miss Weaver, who decided that the news must be broken to Joyce. She wrote to a mutual friend in Paris. Joyce was agonized by the 'news' and need not have been. Certain of Lucia's physical symptoms were compatible with an internal cancer: that was all. Dr Macdonald, who had flown to Paris and seen the effect on Joyce, wrote Miss Weaver a furious letter, forbiding her ever to see Lucia again. Joyce wrote bitterly a letter which affected her so profoundly that she destroyed it.

Lucia returned to Paris with Maria Jolas but could not long be kept out of an institution. In March 1936 she was taken to clinic in a straitjacket, there pronounced dangerous and removed to a nursing home at Ivry, between Paris and the Channel. She remained in their care for fifteen years. The regime was not harsh and she was not 'interned'. The doctors held out some slight hope. Joyce

299

determined to publish the *Chaucer ABC* with Lucia's lettrines, for her birthday. Miss Weaver, who had not succeeded in convincing Joyce of her real affection for his daughter, offered to pay half the cost and was rewarded with a letter from Paris, the first in months:

> My idea is not to persuade her that she is a Cezanne but that on her 29th birthday in the aforesaid madhouse[3] she may see something to persuade her that her whole past has not been a failure. The reason I keep on trying every means to find a solution for her case (which may come at any time as it did with my eyes) is that she may not think that she is left with a blank future as well. I am aware that I am blamed by everybody for sacrificing that precious metal money to such an extent for such a purpose when it could be done so cheaply and quietly by locking her up in an economical mental prison for the rest of her life.
>
> I will not do so as long as I see a single chance of hope for her recovery, nor blame her or punish her for the great crime she has committed in being a victim of one of the most elusive diseases known to men and unknown to medicine . . .

The new alliance between Hitler and Mussolini landed Stanislaus in trouble now in the latest of family misfortunes. The Italians wished to demonstrate their distaste for the British in order to impress their new friends. A simple method was to hound out British citizens living in Italy. Stanislaus was duly handed an expulsion order. Having spent four years in internment for his pro-Italian sympathies he did not think the treatment generous. A grumbling letter to his brother produced small reaction, but a former pupil of theirs, Fulvio Sulvich, Under-Secretary of State, interceded with the Italian Foreign Office and Mussolini was kind enough to allow the order to be rescinded. Stanislaus was to be punished for his nationality merely by unemployment. He was dismissed his post at the University of Trieste. James was importuned to find him work in Paris or Switzerland and made gestures in that direction. Meanwhile, he had a long-standing ambition to fulfil – a trip to Denmark, cultural root of Ibsen and homeplace of that other Scandinavian with whom he identified himself from time to time, Hamlet.

His Danish was good after years of study and a succession of

[3] These four words censored by HSW.

teachers (all but one, however, Norwegian, so that his pronunciation was not impeccable). He was ambushed by a journalist called Vinding, who showed him around Copenhagen (including, naturally, Elsinore) but kept his profession to himself, masquerading as an artist.[4]

'Do you like flowers, Mr Joyce?' the newshound asked.

'No,' said the master. 'I love green growing things, trees and grass. Flowers annoy me.' It began to rain, and Mrs Joyce contributed the biographical detail that she did not like umbrellas.

'Do you like Italy now that Mussolini is there?' Vinding asked, fishing for politics.

'Naturally,' said Joyce. 'Now, as always. Italy is Italy. Not to like it because of Mussolini would be just as absurd as to hate England because of Henry the Eighth.'

He pronounced on various writers, Gide among them.

'Gide is of course a Communist as you know. Some time ago a young man called Armand Petitjean looked him up. When Petitjean was sixteen he began to write a giant work on my *Work in Progress* which he finished long before *my* work was ended. He is twenty now. His book and his interest made him a serious admirer of mine, and he went to Gide with this question: "Maître, when we have communism in France, whatever will we do with Joyce?" Gide thought for a long time before he answered, and finally said, "We'll leave him be."'

He was three-quarters of the way through *Work in Progress*, he told Vinding. The work would go quickly now. Vinding, inevitably, asked him if he placed Ibsen higher than Shakespeare. 'He towers head and shoulders above him when it comes to drama,' said Joyce. 'No one approaches him there. It's very difficult to believe that Ibsen will grow stale. He will renew himself for every generation. His problems will be seen from a new angle as time goes on. There were some who think he was a feminist in *Hedda Gabler*. He was no more a feminist than I am an archbishop.'

Joyce thoroughly enjoyed the trip to Copenhagen and returned to Paris in September armed with new Scandinavian material for *Work in Progress* (HCE in his guise as Earwicker represents the

---

[4] Joyce angrily refused him permission to publish the article he wrote. It appeared only after his death.

Scandinavian foundation of Dublin) and renewed zeal for Ibsen.
This he attempted to communicate to James Stephens by sending
him a copy of Ibsen's early drama *Little Eyolf*. Stephens was not
convinced of Ibsen's dramatic gift but felt 'scandalized' and proud
to think of Joyce navigating the heavy traffic of Paris with his bad
eyesight to deliver the book:

> I take it you sent me this book because of the remarks I made
> to you upon Ibsen. I will agree, with any man who cares to be
> agreed with, that Ibsen is a more than competent stage-
> manager. If a character of his sneezes in the first act, he will
> have a cold in the second act and will die of pneumonia in the
> third . . . The man is a pestilent dramatist, and all his works
> are framed with the desire to make those pay who do not owe,
> and to make them suffer who have not merited it . . . To hell
> with that dark man of the black north, for that is where he
> came from and his literature is as nigh to hellish as the com-
> plete bourgeois can possibly manage.

According to Richard Ellmann, Joyce had himself lost his taste
for serious drama and confined his theatre-going to the opera and
light comedies. He retailed to Samuel Beckett the opening scene
of one such production. A man is eating a bowl of soup in the
dining-room of an hotel. The waiter, looking out of the window,
comments, 'Looks like rain, Sir'. The diner says, 'Tastes like it too'.
In troubled times, Joyce would say in defence of himself and his
work, was it not a service to one's fellow man to make as great
a joke as possible? Listening to a group of intellectuals earnestly
discussing 'literature' he commented irritably to Beckett, 'If only
they'd talk about turnips!' When he was told that his great joke
presented certain difficulties to those anxious to enjoy it, he said,
'The demand that I make of my reader is that he should devote
his whole life to reading my works.'

On other occasions his assessment of his own work was gloomy.
He surprised Arthur Power by ending a conversation on critical
reactions to his work by slumping down in an exhausted manner
and sighing, 'I suppose my work is middle-class'.

He was working many hours a day in an attempt to get *Work in
Progress* finished. He hoped to publish it first on 2 February 1938,
his fifty-sixth birthday, then, when that day passed, 4 July, his
father's birthday. But that day passed too. That month Eugene

Jolas guessed the true title of *Finnegans Wake* with a little assistance from Nora, who alone had shared the secret. Joyce had a standing bet of 1,000 francs with any of his friends who cared to guess. Joyce repeated the offer at dinner one evening and Nora, after a disparaging reference to 'that chop suey he's writing' began to sing a song about Mr Flannigan and Mr Shaniggan. Joyce, alarmed, told her to stop but then clearly made with his lips the outline of the letters 'F' and 'W'. Maria Jolas guessed 'Fair's Wake' and Joyce said, 'Brava! But something was missing'. Eugene Jolas guessed correctly a few days later. Joyce was sad at first, but afterwards gay, and paid Jolas with a bag of ten-franc pieces. The secret was still to be kept until publication. When Faber and Faber inquired into the title of the book they were to publish Joyce answered that they would be told it only when the book was ready for the binders.

He suffered from time to time from bad pains in his stomach which both he and Nora attributed to 'nerves'. One doctor recommended X-rays but Joyce disregarded the advice, which neglect may have cost him his life. 'I don't bother with him any more,' said Nora to David Fleischman (Helen Joyce's son by a previous marriage) one evening that summer. 'He can do what he pleases. But it's terrible in the summer. He doesn't want to go away at all. It'll be like last year. I'll drag him away somewhere and he'll get terrible nervous pains in his stomach. I never get but three words out of him all day these days: in the morning it's "The papers!" at lunch, "What's that?" and the third – Jim, what is the third, I can't remember it? Ah yes, about his bottle of water on the floor: "Don't touch that!"'

She did get him away, to Lausanne, Zurich and Dieppe, and he did suffer terrible stomach cramps, and he did not take medical advice.

'Hip, Hip!' Joyce was able to write to an Italian friend on 18 November 1938. '*Ho finito quel maledetto libro.*' It remained only to correct the proofs of 'the cursed book' and print it, this being no easy undertaking. His publishers had most of it in print already but *Finnegans Wake*, Stanislaus Joyce pointed out, is almost as unprintable as unreadable. There were, as Stanislaus maliciously reminded him, more than a thousand misprints in the first edition of *Finnegans Wake*.

There was the usual fuss to get him a copy by his birthday. After heroic exertions Faber and Faber and their Glasgow printers obliged with an unbound copy by 30 January. His fifty-seventh birthday was a splendid affair. Budgen came over from London. Helen Joyce read the last few pages of the book beautifully and Joyce executed the high-kicking dance he reserved for bucolic moments.

'Lots of fun,' said Joyce to Budgen when he departed.

'At Finnegan's Wake,' answered Budgen.

There was not to be much fun for James Joyce in the two years left to him.

Chapter Twenty-Four

Permis de Sortie

Arthur Power noticed an antique Italian clock in the window of a Paris shop and told Joyce about it. Across the dial were inscribed the words 'Every one hurts and the last one kills'. 'That is good,' Joyce said. 'I must remember that.' He did not need much reminding. The world had little time to pronounce on *Finnegans Wake* before fresh disaster impinged on it, and on Joyce.

Official publication was not until May. The author at first complained at the slow appearance of reviews, suspecting, rightly, that the world was occupied with other things. When criticism was intelligent as well as hostile he did not resent it, but did share that common resentment of performers who get less space than they think appropriate.

The London *Daily Herald* thought one sentence sufficient: 'An Irish stew of verbiage by the author of *Ulysses* with unexpected beauty emerging now and then from the peculiar mixture.' A leading article in *The Times* was more to his taste, 'the only English article perhaps that seems to rise above the stupor with a certain critical ease'. The *Irish Times* had the impertinence to list *Finnegans Wake* as by Sean O'Casey. Joyce pretended not to mind but O'Casey was more forthright in his denunciation of conspiracy: 'I don't think the reference was a misprint. I know many of Dublin's Literary Clique dislike me, and they hate you (why, God only knows), so that "misprint" was a bit of a joke.' O'Casey, in his letter, committed the cardinal sin of inserting an apostrophe in *Finnegans Wake* but was not rebuked.

Herbert Gorman, after nine years' toil, announced that his biography was ready in the summer of 1939. Naturally, having finished it, he wanted it out as quickly as possible. Joyce, who claimed not to have heard from him for eight or nine months, would not allow it. He wished to see first the complete typescript 'and of course the subsequent proofs'. He objected strongly to the suggestion that his father had been financially irresponsible or flamboyant and insisted that passages suggesting that John Joyce had suffered from these vices be struck out. References to his father were duly doctored so that a strong emphasis was placed on the bond between father and son, while the misery he inflicted on the rest of his family was skated over. The resulting prose had a strong flavour of tongue in cheek:

> Those who remember him in Dublin, and he appears to have left his mark on a city that brimmed with impressive and eccentric personalities, assert – albeit with a tender reminiscential glow – that he was an inebriate and a fop, wore a monocle in one eye, was blessed with a quick natural biting wit, was continuously popular and always notorious for his impecuniousness and improvidence.

Some of the succeeding pabulum is rather more distasteful in a peculiarly Edwardian way, considering the date it was written. On May Joyce's death, for instance:

> Emphasis, delicately as it must be put, is necessary here if we are to understand (however fragmentarily) the painful and lonely development of Joyce. His mother's death appears to have been a powerful challenge to his will as well as a great sorrow to his heart. It was Time's remorseless way of testing the integrity of the young man . . . It was, in a way, a test of his inviolability to the usual compromises of the flesh and will.

And so on, as if 'Time' had inflicted cancer on May Joyce at the age of forty-four in order to facilitate the development of the soul of St James Joyce. Joyce might be excused for failing to detect the humbug (after all, he was erecting his own monument) but not Gorman.

The delicate question of Joyce's marriage arose. Gorman had written in his original text that Joyce had been driven out of Dublin by, among other things, the impossibility of living in sin there. But Joyce had developed a fierce bourgeois attachment to the myth of a 1904 marriage, even to the extent of allowing celebration of a bogus wedding anniversary, and would not have it denied. 'The . . . point is a very complicated legal problem which has already caused Mr Joyce heavy expenditure in the matter of legal opinions,' he told Gorman via Léon, 'involving as it did the marriage laws of three different countries. It would be necessary to devote an entire chapter of your book to its elucidation and I doubt whether his solicitors in London would advise him to place the dossier concerning it at your disposal. For the purposes of your book the only way now is to obliterate this passage and any subsequent reference of the same tenor confining yourself to a formal statement.' Mention of Mrs Joyce's marriage subsequently appeared in the index of Gorman's 'definitive biography' but not in the text, a circumstance which may have puzzled some early scholars of the master. To be fair to Joyce, Nora's mother was still alive and would have been upset to read an accurate account of her daughter's marital history. On the other hand, he might have saved himself trouble with Gorman (and his solicitors) by telling the truth. James Joyce, Rimbaudian rebel in his youth, undoubtedly got more and more bourgeois as he got older.

The wretched Gorman suffered other interferences. Helen Joyce makes only the briefest appearance in the book, and that a comment on her taste in clothes, and Lucia's illness could not be mentioned at all. Peculiarly, Joyce did not complain about the insertion of stories he dismissed at other times as legend, such as the episode of being accosted in O'Connell Street by a medical student who vocalizes thus: 'You drunken. . . .!¹ The whole arse of your breeches is gone.' Nor did he complain about Siegmund Feilbogen's being described as an astronomer until after the book came out, in November, and then with unkind glee. As for Gorman, he swore he would never again write the biography of a living person.

The war came no more as a surprise to Joyce than to anyone else in Europe, but like most Europeans he had worried a great deal about it and done nothing to prepare for it. (He had, however, assisted several Jews escape the coming holocaust.) His chief concern was for Lucia. Ivry, on the Seine, was only a few miles from Paris and the war could be expected to reach Paris. He consulted Dr Achille Delmas, director of Lucia's nursing home, who assured him that the institution was to be immediately transferred to the Hôtel Edelweiss at La Baule in Brittany. He and Nora went there to

---

¹ Gorman's ellipse. A Dubliner would undoubtedly say 'you drunken cunt'.

wait for her but found to their alarm on 2 September that the hotel did not intend to receive Delmas's charges. Delmas told him that he expected to secure alternate accommodation within a week or so. Joyce was worried not only about the possibility of a bombardment of Paris but also of the effect of the air-raid alerts on Lucia's nerves. He attempted to find another home for her but could not. There was nothing he could do but wait. He passed some of the time with Dr Daniel O'Brien, of the Rockefeller Foundation, who drank with him. One night, Dr O'Brien reports, in a scene reminiscent of the film *Casablanca*, Joyce thrilled a restaurant full of French and British soldiers with a rendering of the *Marseillaise*. They had heard his voice join theirs and in admiration hoisted him onto a table. He sang it again for them.

'You never saw such an exhibition of one man dominating and thrilling a whole audience,' O'Brien recalled. 'He stood there and sang the "Marseillaise" and they sang it again afterwards with him and if a whole German regiment had attacked at that moment, they would never have got through. That was the feeling. Oh, Joyce and his voice dominated them all!'

Lucia arrived with the other patients two weeks later, Delmas having found accommodation at a place called Pornichet near La Baule. Joyce and Nora stayed for a while to calm her fears until recalled to Paris by a new disaster, the imminent breakdown of his son's marriage. Helen Joyce too had suffered nervous breakdowns and George was living apart from her and resisting the idea of reconciliation. Joyce took his son's part. When Paul Léon, devoted friend of ten years, expressed sympathy for Helen, Joyce punished his impudence by forcing a break with him. He demanded back his contracts, on which Léon had for so long worked for nothing.

Stephen Joyce was sent into the care of Maria Jolas, who had moved her Ecole Bilingue from Paris to the relative safety of St Gérand-le-Puy, near Vichy. Joyce and Nora joined him there on Christmas Eve. Joyce was promptly prostrated by stomach cramps, but would not consult a doctor. He ate nothing at Christmas dinner, restricting himself to an intake of white wine. For years past his friends had noticed his birdlike appearance without suspecting its cause. Joyce had a duodenal ulcer which would kill him in a year.

He passed the last year of his life in that little village,[2] apart from a short spell in Vichy, finding it tedious as he had always found villages tedious. He walked abroad with a pocketful of stones to fend off dogs and indoors maintained a gloomy silence. When Nora complained about it he answered, 'What is there to talk about when you have been married thirty years?' He made no attempt to work, except to hunt misprints in *Finnegans Wake,* but admitted contemplating a new work which would be 'very simple and very short'. The aspect of the war which most interested him (apart from his natural desire to keep himself and his family clear of it) was the Russian attack on Finland and that country's stout defence of itself. But that was because he had prophesied it ('The Finn wakes again'). There were occasional visitors, including Beckett, who could see some point to the war where Joyce could not.

'My unfortunate daughter-in-law has lost her reason and is at present *internée d'office* which is a provisional certificate of lunacy,' he wrote Curran in February. He communicated the same news to Harriet Weaver in March, expecting sympathy, but when she expressed it accused her of prying into his affairs. Helen Joyce was eventually taken back to America by her brother in May and subsequently divorced George.

Lucia remained stranded at Pornichet. Her father's efforts to move her closer to St Gérand-le-Puy were frustrated by the escalation of the war as the Germans invaded first Denmark and Norway, then began their Blitzkrieg on Holland, Belgium and France. With the fall of Paris in June various refugees arrived in the south, among them Beckett, George Joyce and then Paul Léon, exhausted, on the back of a donkey, and managing a joke: 'The Lord Jesus Christ rode into Jerusalem on a donkey,' he said. Joyce made peace.

Léon ought to have known better but returned to Paris in Sep-

---

[2] For the benefit of American readers, who understandably tend to forget that the war began for Europeans in September 1939 and, generally speaking, inconvenienced them more than it did the Americans: Vichy France was technically neutral. Joyce, as a British citizen, could therefore stay there without being interned, but life was uncomfortable because Vichy France was pro-German. He could not return to Paris because that was in the German zone. He wished to go to Switzerland because Switzerland was *genuinely* neutral. The Americans very kindly offered him refuge in their country, but he declined. Apart from his irrational dislike of that country (irrational because he had never been there to test his opinion) he could not face the thought of flying the Atlantic, and no sea-crossings were available.

tember. There he rescued Joyce's papers and books from his flat and bought others at an auction held illegally by Joyce's landlord. These he deposited with the Irish Ambassador with the instruction that, if he did not survive the war, they should be given to the National Library of Ireland under a fifty-year seal (he did not survive. He was arrested by the Germans in 1941 and murdered the following year because he was a Jew).

The fall of France meant the rupture of diplomatic relations between Vichy France and Britain as well as the creation of an occupied zone in the north. Lucia was in that zone and uncomfortably close to the naval base of St Nazaire. Joyce had determined to flee where he had fled before – Switzerland – but getting there meant getting the co-operation of three sets of authorities – German, Vichy French and Swiss. And to accomplish such a move required also money. He could not, because of the economic warfare between Vichy and London, draw even the interest on his British capital (more than three-quarters disappeared in any case) and royalties were slow in coming from America. His funds in Paris were seized by the French when the British seized French funds in London. Miss Weaver had not much money left herself. She was able to arrange a dole of £30 a month via the Irish Minister at Vichy, but not until October. In spite of his murderous circumstances Joyce could still manage a flash of sour wit. When Mary Colum wrote to tell him that J. F. Byrne had written a book he answered, 'It was news to me to hear that Byrne had written a book. I should have been surprised to hear that he had read one.'

The Germans readily granted permission for Lucia to leave France. Joyce then commissioned friends in Zurich to find her a cheap *maison de santé* and eventually succeeded. How to get her there was another question. In August Joyce applied for entry permits into Switzerland and again in September. The Swiss Consulate in Lyons forwarded the applications to the Federal Aliens' Police in Zurich. They were refused. When a friend of Joyce's inquired why he was told it was because Joyce was a Jew.

Eventually the Aliens' Police were persuaded otherwise and the intercession of various prominent Swiss overcame the authorities' objection to the Joyce family, but still they demanded a guarantee of 50,000 Swiss francs, later reduced to 20,000. Swiss friends deposited this and Joyce, after proving with difficulty that he was not

310

indigent, was granted the visas at the end of November.

George had trouble getting out of France since he was not supposed to be there in the first place. He was of military age and had not registered with the authorities. The Irish Minister to Vichy suggested that he adopt Free State citizenship and walk out as a neutral, but he refused. His father applauded his courage. Fortunately a Vichy official was civil enough to stamp his passport, overlooking the absence of a *permis de sortie.*

Another snag was that Joyce's and Nora's passports had expired. George travelled to Vichy and presented them to the American chargé d'affaires. 'But I can't extend British passports,' said that gentleman, with some justification.

'If you can't, who else can?' said George with equal logic. The American stamped the passports.

By now Lucia's exit permit had expired. Joyce decided to travel on to Zurich and arrange her removal from there.

On 14 December, after travelling through the night they reached the Swiss border and got across, no matter how dubious their documents. Next day they arrived in Lausanne and unpacked their bags at the Hôtel de la Paix. 'Jim, look at this mess,' said Nora. 'There's green ink over everything.' A bottle had spilt. Joyce, cheerfully lighting up a cigarette, was unable to regard that as a disaster.

On 17 December they were back in the familiar and pleasant city of Zurich, installed in a pension. They had a convivial Christmas dinner with friends. On 10 January 1941, after celebrating a friend's birthday, Joyce was again overcome with stomach cramps and was given morphine.

The following morning he was taken, still in great pain, to the Red Cross Hospital and X-rayed. The doctors discovered a perforated ulcer. They suspected the ulcer had been present for several years. Even now Joyce resisted the idea of an operation, but George talked him into it. The operation, which took place on Saturday morning, seemed to have been successful.

'I thought I wouldn't get through it,' Joyce said to Nora when he woke up. On Sunday morning he needed transfusions. Nora said, optimistically, 'Jim is tough.' On Sunday afternoon he passed into a coma. When he awoke for a moment he asked that Nora sleep beside him as he had slept beside her during her illnesses. But the doctors told her and George to go home. At one in the morning he

311

awoke again and asked for his wife and son, then lapsed once more into coma. By the time they were called and had arrived at the hospital he had died.

He was buried two days later in the Fluntern Cemetery, near the zoo, with snow on the ground. When she was offered the services of a priest, Nora said, 'I couldn't do that to him.' There were speeches by Lord Derwent, the British Minister, by the poet Max Geillinger and by Heinrich Straumann, Professor of English at the University of Zurich, who had so recently done him the favour of telling the Federal Alien's Police he was a man of genius worthy of entry into Switzerland. A tenor sang an aria of Monteverdi's *Addio terra, addio cielo.*

Nora had a last look at her dead husband through the glass window in the coffin, then held out her hand as it was lowered. A deaf old man who was a boarder at their pension asked, 'Who is buried here?' 'Herr Joyce,' said the undertaker. 'Who is it?' said the old man again. 'Herr Joyce!' shouted the undertaker as the coffin came to rest at the bottom of the grave. But Joyce did not wake.

When Lucia heard of his death she said, 'What is he doing under the ground, that idiot? When will he decide to come out? He's watching us all the time.'

Frank Budgen read the news in the *Evening Standard* in an air-raid dug-out in London. Miss Weaver heard it on the BBC news and sent Nora £250 she had been about to send her husband.

Stanislaus Joyce became physically ill when he heard of his brother's death, and bitterly regretted having refused his offer of a copy of *Finnegans Wake.* He had always celebrated Bloomsday, 16 June. He died on that day in 1955.

Nora Joyce lived on in Zurich until 1951. She would tell anyone who asked her opinion that Jim had been the greatest writer in the world. The cross she had so often complained of bearing seemed in retrospect not so heavy. 'Things are very dull now. There was always something doing when he was about.'

She had poverty still to keep her company and remind her of their days together. 'I am afraid I will sooner or later have to sell my manuscript of "Chamber Music" written in Dublin in the year 1909 and dedicated to me . . .' she wrote the Colums a little before her death. 'If you know anybody who you think will be interested in buying such a work would you kindly let me know.'

312

She allowed herself some slight consolations of religion and was rewarded by having an ignorant priest call her a 'great sinner' in the gracious oration he delivered at her graveside. She had visited her husband's grave every day she was well enough. She said she liked to think of him listening to the lions roaring in the distance. On a visit to Paris she complained to Mrs Arthur Power as she got into a taxi, 'O, this too, too solid flesh'.

Her last great gesture towards her husband was to prevent Harriet Weaver donating the manuscript of *Finnegans Wake* to the National Library of Ireland. It went instead to the British Museum. Nora had asked the Irish Government to do James Joyce the honour of moving his remains to Ireland. They declined what would have done themselves more honour. Nora and James both rest still in Fluntern Cemetery. (The Swiss have erected a passable statue. The Irish might at least do the same, in Dublin.)

Ireland has changed a little, and will change more. Certainly James Joyce gets the credit for some part of the small but hopeful and continuing intellectual improvement of his country. It was too great a task even for his genius to forge single-handedly a conscience for the Irish, but he wrought a more important change in the world. He changed literature.

Appendix
Syphilis and Joyce's Eyesight

James Joyce undoubtedly contracted venereal disease on several occasions but there is no positive proof that he ever had syphilis. His father, however, most certainly had it, and Joyce could have inherited it. Dr F. R. Walsh of Kilkenny contributed an illuminating article on the subject to the *Irish Medical Times* of 9 May 1975.

John Joyce, in his old age, was in the habit of consorting with medical students. In 1919/20 he confessed to Dr Walsh, then a student, that while himself a student at Queen's College, Cork, in 1867 (see p. 10) he had discovered a syphilitic chancre and treated it himself by the then usual method – cauterizing with carbolic – which might remove the symptom but by no means guaranteed a cure. Eye failure can be a consequence of syphilis (Dr Walsh quotes W. A. Boyd, *Text Book of Pathology* [1961], to the effect that 'there is no symptom which it cannot cause, no syndrome for which it may not be responsible'). John Joyce was himself treated for iritis and conjunctivitis in 1909 (p. 165). His first child lived only a few days, two were stillborn, two did not survive adolescence and the last, like the first, died after a few days. May Joyce died at the age of forty-four of a disease which was variously diagnosed as cancer of the liver and cirrhosis. Syphilis, too, can attack the interior organs. James Joyce died of a perforated duodenal ulcer and the peritonitis which followed an unsuccessful operation. Gastric syphilis, says Dr Walsh, is rare but not unknown: 'It does occur in the form of single or multiple ulcerated gummas with simulate peptic ulcer symptoms. Bailey and Love – "Practice of Surgery" – say the differential diagnosis is difficult. Erosion of a mucosal gumma could presumably lead to ulceration, haemorrhage and perforation – an unlikely, but possible event.'

It is possible therefore, if impossible to prove, that John Joyce, that amiable ruffian, carried in his blood an agency which, untreated, blinded – perhaps even helped to kill – James Joyce and could conceivably also have killed his own wife and several of his children.

Dr Walsh has made a considerable study of James Joyce's medical history and finds it surprising that he was not, when his eyes were being treated in middle age, ever tested for syphilis. He advances the theory that it simply never occurred to Dr Vogt of Zurich to suggest such a thing to so eminent a man of letters.

Bibliography

WORKS BY JAMES JOYCE (dates refer to first complete publication)

The Holy Office, Trieste, 1905
Chamber Music, London, 1907
Gas From a Burner, Trieste, 1912
Dubliners, London, 1914
A Portrait of the Artist as a Young Man, New York, 1916
Exiles, London, 1918
Ulysses, Paris, 1922
Pomes Penyeach, Paris, 1927
Finnegans Wake, London and New York, 1939
Epiphanies, Buffalo, New York, 1956
The Letters of James Joyce, Volume 1, ed. Stuart Gilbert, London, 1957
The Critical Writings of James Joyce, ed. Ellsworth Mason and Richard Ellmann, London and New York, 1959
The Letters of James Joyce, Volumes II and III, ed. Richard Ellmann, London, 1966
Giacomo Joyce, London, 1968

All of these works are easily available on both sides of the Atlantic, most in paperback. *The Essential James Joyce*, edited by Harry Levin (London, 1948, 1963), contains five episodes of *Ulysses*, the whole of *A Portrait of the Artist as a Young Man*, the whole of *Exiles*, *Chamber Music*, *Pomes Penyeach*, *The Holy Office*, *Gas From a Burner*, *Dubliners*, three episodes of *Finnegans Wake*, and the last poem, *Ecce Puer*. For those unwilling to tackle *Finnegans Wake* without preparation, there is *A Shorter Finnegans Wake*, edited by Anthony Burgess (London, 1966).

As regards the letters, Harriet Shaw Weaver censored many of Joyce's to her, and destroyed others. Going through these letters in the British Library is a sad business. Neat little notes in Miss Weaver's handwriting testify to the many letters she destroyed, always because they dealt too intimately with Joyce's family affairs.

CRITICAL WORKS ON JAMES JOYCE

Beckett, Samuel, *et al.: Our Examination Round His Factification For Incamination of Work in Progress*, Paris, 1929

Burgess, Anthony: *Here Comes Everybody*, London, 1969

——: *Joysprick, An Introduction to the Language of James Joyce*, London, 1973

Campbell, J. and Robinson, H. M.: *A Skeleton Key to 'Finnegans Wake'*, New York, 1944

Dalton, J. P. and Hart, C.: *Twelve and a Tilly* (essays on the occasion of the 25th anniversary of *Finnegans Wake*), London, 1966

Ellmann, Richard: *Ulysses on the Liffey*, London, 1972

Field, Saul and Levitt, Morton, P.: *Bloomsday*, London, 1973

Gilbert, Stuart: *James Joyce's 'Ulysses': A Study*, New York, 1930, London, 1952

Levin, Harry: *James Joyce: A Critical Introduction* (2nd ed.), London, 1960

Wilson, Edmund: *Axel's Castle: A Study in the Imaginative Literature of 1870–1930*, New York, 1931

REMINISCENCES OF JOYCE, AND OTHER BIOGRAPHICAL WORKS CONCERNING HIM

Anderson, Chester G.: *James Joyce and his world*, London, 1967

Beach, Sylvia: *Shakespeare and Company*, London, 1960

Budgen, Frank: *James Joyce and the Making of 'Ulysses'* (containing *Further Recollections of James Joyce*), Indiana, 1960

——: *Myselves When Young*, London, 1970

Colum, Padraic and Mary: *Our Friend James Joyce*, London, 1959

Ellmann, Richard: *James Joyce*, London, 1959

Gillet, Louis: *Claybook for James Joyce*, London and New York, 1958

Gorman, Herbert: *James Joyce*, London, 1941

Healey, George Harris (ed.): *The Dublin Diary of Stanislaus Joyce*, London, 1962

Hemingway, Ernest: *A Moveable Feast*, London, 1964

Hotchner, A. E.: *Papa Hemingway*, London, 1966

Hutchins, Patricia: *James Joyce's Dublin*, London, 1950

——: *James Joyce's World*, London, 1957

Joyce, Stanislaus: *My Brother's Keeper*, London, 1958

Lewis, Wyndham: *Blasting and Bombardiering*, London, 1937

Lyons, J. B.: *James Joyce in Medicine*, Dublin, 1973

McAlmon, Robert: *Being Geniuses Together* (revised and with supplementary chapters by Kay Boyle), London, 1970

O'Connor, Ulick: *Oliver St. John Gogarty A Poet and His Times*, London, 1964

—— (ed.): *The Joyce We Knew* (Eugene Sheehy, William G. Fallon, Padraic Colum, Arthur Power), Cork, 1967

Paige, D. D. (ed.): *The Letters of Ezra Pound 1907–1941*, New York, 1959, London, 1951

Power, Arthur: *From the Old Waterford House*, London, 1945.

——: *Conversations with James Joyce*, London, 1974

Read, Forrest (ed.): *Pound/Joyce Letters of Ezra Pound to James Joyce*, New York, 1967, London, 1968

Sheehy, Eugene: *May It Please the Court*, Dublin, 1951

Slocum, John J. and Cahoon, Herbert: *A Bibliography of James Joyce 1882–1941*, New Haven, 1953

Sullivan, Kevin: *Joyce Among the Jesuits*, New York, 1968

Svevo, Italo (Ettore Schmitz): *James Joyce*, New York, 1950

Walsh, F. R.: 'New Light on James Joyce's Medical Problems' article in *Irish Medical Times*, 9 May, 1975

Acknowledgements

My thanks to: Mr and Mrs Arthur Power for their hospitality to me in Dublin, and for their reminiscences; the late Frank Budgen for an interview granted to me in 1970; Ulick O'Connor for advice and very useful information on Gogarty and his friendship with Joyce; Morris Ernst of New York; Dermot Gallagher of the Irish Embassy in London for certain arcane information, hospitality, and admission to his card table; Dr J. B. Lyons of Dublin and Dr F. R. Walsh of Kilkenny for their opinions of Joyce's health; Miss Jane Lidderdale for her courteous answers to my enquiries; Faber and Faber Ltd for making available to me certain unobtainable texts; Mr T. J. Keating of Dublin, Keeper of the Joyce Tower at Sandycove, for courteous answers to questions; Mr Alf Mac Lochlainn, Keeper of Printed Books at the National Library of Ireland, for explaining to me his regret that neither I nor anyone else may see the unpublished Joyce papers there until 1991; that splendid institution, the British Library; Mr Leslie Mallory of Dublin for his story about the front door of No 7 Eccles Street, and for other entertaining anecdotes; the late Martin O'Cadhain for (probably) pulling my leg about the derivation of the surname Barnacle; Mr Toby Buchan of Davis-Poynter Ltd for dealing with my tortuous original typescript; all of my friends who helped and encouraged me, most particularly Miss Paddy Frost.

In addition, I am grateful to the following for permission to use copyright material: The Society of Authors as the literary representative of the Estate of James Joyce; the Society of Authors on behalf of the Bernard Shaw Estate; Messrs Jonathan Cape Ltd and the Society of Authors on behalf of the James Joyce Estate; Messrs Faber and Faber Ltd; Messrs Victor Gollancz Ltd; the Estate of H. G. Wells; Dr Arthur Wiederkehr of Zurich as the literary representative of the estate of Professor Alfred Vogt and the Society of Authors on behalf of the James Joyce Estate; M. B. Yeats, Miss Ann Yeats, and Messrs Macmillan Ltd of London and Basingstoke.

Index

321

Lewis, Wyndham, 288-9, 233, 234, 235, 244, 256
Lichtensteiger, Nellie, *see* Joyce, Mrs Stanislaus
Lidwell, John, 182-4
Linati, Carlo, 197
Little Review, The, 207, 211, 223, 230
Loy, Mina, 242
Lugné-Poë, Aurélien-Marie, 226, 236
Lyons, Dr J. B., 92n; Works, *James Joyce in Medicine*, 92n

Macdonald, Dr, 299
Machnich, Antonio, 163-4
Maeterlinck, Maurice, 35, 72, 89, 226
Magee, William, *see* Eglington, John
Maillard, Dr G., 291
Malacrida, Herr, 112
Mallory, Leslie, 238n
Mangan, James Clarence, 55, 68, 90, 141
Marsden, Dora, 191, 271 and n
Marsh, Edward, 204
Martin, Jules (Juda de Vries), 205-8
Martyn, Edward, 59
Matthews, Charles, 57
Matthews, Elkin, publisher, 137, 141, 143, 147, 190, 203; agrees to publish *Chamber Music*, 137, 139
Maunsel & Co., publishers, 94, 104, 147, 155, 156, 176, 184
Maupassant, Guy de, 125, 143
Mayer, Teodoro, 195-6
McAlmon, Robert, 235, 236, 237, 241-4, 247, 257, 267, 268, 273, 281-2; Works, *Being Geniuses Together*, 267q.
McCarthy, Desmond, 283-4
McCormack, John, 92, 275, 296
McCormick, Mrs Harold, 206, 208, 220, 224, 228; withdraws money for Joyce, 220-1
McKernan, Mrs, landlady, 93-4, 100, 105
Mencken, H. L., 191, 198
Milhaud, Darius, 292
Mitford, Nancy, 295n
Monnier, Adrienne, 227, 228n,

230-1, 237, 243, 259, 268, 281, 286; organizes sèance, 281
Moore, George, 35, 59-60, 75, 104, 116, 187, 204, 268, 274
Morel, Auguste, 259
Mulvey, Willie, 99-100
Munro, Fred, 276, 280, 282
Murray, John, father of Mary Jane, 11-12
Murray, John, brother of Mary Jane, 83
Murray, Josephine, aunt to James Joyce, 79, 93, 114, 121, 127, 187, 222, 248; attempts to feed Joyce children, 85, death of, 260
Murray, Kathleen, 85, 250
Murray, Mary Jane (May), *see* Joyce, Mrs John Stanislaus
Murray, Middleton, 246

Nation and Athenaeum, 141, 204, 246; review of *Ulysses*, 246
National Library, 69, 70, 71, 83, 91, 94, 109
National Theatre Society, 72, 100
New Freewoman, The, 190, 192, 203
New Statesman, 193
New York Herald, 277
Newman, Cardinal, 35, 42
Nicolson, Sir Harold, 283-4, 286
Northern Whig, 176
Nouvelle Revue Française, 230
Novak, Francesco, 163-4, 172, 174
Nutting, Myron, 240

O'Brien, Dr Daniel, 308
O'Brien, Flann, 82n
O'Brien, Miss, 175
Observer, The, 246
O'Cadhain, Martin, 97n
O'Casey, Sean, 285, 305
O'Connell, Daniel, 9
O'Connell, William, 17
O'Connor, Frank, 267, 268
O'Connor, T. P., 50
O'Connor, Ulick, 92n, 106n, 107, 154n
O'Donnell, George, 36
O'Flaherty, Liam, 184n
O'Halloran, Mary, 99
O'Shea, Mrs Kitty, 19